Please renew/return this item by the last date shown.

So that your telephone call is charged at local rate, please call the numbers as set out below:

	From Area codes 01923 or 020:	From the rest of Herts:
Renewals:	01923 471373	01438 737373
Enquiries:	01923 471333	01438 737333
Textphone:	01923 471599	01438 737599

L32   www.hertsdirect.org/librarycatalogue

THE GUINNESS
RUGBY LEAGUE
FACT BOOK

THE GUINNESS
RUGBY LEAGUE
FACT BOOK

ROBERT GATE

GUINNESS PUBLISHING

Editor: Charles Richards
Design: Steve Leaning
Cover design: Ad Vantage Studios

Published in Great Britain by Guinness Publishing Ltd,
33 London Road, Enfield, Middlesex

Front cover: *Top* Halifax, Challenge Cup winners 1939 *Middle* Ellery
Hanley (Wigan) v Warrington, Challenge Cup Final 1990 *Bottom* Mal
Meninga (Australia)

Typeset in Baskerville and Helvetica by
Ace Filmsetting Ltd, Frome, Somerset

Printed and bound in Great Britain by The Bath Press, Bath

'Guinness' is a registered trademark of Guinness Publishing Ltd

British Library Cataloguing in Publication Data
Gate, Robert
  The Guinness Rugby League fact book
  1. Rugby League football, history
  I. Title
  796.33309

ISBN 0-85112-949-8

ABOUT THE AUTHOR

Robert Gate lives in Pennine Yorkshire with his wife Myfanwy and dog Lucy who try to help him to control an acre of tumbling moorland. As that is too hard, he consoles himself by writing books about Rugby League. *The Guinness Rugby League Fact Book* is his eighth book, following *Gone North – Welshmen in Rugby League (Vols I and II)*, *The Struggle For The Ashes*, *Champions – A Celebration of the Rugby League Championship 1895–1987*, *The Rugby League Quiz Book*, *Rugby League – An Illustrated History* and *An Illustrated History of Saints v Wigan Derby Matches*. Robert is the Rugby League's official historian and archivist, a founder member of the Rugby League Record Keepers Club and a contributor to *Open Rugby* and *Code 13* magazines.

ACKNOWLEDGEMENTS

Many individuals have helped in the compilation of this book. I am particularly indebted to Michael Latham who read the manuscript, pointed out errors and made valuable suggestions for improvements.

The photographic content has been derived from many sources. Chief amongst these is *The Rugby Leaguer* newspaper, which has given permission to use many of its colour and black and white photographs. Freelance photographer Andrew Cudbertson has supplied the majority of the modern colour photographs.

Other individuals who have furnished assistance in the form of illustrations or verification of facts are Timothy Auty, May Barrett, Steve Calline, Norman Carr, Donald Clist, Bill Dalton, Ernie Day, John Edwards, Halifax *Evening Courier*, Harold Farrimond, Tom Fleet, Raymond Fletcher, Bob Fox, Les Hoole, David Howes, Michael Inman, Eddie Jarrett, Curtis Johnstone, David Kay, Phil Lyon, Dave Makin, Chris Park, Darrell Platt, Barry Rennison, Mick Rhodes, The Rugby Football League, David Thorpe, the late and sorely missed Tom Webb, Donald Walton and Nigel Williams.

Perhaps the person to whom I owe most thanks is Irvin Saxton, founder and secretary of the Rugby League Record Keepers Club. Irvin founded the RLRKC in 1973 and has since provided an invaluable mechanism for the compilation and verification of the game's records, which hitherto simply had not existed. Through his organisation, local Rugby League historians have been encouraged to pool their research and expertise to vastly improve our knowledge of the game's history and records. Without Irvin's persistence in nurturing the RLRKC, many people would still be whistling in the dark with regard to Rugby League record keeping.

CONTENTS

INTRODUCTION &
   AUTHOR'S NOTES 7

RUGBY LEAGUE MILESTONES 8

RUGBY LEAGUE
   CLUB DIRECTORY 16
Barrow 16
Batley 17
Bradford Northern 18
Bramley 19
Carlisle 19
Castleford 20
Chorley 20
Dewsbury 21
Doncaster 21
Featherstone Rovers 22
Fulham 23
Halifax 23
Huddersfield 25
Hull 26
Hull Kingston Rovers 28
Hunslet 29
Keighley 29
Leeds 32
Leigh 32
Nottingham City 33
Oldham 36
Rochdale Hornets 37
Ryedale–York 37
St Helens 38
Salford 40
Scarborough 40
Sheffield Eagles 40
Sutton (Highfield) 41
Swinton 42
Trafford Borough 43
Wakefield Trinity 43
Warrington 44
Whitehaven 45
Widnes 48
Wigan 48
Workington Town 52

CURRENT COMPETITIONS:
RESULTS HISTORY & RECORDS 53
The Rugby League Championship 53
First Division Premiership Trophy 55
Second Division Championship 58
Second Division Premiership 59
The Rugby League Challenge Cup 59
The Lancashire Challenge Cup 72
The Yorkshire Challenge Cup 78

The Regal Trophy 84
The Rugby League Charity Shield 87
Cup Finals Man-of-the-Match Awards 88
The Roses Match 90
Reserve Team Rugby League 96

DEFUNCT COMPETITIONS:
RESULTS HISTORY & RECORDS 98
The BBC2 Floodlit Trophy 98
The Northern Rugby League Championship .. 101
The Lancashire and Yorkshire League
   Championships 107
'One-Season Wonders' 110

INDIVIDUAL RECORDS IN RUGBY
LEAGUE 111

OTHER RUGBY LEAGUE RECORDS . 160

GREAT BRITAIN: TEST MATCH
RESULTS 162
Great Britain v Australia 162
Great Britain v New Zealand 171
Great Britain v France 178
Great Britain v Papua New Guinea 183
Incoming Tours 184
Other International Matches 185

BRITISH INTERNATIONAL
RECORDS 189

GREAT BRITAIN TOURISTS 198

THE WORLD CUP 212

PLAYER FEATURES:
Eric Batten 70
Brian Bevan 122
Billy Boston 50
Joe Ferguson 34
Neil Fox 132
Bob Haigh 154
Lewis Jones 30
Mick Martyn 114
Roger Millward 202
Albert Rosenfeld 144
Jim Sullivan 126
Mick Sullivan 192
David Watkins 136

INDEX 221

INTRODUCTION

Rugby League is a sport which, next arguably to cricket, most readily provides its followers with a constant stream of facts and figures to digest. Records of one sort or another are created almost every season. Some records, of course, seem unassailable, such as Albert Rosenfeld's 80 tries in a season, set before the Great War. Brian Bevan's monumental record of 796 career tries now seems to beggar betterment, but who is to say that Martin Offiah or some other future genius will not surpass the great Bev's mark? For long enough no-one seriously believed that Jim Sullivan's mountainous 6000-odd points would ever be challenged – but then along came Neil Fox!

It is almost axiomatic that records are made to be broken, but as Rugby League enters the last decade of the 20th century it may well be that changes in the game's structure will render most past records obsolete. The proposed change to three divisions will certainly have a profound effect on the game, and not least affected will be the record keepers who will be presented with a new set of circumstances in which to make their calculations and comparisons.

Record keeping under present conditions is perilous enough. Some people still work out currency in terms of pounds, shillings and pence; Rugby League statisticians have had to cope with the introduction of four-point tries, one-point drop goals, substitutes, sin-binnings and two divisions, the latter three times! Nowadays, as more and more local historians turn their attention to sports, the accumulated errors and false information of past record keepers are coming to light, and fine tuning of records has become increasingly necessary. Sharp-eyed readers will no doubt notice discrepancies from previous works in this volume. The author would welcome notification of any inadvertent omissions.

AUTHOR'S NOTES

All statistics relate to first-class fixtures in British Rugby League or to first-class games involving British teams overseas. No friendly fixtures have been included. Figures apply to the period ending 13 May 1991.

When referring to players' individual appearance records, substitute appearances are listed as additional to full playing records. For example, AN Other 35+2 signifies that the player made 35 full appearances and played twice after coming on to the field as a substitute, for an overall total of 37 games. Non-playing substitutions are not recorded. Players who appeared in and scored in Second World War matches as guests for clubs other than their own have had those appearances and scores included in their career totals. First World War games from September 1915 to January 1919 were unofficial and are excluded from records.

In the section relating to Test matches it should be noted that the term 'Great Britain' has been used throughout, although British Test XIIIs were originally styled 'The Northern Union'. From around 1924 to 1947 the Test team was simply styled 'England' despite the fact that Scots and Welshmen often gained inclusion. The title 'Great Britain' was first used in the home series against New Zealand in 1947.

It should be noted that in several cases clubs have been treated as being in continuous existence despite changes in name or location. Clubs which fall into this category are:

Bradford Northern	ex-Bradford
Highfield	ex-Wigan Highfield/London Highfield/ Liverpool Stanley/Liverpool City/ Huyton/Runcorn Highfield
Huddersfield	ex-Huddersfield/Huddersfield Barracudas
Hunslet	ex-Hunslet/New Hunslet
Nottingham City	ex-Mansfield Marksman
Ryedale–York	ex-York
Trafford Borough	ex-Blackpool Borough/Springfield Borough/Chorley Borough

RUGBY LEAGUE MILESTONES

PRE-NORTHERN UNION

1871 Foundation of the English Rugby Football Union.

1877 Inauguration of the Yorkshire Challenge Cup ('T'Owd Tin Pot'). First winners are Halifax.

1880s Massive growth in numbers and playing strength of northern clubs, particularly in Lancashire and Yorkshire.

1892 Introduction of leagues, despite the opposition of the Rugby Football Union. Formation of the Lancashire Club Championship and the Yorkshire Senior Competition. Salford and Bradford are the respective first winners.

1893 (20 Sep) The RFU reject the northern clubs' proposal that players be allowed to receive broken-time payments.

THE NORTHERN UNION

1895 (29 Aug) 22 clubs from Cheshire, Lancashire and Yorkshire secede from the RFU and form the Northern Rugby Football Union. The decision is made at the George Hotel, Huddersfield. Broken-time payments of six shillings permitted. Professionalism per se still ruled illegal.

(7 Sep) First league fixtures played.

1895 Oldham's Joseph Platt becomes Secretary of the Northern Union. Inauguration of the County Championship – Cheshire, Lancashire and Yorkshire compete. Lancashire are the first winners.

(9 Dec) First rule changes include penalty for half-backs not behind rearmost forward at scrums.

1896 Manningham are the first Champions of the Northern Union.

1897 (24 Apr) Batley defeat St Helens in the first Challenge Cup Final.

Line-out abolished and replaced by punt-in from touch. All goals worth two points. Touch judges allowed to report foul play to referees.

1898 Professionalism in strictly regulated working clauses allowed.

1900 Abolition of the charge at goal kicks.

1901 Accidental knock-on allowed – play on if the ball is caught before touching the ground. Transfer system rationalised – Bramley's James Lomas is signed by Salford in the first £100 transfer.

1901–02 Broughton Rangers become the first club to win both Cup and League in a season.

1902 Punt-in abolished and replaced by the 10-yard scrum.

1902–03 Two divisions introduced.

1904 (5 Apr) First Northern Union international match: England 3 Other Nationalities 9 at Wigan.

1905 Open professionalism allowed.

(4 Mar) Hull KR winger George 'Tich' West scores a record 11 tries and 53 points against Brookland Rovers in a Challenge Cup tie.

Two divisions experiment ended.

1905–06 Lancashire and Yorkshire Challenge Cups inaugurated. Wigan and Hunslet are the respective first winners.

1906 (12 Jun) Teams reduced from 15 to 13 players. Play-the-ball rule defined. Ball-back rule introduced vis-à-vis direct kicking to touch.

1906–07 Top four play-off introduced to decide the Championship.

(20 Apr 1907) Halifax defeat Oldham in the first Championship Final.

1907 Lancashire and Yorkshire League Championships inaugurated. Oldham and Hunslet are the respective first winners.

1907–08 First tour of Britain by New Zealand ('The All Golds') organised by AH Baskerville.

(9 Oct 1907) New Zealand win their first game against Bramley.

(25 Jan 1908) First ever Test match – The Northern Union 14 New Zealand 6 at Headingley. Hunslet become the first club to win All Four Cups. Their captain

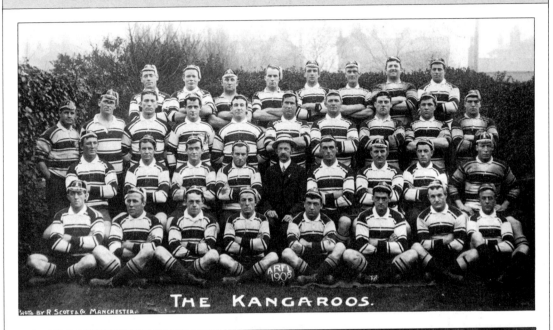

Top *The first Australian touring team 1908–09.*
Above *Hunslet 1905, first winners of the Yorkshire Cup.* BACK: *Glew, Wray, Jukes, Uttley, Hannah, Williamson, Everson, Walsh, Shooter.* MIDDLE: *Eagers, Wilcox, A Goldthorpe, W Goldthorpe, Brooks, Wilson.* FRONT: *Jackson, W Ward, Place, C Ward.*

Albert Goldthorpe becomes the first player to kick 100 goals in a season.

1908 (20 Apr) First Wales–England international. Wales win 35–18 at Tonypandy.

First season of Sydney Premiership.

1908–09 First tour of Britain by Australia organised by JJ Giltinan.

(3 Oct 1908) Australia win their first game against Mid-Rhondda.

(12 Dec 1908) First Ashes Test at Park Royal, London, is drawn 22–22.

1910 First Lions tour of Australasia, led by Salford's James Lomas.

1911 Compulsory numbering of jerseys introduced. Games to last statutory 80 minutes – previously clubs could agree to play less. Australia win the Ashes for the first time.

1913 (12 Apr) Leeds defeat Coventry 102–0, a record score for a league fixture.

1913–14 Huddersfield winger Albert Rosenfeld scores 80 tries this season, a record which remains unbeaten.

1914 (28 Feb) Huddersfield beat Swinton Park 119–2 in the Challenge Cup, a record score for a first-class fixture.

(4 Jul) Great Britain win the Ashes despite being reduced to 10 men in the 'Rorke's Drift Test' at Sydney.

1914–15 Huddersfield become the second club to win All Four Cups in a season.

1915–19 The game is played throughout the First World War on a friendlies-only basis.

1919 (Jan) Lancashire and Yorkshire League matches and county cup-ties resumed on an official basis.

1919–20 Huddersfield forward Ben Gronow becomes the first player to score 300 points in a season.

1920 John Wilson succeeds Joseph Platt as Northern Union Secretary.

1921 Harold Buck, Hunslet's winger, transferred to Leeds in

Harold Buck, the Hunslet winger transferred to Leeds in 1921.

the first reputed £1000 deal.

1922 Great Britain regain the Ashes – they would retain them until 1950.

THE RUGBY FOOTBALL LEAGUE

1922 The Northern Union changes its title to the Northern Rugby Football League. Abolition of the goal from a mark.

1925 (14 Feb) Jim Sullivan kicks a record 22 goals for Wigan against Flimby & Fothergill in a Challenge Cup tie.

1927 First broadcast of a Challenge Cup Final – Oldham v Swinton at Wigan. International transfer ban lifted.

1927–28 Swinton become the third and final club to win All Four Cups.

1929 (4 May) Wigan defeat Dewsbury in Wembley's first Challenge Cup Final.

1930 Loose-forward compelled to pack behind and between second-rowers. He could previously pack on either side of the scrum.

1932 (2 Jan) Warrington–Halifax match is the first league fixture to be broadcast.

(6 Jun) World record Test match crowd of 70 204 see Great Britain defeat Australia 8–6 at Sydney Cricket Ground.

1932–33 Jim Hoey (Widnes) becomes the first man to play and score in every club match in a season.

1933 Wigan Highfield become Rugby League's first London club, changing their name to London Highfield and playing at the White City Stadium. The experiment lasts one season.

(Dec 31) England meet Australia in Paris to launch the game in France.

1934 (March) A French team under Jean Galia makes a six-match tour of England.

(13 Apr) First England–France international in Paris.

1933–34 Jim Sullivan, the Wigan full-back, becomes the first player to score over 400 points in a season.

1935 Triangular international tournament between England, France and Wales established.

1935 (1 Jan) First Wales–France international at Bordeaux.

(22 Apr) First England–France amateur international in Paris. The Rugby Football League moves its administration to 180 Chapeltown Road, Leeds.

1935–37 Renewed attempts to establish the game in London, with clubs at Acton & Willesden and Streatham & Mitcham.

1938 Introduction of the drop-out from under the posts after defender makes the ball dead.

1939 (13 May) Record British pre-war attendance of 69 504 for the Castleford–Salford Championship Final at Maine Road, Manchester.

1939–45 Rugby League continues to play competitive fixtures throughout the war. Guest system of registering players often causes problems.

1940 (13 Apr) Swinton forward Martin Hodgson kicks a goal from 77¾ yards against Rochdale Hornets, the longest recorded goal in the game's history.

1942–43 (23 Jun 1943) Dewsbury's Championship title declared null and void after the club had fielded an ineligible player.

1943 (23 Jan) Northern Command Rugby League defeat Northern Command Rugby Union 18–11 at Headingley under Rugby Union laws.

1944 (24 Apr) Rugby League Combined Services defeat Rugby Union Combined Services 15–10 at Odsal under Rugby Union laws.

1945 Professional Rugby League introduced to Cumberland with the formation of Workington Town.

1946 William Fallowfield suc-

Above *Jean Galia, one of the founding fathers of French Rugby League, pictured with Warrington secretary Bob Anderton.*

Below *Wembley, 1948 – George VI becomes the first reigning monarch to attend a Rugby League fixture. He is seen shaking hands with the Bradford Northern and Great Britain captain Ernest Ward.*

ceeds John Wilson as Secretary of the Rugby Football League.

1946–47 Rugby League's longest season – severe winter weather causes a huge log-jam of fixtures which sees the Championship Final delayed until 21 June.

1947 First £2000 transfer – Batley forward Bill Hudson to Wigan.

1948 International Board founded at Bordeaux. George VI becomes first reigning monarch to attend a Rugby League match – he presents the Challenge Cup at the Wigan–Bradford Northern final.

1949 Bradford Northern become the first club to appear in three consecutive Wembley Challenge Cup Finals. Southern Amateur Rugby League formed. Welsh Rugby League formed.

1950 Great Britain lose the Ashes for the first time since 1920.

Below *The American 'All Star' touring team of 1953.*

(Aug–Sep) Italian touring team under Vincenzo Bertoletto play six fixtures in England. (The Italians also toured in April 1954.)

First £5000 transfer – Leigh sign Wigan hooker Joe Egan.

1951 (10 Nov) First televising of a Test match – Great Britain v New Zealand at Swinton. Reintroduction of international transfer ban.

1952 (12 Jan) First league fixture to be televised is Wigan v Wakefield Trinity.

(19 Apr) First national television broadcast of a Wembley Cup Final – Featherstone Rovers v Workington Town.

1953–54 American All Stars tour Australia, New Zealand and France.

1954 (5 May) World record attendance at a Rugby League match – 102 569 at the Halifax–Warrington Challenge Cup Final replay at Odsal Stadium, Bradford. Warrington are the winners, 8–4.

Lewis Jones sets a Lions record by scoring 278 points on the

Australasian tour. Great Britain win the inaugural World Cup in France.

1956–57 Leeds centre Lewis Jones sets a record for points in a season – 496. Hull win European Club Championship in a four-team tournament with Albi, Carcassonne and Halifax.

1957 World Cup staged in Australia for the first time. Great Britain and France play in three exhibition games in South Africa on the homeward journey.

1957–58 Oldham full-back Bernard Ganley becomes the first player to kick 200 goals in a season.

1958 First £10 000 transfer – Workington Town winger Ike Southward signed by Oldham.

1958–59 St Helens become the first team to score 1000 points in league games in a season (1005).

1959 (23 Mar) Record 47 477 crowd attend Wigan–St Helens league fixture.

Abolition of tap penalty.

1960 (21 May) 83 190 attend Wakefield Trinity–Wigan Cham-

FIRST AUSTRALIAN TOUR 1953
AMERICAN "ALL STARS" RUGBY LEAGUE TEAM

Back Row: W. Moore (Masseur), E. Crossman, P. Henry, H. Han, A. E. Kirkland, Mr. N. Robinson (Coach).
3rd Row: S. Naumu, G. Kerkorian, G. Kauffman, W. Albans, S. Drakulvitch, Ray Terry (Asst. Manager), F. Mandulav.
2nd Row: E. Demiriiian, I. Bonetti, R. Bucklev, Mike Dimitro (Manager), V. Iones, A. D. Kirkland, X. Mena.
Front: A. Abaiian, S. Walker.

John Berriman.

A world record Rugby League crowd of 102 569 attended the Challenge Cup Final Replay of 1954 at Odsal. Here Halifax full-back Tuss Griffiths kicks a goal, but his team went down 4–8 to Warrington.

pionship Final at Odsal.

World Cup staged in England for the first time. Great Britain are the winners.

1962 Short tours of South Africa made by Wakefield Trinity and Great Britain. Two divisions reintroduced – experiment lasts only two seasons. Introduction of Eastern and Western Division Championships – also abandoned after two seasons.

1962–63 Bad weather causes league programme to be extended to 1 June.

1963 South African Rugby League team tours Australia and New Zealand. Leeds are the first Rugby League club to install undersoil heating.

(9 Nov) Record 12–50 defeat for Great Britain, against Australia at Swinton.

Australia win the Ashes in England for the first time since 1911–12.

1964 Substitutions allowed up to half-time, but only for injured players.

1964–65 Return to single league. Introduction of top 16 play-off to decide Championship. First winners are Halifax.

1965 Substitutions allowed for any reason up to half-time.

1965–66 Inauguration of BBC2 Floodlit Trophy Competition. First winners are Castleford.

1966 Foundation of English Schools Rugby League.

Introduction of five-yard rule at play-the-ball. Four-tackle rule introduced. Double penalty introduced – i.e. tap penalty after penalty kick to touch.

1967 (17 Dec) First Sunday fixtures staged – Bradford Northern v York and Leigh v Dewsbury.

1968 (15 Mar) First University match – Leeds 45 Liverpool 13 – played at Widnes.

New Zealand co-host the World Cup with Australia.

1969 Substitution allowed for full 80 minutes. Formation of Universities Rugby League Association.

1969–70 Demise of the Lancashire and Yorkshire League Championships. Last winners are Wigan and Leeds respectively.

1970 Great Britain win the Ashes in Australia, a feat never since emulated. England stages the World Cup.

1970–71 Bob Haigh (Leeds) creates a try-scoring record for a forward with 40 tries in the season.

1971 New Zealand win a Test series in Britain for the first time since 1907–08.

1971–72 Inauguration of John Player Trophy (currently Regal Trophy). First winners are Halifax.

1972 Great Britain win the World Cup in France.

Introduction of six-tackle rule. Use of time-keepers and hooter introduced. Inauguration of Colts League.

1972–73 Salford's David Watkins kicks a record 221 goals in a season.

MILESTONES

1973 (4 Mar) Establishment of the British Amateur Rugby League Association (BARLA), based in Huddersfield – previously the amateur game had been administered by the Rugby Football League.

1973–74 Modern era of two divisions began.

1974 First BARLA National Cup won by Leigh Miners. Drop goal devalued to one point. David Oxley succeeds Bill Fallowfield as Secretary of the Rugby Football League.

David Howes becomes the Rugby Football League's first full-time Public Relations Officer. National Coaching Scheme inaugurated.

1975 Premiership Trophy introduced – first winners are Leeds.

Great Britain split into England and Wales for World Championship, which for the first time is played in both hemispheres. Australia win the tournament.

(6 Jul) First visit of a British team to Papua-New Guinea. England beat Papua-New Guinea 40–12 at Port Moresby.

1976 St Helens become the first

Second Test, 1982 – Australian captain Max Krilich leaves Bob Eccles and John Dalgreen in his wake as Britain surrender 27–6 at Wigan. Krilich's Kangaroos were the first touring team to win all their fixtures, and were immortalised as 'The Invincibles'.

British club to play in Australia and New Zealand. Introduction of differential penalty for scrum offences.

1977 World Cup played in Australia and New Zealand. Renewal of international transfer ban to stop migration of British players to Australia.

First amateur tour of Australasia, by BARLA Under-18s.

1978 Papua-New Guinea becomes the fifth member of the International Board. First £20 000 transfer – Castleford half-back Clive Pickerill signs for Hull.

1979 Australia beat Great Britain 3-0 for the first time in an Ashes series. First tour by Papua-New Guinea – they play BARLA opponents only.

1980 Relaunch of professional Rugby League in London. Fulham admitted to the Second Division.

1981 (26 Apr) First Rugby League varsity match at Fulham – Cambridge University 9 Oxford University 16.

Relaunch of professional Rugby League in Wales. Cardiff City Blue Dragons admitted to the Second Division.

1982 Abandonment of the County Championship after 87 years. Max Krilich's Australians become the first touring team to win every game in Great Britain. They earn the title 'Invincibles'.

1983 Introduction of the sin-bin. Try revalued at four points. Introduction of the handover on the sixth tackle. International transfer ban lifted.

1984 Alliance League introduced for reserve teams.

1985 Inauguration of the Rugby League Charity Shield. First winners are Wigan. 'War of the Roses' matches launched – first winners are Yorkshire. Promotion and relegation places reduced from four to three.

1986 Introduction of the 'free gang-way' between BARLA and the RFU. New Zealand host and win the first Student Rugby League World Cup. First £100 000 transfer – Wigan sign Joe Lydon from Widnes. BARLA launch the National Amateur Rugby League. Australians, under Wally Lewis, are again undefeated through their European tour.

1987 (2 May) First £1 000 000 gate taken at a Rugby League match – Halifax v St Helens Challenge Cup Final at Wembley. Second Division Premiership introduced. First winners are Swinton. First £150 000 transfer – Leeds sign Lee Crooks from Hull. Papua-New Guinea tour Britain – they meet professional teams for the first time.

(7 Oct) Wigan defeat Manly 8-2 in the first World Club Challenge.

Establishment of the Rugby League Foundation, a joint venture by the RFL and BARLA to develop the game. Freedom of contract for players introduced. Transfer tribunal introduced.

1987-88 First Division reduced from 16 to 14 clubs.

1988 Colts competitions scrapped. District Development Associations founded. Rugby Football League establish a six-man Board of Directors to administer the game. Fred Lindop becomes the League's first Controller of Referees. Rugby League Hall of Fame inaugurated.

1989 (10 Jun) Warrington play Wigan in a promotional game in Milwaukee, USA.

Featherstone Rovers transfer Graham Steadman to Castleford for British record fee of £170 000.

(4 Oct) Widnes beat Canberra 30-18 at Old Trafford in the World Club Challenge.

1990 Wigan become the first club to win three consecutive Wembley Challenge Cup Finals. Rugby League introduced into USSR. Russians tour Britain.

(27 Oct) Record British Test crowd of 54 569 attend Great Britain–Australia Test at Wembley. Ashes series attracts record British Test aggregate – 133 784.

1991 Introduction of Scarborough as 36th member club allows the Rugby Football League to formulate a three-divisions system.

(May) Fulham and Ryedale-York make promotional tour of the USSR.

1990-91 Wigan become the first club to win four consecutive Challenge Cup Finals. They are also the first to perform the League and Cup double in consecutive seasons.

BARROW

Ground	Craven Park
Colours	Royal blue and white jerseys, white shorts
First home game	8 Sep 1900 v Oldham, lost 3–6
First away game	1 Sep 1900 v Runcorn, lost 5–10
Record crowd	22 651 v Salford, 15 Apr 1938
Highest score	83–3 v Maryport, 19 Feb 1938
Highest against	0–90 v Leeds, 11 Feb 1990

INDIVIDUAL RECORDS

Tries – match	6	V Cumberbatch v Batley, 21 Nov 1936
	6	J Thornburrow v Maryport, 19 Feb 1938
	6	F Castle v York, 29 Sep 1951
Goals – match	12	F French v Maryport, 19 Feb 1938
	12	W Horne v Cardiff, 8 Sep 1951
	12	S Tickle v Kent Invicta, 8 Apr 1984
Points – match	28	K Jarrett v Doncaster, 25 Aug 1970
	28	S Tickle v Kent Invicta, 8 Apr 1984
	28	D Marwood v Runcorn H, 16 Apr 1989
Tries – season	50	J Lewthwaite, 1956–57
Goals – season	135	J Ball, 1956–57
Points – season	305	I Ball, 1979–80
Tries – career	352	J Lewthwaite, 1943–57
Goals – career	741	W Horne, 1943–59
Points – career	1818	W Horne, 1943–59
Games – career	500	J Lewthwaite, 1943–57

GREAT BRITAIN CAPS

W Burgess snr, W Burgess jnr, D Cairns, C Camilleri, C Carr, F Castle, R Francis, H Gifford, D Goodwin, J Grundy, P Hogan, W Horne, P Jackson, J Jones, B Knowelden, E Szymala, E Toohey, L Troup, J Woods

CLUB HONOURS

Challenge Cup Winners	1954–55
Runners-up	1937–38, 1950–51, 1956–57, 1966–67
Lancashire Cup Winners	1954–55, 1983–84
Runners-up	1937–38
Lancashire League Runners-up	1932–33, 1937–38, 1945–46, 1956–57
Regal Trophy Runners-up	1980–81
Division Two Champions	1975–76, 1983–84
Promotion	1904–05, 1977–78, 1979–80, 1985–86, 1988–89

One of British Rugby League's most artful stand-offs, Willie Horne scored a club record 1818 points for Barrow (1943–59).

BATLEY

Ground	Mount Pleasant
Colours	Deep orange chevron on maroon jersey with white trim, white shorts
First home game	7 Sep 1895 v Hull, won 7–3
First away game	14 Sep 1895 v Manningham, lost 3–5
Record crowd	23 989 v Leeds, 14 Mar 1925
Highest score	52–8 v Widnes, 27 Mar 1909
Highest against	9–78 v Wakefield T, 26 Aug 1967

INDIVIDUAL RECORDS

Tries – match	5 J Oakland v Bramley, 19 Dec 1908
	5 T Brannan v Swinton, 17 Jan 1920
	5 J Wale v Bramley, 4 Dec 1926
	5 J Wale v Cottingham, 12 Feb 1927
Goals – match	9 WP Davies v Widnes, 27 Mar 1909
	9 S Thompson v Keighley, 20 Sep 1958
Points – match	26 J Perry v Liverpool C, 16 Sep 1951
Tries – season	29 J Tindall, 1912–13
Goals – season	120 S Thompson, 1958–59
Points – season	281 J Perry, 1950–51
Tries – career	123 WP Davies, 1897–1912
Goals – career	463 WP Davies, 1897–1912
Points – career	1297 WP Davies, 1897–1912
Games – career	421 WP Davies, 1897–1912

GREAT BRITAIN CAPS

N Field, F Gallagher, C Gibson, J Oliver

CLUB HONOURS

Championship Winners	1923–24
Challenge Cup Winners	1896–97, 1897–98, 1900–01
Yorkshire Cup Winners	1912–13
Runners-up	1909–10, 1922–23, 1924–25, 1952–53
Yorkshire League Winners	1898–99, 1923–24
Runners-up	1899–1900, 1925–26

Winger Jack Perry set Batley's points record for a season by claiming 281 in 1950–51. He is pictured in Yorkshire cap and jersey.

BRADFORD NORTHERN

Ground	Odsal Stadium
Colours	White jerseys with red, black and amber chevrons, black shorts
First home game	7 Sep 1895 v Wakefield T, won 11–0
First away game	14 Sep 1895 v Tyldesley, won 8–6
Record crowd	69 429 v Huddersfield, 14 Mar 1953
Ground record	102 569, Halifax v Warrington, Challenge Cup Final replay, 5 May 1954
Highest score	72–9 v Doncaster, 4 Nov 1973
	72–12 v Hunslet, 7 Oct 1984
Highest against	18–75 v Leeds, 14 Sep 1931

INDIVIDUAL RECORDS

Tries – match	7	J Dechan v Bramley, 13 Oct 1906
Goals – match	14	J Phillips v Batley, 6 Sep 1952
Points – match	36	J Woods v Swinton, 13 Oct 1985
Tries – season	63	J McLean, 1951–52
Goals – season	173	E Tees, 1971–72
Points – season	364	E Tees, 1971–72
Tries – career	261	J McLean, 1950–56
Goals – career	778	K Mumby, 1973–90
Points – career	1818	K Mumby, 1973–90
Games – career	573+4	K Mumby, 1973–90

GREAT BRITAIN CAPS

D Barends, E Batten, I Brooke, L Casey, G Cordle, W Davies, K Fairbank, A Fisher, P Ford, T Foster, J Grayshon, E Hanley, D Hobbs, R Jasiewicz, J Kitching, A Mann, K Mumby, B Noble, T Price, J Rae, W Ramsey, A Rathbone, A Redfearn, D Redfearn, K Skerrett, T Smales, H Smith, J Thompson, K Traill, E Ward, F Whitcombe

Yorkshire Cup Final, 1982 – Bradford Northern full-back Keith Mumby kicks to touch. Mumby was transferred to Sheffield Eagles in 1990 having made a record 577 appearances for Bradford.

CLUB HONOURS

Championship Winners	1903–04, 1939–40, 1940–41, 1944–45, 1979–80, 1980–81
Runners-up	1904–05, 1941–42, 1947–48, 1951–52, 1977–78
Challenge Cup Winners	1905–06, 1943–44, 1946–47, 1948–49
Runners-up	1897–98, 1944–45, 1947–48, 1972–73
Premiership Winners	1977–78
Runners-up	1978–79, 1979–80, 1989–90
Yorkshire Cup Winners	1906–07, 1940–41, 1941–42, 1943–44, 1945–46, 1948–49, 1949–50, 1953–54, 1965–66, 1978–79, 1987–88, 1989–90
Runners-up	1913–14, 1981–82, 1982–83
Yorkshire League Winners	1899–1900, 1900–01, 1939–40, 1940–41, 1947–48
Runners-up	1897–98, 1948–49, 1951–52
Regal Trophy Winners	1974–75, 1979–80
Runners-up	1990–91
Division Two Champions	1973–74

BRAMLEY

Ground	McLaren Field
Colours	Black and yellow jerseys with white bands, black shorts
First home game	12 Sep 1896 v Batley, won 10–5
First away game	5 Sep 1896 v Heckmondwike, drew 0–0
Record crowd	12 600 v Leeds, 7 May 1947
Highest score	62–14 v Dewsbury, 30 Oct 1988
Highest against	7–92 v Australians, 9 Nov 1921

INDIVIDUAL RECORDS

Tries – match	7	J Sedgewick v Normanton, 16 Apr 1906
Goals – match	11	B Ward v Doncaster, 1 Sep 1974
Points – match	28	B Ward v Doncaster, 1 Sep 1974
Tries – season	34	P Lister, 1985–86

Peter Lister, Bramley's most prolific try-scorer with 140 (1982–91).

Goals – season	130	J Wilson, 1961–62
Points – season	276	G Langfield, 1956–57
Tries – career	140	P Lister, 1982–91
Goals – career	926	J Wilson, 1953–64
Points – career	1903	J Wilson, 1953–64
Games – career	406+4	J Wolford, 1962–76

CLUB HONOURS

BBC2 Floodlit Trophy Winners	1973–74
Promotion	1976–77

CARLISLE

Ground	Gillford Park
Colours	Royal blue jerseys with red and white stripes, red shorts
First home game	16 Aug 1981 v Wigan, lost 6–9
First away game	30 Aug 1981 v Bramley, won 10–4
Record crowd	5903 v Workington T, 6 Sep 1981
Highest score	60–0 v Nottingham C, 11 Mar 1990
Highest against	0–112 v St Helens, 14 Sep 1986

INDIVIDUAL RECORDS

Tries – match	4	G Peacham v Workington T, 25 Jan 1987
	4	K Pape v Rochdale H, 11 Feb 1987
Goals – match	10	B Vickers v Nottingham C, 11 Mar 1990
Points – match	24	B Vickers v Nottingham C, 11 Mar 1990
Tries – season	25	M Morgan, 1981–82
	25	G Peacham, 1984–85
Goals – season	113	S Ferres, 1981–82
Points – season	242	S Ferres, 1981–82
Tries – career	132	K Pape, 1984–91
Goals – career	288	B Vickers, 1988–91
Points – career	594	B Vickers, 1988–91
Games – career	225	K Pape, 1984–91

CLUB HONOURS

Promotion   1981–82

CASTLEFORD

Ground	Wheldon Road
Colours	White jerseys with black and amber bands, amber shorts
First home game	1 Sep 1926 v Rochdale H, lost 0–3
First away game	28 Aug 1926 v Hull, lost 0–22
Record crowd	25 449 v Hunslet, 3 Mar 1935
Highest score	94–12 v Huddersfield, 18 Sep 1988
Highest against	12–62 v St Helens, 16 Apr 1986

INDIVIDUAL RECORDS

Tries – match	5	D Foster v Hunslet, 10 Nov 1972
	5	J Joyner v Millom, 16 Sep 1973
	5	S Fenton v Dewsbury, 27 Jan 1978
	5	I French v Hunslet, 9 Feb 1986
	5	S Ellis v Whitehaven, 10 Dec 1989
Goals – match	17	G Lloyd v Millom, 16 Sep 1973
Points – match	43	G Lloyd v Millom, 16 Sep 1973
Tries – season	36	K Howe, 1963–64
Goals – season	158	G Lloyd, 1976–77
Points – season	334	R Beardmore, 1983–84
Tries – career	206	A Hardisty, 1958–71
Goals – career	875	A Lunn, 1951–63
Points – career	1870	A Lunn, 1951–63
Games – career	581+22	J Joyner, 1973–91

GREAT BRITAIN CAPS

A Atkinson, K Beardmore, W Bryant, J Croston, B Cunniffe, W Davies, D Edwards, S Ellis, K England, A Hardisty, D Hartley, K Hepworth, S Irwin, J Joyner, B Lockwood, A Marchant, R Millward, S Norton, D Plange, M Reilly, P Small, G Steadman, G Stephens, D Walton, J Ward, K Ward

CLUB HONOURS

Championship Runners-up	1938–39, 1968–69
Challenge Cup Winners	1934–35, 1968–69, 1969–70, 1985–86
Premiership Runners-up	1983–84
Yorkshire Cup Winners	1977–78, 1981–82, 1986–87, 1990–91
Runners-up	1948–49, 1950–51, 1968–69, 1971–72, 1983–84, 1985–86, 1987–88, 1988–89
Yorkshire League Winners	1932–33, 1938–39, 1964–65
Runners-up	1936–37, 1965–66, 1968–69, 1969–70
Eastern Division Runners-up	1963–64
Regal Trophy Winners	1976–77
BBC2 Floodlit Trophy Winners	1965–66, 1966–67, 1967–68, 1976–77
Charity Shield Runners-up	1986–87

CHORLEY

Ground	Victory Park
Colours	Black jerseys with gold and red hoops, black shorts
First home game	30 Aug 1989 v Trafford B, won 12–6
First away game	3 Sep 1989 v Swinton, lost 4–48
Record crowd	*At Victory Park* 2851 v Oldham, 21 Jan 1990
	At home game 5026 v Wigan, 15 Sep 1989 (played at Leigh)
Highest score	46–12 v Runcorn, 1 Jan 1990
Highest against	16–66 v Oldham, 18 Feb 1990
	5–66 v Leigh, 2 Dec 1990

INDIVIDUAL RECORDS

Tries – match	3	G Bimson v Runcorn H, 1 Jan 1990
	3	M Knight v Nottingham C, 8 Apr 1990

Goals – match	6	M Smith v Runcorn H, 1 Jan 1990
	6	M Smith v Nottingham C, 8 Apr 1990
Points – match	12	G Bimson v Runcorn H, 1 Jan 1990
	12	M Knight v Nottingham C, 8 Apr 1990
	12	M Smith v Runcorn H, 1 Jan 1990
	12	M Smith v Nottingham C, 8 Apr 1990
	12	D Wood v Ryedale–York, 24 Mar 1991
Tries – season	10	D Bacon, 1989–90
Goals – season	73	M Smith, 1989–90
Points – season	142	M Smith, 1989–90
Tries – career	14	M Knight, 1989–91
	14	A Whittaker, 1989–91
Goals – career	132	M Smith, 1989–91
Points – career	257	M Smith, 1989–91
Games – career	57+2	M Smith, 1989–91

DEWSBURY

Ground	Owl Lane*
Colours	Red, amber and black hooped jerseys, white shorts
First home game	7 Sep 1901 v Sowerby Bridge, won 3–0
First away game	14 Sep 1901 v Goole, won 10–3
Record crowd	26 584 v Halifax, 30 Oct 1920
Highest score	72–0 v Doncaster, 7 Oct 1984
Highest against	0–82 v Widnes, 30 Nov 1986

INDIVIDUAL RECORDS

Tries – match	8	D Thomas v Liverpool C, 13 Apr 1907
Goals – match	10	J Ledgard v Yorkshire Amateurs, 13 Sep 1947
	10	N Stephenson v Blackpool B, 28 Aug 1972
	10	C Wilkinson v Huddersfield, 27 Mar 1989
Points – match	29	J Lyman v Hull, 22 Apr 1919
Tries – season	40	D Thomas, 1906–07
Goals – season	145	N Stephenson, 1972–73
Points – season	368	N Stephenson, 1972–73
Tries – career	144	J Lyman, 1913–31
Goals – career	863	N Stephenson, 1968–86
Points – career	2082	N Stephenson, 1968–86
Games – career	454	J Lyman, 1913–31

* Dewsbury are to play at Mount Pleasant, Batley, in 1991–92. The club hopes to commence playing at Owl Lane when building permission is granted.

GREAT BRITAIN CAPS

A Bates, F Gallagher, J Ledgard, R Pollard, M Stephenson, H Street

CLUB HONOURS

Championship Winners	1941–42, 1942–43 (void), 1972–73
Runners-up	1946–47
Challenge Cup Winners	1911–12, 1942–43
Runners-up	1928–29
Yorkshire Cup Winners	1925–26, 1927–28, 1942–43
Runners-up	1918–19, 1921–22, 1940–41, 1972–73
Yorkshire League Winners	1946–47
BBC2 Floodlit Trophy Runners-up	1975–76
Division Two Champions	1904–05
Promotion	1976–77, 1984–85

DONCASTER

Ground	Tattersfield
Colours	Blue and gold jerseys, blue shorts
First home game	18 Aug 1951 v Wakefield T, won 10–3
First away game	22 Aug 1951 v Featherstone R, lost 5–19
Record crowd	10 000 v Bradford N, 16 Feb 1952
Highest score	58–2 v Bramley, 6 Jan 1991
Highest against	3–75 v Leigh, 28 Mar 1976

INDIVIDUAL RECORDS

Tries – match	4	V Grace v Rochdale H, 4 Oct 1952
	4	B Tasker v Leeds, 26 Oct 1963
	4	J Buckton v Rochdale H, 30 Aug 1981
	4	A Kemp v Carlisle, 23 Nov 1986
	4	N Turner v Keighley, 22 Oct 1989
Goals – match	9	D Towle v York, 9 Sep 1967
	9	D Carroll v Bramley, 6 Jan 1991
Points – match	20	K Jones v Whitehaven, 13 Mar 1988
	20	D Noble v Dewsbury, 2 Oct 1988
Tries – season	21	M Roache, 1989–90
Goals – season	118	D Noble, 1985–86
Points – season	250	D Noble, 1986–87
Tries – career	72	N Turner, 1985–89
Goals – career	845	D Noble, 1974–89
Points – career	1741	D Noble, 1974–89
Games – career	307+15	D Noble, 1974–89

FEATHERSTONE ROVERS

Ground	Post Office Road
Colours	Blue and white hooped jerseys, blue shorts
First home game	3 Sep 1921 v Hull, lost 9–21
First away game	27 Aug 1921 v Bradford N, won 17–3
Record crowd	17 531 v St Helens, 21 Mar 1959
Highest score	86–18 v Keighley, 17 Sep 1989
Highest against	2–70 v Halifax, 14 Apr 1941

INDIVIDUAL RECORDS

Tries – match	6	M Smith v Doncaster, 13 Apr 1968
	6	C Bibb v Keighley, 17 Sep 1989
Goals – match	13	M Knapper v Keighley, 17 Sep 1989
Points – match	30	M Knapper v Keighley, 17 Sep 1989
Tries – season	31	C Woolford, 1958–59
Goals – season	163	S Quinn, 1979–80
Points – season	375	S Quinn, 1979–80
Tries – career	162	Don Fox, 1953–65
Goals – career	1210	S Quinn, 1976–88
Points – career	2656	S Quinn, 1976–88
Games – career	440	J Denton, 1921–34

GREAT BRITAIN CAPS

T Askin, C Bibb, J Bridges, T Clawson, M Dixon, S Evans, Deryck Fox, Don Fox, D Hobbs, G Jordan, A Morgan, S Nash, P Newlove, P Smith, J Thompson

Challenge Cup semi-final, 1974 – Featherstone scrum-half Steve Nash, a veteran of 24 Test matches (1971–82), gets the ball away from a scrum as Rovers beat Leigh 21–14 at Leeds.

CLUB HONOURS

Championship Winners	1976–77
Runners-up	1927–28, 1975–76
Challenge Cup Winners	1966–67, 1972–73, 1982–83
Runners-up	1951–52, 1973–74
Yorkshire Cup Winners	1939–40, 1959–60
Runners-up	1928–29, 1963–64, 1966–67, 1969–70, 1970–71, 1976–77, 1977–78, 1989–90
Yorkshire League Runners-up	1927–28, 1961–62
Division Two Champions	1979–80
Promotion	1987–88
Division Two Premiership Runners-up	1987–88
Captain Morgan Trophy Runners-up	1973–74

FULHAM

Ground	Crystal Palace National Sports Centre
Colours	Red and white chevrons on black jerseys, black shorts
First home game	14 Sep 1980 v Wigan, won 24–5
First away game	21 Sep 1980 v Keighley, lost 13–24
Record crowd	15 013 v Wakefield T, 15 Feb 1981
Highest score	61–22 v Huddersfield, 23 Oct 1988
Highest against	6–72 v Whitehaven, 14 Sep 1986

INDIVIDUAL RECORDS

Tries – match	3	Fifteen instances
Goals – match	11	S Guyett v Huddersfield, 23 Oct 1988
	11	G Pearce v Runcorn H, 26 Aug 1990
Points – match	22	A Platt v Mansfield M, 10 May 1986
	22	G Pearce v Runcorn H, 26 Aug 1990
Tries – season	27	J Crossley, 1982–83
Goals – season	136	S Diamond, 1982–83
Points – season	308	S Diamond, 1982–83
Tries – career	73	H M'Barki, 1981–91
Goals – career	309	S Diamond, 1981–84
Points – career	691	S Diamond, 1981–84
Games – career	146+12	H M'Barki, 1981–91

GREAT BRITAIN CAP

J Dalgreen

CLUB HONOURS

Division Two Champions	1982–83
Promotion	1980–81

HALIFAX

Ground	Thrum Hall
Colours	Blue and white hooped jerseys, white shorts
First home game	21 Sep 1895 v Widnes, won 6–0
First away game	7 Sep 1895 v Liversedge, won 5–0
Record crowd	29 153 v Wigan, 21 Mar 1959
Highest score	82–8 v Runcorn H, 14 Oct 1990
Highest against	0–64 v Wigan, 7 Mar 1923

INDIVIDUAL RECORDS

Tries – match	8	K Williams v Dewsbury, 9 Nov 1957
Goals – match	14	B Burton v Hunslet, 27 Aug 1972
Points – match	31	B Burton v Hunslet, 27 Aug 1972
Tries – season	48	J Freeman, 1956–57
Goals – season	147	T Griffiths, 1955–56
Points – season	298	C Whitfield, 1986–87
Tries – career	290	J Freeman, 1954–67
Goals – career	1028	R James, 1961–71
Points – career	2191	R James, 1961–71
Games – career	481	S Kielty, 1946–58

GREAT BRITAIN CAPS

A Ackerley, A Bassett, J Beames, N Bentham, H Beverley, O Burgham, A Daniels, W Davies, C Dixon, P Dixon, P Eccles, T Fogerty, A Halmshaw, N James, R Lloyd, A Milnes, S Prosser, D Rees, C Renilson, J Riley, K Roberts, A Robinson, D Schofield, J Shaw, C Stacey, J Thorley, J Wilkinson, F Williams, D Willicombe

CLUB HONOURS

Championship Winners	1902–03, 1906–07, 1964–65, 1985–86
Runners-up	1895–96, 1942–43, 1944–45, 1952–53, 1953–54, 1955–56, 1965–66

Challenge Cup Winners	1902–03, 1903–04, 1930–31, 1938–39, 1986–87		1955–56, 1957–58
		Runners-up	1895–96, 1900–01, 1907–08, 1909–10, 1949–50, 1950–51, 1954–55, 1964–65
Runners-up	1920–21, 1940–41, 1941–42, 1948–49, 1953–54, 1955–56, 1987–88		
		Eastern Division Winners	1963–64
		Regal Trophy Winners	1971–72
Premiership Runners-up	1985–86	Runners-up	1989–90
Yorkshire Cup Winners	1908–09, 1944–45, 1954–55, 1955–56, 1963–64	Promotion	1973–74, 1979–80, 1981–82, 1983–84, 1990–1991
Runners-up	1905–06, 1907–08, 1941–42, 1979–80	Division Two Premiership	
		Runners-up	1990–91
Yorkshire League Winners	1908–09, 1920–21, 1952–53, 1953–54,	Charity Shield Winners	1986–87
		Runners-up	1987–88

Left *Halifax left-winger Johnny Freeman scored a record 290 tries for his club. No player has ever scored as many tries as Freeman and yet failed to win an international or Test cap.*

HUDDERSFIELD

Ground	Fartown
Colours	Claret and gold jerseys, white shorts
First home game	14 Sep 1895 v Wakefield T, drew 10–10
First away game	21 Sep 1895 v Broughton R, lost 3–10
Record crowd	32 912 v Wigan, 4 Mar 1950
Ground record	35 136 Leeds v Wakefield T, Challenge Cup semi-final, 19 Apr 1947
Highest score	119–2 v Swinton Park, 28 Feb 1914
Highest against	12–94 v Castleford, 18 Sep 1988

INDIVIDUAL RECORDS

Tries – match	10	L Cooper v Keighley, 17 Nov 1951
Goals – match	18	M Holland v Swinton Park, 28 Feb 1914
Points – match	39	M Holland v Swinton Park, 28 Feb 1914
Tries – season	80	A Rosenfeld, 1913–14
Goals – season	147	B Gronow, 1919–20
Points – season	332	P Devery, 1952–53
Tries – career	420	L Cooper, 1947–55
Goals – career	958	F Dyson, 1949–63
Points – career	2072	F Dyson, 1949–63
Games – career	485	D Clark, 1909–29

GREAT BRITAIN CAPS

J Bowden, K Bowman, B Briggs, S Brogden, J Chilcott, D Clark, D Close, R Cracknell, J Davies, F Dyson, B Gronow, F Longstaff, K Loxton, S Moorhouse, R Nicholson, J Rogers, K Senior, T Smales, M Sullivan, G Thomas, D Valentine, R Valentine, H Wagstaff, H Young

CLUB HONOURS

Championship Winners		1911–12, 1912–13, 1914–15, 1928–29, 1929–30, 1948–49, 1961–62
	Runners-up	1913–14, 1919–20, 1922–23, 1931–32, 1945–46, 1949–50
Challenge Cup Winners		1912–13, 1914–15, 1919–20, 1932–33, 1944–45, 1952–53
	Runners-up	1934–35, 1961–62
Yorkshire Cup Winners		1909–10, 1911–12, 1913–14, 1914–15, 1918–19, 1919–20, 1926–27, 1931–32, 1938–39, 1950–51, 1952–53, 1957–58
	Runners-up	1910–11, 1923–24, 1925–26, 1930–31, 1937–38, 1942–43, 1949–50, 1960–61
Yorkshire League Winners		1911–12, 1912–13, 1913–14, 1914–15, 1919–20, 1921–22, 1928–29, 1929–30, 1948–49, 1949–50, 1951–52
	Runners-up	1922–23, 1923–24, 1930–31, 1931–32, 1939–40, 1945–46, 1946–47, 1947–48, 1952–53
Eastern Division Runners-up		1962–63
Division Two Champions		1974–75
Promotion		1977–78

Lionel Cooper skirts the Whitehaven cover in 1951. Altogether the Huddersfield winger scored a phenomenal 441 tries (1947–55) to earn fifth place in the all-time try-scoring lists.

HULL

Ground   The Boulevard
Colours   Black and white irregular
                hooped jerseys, black shorts
First home game 21 Sep 1895 v Liversedge,
                won 3–0
First away game 7 Sep 1895 v Batley, lost 3–7
Record crowd   28 798 v Leeds, 7 Mar 1936
Highest score   86–0 v Elland, 1 Apr 1899
Highest against 2–64 v St Helens, 17 Feb
                1988

INDIVIDUAL RECORDS

Tries – match	7	C Sullivan v Doncaster, 15 Apr 1968
Goals – match	14	J Kennedy v Rochdale H, 7 Apr 1921
	14	G Lloyd v Oldham, 10 Sep 1978
Points – match	36	J Kennedy v Keighley, 29 Jan 1921
Tries – season	52	J Harrison, 1914–15
Goals – season	170	G Lloyd, 1978–79
Points – season	369	G Lloyd, 1978–79
Tries – career	250	C Sullivan, 1961–85
Goals – career	687	J Oliver, 1928–45
Points – career	1842	J Oliver, 1928–45
Games – career	501	E Rogers, 1906–25

GREAT BRITAIN CAPS

W Batten, H Bowman, F Boylen, R Coverdale, M Crane,
L Crooks, A Dannatt, G Divorty, J Drake, W Drake,
P Eastwood, S Evans, V Farrar, R Gemmell, E Gwynne,
T Harris, K Harrison, M Harrison, W Holder, L Jackson,
A Keegan, E Morgan, S Norton, W Proctor, P Rose,
G Schofield, T Skerrett, W Stone, C Sullivan, H Taylor,
R Taylor, D Topliss, J Whiteley

CLUB HONOURS

Championship Winners	1919–20, 1920–21, 1935–36, 1955–56, 1957–58, 1982–83
Runners-up	1956–57, 1981–82, 1983–84
Challenge Cup Winners	1913–14, 1981–82
Runners-up	1907–08, 1908–09, 1909–10, 1921–22, 1922–23, 1958–59, 1959–60, 1979–80, 1982–83, 1984–85
Premiership Winners	1990–91
Runners-up	1980–81, 1981–82, 1982–83, 1988–89

Above Hull's Ned Rogers holds the club appearances record with a total of 501 between 1906 and 1925.

Right *Two of the game's most durable forwards clash in the Challenge Cup semi-final of 1982. Mal Reilly (Castleford) takes a grip on Hull's Trevor Skerrett. Skerrett cost Hull a record £40 000 from Wakefield Trinity in 1980.*

Yorkshire Cup Winners	1923–24, 1969–70, 1982–83, 1983–84, 1984–85
Runners-up	1912–13, 1914–15, 1920–21, 1927–28, 1938–39, 1946–47, 1953–54, 1954–55, 1955–56, 1959–60, 1967–68, 1986–87
Yorkshire League Winners	1918–19, 1922–23, 1926–27, 1935–36
Runners-up	1898–99, 1913–14, 1919–20, 1920–21, 1921–22, 1934–35, 1940–41, 1953–54, 1955–56, 1956–57, 1957–58, 1959–60
Regal Trophy Winners	1981–82
Runners-up	1975–76, 1984–85
BBC2 Floodlit Trophy Winners	1979–80
Division Two Champions	1976–77, 1978–79

HULL KINGSTON ROVERS

Ground	Craven Park
Colours	Blue trimmed red band on white jerseys, white shorts
First home game	16 Sep 1899 v Hull, won 8–2
First away game	2 Sep 1899 v Bradford, lost 0–3
Record crowd	27 670 v Hull, 3 Apr 1953
Highest score	100–6 v Nottingham C, 19 Aug 1990
Highest against	0–68 v Halifax, 3 Apr 1956

Hull KR full-back Laurie Osbourne landed over 700 goals for his club (1920–32) and captained Rovers to the 1924–25 Championship.

INDIVIDUAL RECORDS

Tries – match	11	G West v Brookland R, 4 Mar 1905
Goals – match	14	A Carmichael v Merthyr Tydfil, 8 Oct 1910
	14	M Fletcher v Whitehaven, 18 Mar 1990
	14	C Armstrong v Nottingham C, 19 Aug 1990
Points – match	53	G West v Brookland R, 4 Mar 1905
Tries – season	45	G Prohm, 1984–85
Goals – season	199	M Fletcher, 1989–90
Points – season	450	M Fletcher, 1989–90
Tries – career	207	R Millward, 1966–80
Goals – career	1192	C Kellett, 1956–67
Points – career	2489	C Kellett, 1956–67
Games – career	481+8	M Smith, 1975–91

GREAT BRITAIN CAPS

D Bishop, C Burton, A Burwell, L Casey, G Clark, A Dockar, G Fairbairn, J Feetham, P Flanagan, F Foster, D Hall, P Harkin, S Hartley, P Hogan, R Holdstock, W Holliday, D Laws, B Lockwood, P Lowe, R Millward, H Poole, P Rose, M Smith, B Tyson, D Watkinson, C Young

CLUB HONOURS

Championship Winners		1922–23, 1924–25, 1978–79, 1983–84, 1984–85
	Runners-up	1920–21, 1967–68, 1982–83
Challenge Cup Winners		1979–80
	Runners-up	1904–05, 1924–25, 1963–64, 1980–81, 1985–86
Premiership Winners		1980–81, 1983–84
	Runners-up	1984–85
Yorkshire Cup Winners		1920–21, 1929–30, 1966–67, 1967–68, 1971–72, 1974–75, 1985–86
	Runners-up	1906–07, 1911–12, 1933–34, 1962–63, 1975–76, 1980–81, 1984–85
Yorkshire League Winners		1924–25, 1925–26
	Runners-up	1911–12, 1912–13, 1966–67, 1967–68
Eastern Division Winners		1962–63
Regal Trophy Winners		1984–85
	Runners-up	1981–82, 1985–86
BBC2 Floodlit Trophy Winners		1977–78
	Runners-up	1979–80
Division Two Champions		1989–90
Promotion		1974–75
Division Two Premiership Runners-up		1989–90
Charity Shield Runners-up		1985–86

HUNSLET

Ground	Elland Road
Colours	Myrtle, white and flame jerseys, myrtle shorts
First home game	14 Sep 1895 v Oldham, won 16–8
First away game	7 Sep 1895 v Warrington, lost 4–5
Record crowd	24 700 v Wigan, 15 Mar 1924
Ground record	54 112, Hunslet v Leeds, Championship Final, 30 Apr 1938. At this time Elland Road was purely a soccer ground
Highest score	75–5 v Broughton Rec, 20 Mar 1897
Highest against	8–76 v Halifax, 27 Aug 1972

INDIVIDUAL RECORDS

Tries – match	7	G Dennis v Bradford N, 20 Jan 1934
Goals – match	12	W Langton v Keighley, 18 Aug 1959
Points – match	28	T Lumb v Runcorn H, 7 Oct 1990
Tries – season	34	A Snowden, 1956–57
Goals – season	181	W Langton, 1958–59
Points – season	380	W Langton, 1958–59
Tries – career	154	F Williamson, 1943–55
Goals – career	1044	W Langton, 1955–66
Points – career	2202	W Langton, 1955–66
Games – career	572	J Walkington, 1927–48
	569+10	G Gunney, 1951–73

GREAT BRITAIN CAPS

W Batten, H Beverley, A Burnell, H Crowther, J Evans, K Eyre, B Gabbitas, G Gunney, D Hartley, J Higson, D Jenkins, A Jenkinson, W Jukes, B Prior, W Ramsey, B Shaw, G Shelton, F Smith, S Smith, C Thompson, L White, R Williams, H Wilson

CLUB HONOURS

Championship Winners	1907–08, 1937–38
Runners-up	1905–06, 1958–59
Challenge Cup Winners	1907–08, 1933–34
Runners-up	1898–99, 1964–65
Yorkshire Cup Winners	1905–06, 1907–08, 1962–63
Runners-up	1908–09, 1929–30, 1931–32, 1944–45, 1956–57, 1965–66
Yorkshire League Winners	1897–98, 1907–08, 1931–32
Runners-up	1910–11, 1933–34, 1937–38, 1958–59
Division Two Champions	1962–63, 1986–87
Promotion	1976–77, 1978–79, 1983–84
Division Two Premiership Runners-up	1986–87

KEIGHLEY

Ground	Lawkholme Lane
Colours	Scarlet and emerald green chevrons on white jerseys, white shorts
First home game	21 Sep 1901 v Wakefield T, won 7–6
First away game	7 Sep 1901 v Bramley, won 9–2
Record crowd	14 500 v Halifax, 3 Mar 1951
Highest score	67–0 v Castleford, 13 Jan 1906
Highest against	2–92 v Leigh, 30 Apr 1986

INDIVIDUAL RECORDS

Tries – match	5	I Jagger v Castleford, 13 Jan 1906
	5	S Stacey v Liverpool C, 9 Mar 1907
Goals – match	11	R Walker v Castleford, 13 Jan 1906
	11	H Cook v Hull KR, 31 Oct 1953
Points – match	24	J Phillips v Halifax, 5 Oct 1957
Tries – season	30	J Sherburn, 1934–35
Goals – season	155	B Jefferson, 1973–74
Points – season	331	B Jefferson, 1973–74
Tries – career	155	S Stacey, 1904–20
Goals – career	967	B Jefferson, 1965–77
Points – career	2116	B Jefferson, 1965–77
Games – career	372	H Tempest, 1902–15
	372	D McGoun, 1925–38

GREAT BRITAIN CAP

T Hollindrake

CLUB HONOURS

Challenge Cup Runners-up	1936–37
Yorkshire Cup Runners-up	1943–44, 1951–52
Division Two Champions	1902–03
Promotion	1962–63, 1973–74

LEWIS JONES

The Golden Boy's Golden Season

Lewis Jones was one of those players who come along once in a life-time, one upon whom the title 'genius' comfortably rests. A match-winner throughout his career, Jones left an indelible impression on all who beheld his artistry, whether at centre, stand-off or full-back. A creator of tries, a scorer of tries, a supreme place-kicker, a deft dropper of goals, an inspirational captain, a moody maestro – Benjamin Lewis Jones was all of these and more. He was idolised in Leeds, with whom he played all his English Rugby League after joining them for a reputed £6000 in 1952.

His career had begun in Welsh schoolboy Rugby Union in his native Gorseinon and he had graduated to senior football with Neath, Devonport Services and Llanelli. He was only 18 when he won the first of 10 caps for Wales in 1950, a year in which he was called out to New Zealand and Australia for the British Lions tour, as a replacement for the injured Irish full-back GW Norton. By the time Leeds lured him to League he had been christened the 'Golden Boy' of Rugby Union.

After an unfortunate injury-ridden start to his professional career, Lewis soon became a crowd-puller with extraordinary displays of attacking rugby and prodigious kicking feats. By 1953 he had become a dual international for Wales and in 1954 he became a British Lion under Rugby League auspices. His performances in Australia and New Zealand brought him a record 127 goals and 278 points and enhanced his already burgeoning box-office appeal.

Jones experienced his most successful season, however, in 1956–57 when he shattered the record of Wigan full-back Jim Sullivan who had amassed 406 points in 1933–34. By the season's end Lewis had piled up 496 points to create a world record which has still not been bettered. In the course of creating the new record, all manner of club and Rugby League records were swept away by this Merlinesque magician.

The first record to fall, in only the second game of the season, was that of most points in a match for Leeds. Jones collected 31 of Leeds' points (3 tries, 11 goals) – another record which still stands – in a 40–14 victory at Bradford. It was to be his biggest haul of the season. The Test selectors were somehow unmoved by Jones' tall scoring in the first half of the season and left him out of the Ashes series altogether. Jones' reply was to keep on scoring. By the turn of the year he had 234 points to his credit but 1957 would see him accelerate his points gathering.

The Test selectors were unable to ignore him any longer and he was reinstated at centre for all three Tests against

LEWIS JONES 1956–57

1956	Match		Points	1957	Match		Points
17 Aug	Halifax	H	6	5 Jan	Hull	H	16
22 Aug	Bradford N	A	31	12 Jan	Warrington	A	9
25 Aug	Wigan	A	8	19 Jan	St Helens	H	13
27 Aug	Featherstone R	H	11	26 Jan	GB v France	**	21
1 Sep	Wakefield T (YC)	A	9	2 Feb	Huddersfield	H	12
8 Sep	Dewsbury	A	12	9 Feb	Wigan (CC)	H	7
15 Sep	Warrington	H	14	16 Feb	York	A	17
22 Sep	Huddersfield	A	6	23 Feb	Warrington (CC)	H	13
29 Sep	York	H	12	27 Feb	Castleford	H	11
3 Oct	Rest v GB	*	8	3 Mar	GB v France	† †	13
6 Oct	Batley	A	14	9 Mar	Halifax (CC)	A	10
13 Oct	Australians	H	DNP	16 Mar	Wakefield T	H	13
20 Oct	Hull KR	A	DNP	20 Mar	Bradford N	H	13
27 Oct	Wigan	H	4	23 Mar	Hull	A	4
29 Oct	RL v Australia	†	6	30 Mar	Whitehaven (CC)	*	2
3 Nov	Hunslet	A	2	3 Apr	Wakefield T	A	6
10 Nov	Barrow	H	12	6 Apr	St Helens	A	0
17 Nov	Halifax	A	8	10 Apr	GB v France	§	17
24 Nov	Keighley	H	15	12 Apr	Hull KR	H	DNP
1 Dec	Barrow	A	8	13 Apr	Dewsbury	H	18
8 Dec	Bramley	A	10	19 Apr	Hunslet	H	16
15 Dec	Doncaster	H	8	20 Apr	Featherstone R	A	4
22 Dec	Bradford N	H	5	22 Apr	Castleford	A	4
	(Abandoned)			23 Apr	Bramley	H	17
25 Dec	Batley	H	19	4 May	Oldham (PO)	A	6
29 Dec	Keighley	A	6	11 May	Barrow (CC)	§ §	0

*	At Odsal	**	At Headingley
†	At Leigh	† †	At Toulouse
DNP	Did not play	§	At St Helens
YC	Yorkshire Cup	§ §	At Wembley
PO	Championship Play-off	CC	Challenge Cup

Lewis Jones in action against Barrow at Wembley in 1957. Test centre Phil Jackson misses the tackle.

France. His scoring in them was phenomenal – 51 points from 3 tries and 21 goals. The first Test, on his home ground at Headingley on 26 January 1957, produced a British Test record of 21 points for the golden boy. The second at Toulouse saw Jones conjure a 75-yard try to help Britain salvage a 19–19 draw, 13 of the points falling to him. On 6 April Jones failed to score for the first time that season as Leeds were swamped 3–44 at St Helens, but four days later on the same ground he was a hero after grabbing 17 points in the third Test against the

French.

Leeds were progressing through the Challenge Cup rounds and on 30 March met Whitehaven in the semi-final at Odsal; they had to struggle desperately to beat the Cumbrians 10–9, but two goals from Jones pushed him past Jim Sullivan's record 406 points and Leeds were at Wembley.

Five goals in a 28–13 local derby victory over Hunslet on 19 April at Headingley took Jones past the club record for a season of 150 goals, kicked by Bert Cook, a New Zealand full-back, in 1950–51. Cook's club

record of 312 points had long since been picked off by the relentless Welshman. Three goals at Oldham in the Championship semi-final on 4 May brought Jones level with Sullivan's all-time goals record of 194 in a season, an achievement not recognised at the time. Logic said the record would be Jones' alone the following week when Leeds met Barrow at Wembley in the final game of the season. Logic flew out of the window. Leeds won all right, 9–7, but Lewis Jones failed to score!

LEEDS

Ground	Headingley
Colours	Blue and amber jerseys, white shorts
First home game	21 Sep 1895 v Brighouse R, won 3–0
First away game	7 Sep 1895 v Leigh, won 6–3
Record crowd	40 175 v Bradford N, 21 May 1947
Highest score	102–0 v Coventry, 12 Apr 1913
Highest against	0–71 v Wakefield T, 12 Sep 1945

INDIVIDUAL RECORDS

Tries – match	8	F Webster v Coventry, 12 Apr 1913
	8	E Harris v Bradford N, 14 Sep 1931
Goals – match	13	L Jones v Blackpool B, 19 Aug 1957
Points – match	31	L Jones v Bradford N, 22 Aug 1956
Tries – season	63	E Harris, 1935–36
Goals – season	166	L Jones, 1956–57
Points – season	431	L Jones, 1956–57
Tries – career	393	E Harris, 1930–39
Goals – career	1244	L Jones, 1952–64
Points – career	2920	L Jones, 1952–64
Games – career	604+17	J Holmes, 1968–89

GREAT BRITAIN CAPS

L Adams, J Atkinson, J Bacon, R Batten, J Birch, S Brogden, J Brough, G Brown, M Clark, T Clawson, D Creasser, L Crooks, W Davies, K Dick, R Dickinson, P Dixon, L Dyl, A Fisher, P Ford, R Gemmell, C Gibson, J Grayshon, R Haigh, D Hallas, F Harrison, D Heron, J Holmes, S Hynes, W Jarman, D Jeanes, D Jenkins, L Jones, K Jubb, J Lowe, P Medley, I Owens, S Pitchford, H Poole, R Powell, D Prosser, Keith Rayne, Kevin Rayne, B Risman, D Robinson, D Rose, G Schofield, B Seabourne, B Shaw, M Shoebottom, B Simms, A Smith, S Smith, D Stephenson, J Stevenson, S Stockwell, A Terry, A Thomas, P Thomas, J Thompson, A Turnbull, H Waddell, D Ward, W Ward, F Webster, R Williams, H Woods, G Wriglesworth, F Young

CLUB HONOURS

Championship Winners	1960–61, 1968–69, 1971–72
Runners-up	1914–15, 1928–29, 1929–30, 1930–31, 1937–38, 1969–70,
Challenge Cup Winners	1972–73, 1989–90 1909–10, 1922–23, 1931–32, 1935–36, 1940–41, 1941–42, 1956–57, 1967–68, 1976–77, 1977–78
Runners-up	1942–43, 1946–47, 1970–71, 1971–72
Premiership Winners	1974–75, 1978–79
Yorkshire Cup Winners	1921–22, 1928–29, 1930–31, 1932–33, 1934–35, 1935–36, 1937–38, 1958–59, 1968–69, 1970–71, 1972–73, 1973–74, 1975–76, 1976–77, 1979–80, 1980–81, 1988–89
Runners-up	1919–20, 1947–48, 1961–62, 1964–65
Yorkshire League Winners	1927–28, 1930–31, 1933–34, 1934–35, 1936–37, 1937–38, 1950–51, 1954–55, 1956–57, 1960–61, 1966–67, 1967–68, 1968–69, 1969–70
Runners-up	1914–15, 1918–19, 1924–25, 1926–27, 1928–29, 1929–30, 1935–36, 1938–39
Yorkshire Senior Competition Winners	1901–02
Regal Trophy Winners	1972–73, 1983–84
Runners-up	1982–83, 1987–88
BBC2 Floodlit Trophy Winners	1970–71
Promotion	1902–03

LEIGH

Ground	Hilton Park
Colours	Cherry and white hooped jerseys, red shorts
First home game	7 Sep 1895 v Leeds, lost 3–6
First away game	14 Sep 1895 v Stockport, won 10–3
Record crowd	31 326 v St Helens, 14 Mar 1953
Highest score	92–2 v Keighley, 30 Apr 1986
Highest against	8–60 v Salford, 25 May 1940

INDIVIDUAL RECORDS

Tries – match	6	J Wood v York, 4 Oct 1947
Goals – match	15	M Stacey v Doncaster, 28 Mar 1976

Points – match	38	J Woods v Blackpool B, 11 Sep 1977
Tries – season	49	S Halliwell, 1985–86
Goals – season	173	C Johnson, 1985–86
Points – season	400	C Johnson, 1985–86
Tries – career	189	M Martyn, 1954–67
Goals – career	1043	J Ledgard, 1948–58
Points – career	2272	J Woods, 1976–90
Games – career	503	A Worrall, 1920–38

GREAT BRITAIN CAPS

K Ashcroft, J Cartwright, D Chisnall, J Darwell, S Donlan, D Drummond, P Foster, C Johnson, F Kitchen, J Ledgard, G Lewis, M Martyn, W Mooney, S Owen, C Pawsey, W Robinson, J Walsh, W Winstanley, J Woods

CLUB HONOURS

Championship Winners	1905–06, 1981–82
Challenge Cup Winners	1920–21, 1970–71

Prop forward Albert Worrall holds the Leigh career appearances record with 503 (1920–38).

Lancashire Cup Winners	1952–53, 1955–56, 1970–71, 1981–82
Runners-up	1905–06, 1909–10, 1920–21, 1922–23, 1949–50, 1951–52, 1963–64, 1969–70
Lancashire League Runners-up	1918–19, 1949–50, 1952–53
BBC2 Floodlit Trophy Winners	1969–70, 1972–73
Runners-up	1967–68, 1976–77
Division Two Champions	1977–78, 1985–86, 1988–89
Promotion	1963–64, 1975–76
ITA Trophy Runners-up	1955–56

NOTTINGHAM CITY

Ground	Harvey Hadden Stadium
Colours	Green and yellow jerseys, green shorts
First home game	9 Sep 1984 v Wakefield T, won 15–0
First away game	2 Sep 1984 v Runcorn H, won 35–6
Record crowd	2545 v Halifax, 1 Oct 1989
Highest score	54–10 v Doncaster, 4 Nov 1984
Highest against	6–100 v Hull KR, 19 Aug 1990

INDIVIDUAL RECORDS

Tries – match	4	K Whiteman v Doncaster, 4 Nov 1984
Goals – match	7	B Holden v Keighley, 10 Mar 1985
	7	W Sanchez v Hunslet, 2 Oct 1988
Points – match	18	B Holden v Keighley, 10 Mar 1985
	18	M Howarth v Dewsbury, 17 Jan 1988
Tries – season	13	S Nicholson, 1984–85
	13	K Whiteman, 1984–85
Goals – season	63	C Sanderson, 1984–85
Points – season	136	C Sanderson, 1984–85
Tries – career	26	C Willis, 1984–91
Goals – career	79	C Sanderson, 1984–86
Points – career	195	D Oates, 1986–91
Games – career	103+12	C Willis, 1984–91

Note – The club began life as Mansfield Marksman in 1984–85. It became Nottingham City in 1989–90.

JOE FERGUSON

Rugby League's Most Durable Forward

Rugby League is undoubtedly the most physically tough of all team games, and forwards have always borne the brunt of the attendant punishment and pain. In the earliest days of the game, forwards had to be exceptionally robust to cope with the incessant scrummaging, dribbling and tackling they were required to undertake. All too frequently, injury has prematurely ended the careers of packmen. Yet there have been those who have to all intents and purposes seemed indestructible, despite the mayhem which sometimes engulfed them.

Foremost amongst these men of iron was Joe Ferguson, a Cumbrian forward who despite playing in the game's earliest era holds records which still stand. No forward has appeared in more first-class fixtures than Ferguson's 677 between 1899 and 1923. Oddly enough he began his career as far away from the forwards as possible, as a full-back in Cumberland junior rugby with Brookland Rovers, and he was a good enough footballer to revert to full-back for a handful of games for Oldham in 1904. But it was as a hooking forward that Joe Ferguson made his name – the term 'hooker' was not generally current until after the First World War.

Joining Oldham in 1899 he quickly established himself in the first team and became one of the most inspirational pack leaders in the game. During his time at the Watersheddings, Oldham were invariably amongst the leading clubs and Ferguson was the recipient of caps and cups aplenty. The only trophy that he never held aloft as Oldham captain was in fact the Challenge Cup, having been in defeated teams in the finals of 1907 against Warrington and 1912 against Dewsbury. Oldham reached the Championship Final in five consecutive seasons (1906–07 to 1910–11) and Joe played in all five, the first three being lost. The last two, under his captaincy, brought 13–7 and 20–7 victories over Jim Leytham's great Wigan side. Oldham won four Lancashire League Championships and appeared in eight Lancashire Cup Finals (four successful) in Ferguson's days with the 'Spindles'.

Apart from his skills as a forward, Joe was a splendid goalkicker, capable of bisecting the sticks from enormous distances. One of his greatest goals, a drop from half-way, won the Lancashire Cup for Oldham in 1910 when Swinton were pipped 4–3. In 1904–05 and 1905–06 he was the leading goal-kicker in the Northern Union and won many a game for his club and representative teams.

Joe Ferguson had the singular distinction of playing for England at 12-, 13- and 15-a-side.

He was a member of the England team which drew 3–3 against Other Nationalities in the Northern Union's first ever international, at Wigan on 5 April 1904, when experimental teams of 12 participated. On 2 January 1905 he kicked three goals in a 26–11 victory over Other Nationalities at Bradford Park Avenue in the game's first 15-a-side international, and following the game's move to 13-a-side in 1906 he had the distinction of captaining England to victories over New Zealand in 1908 and Wales in 1909. He was among the first choices for Great Britain's initial tour of Australasia in 1910, but turned down the invitation for business reasons.

As a county player Ferguson created a record which, unless county matches come back into vogue, is almost certain to remain unbeaten. From 1900 to 1905 he played 15 times for Lancashire, through his residential qualification, and then represented his native Cumberland in a further 31 matches between 1905 and 1922. His record of 46 county caps has never been challenged. Yet another record is attributed to this remarkable hooker, for when he played his last game for Oldham, at St Helens on 14 April 1923, he was 44 years and 48 days of age. No record of an older player appearing in first-class Rugby League has yet been authenticated.

JOE FERGUSON'S CAREER

Season	OLDHAM Games	Tries	Goals	County	Games	Tries	Goals
1899–1900	20	0	0	LANCS	0	0	0
1900–01	27	1	10	LANCS	2	0	7
1901–02	27	0	14	LANCS	3	0	0
1902–03	35	0	18	LANCS	4	0	0
1903–04	33	0	25	LANCS	3	0	0
1904–05	36	1	44	LANCS	3	0	0
1905–06	41	2	50	CUMB	3	0	0
1906–07	42	11	70	CUMB	2	0	1
1907–08	39	7	55	CUMB	3	0	5
1908–09	36	11	23	CUMB	3	0	0
1909–10	35	5	23	CUMB	2	0	0
1910–11	38	1	13	CUMB	2	0	2
1911–12	37	9	15	CUMB	3	1	3
1912–13	32	3	40	CUMB	2	0	1
1913–14	34	2	23	CUMB	2	0	1
1914–15	35	3	40				
GREAT WAR							
1918–19	13	3	9				
1919–20	32	1	41	CUMB	2	0	4
1920–21	18	0	15	CUMB	2	0	6
1921–22	7	2	4	CUMB	3	1	7
1922–23	9	0	8	CUMB	2	0	1
Totals	626	62	540		46	2	38

Joe Ferguson played 682 first-class games, 677 in the pack. His scoring aggregate was 66 tries, 582 goals, 1362 points.

OLDHAM

Ground	Watersheddings
Colours	Red and white hooped jerseys, red shorts
First home game	21 Sep 1895 v Tyldesley, lost 3–11
First away game	14 Sep 1895 v Hunslet, lost 8–16
Record crowd	28 000 v Huddersfield, 24 Feb 1912
Highest score	67–6 v Liverpool C, 4 Apr 1959
Highest against	11–67 v Hull KR, 24 Sep 1978

Tries – season	49	R Farrar, 1921–22
Goals – season	200	B Ganley, 1957–58
Points – season	412	B Ganley, 1957–58
Tries – career	173	A Davies, 1950–61
Goals – career	1365	B Ganley, 1951–61
Points – career	2775	B Ganley, 1951–61
Games – career	626	J Ferguson, 1899–1923

GREAT BRITAIN CAPS

A Avery, C Bott, A Brough, T Clawson, A Davies, E Davies, T Flanagan, D Foy, B Ganley, A Goodway, W Hall, H Hilton, D Hobbs, D Holland, R Irving, K Jackson, E Knapman, S Little, T Llewellyn, J Lomas, W Longworth, L McIntyre, T O'Grady, J Oster, D Parker, D Phillips, F Pitchford, T Rees, S Rix, R Sloman, A Smith, I Southward, L Thomas, D Turner, G Tyson, H Waddell, T White, C Winslade, A Wood, M Worrall

INDIVIDUAL RECORDS

Tries – match	7	J Miller v Barry, 31 Oct 1908
Goals – match	14	B Ganley v Liverpool C, 4 Apr 1959
Points – match	30	A Johnson v Widnes, 9 Apr 1928

CLUB HONOURS

Championship Winners	1904–05, 1909–10, 1910–11, 1956–57
Runners-up	1906–07, 1907–08, 1908–09, 1921–22, 1954–55

Challenge Cup Winners	1898–99, 1924–25, 1926–27
Runners-up	1906–07, 1911–12, 1923–24, 1925–26
Lancashire Cup Winners	1907–08, 1910–11, 1913–14, 1919–20, 1924–25, 1933–34, 1956–57, 1957–58, 1958–59
Runners-up	1908–09, 1911–12, 1918–19, 1921–22, 1954–55, 1966–67, 1968–69, 1986–87, 1989–90
Lancashire League Winners	1897–98. 1900–01. 1907–08, 1909–10, 1921–22, 1956–57, 1957–58
Runners-up	1895–96, 1896–97, 1898–99, 1899–1900, 1908–09, 1910–11, 1911–12, 1923–24, 1954–55
Division Two Champions	1963–64, 1981–82, 1987–88
Promotion	1974–75, 1979–80, 1989–90
Division Two Premiership Winners	1987–88, 1989–90

ROCHDALE HORNETS

Ground	Spotland
Colours	Blue jerseys with red and white band, white shorts
First home game	28 Sep 1895 v Bradford, lost 3–14
First away game	7 Sep 1895 v St Helens, lost 3–8
Record crowd	26 664 v Oldham, 25 Mar 1922
Ground record	41 831, Oldham v Wigan, Challenge Cup Final, 12 Apr 1924
Highest score	92–0 v Runcorn H, 5 Nov 1989
Highest against	2–79 v Hull, 7 Apr 1921

Left Oldham's record try-scorer Alan Davies beats the Wigan Test second-rower Norman Cherrington for one of his 173 club tries (1950–61).

INDIVIDUAL RECORDS

Tries – match	5	J Corsi v Barrow, 31 Dec 1921
	5	J Corsi v Broughton Moor, 25 Feb 1922
	5	J Williams v St Helens, 4 Apr 1933
	5	N Brelsford v Whitehaven, 3 Sep 1972
Goals – match	14	S Turner v Runcorn H, 5 Nov 1989
Points – match	32	S Turner v Runcorn H, 5 Nov 1989
Tries – season	30	J Williams, 1934–35
Goals – season	115	K Harcombe, 1985–86
Points – season	243	S Turner, 1988–89
Tries – career	103	J Williams, 1931–37
Goals – career	741	W Gowers, 1922–46
Points – career	1497	W Gowers, 1922–46
Games – career	456	W Gowers, 1922–46

GREAT BRITAIN CAPS

J Baxter, J Bennett, J Bowers, T Fogerty, E Jones, M Price, J Robinson, T Woods

CLUB HONOURS

Challenge Cup Winners	1921–22
Lancashire Cup Winners	1911–12, 1914–15, 1918–19
Runners-up	1912–13, 1919–20, 1965–66
Lancashire League Winners	1918–19
Runners-up	1914–15, 1919–20
Regal Trophy Runners-up	1973–74
BBC2 Floodlit Trophy Runners-up	1971–72
Promotion	1975–76, 1977–78, 1989–90

RYEDALE–YORK

Ground	Ryedale Stadium
Colours	Amber, black and white jerseys, white shorts
First home game	7 Sep 1901 v Goole, won 15–3
First away game	21 Sep 1901 v Sowerby Bridge, won 7–2
Record crowd	14 689 v Swinton, 10 Feb 1934
Highest score	70–8 v Keighley, 11 Mar 1990
Highest against	3–75 v Warrington, 23 Sep 1950

INDIVIDUAL RECORDS

Tries – match	6	R Hardgrave v Bramley, 5 Jan 1935
	6	D Kettlestring v Keighley, 11 Mar 1990
Goals – match	11	V Yorke v Whitehaven, 6 Sep 1958
	11	C Gibson v Dewsbury, 28 Sep 1980
Points – match	26	G Steadman v Batley, 25 Nov 1984
	26	G Sullivan v Keighley, 11 Mar 1990
Tries – season	35	J Crossley, 1980–81
Goals – season	146	V Yorke, 1957–58
Points – season	318	G Steadman, 1984–85
Tries – career	167	P Foster, 1955–67
Goals – career	1060	V Yorke, 1954–67
Points – career	2159	V Yorke, 1954–67
Games – career	449	W Hargreaves, 1952–65

GREAT BRITAIN CAPS

E Dawson, H Field, G Smith, J Stevenson, M Sullivan, B Watts, L White

CLUB HONOURS

Challenge Cup Runners-up	1930–31
Yorkshire Cup Winners	1922–23, 1933–34, 1936–37
Runners-up	1935–36, 1957–58, 1978–79
Yorkshire League Runners-up	1932–33
Division Two Champions	1980–81
Promotion	1973–74, 1978–79, 1984–85

ST HELENS

Ground	Knowsley Road
Colours	Red chevrons on white jerseys, white shorts
First home game	7 Sep 1895 v Rochdale H, won 8–3
First away game	21 Sep 1895 v Batley, drew 3–3
Record crowd	35 695 v Wigan, 26 Dec 1949
Highest score	112–0 v Carlisle, 14 Sep 1986
Highest against	3–78 v Warrington, 12 Apr 1909

INDIVIDUAL RECORDS

Tries – match	6	A Ellaby v Barrow, 5 Mar 1932
	6	S Llewellyn v Castleford, 3 Mar 1956
	6	S Llewellyn v Liverpool C, 20 Aug 1956
	6	T Vollenhoven v Wakefield T, 21 Dec 1957
	6	T Vollenhoven v Blackpool B, 23 Apr 1962
	6	F Myler v Maryport, 1 Sep 1969
	6	S Cooper v Hull, 17 Feb 1988
Goals – match	16	P Loughlin v Carlisle, 14 Sep 1986
Points – match	40	P Loughlin v Carlisle, 14 Sep 1986
Tries – season	62	T Vollenhoven, 1958–59
Goals – season	214	K Coslett, 1971–72
Points – season	452	K Coslett, 1971–72
Tries – career	392	T Vollenhoven, 1957–68
Goals – career	1639	K Coslett, 1962–76
Points – career	3413	K Coslett, 1962–76
Games – career	519+12	K Coslett, 1962–76

GREAT BRITAIN CAPS

C Arkwright, L Aston, W Benyon, T Bishop, F Carlton, E Chisnall, E Cunningham, R Dagnall, D Eckersley, A Ellaby, L Fairclough, J Fieldhouse, A Fildes, A Frodsham, P Gorley, D Greenall, P Groves, R Haggerty, M Hicks, N Holding, R Huddart, L Jones, A Karalius, V Karalius, K Kelly, B Ledger, P Loughlin, J Mantle, S McCormick, T McKinney, R Mathias, G Moses, A Murphy, F Myler, G Nicholls, H Pinner, A Platt, A Prescott, A Rhodes, J Stott, M Sullivan, J Tembey, A Terry, J Walsh, K Ward, J Warlow, C Watson

CLUB HONOURS

Championship Winners	1931–32, 1952–53, 1958–59, 1965–66, 1969–70, 1970–71, 1974–75
Runners-up	1962–63, 1964–65, 1966–67, 1971–72, 1973–74, 1976–77, 1984–85, 1986–87, 1987–88
Challenge Cup Winners	1955–56, 1960–61, 1965–66, 1971–72, 1975–76
Runners-up	1896–97, 1914–15, 1929–30, 1952–53, 1977–78, 1986–87, 1988–89, 1990–91
Premiership Winners	1975–76, 1976–77, 1984–85
Runners-up	1974–75, 1987–88

Lancashire Cup Winners	1926–27, 1953–54, 1960–61, 1961–62, 1962–63, 1963–64, 1964–65, 1967–68, 1968–69, 1984–85
Runners-up	1932–33, 1952–53, 1956–57, 1958–59, 1959–60, 1970–71, 1982–83
Lancashire League Winners	1929–30, 1931–32, 1952–53, 1959–60, 1964–65, 1965–66, 1966–67, 1968–69

Runners-up	1953–54, 1955–56, 1957–58, 1958–59, 1960–61, 1967–68
Western Division Winners	1963–64
Regal Trophy Winners	1987–88
BBC2 Floodlit Trophy Winners	1971–72, 1975–76
Runners-up	1965–66, 1968–69, 1970–71, 1977–78, 1978–79
Club Championship Runners-up	1973–74
Promotion	1903–04

St Helens' record try-scorer, Tom Vollenhoven.

SALFORD

Ground	The Willows
Colours	Red and white jerseys, red shorts
First home game	12 Sep 1896 v Oldham, lost 0–9
First away game	5 Sep 1896 v Widnes, lost 0–10
Record crowd	26 470 v Warrington, 13 Feb 1937
Highest score	78–0 v Liverpool C, 2 Feb 1907
Highest against	0–65 v Castleford, 1 Apr 1990

INDIVIDUAL RECORDS

Tries – match	6	F Miles v Lees, 5 Mar 1898
	6	E Bone v Goole, 29 Mar 1902
	6	J Hilton v Leigh, 7 Oct 1939
Goals – match	13	A Risman v Bramley, 5 Apr 1933
	13	A Risman v Broughton R, 18 May 1940
	13	D Watkins v Keighley, 7 Jan 1972
	13	S Rule v Doncaster, 4 Sep 1981
Points – match	39	J Lomas v Liverpool C, 2 Feb 1907
Tries – season	46	K Fielding, 1973–74
Goals – season	221	D Watkins, 1972–73
Points – season	493	D Watkins, 1972–73
Tries – career	297	M Richards, 1969–83
Goals – career	1241	D Watkins, 1967–79
Points – career	2907	D Watkins, 1967–79
Games – career	496+2	M Richards, 1969–83

GREAT BRITAIN CAPS

W Burgess, P Charlton, M Coulman, G Curran, E Curzon, T Danby, C Dixon, A Edwards, J Feetham, K Fielding, K Gill, J Gore, C Hesketh, B Hudson, E Jenkins, J Lomas, T McKinney, A Middleton, S Nash, M Richards, A Risman, J Spencer, J Ward, S Warwick, D Watkins, W Watkins, P Williams, W Williams

CLUB HONOURS

Championship Winners	1913–14, 1932–33, 1936–37, 1938–39, 1973–74, 1975–76
Runners-up	1901–02, 1902–03, 1903–04, 1933–34
Challenge Cup Winners	1937–38
Runners-up	1899–1900, 1901–02, 1902–03, 1905–06, 1938–39, 1968–69
Premiership Runners-up	1975–76
Lancashire Cup Winners	1931–32, 1934–35, 1935–36, 1936–37, 1972–73
Runners-up	1929–30, 1938–39, 1973–74, 1974–75, 1975–76, 1988–89, 1990–91
Lancashire League Winners	1932–33, 1933–34, 1934–35, 1936–37, 1938–39
Runners-up	1913–14, 1929–30, 1931–32, 1939–40, 1969–70
Regal Trophy Runners-up	1972–73
BBC2 Floodlit Trophy Winners	1974–75
Division Two Champions	1990–91
Division Two Premiership Winners	1990–91
Promotion	1982–83, 1984–85

SCARBOROUGH PIRATES

Ground	McCain Stadium
Colours	Royal purple and gold
First season	1991–92

SHEFFIELD EAGLES

Ground	Don Valley Stadium
Colours	White and gold chevrons on red jerseys, white shorts
First home game	2 Sep 1984 v Rochdale H, won 29–10
First away game	20 Sep 1984 v Runcorn H, lost 6–13
Record crowd	8636 v Widnes, 8 Oct 1989
Highest score	80–8 v Wigan St Patricks, 13 Nov 1988
Highest against	11–62 v Warrington, 9 Feb 1986

INDIVIDUAL RECORDS

Tries – match	5	D Powell v Mansfield M, 2 Jan 1989
Goals – match	12	R Rafferty v Fulham, 21 Sep 1986
Points – match	32	R Rafferty v Fulham, 21 Sep 1986

Tries – season	28 D Powell, 1988–89
Goals – season	148 M Aston, 1988–89
Points – season	307 M Aston, 1988–89
Tries – career	82 D Powell, 1984–91
Goals – career	333 M Aston, 1986–91
Points – career	726 M Aston, 1986–91
Games – career	212+2 D Powell, 1984–91

GREAT BRITAIN CAPS

M Aston, D Powell

CLUB HONOURS

Promotion	1988–89
Division Two Premiership	
Winners	1988–89

(SUTTON) HIGHFIELD

Ground	Hoghton Road
Colours	Red jerseys with green, black, blue and yellow shoulder bands, black shorts
First home game	2 Sep 1922 v Wigan, lost 10–25
First away game	16 Sep 1922 v St Helens, lost 5–21

Below Liverpool Stanley, c. 1936. Stanley were the most successful incarnation of the club which was to become Highfield in 1991.

Record crowd	14 000 v Widnes, 2 May 1936
Highest score	59–11 v Bramley, 4 May 1934
Highest against	2–92 v Wigan, 13 Nov 1988
	0–92 v Rochdale H, 5 Nov 1989

INDIVIDUAL RECORDS

Tries – match	5 J Maloney v Bramley, 25 Apr 1931
Goals – match	11 P Wood v Batley, 21 Oct 1984
Points – match	30 N Barrow v Keighley, 31 Mar 1991
Tries – season	28 J Maloney, 1930–31
Goals – season	126 P Wood, 1984–85
Points – season	240 P Wood, 1984–85
Tries – career	204 J Maloney, 1926–45
Goals – career	304 W Hunt, 1955–66
Points – career	731 W Hunt, 1955–66
Games – career	413 J Maloney, 1926–45

GREAT BRITAIN CAPS

R Ashby, W Belshaw, N Bentham, H Woods

CLUB HONOURS

Lancashire League Winners	1935–36
Runners-up	1936–37

Note – The club joined the Rugby Football League in 1922-23 as Wigan Highfield, and subsequently became London Highfield (1933–34), Liverpool Stanley (1934–35), Liverpool City (1951–52), Huyton (1968–69) and Runcorn Highfield (1984–85). Scheduled to commence operations in Sutton, St Helens as Highfield in 1991–92.

SWINTON

Ground	Station Road
Colours	Blue jerseys with white chevrons, white shorts
First home game	5 Sep 1896 v Warrington, won 17–6
First away game	12 Sep 1896 v Runcorn, drew 0–0
Record crowd	26 891 v Wigan, 12 Feb 1964
Ground record	44 621, Warrington v Wigan, Challenge Cup semi-final, 7 Apr 1951
Highest score	76–4 v Pontefract, 8 Sep 1906
Highest against	3–76 v Huddersfield, 20 Apr 1946
	16–76 v Castleford, 6 Mar 1988

INDIVIDUAL RECORDS

Tries – match	5	M Bevan v Morecambe, 10 Sep 1898
	5	W Wallwork v Widnes, 15 Dec 1900
	5	J Evans v Bradford N, 30 Sep 1922
	5	H Halsall v St Helens, 24 Jan 1925
	5	R Cracknell v Whitehaven Rec, 11 Feb 1928
	5	R Lewis v Keighley, 12 Jan 1946
	5	J Stopford v Bramley, 22 Dec 1962
	5	A Buckley v Salford, 8 Apr 1964
	5	J Ropati v Nottingham C, 21 Jan 1990
Goals – match	12	K Gowers v Liverpool C, 3 Oct 1959
Points – match	29	B McMahon v Dewsbury, 15 Aug 1959
Tries – season	42	J Stopford, 1963–64
Goals – season	128	A Blan, 1960–61
Points – season	283	A Blan, 1960–61
Tries – career	197	F Evans, 1921–31
Goals – career	970	K Gowers, 1954–73
Points – career	2105	K Gowers, 1954–73
Games – career	593+8	K Gowers, 1954–73

GREAT BRITAIN CAPS

T Armitt, A Buckley, F Butters, W Davies, B Evans, F Evans, J Evans, K Gowers, H Halsall, M Hodgson, R Morgan, W Rees, D Robinson, J Stopford, J Wright

CLUB HONOURS

Championship Winners	1926–27, 1927–28, 1930–31, 1934–35, 1962–63, 1963–64
Runners-up	1924–25, 1932–33, 1939–40
Challenge Cup Winners	1899–1900, 1925–26, 1927–28
Runners-up	1926–27, 1931–32
Lancashire Cup Winners	1925–26, 1927–28, 1939–40, 1969–70
Runners-up	1910–11, 1923–24, 1931–32, 1960–61, 1961–62, 1962–63, 1964–65, 1972–73
Lancashire League Winners	1924–25, 1927–28, 1928–29, 1930–31, 1939–40, 1960–61
Runners-up	1897–98, 1900–01, 1922–23, 1925–26, 1926–27, 1934–35, 1938–39, 1965–66
Western Division Runners-up	1963–64
BBC2 Floodlit Trophy Runners-up	1966–67
Division Two Champions	1984–85
Promotion	1974–75, 1986–87, 1990–91
Division Two Premiership Winners	1986–87
Runners-up	1988–89

Left *Swinton's half-back Bryn Evans was a double Great Britain tourist, made ten Test appearances (1926–33) and played 464 games for his club (1920–36).*

TRAFFORD BOROUGH

Ground	Moss Lane
Colours	Royal blue and red jerseys, blue shorts
First home game	17 Aug 1954 v Batley, lost 7–10
First away game	14 Aug 1954 v Salford, lost 3–40
Record crowd	21 000 v Leigh, 9 Mar 1957
Highest score	56–2 v Runcorn H, 1 Jan 1989
Highest against	8–77 v Wigan, 26 Oct 1963

INDIVIDUAL RECORDS

Tries – match	4	T Wilkshire v Bradford N, 14 Jan 1961
	4	J Stockley v Doncaster, 1 Apr 1984
	4	T Frodsham v Bridgend, 14 Apr 1985
	4	T Frodsham v Mansfield M, 30 Nov 1986
Goals – match	11	N Turley v Carlisle, 26 Apr 1984
Points – match	27	N Turley v Carlisle, 26 Apr 1984
Tries – season	30	T Frodsham, 1985–86
Goals – season	98	M Smith, 1987–88
Points – season	201	P Fearis, 1957–58
Tries – career	82	J Johnson, 1969–76
Goals – career	334	T McCarrick, 1963–69
Points – career	689	T McCarrick, 1963–69
Games – career	322+18	P Gamble, 1973–88

CLUB HONOURS

Regal Trophy Runners-up	1976–77
Promotion	1978–79

Note – The club began as Blackpool Borough in 1954–55, moving to Wigan in 1987–88 to become Springfield Borough before transferring to Chorley as Chorley Borough in 1988–89. In 1989–90 a final move was made to Altrincham under the title Trafford Borough.

WAKEFIELD TRINITY

Ground	Belle Vue
Colours	Blue jerseys with red and white hoops, white shorts
First home game	21 Sep 1895 v Wigan, won 13–9
First away game	7 Sep 1895 v Bradford, lost 0–11
Record crowd	28 254 v Wigan, 24 Mar 1962
Ground record	37 906, Huddersfield v Leeds, Challenge Cup semi-final, 21 Mar 1936
Highest score	78–9 v Batley, 26 Aug 1967
Highest against	6–72 v Wigan, 29 Mar 1987

INDIVIDUAL RECORDS

Tries – match	7	F Smith v Keighley, 25 Apr 1959
	7	K Slater v Hunslet, 6 Feb 1971
Goals – match	12	N Fox v Batley, 26 Aug 1967
	12	N Fox v Workington T, 19 Sep 1970
	12	B Ward v Hunslet, 6 Feb 1971
Points – match	33	N Fox v Batley, 26 Aug 1967
Tries – season	38	F Smith, 1959–60
	38	D Smith, 1973–74
Goals – season	163	N Fox, 1961–62
Points – season	407	N Fox, 1961–62
Tries – career	272	N Fox, 1956–74
Goals – career	1836	N Fox, 1956–74
Points – career	4488	N Fox, 1956–74
Games – career	605	H Wilkinson, 1930–49

GREAT BRITAIN CAPS

I Brooke, N Fox, R Haigh, W Horton, D Jeanes, B Jones, H Kershaw, F Mortimer, H Murphy, T Newbould, J Parkin, C Pollard, E Pollard, H Poynton, D Robinson, G Round, T Skerrett, S Smith, D Topliss, D Turner, D Vines, J Wilkinson

CLUB HONOURS

Championship Winners	1966–67, 1967–68
Runners-up	1959–60, 1961–62
Challenge Cup Winners	1908–09, 1945–46, 1959–60, 1961–62, 1962–63
Runners-up	1913–14, 1967–68, 1978–79

WARRINGTON

Yorkshire Cup Winners	1910–11, 1924–25, 1946–47, 1947–48, 1951–52, 1956–57, 1960–61, 1961–62, 1964–65
Runners-up	1926–27, 1932–33, 1934–35, 1936–37, 1939–40, 1945–46, 1958–59, 1973–74, 1974–75, 1990–91
Yorkshire League Winners	1909–10, 1910–11, 1945–46, 1958–59, 1959–60, 1961–62, 1965–66
Runners-up	1960–61
Regal Trophy Runners-up	1971–72
Division Two Champions	1903–04
Promotion	1982–83, 1985–86, 1987–88

Ground	Wilderspool
Colours	Primrose and blue hooped jerseys, blue shorts
First home game	7 Sep 1895 v Hunslet, won 5–4
First away game	21 Sep 1895 v Bradford, lost 0–23
Record crowd	34 304 v Wigan, 22 Jan 1949
Ground record	35 000, Leigh v Wigan, Lancashire Cup Final, 29 Oct 1949
Highest score	78–3 v St Helens, 12 Apr 1909
Highest against	14–68 v Hunslet, 10 Apr 1928

INDIVIDUAL RECORDS

Tries – match	7	B Bevan v Leigh, 29 Mar 1948
	7	B Bevan v Bramley, 22 Apr 1953
Goals – match	14	H Palin v Liverpool C, 13 Sep 1950
Points – match	33	G Thomas v St Helens, 12 Apr 1909
Tries – season	66	B Bevan, 1952–53
Goals – season	170	S Hesford, 1978–79
Points – season	363	H Bath, 1952–53
Tries – career	740	B Bevan, 1945–62
Goals – career	1159	S Hesford, 1975–85
Points – career	2416	S Hesford, 1975–85
Games – career	620	B Bevan, 1945–62

GREAT BRITAIN CAPS

J Arkwright, K Ashcroft, W Aspinall, W Belshaw, N Bentham, J Bevan, T Blinkhorn, E Brooks, J Challinor, N Courtney, W Cunliffe, G Dickenson, W Dingsdale, D Drummond, R Duane, R Eccles, K Ellis, J Featherstone, M Forster, E Fraser, L Gilfedder, R Greenough, A Gregory, M Gregory, G Helme, K Holden, A Johnson, K Kelly, T McKinney, J Miller, A Murphy, A Naughton, T O'Grady, H Palin, K Parr, A Pimblett, R Price, R Ryan, R Ryder, F Shugars, G Skelhorne, G Thomas, D Whitehead, J Woods

CLUB HONOURS

Championship Winners	1947–48, 1953–54, 1954–55
Runners-up	1925–26, 1934–35, 1936–37, 1948–49, 1950–51, 1960–61, 1978–79, 1980–81
Challenge Cup Winners	1904–05, 1906–07, 1949–50, 1953–54, 1973–74
Runners-up	1900–01, 1903–04, 1912–13, 1927–28, 1932–33, 1935–36, 1974–75, 1989–90
Premiership Winners	1985–86
Runners-up	1976–77, 1986–87
Club Championship Winners	1973–74
Lancashire Cup Winners	1921–22, 1929–30, 1932–33, 1937–38, 1959–60, 1965–66, 1980–81, 1982–83, 1989–90
Runners-up	1906–07, 1948–49, 1950–51, 1967–68, 1985–86, 1987–88
Lancashire League Winners	1937–38, 1947–48, 1948–49, 1950–51, 1953–54, 1954–55, 1955–56, 1967–68
Runners-up	1920–21, 1940–41, 1951–52, 1964–65
Regal Trophy Winners	1973–74, 1977–78, 1980–81, 1990–91
Runners-up	1978–79, 1986–87
BBC 2 Floodlit Trophy Runners-up	1974–75
Captain Morgan Trophy Winners	1973–74
ITA Trophy Winners	1955–56

WHITEHAVEN

Ground	Recreation Ground
Colours	White, chocolate, royal blue and gold jerseys, white shorts
First home game	21 Aug 1948 v Hull, won 5–0
First away game	28 Aug 1948 v Batley, lost 9–15
Record crowd	18 500 v Wakefield T, 19 Mar 1960
Highest score	72–6 v Fulham, 14 Sep 1986
Highest against	10–92 v Hull KR, 18 Mar 1990

INDIVIDUAL RECORDS

Tries – match	6	V Gribbin v Doncaster, 18 Nov 1984
Goals – match	11	W Holliday v Hunslet, 31 Mar 1962
Points – match	25	W Holliday v Hunslet, 31 Mar 1962
Tries – season	29	W Smith, 1956–57
Goals – season	141	J McKeown, 1956–57
Points – season	291	J McKeown, 1956–57
Tries – career	148	W Smith, 1950–62
Goals – career	1050	J McKeown, 1948–61
Points – career	2133	J McKeown, 1948–61
Games – career	417	J McKeown, 1948–61

GREAT BRITAIN CAPS

V Gribbin, W Holliday, R Huddart, P Kitchin, A Walker

CLUB HONOURS

Promotion	1980–81, 1982–83

Left *Australian second-rower Harry Bath still holds the Warrington points-in-a-season record with 363 amassed in 1952–53.*

Overleaf *One of League's most successful converts from Welsh Rugby Union, John Bevan scored 201 tries for Warrington (1973–86).*

WIDNES

Ground	Naughton Park
Colours	White jerseys with black trim, black shorts
First home game	14 Sep 1895 v Leeds, won 11–8
First away game	7 Sep 1895 v Runcorn, lost 4–15
Record crowd	24 205 v St Helens, 16 Feb 1961
Highest score	82–0 v Dewsbury, 30 Nov 1986
Highest against	5–60 v Oldham, 9 Apr 1928

INDIVIDUAL RECORDS

Tries – match	5	E Cunningham v Doncaster, 15 Feb 1981
	5	J Basnett v Hunslet, 17 Oct 1981
	5	J Basnett v Hull KR, 2 Nov 1986
	5	D Hulme v Dewsbury, 30 Nov 1986
	5	A Currier v Featherstone R, 25 Sep 1988
	5	M Offiah v Warrington, 15 Mar 1989
Goals – match	11	R Whitfield v Oldham, 28 Oct 1965
Points – match	34	A Currier v Featherstone R, 25 Sep 1988
	34	J Davies v Whitehaven, 26 Aug 1990
Tries – season	58	M Offiah, 1988–89
Goals – season	140	M Burke, 1978–79
Points – season	342	J Davies, 1990–91
Tries – career	234	M Aspey, 1964–80
Goals – career	1083	R Dutton, 1966–78
Points – career	2195	R Dutton, 1966–78
Games – career	587+4	K Elwell, 1969–86

GREAT BRITAIN CAPS

M Adams, J Basnett, K Bentley, M Burke, F Collier,
A Currier, J Davies, R Dutton, K Elwell, R Eyres,
J Fieldhouse, R French, L Gorley, A Gregory, I Hare,
A Higgins, F Higgins, L Holliday, E Hughes, D Hulme,
P Hulme, A Johnson, V Karalius, G Kemel, D Laughton,
J Lydon, T McCue, J Measures, J Mills, A Myler, F Myler,
G Nicholls, M Offiah, D O'Neill, M O'Neill, H Pinner,
G Shaw, N Silcock, A Tait, J Warlow, D Wright, S Wright

CLUB HONOURS

Championship Winners	1977–78, 1987–88, 1988–89
Runners-up	1935–36, 1979–80, 1990–91
Challenge Cup Winners	1929–30, 1936–37, 1963–64, 1974–75, 1978–79, 1980–81, 1983–84
Runners-up	1933–34, 1949–50, 1975–76, 1976–77, 1981–82
Premiership Winners	1979–80, 1981–82, 1982–83, 1987–88, 1988–89, 1989–90
Runners-up	1977–78, 1990–91
Lancashire Cup Winners	1945–46, 1974–75, 1975–76, 1976–77, 1978–79, 1979–80, 1990–91
Runners-up	1928–29, 1939–40, 1955–56, 1971–72, 1981–82, 1983–84
Lancashire League Winners	1919–20
Runners-up	1935–36, 1946–47
Lancashire Senior Competition Runners-up	1901–02
Western Division Runners-up	1962–63
Regal Trophy Winners	1975–76, 1978–79
Runners-up	1974–75, 1977–78, 1979–80, 1983–84, 1988–89
BBC2 Floodlit Trophy Winners	1978–79
Runners-up	1972–73, 1973–74
Charity Shield Winners	1988–89, 1989–90, 1990–91

WIGAN

Ground	Central Park
Colours	Cherry and white hooped jerseys, cherry shorts
First home game	28 Sep 1895 v Tyldesley, drew 0–0
First away game	7 Sep 1895 v Broughton R, won 9–0
Record crowd	47 477 v St Helens, 27 Mar 1959
Highest score	116–0 v Flimby & Fothergill, 14 Feb 1925
Highest against	3–58 v Leeds, 14 Oct 1972

INDIVIDUAL RECORDS

Tries – match	7	J Ring v Flimby & Fothergill, 14 Feb 1925
	7	J Ring v Salford, 13 Apr 1925
	7	J Ring v Pemberton R, 12 Feb 1927
	7	G Ratcliffe v Liverpool S, 23 Aug 1947
	7	W Boston v Dewsbury, 20 Aug 1955
	7	W Boston v Salford, 30 Apr 1962
	7	G Vigo v St Helens, 21 Aug 1976
Goals – match	22	J Sullivan v Flimby & Fothergill, 14 Feb 1925
Points – match	44	J Sullivan v Flimby & Fothergill, 14 Feb 1925
Tries – season	62	J Ring, 1925–26
Goals – season	176	F Griffiths, 1958–59
Points – season	394	F Griffiths, 1958–59
Tries – career	478	W Boston, 1953–68
Goals – career	2317	J Sullivan, 1921–46
Points – career	4883	J Sullivan, 1921–46
Games – career	774	J Sullivan, 1921–46

GREAT BRITAIN CAPS

R Ashby, E Ashcroft, E Ashton, W Ashurst, F Barton, J Barton, J Bennett, D Betts, D Bevan, W Blan, D Bolton, W Boston, T Bradshaw, F Carlton, B Case, N Cherrington, C Clarke, P Clarke, P Coldrick, F Collier, J Cunliffe, M Dermott, S Edwards, J Egan, R Evans, G Fairbairn, T Fogerty, P Ford, W Francis, D Gardiner, K Gee, H Gill, A Goodway, R Goulding, J Gray, A Gregory, S Hampson, E Hanley, C Hill, D Hill, J Hilton, T Howley, W Hudson, D Hurcombe, B Jenkins, K Jones, R Kinnear, N Kiss, D Laughton, J Lawrenson, J Leytham, I Lucas, J Lydon, B McTigue, J Miller, J Morley, A Platt, I Potter, J Price, R Ramsdale, G Ratcliffe, J Ring, D Robinson, M Ryan, W Sayer, J Sharrock, N Silcock, R Silcock, D Stephenson, J Sullivan, M Sullivan, G Thomas, J Thomas, S Wane, E Ward, L White, D Willicombe, W Winstanley

CLUB HONOURS

Championship Winners	1908–09, 1921–22, 1925–26, 1933–34, 1943–44, 1945–46, 1946–47, 1949–50, 1951–52, 1959–60, 1986–87, 1989–90, 1990–91
Runners-up	1909–10, 1910–11, 1911–12, 1912–13, 1923–24, 1940–41, 1963–64, 1970–71, 1974–75, 1985–86

Challenge Cup Winners	1923–24, 1928–29, 1947–48, 1950–51, 1957–58, 1958–59, 1964–65, 1984–85, 1987–88, 1988–89, 1989–90, 1990–91
Runners-up	1910–11, 1919–20, 1943–44, 1945–46, 1960–61, 1962–63, 1965–66, 1969–70, 1983–84
Premiership Winners	1986–87
Lancashire Cup Winners	1905–06, 1908–09, 1909–10, 1912–13, 1922–23, 1928–29, 1938–39, 1946–47, 1947–48, 1948–49, 1949–50, 1950–51, 1951–52, 1966–67, 1971–72, 1973–74, 1985–86, 1986–87, 1987–88, 1988–89
Runners-up	1913–14, 1914–15, 1925–26, 1927–28, 1930–31, 1934–35, 1935–36, 1936–37, 1945–46, 1953–54, 1957–58, 1977–78, 1980–81, 1984–85
Lancashire League Winners	1908–09, 1910–11, 1911–12, 1912–13, 1913–14, 1914–15, 1920–21, 1922–23, 1923–24, 1925–26, 1940–41, 1945–46, 1946–47, 1949–50, 1951–52, 1958–59, 1961–62, 1969–70
Runners-up	1909–10, 1921–22, 1924–25, 1928–29, 1930–31, 1933–34, 1947–48, 1948–49, 1959–60, 1968–69
Lancashire Senior Competition Winners	1901–02
Regal Trophy Winners	1982–83, 1985–86, 1986–87, 1988–89, 1989–90
BBC2 Floodlit Trophy Winners	1968–69
Runners-up	1969–70
Promotion	1980–81
Charity Shield Winners	1985–86, 1987–88
Runners-up	1988–89, 1989–90, 1990–91

BILLY BOSTON

Fastest Try Centurion

Billy Boston (right) moves to tackle Australia's Norm Provan in a 1954 Test.

When Widnes' winger Martin Offiah scored the 100th try of his short Rugby League career in a game against Featherstone Rovers on 19 February 1989, he was deservedly praised to the sky. It had taken him a mere 17½ months and was hailed as the fastest century of tries in the history of the sport. The previous record holder had been St Helens' super Springbok Tom Vollenhoven, who had taken

18½ months to achieve the century. The Voll had crashed the century barrier in the grand manner, the first of three tries in the Championship Final of 1959 giving him his 100th touchdown, a 75-yarder which ranks as one of the all-time classics.

In terms of calendar time Offiah's and Vollenhoven's are certainly the quickest centuries on record but in real terms nei-

ther matched the swiftness of Billy Boston's 'ton'. Boston took over 21 months before hitting 100 tries in September 1955 but passed the target in only 68 games. Vollenhoven had needed 76 games and Offiah 80.

Boston, a Welshman from Butetown, Cardiff, had joined Wigan from Army Rugby Union in 1953 and became arguably the most charismatic winger Rugby League has ever seen. In his later years he put weight on to such an extent that he could have been mistaken for a prop, but retained such a tremendous burst of speed and nimbleness of foot that it hardly seemed to matter. In his earliest days he was everything a wingman should be – quick, powerful, alert, agile and determined – and the tries came in torrents.

Billy opened his scoring blitz with a try against Barrow on his Wigan debut, on 21 November 1953. Playing intermittently because of his Army commitments, the novice wing proceeded to score two tries in his second match, a 55–10 hammering of Liverpool City, three in his third against Swinton and four in his fifth, a 45–0 romp against Batley. It was obvious that an extraordinary talent had entered the game. Wigan were a good side, but not the pre-eminent force of a couple of seasons before. Had Boston played in that team he may have scored even more heavily. As it was, defences found him almost unmanageable and the international selectors were impressed enough to pick him for the 1954 Lions tour after only half a dozen games.

Boston was only 19 when he toured Australasia in 1954, the youngest tourist up to that time. Age and reputations meant nothing to him. Following a calamitous 12–37 defeat in the First Test against Australia, Billy was drafted into the Test team for the Second and scored twice in a 38–21 victory at Brisbane. He played in all the remaining Tests, equalling the British Test record by scoring four tries against New Zealand at Auckland in the First Test despite atrocious muddy conditions. The tour ended with him breaking Tom Danby's Lions record of 34 tries set in 1950, Boston having rattled up 36 tries in 18 appearances. His 50th try

had come in only his 26th first-class game when he had scored four against Canterbury.

Returning to domestic football in 1954–55 Billy scored 31 tries in 31 games to top the Wigan try-scorers. For the young winger and for his illustrious club it was a relatively quiet season. Billy played for Wales against a French B XIII at Nantes in May 1955, but declined a place in the Great Britain squad which won the first World Cup in France in the autumn of 1954.

The 1955–56 campaign began dramatically for Billy, who equalled Johnny Ring's club record by scoring seven tries in a 52–5 victory over Dewsbury at Central Park on the opening day of the season. Three days later he bagged four in a 31–6 romp at Blackpool Borough and in his first six games he tallied 16 tries for Wigan to bring him on to the 98 tries mark. The 100th try arrived on Monday 12 September 1955, appropriately enough on home ground at Central Park. Billy was not adorned in the cherry and white of Wigan, however, but in the green of the Other Nationalities who were engaging England in International combat. By the 27th minute Billy had hit the century with the second of three tries in a 33–16 rout of the English. Billy would go on for a further 15 years bashing and bamboozling Rugby League defences the world over before bowing out with a grand total of 571 tries.

BILLY BOSTON'S RECORD HUNDRED TRIES

1953	Opponents		Tries
21 Nov	Barrow		1
12 Dec	Liverpool C		2
1954			
2 Jan	Swinton		3
6 Feb	Latchford Albion	CC	2
27 Feb	Batley		4
16 Apr	St Helens		1
19 Apr	Salford		1
27 Apr	GB v France		1

LIONS TOUR

19 May	Western Division	2
29 May	Sydney	1
14 Jun	Brisbane	1
19 Jun	Queensland	3
20 Jun	Wide-Bay	4
22 Jun	Southern Zone	1
27 Jun	North Queensland	4
3 Jul	Australia	2
4 Jul	Toowoomba	1
7 Jul	North Coast	6
24 Jul	New Zealand	4
27 Jul	Wellington	3
7 Aug	Canterbury	4
25 Sep	Bradford N	1
9 Oct	Widnes	2
16 Oct	Whitehaven	1
23 Oct	Blackpool B	3
30 Oct	Leigh	1
13 Nov	Leigh	2
18 Dec	Liverpool C	3
25 Dec	Salford	2
1955		
1 Jan	Warrington	1
22 Jan	Belle Vue Rangers	3
29 Jan	Widnes	2
5 Mar	Swinton	4
12 Mar	Barrow	1
19 Mar	Warrington	2
8 Apr	St Helens	1
11 Apr	Salford	2
20 Aug	Dewsbury	7
23 Aug	Blackpool B	4
31 Aug	Liverpool C	2
10 Sep	Wakefield T	3
12 Sep	Other Nats v England	3

CC Challenge Cup

WORKINGTON TOWN

Ground	Derwent Park
Colours	White jerseys with blue band, white shorts
First home game	25 Aug 1945 v Broughton R, won 27–5
First away game	1 Sep 1945 v Keighley, lost 0–13
Record crowd	20 403 v St Helens, 8 Mar 1952
Highest score	62–15 v Hunslet, 20 Apr 1964
Highest against	0–68 v Wigan, 18 Jan 1987

INDIVIDUAL RECORDS

Tries – match	7	I Southward v Blackpool B, 17 Sep 1955
Goals – match	11	I MacCorquodale v Blackpool B, 6 Jan 1973
Points – match	33	I Southward v Blackpool B, 17 Sep 1955
Tries – season	49	J Lawrenson, 1951–52
Goals – season	186	L Hopkins, 1981–82
Points – season	438	L Hopkins, 1981–82
Tries – career	274	I Southward, 1952–68
Goals – career	809	I MacCorquodale, 1972–80
Points – career	1800	I MacCorquodale, 1972–80
Games – career	415+4	P Charlton, 1961–80

GREAT BRITAIN CAPS

E Bowman, P Charlton, B Edgar, N Herbert, W Martin, V McKeating, A Pepperell, I Southward, G Wilson

CLUB HONOURS

Championship Winners	1950–51
Runners-up	1957–58
Challenge Cup Winners	1951–52
Runners-up	1954–55, 1957–58
Lancashire Cup Winners	1977–78
Runners-up	1976–77, 1978–79, 1979–80
Lancashire League Runners-up	1950–51, 1961–62, 1966–67
Western Division Winners	1962–63
Promotion	1975–76, 1981–82, 1983–84

Cumbrian winger Ike Southward struggles with Featherstone's Terry Clawson and Jackie Fennell. Southward twice cost clubs world record fees. In 1958–59 Oldham paid £10 650 to Workington for his services only to transfer him back two years later to Town for £11 002/10/–.

CURRENT COMPETITIONS: RESULTS HISTORY & RECORDS

THE RUGBY LEAGUE CHAMPIONSHIP

Various methods have been used to determine Rugby League's champion teams since 1895. Since 1973–74 the team finishing at the top of the First Division has automatically been declared the Champions. This eminently logical state of affairs also applied in two other short-lived experiments with two divisions, firstly in seasons 1902–03, 1903–04 and 1904–05 and latterly in 1962–63 and 1963–64.

In the game's first season, 1895–96, all 22 clubs played each other at home and away with Manningham just pipping Halifax for the Championship of 'The Northern Rugby Football League'. For the following five seasons the clubs played only county competitions (Lancashire and Yorkshire Senior Competitions) and no overall champion team was decided. In 1901–02, however, a super league of 14 clubs was formed, Broughton Rangers easily winning the title ahead of Salford. When the two-division experiment of 1902–05 was ended, the 1905–06 Championship was decided on a percentage basis as

clubs played wildly differing numbers of matches before Leigh emerged as Champions. The unsatisfactory nature of this system was modified in 1906–07 with the introduction of the top four play-off. This system allowed the Championship to be decided via semi-finals and a Championship Final played on a neutral ground. It was the source of many a classic encounter and undoubtedly created a great deal of excitement and interest for the clubs involved in the chase for a place in the top four. The game basically stuck to this formula until 1964–65 when the play-offs were extended to the top 16, a format which ran until two divisions in their present form were re-introduced in 1973–74.

Wigan celebrate their lifting of the 1989–90 Championship, for a record 12th time. They retained their title the following season.

RUGBY LEAGUE CHAMPIONSHIP WINNERS AND RUNNERS-UP

Year	Winners	Runners-up	Year	Winners	Runners-up
1895–96	Manningham	Halifax	1950–51	Workington Town	Warrington
1896–1901	*No competition*		1951–52	Wigan	Bradford N
1901–02	Broughton Rangers	Salford	1952–53	St Helens	Halifax
1902–03	Halifax	Salford	1953–54	Warrington	Halifax
1903–04	Bradford*	Salford	1954–55	Warrington	Oldham
1904–05	Oldham	Bradford	1955–56	Hull	Halifax
1905–06	Leigh	Hunslet	1956–57	Oldham	Hull
1906–07	Halifax	Oldham	1957–58	Hull	Workington Town
1907–08	Hunslet	Oldham	1958–59	St Helens	Hunslet
1908–09	Wigan	Oldham	1959–60	Wigan	Wakefield T
1909–10	Oldham	Wigan	1960–61	Leeds	Warrington
1910–11	Oldham	Wigan	1961–62	Huddersfield	Wakefield T
1911–12	Huddersfield	Wigan	1962–63	Swinton	St Helens
1912–13	Huddersfield	Wigan	1963–64	Swinton	Wigan
1913–14	Salford	Huddersfield	1964–65	Halifax	St Helens
1914–15	Huddersfield	Leeds	1965–66	St Helens	Halifax
1915–19	*No competition*		1966–67	Wakefield T	St Helens
1919–20	Hull	Huddersfield	1967–68	Wakefield T	Hull KR
1920–21	Hull	Hull KR	1968–69	Leeds	Castleford
1921–22	Wigan	Oldham	1969–70	St Helens	Leeds
1922–23	Hull KR	Huddersfield	1970–71	St Helens	Wigan
1923–24	Batley	Wigan	1971–72	Leeds	St Helens
1924–25	Hull KR	Swinton	1972–73	Dewsbury	Leeds
1925–26	Wigan	Warrington	1973–74	Salford	St Helens
1926–27	Swinton	St Helens Recs	1974–75	St Helens	Wigan
1927–28	Swinton	Featherstone R	1975–76	Salford	Featherstone R
1928–29	Huddersfield	Leeds	1976–77	Featherstone R	St Helens
1929–30	Huddersfield	Leeds	1977–78	Widnes	Bradford N
1930–31	Swinton	Leeds	1978–79	Hull KR	Warrington
1931–32	St Helens	Huddersfield	1979–80	Bradford N	Widnes
1932–33	Salford	Swinton	1980–81	Bradford N	Warrington
1933–34	Wigan	Salford	1981–82	Leigh	Hull
1934–35	Swinton	Warrington	1982–83	Hull	Hull KR
1935–36	Hull	Widnes	1983–84	Hull KR	Hull
1936–37	Salford	Warrington	1984–85	Hull KR	St Helens
1937–38	Hunslet	Leeds	1985–86	Halifax	Wigan
1938–39	Salford	Castleford	1986–87	Wigan	St Helens
1939–40	Bradford N	Swinton	1987–88	Widnes	St Helens
1940–41	Bradford N	Wigan	1988–89	Widnes	Wigan
1941–42	Dewsbury	Bradford N	1989–90	Wigan	Leeds
1942–43	Dewsbury**	Halifax	1990–91	Wigan	Widnes
1943–44	Wigan	Dewsbury			
1944–45	Bradford N	Halifax			
1945–46	Wigan	Huddersfield			
1946–47	Wigan	Dewsbury			
1947–48	Warrington	Bradford N			
1948–49	Huddersfield	Warrington			
1949–50	Wigan	Huddersfield			

* In 1903–04 Bradford and Salford finished level at the top of the league and played off for the title at Halifax on 28 April 1904. Bradford won 5–0.

** In 1942–43 the Championship was declared void after Dewsbury were found guilty of playing an ineligible player in the Championship Final.

CHAMPIONSHIP HONOURS TABLE

Club	Champions	Runners-up	Club	Champions	Runners-up
Wigan	13	11	Hunslet	2	2
St Helens	7	9	Wakefield Trinity	2	2
Huddersfield	7	6	Leigh	2	–
Bradford Northern	6	5	Featherstone Rovers	1	2
Hull	6	3	Workington Town	1	1
Salford	6	4	Batley	1	–
Swinton	6	3	Broughton Rangers	1	–
Hull KR	5	3	Manningham	1	–
Halifax	4	7	Castleford	–	2
Oldham	4	5	St Helens Recs	–	1
Leeds	3	8			
Warrington	3	8	**Note** – Bradford Northern's record includes success as		
Widnes	3	3	Bradford, whilst the void Championship of 1942–43 is		
Dewsbury	3	2	included in Dewsbury's record.		

FIRST DIVISION PREMIERSHIP TROPHY

When the two division system was introduced in 1973–74 there was no necessity to continue with championship play-offs. The Rugby Football League, however, continued the tradition of staging end-of-season play-offs by instituting the Premiership in 1974–75. In its earliest days, 16 clubs took part in the competition but it quickly developed into a knock-out tournament for the top eight first division clubs. The competition is seeded in that the highest placed clubs receive home ties, the final being staged on a neutral ground.

PREMIERSHIP FINALS

1974–75 *17 May, at Wigan, 14 531*

LEEDS	26	T: Atkinson 2, Smith, Mason, Hynes
		G: Marshall 3, Holmes 2, Hynes (DG)
ST HELENS	11	T: Heaton, Mathias, Jones
		G: Coslett

1975–76 *22 May, at Swinton, 18 082*

ST HELENS	15	T: Glynn, Chisnall, Karalius
		G: Pimblett 3
SALFORD	2	G: Watkins 2 (2DG)

1976–77 *28 May, at Swinton, 11 718*

ST HELENS	32	T: K Gwilliam, James, Pimblett, Mathias, Benyon, Cunningham
		G: Pimblett 7
WARRINGTON	20	T: Weavill, A Gwilliam, Gordon, B Philbin
		G: Hesford 4

1977–78 *20 May, at Swinton, 16 813*

BRADFORD NORTHERN	17	T: Haigh, Barends, Roe, D Redfearn
		G: Mumby 2, Wolford (DG)
WIDNES	8	T: Aspey 2
		G: Woods

1978–79 *27 May, at Huddersfield, 19 486*

LEEDS	24	T: D Smith, Ward, A Smith
		G: Dick 8 (1DG)
BRADFORD NORTHERN	2	G: Ferres

1979–80 *17 May, at Swinton, 10 215*

WIDNES	19	T: Bentley, Gorley, Wright, Elwell, Aspey
		G: Burke, Eckersley (DG), Elwell (DG)
BRADFORD NORTHERN	5	T: D Redfearn
		G: Mumby

1980–81 *16 May, at Headingley, 29 448*

HULL KR	11	T: Smith, Hogan, Hartley
		G: Hubbard
HULL	7	T: Crane
		G: Woods 2

1981–82 *15 May, at Headingley, 12 100*

WIDNES	23	T: Wright, Adams, Burke, Hughes, Basnett
		G: Burke 4
HULL	8	T: Crooks
		G: Crooks 3 (1DG)

Hull forwards Charlie Stone and Keith Bridges are outpaced by Widnes captain Eric Hughes in the 1983 Final.

1982-83 *14 May, at Headingley, 17 813*
WIDNES	22	T: Basnett 2, Gregory, A Myler
		G: Lydon 5
HULL	10	T: Topliss, O'Hara
		G: Crooks 2

1983-84 *12 May, at Headingley, 12 515*
HULL KR	18	T: Prohm, Laws, Smith, Dorahy
		G: Dorahy
CASTLEFORD	10	T: Kear
		G: R Beardmore 3

1984-85 *11 May, at Elland Road, 15 518*
ST HELENS	36	T: Meninga 2, Ledger 2, Veivers, Pinner, Ainsworth
		G: Day 4
HULL KR	16	T: Laws, Fairbairn, Robinson
		G: Fairbairn 2

1985-86 *18 May, at Elland Road, 13 683*
WARRINGTON	38	T: Boyd 2, Forster, Bishop, Jackson, Tamati, Johnson
		G: Bishop 5
HALIFAX	10	T: C Anderson
		G: Whitfield 3

1986-87 *17 May, at Old Trafford, 38 756*
WIGAN	8	T: Lydon
		G: Stephenson, Gill
WARRINGTON	0	

1987-88 *15 May, at Old Trafford, 35 252*
WIDNES	38	T: Wright 2, D Hulme 2, Tait, McKenzie, Sorensen
		G: Currier 4, Platt
ST HELENS	14	T: Haggerty, Ledger
		G: Loughlin 3

1988-89 *14 May, at Old Trafford, 40 194*
WIDNES	18	T: Currier, Wright, Offiah
		G: Davies 3
HULL	10	T: Welham
		G: Pearce 3

1989-90 *13 May, at Old Trafford, 40 796*
WIDNES	28	T: Currier 2, Tait 2, Holliday
		G: Davies 4
BRADFORD NORTHERN	6	T: Marchant
		G: Mumby

1990-91 *12 May, at Old Trafford, 42 043*
HULL	14	T: Gay, Walker, Nolan
		G: Eastwood
WIDNES	4	T: Offiah

PREMIERSHIP HONOURS

Club	Premiers	Runners-up
Widnes	6	2
St Helens	3	2
Hull KR	2	1
Leeds	2	–
Hull	1	4
Bradford N	1	3
Warrington	1	2
Wigan	1	–
Castleford	–	1
Halifax	–	1
Salford	–	1

PREMIERSHIP FINAL RECORDS

Most finals	8	Widnes
Most wins	6	Widnes
Most consecutive finals	4	Widnes
Most consecutive wins	3	Widnes
Highest score	38	Warrington v Halifax, 1986
	38	Widnes v St Helens, 1988
Highest aggregate	52	St Helens 32 Warrington 20, 1977
	52	St Helens 36 Hull KR 16, 1985
	52	Widnes 38 St Helens 14, 1988
Lowest aggregate	8	Wigan 8 Warrington 0, 1987
Largest crowd	42 043	Hull v Widnes, 1991
Smallest crowd	10 215	Bradford N v Widnes, 1980
Highest receipts	£384 300	Hull v Widnes, 1991

PLAYERS' RECORDS IN ALL FINALS

Most appearances	6	M O'Neill (Widnes) 1980, 1982, 1983, 1988, 1989, 1990
Most tries	3	M Aspey (Widnes) 1978, 1980
	3	J Basnett (Widnes) 1982, 1983
	3	B Ledger (St Helens) 1985, 1988
	3	D Wright (Widnes) 1988, 1989
	3	A Tait (Widnes) 1988, 1990
	3	A Currier (Widnes) 1989, 1990
Most goals	10	G Pimblett (St Helens) 1976, 1977
Most points	23	G Pimblett (St Helens) 1976, 1977

PLAYERS' RECORDS IN ONE FINAL

Most tries		Ten players have scored two tries in a final
Most goals	8	K Dick (Leeds) v Bradford N, 1979
Most points	17	G Pimblett (St Helens) v Warrington, 1977

Premiership Final, 1986 – Halifax prop Geoff Robinson leaves Warrington stand-off Paul Bishop grasping fresh air. Bishop had the last laugh, however, claiming 14 points in Warrington's record 38–10 triumph.

SECOND DIVISION CHAMPIONSHIP

Rugby League has operated a two division system in three distinct eras. The first experiment was conducted in seasons 1902–03, 1903–04 and 1904–05 and repeated in seasons 1962–63 and 1963–64. Two divisions has been the system in vogue from 1973–74 to date. In the first two eras of two divisions, only the Second Division Champions and runners-up were promoted. From 1973–74 to 1984–85 the top four clubs were promoted. Since then, with the exception of 1986–87 (two clubs promoted), three clubs per season have been promoted.

Hunslet were the first winners of the new Second Division in 1962–63. Here Geoff Gunney prepares to face Wakefield three-quarters Ken Hirst and Gert Coetzer in a game at Parkside in 1964.

SECOND DIVISION CHAMPIONS, RUNNERS-UP & PROMOTED CLUBS

Year	Champions	Runners-up	Also promoted
1902–03	Keighley	Leeds	
1903–04	Wakefield T	St Helens	
1904–05	Dewsbury	Barrow	
1962–63	Hunslet	Keighley	
1963–64	Oldham	Leigh	
1973–74	Bradford N	York	Keighley, Halifax
1974–75	Huddersfield	Hull KR	Oldham, Swinton
1975–76	Barrow	Rochdale H	Workington T, Leigh
1976–77	Hull	Dewsbury	Bramley, New Hunslet
1977–78	Leigh	Barrow	Rochdale H, Huddersfield
1978–79	Hull	New Hunslet	York, Blackpool B
1979–80	Featherstone R	Halifax	Oldham, Barrow
1980–81	York	Wigan	Fulham, Whitehaven
1981–82	Oldham	Carlisle	Workington T, Halifax
1982–83	Fulham	Wakefield T	Salford, Whitehaven
1983–84	Barrow	Workington T	Hunslet, Halifax
1984–85	Swinton	Salford	York, Dewsbury
1985–86	Leigh	Barrow	Wakefield T
1986–87	Hunslet	Swinton	
1987–88	Oldham	Featherstone R	Wakefield T
1988–89	Leigh	Barrow	Sheffield E
1989–90	Hull KR	Rochdale H	Oldham
1990–91	Salford	Halifax	Swinton

SECOND DIVISION PREMIERSHIP

The Second Division Premiership was inaugurated in 1986–87. The final, the culmination of a seeded knock-out competition for the top eight clubs in the division, is played at Old Trafford, Manchester immediately before the final of the First Division Premiership.

SECOND DIVISION PREMIERSHIP FINALS

1986-87 *17 May*

SWINTON	27	T: Grima, Lee, Bate, Ainsworth, Derbyshire
		G: Rippon 3, L Holliday (DG)
HUNSLET	10	T: Bateman 2
		G: Platt

1987-88 *15 May*

OLDHAM	28	T: Foy 2, Walsh, Flanagan, Meadows
		G: McAlister 4
FEATHERSTONE R	26	T: Steadman 2, Sykes, Bannister
		G: Quinn 5

1988-89 *14 May*

SHEFFIELD EAGLES	43	T: Powell 3, Cook, McDermott, Aston, Broadbent
		G: Aston 8 (1DG)
SWINTON	18	T: Frodsham, Melling, Ranson
		G: Myler 3

1989-90 *13 May*

OLDHAM	30	T: Lord, Ford, Henderson, Irving, Ruane, Martyn
		G: Hyde 2, Platt
HULL KR	29	T: Parker 2, Clark, Lyman, Harrison
		G: Fletcher 4, Parker (DG)

1990-91 *12 May*

SALFORD	27	T: Kerry 2, Gilfillan, Evans
		G: Kerry 5 (1DG) Cassidy (DG), Lee (DG)
HALIFAX	20	T: Southernwood, Hill, Wilson, Wood
		G: Platt 2

THE RUGBY LEAGUE CHALLENGE CUP

Inaugurated in 1897 as 'The Northern Rugby Football Union Challenge Cup', this competition is undoubtedly the most glamorous in the game. Fifty-two clubs entered the first competition, the first ties being played on 20 March 1897. Since 1929 the Challenge Cup Final has been played at Wembley Stadium, excluding war years.

Challenge Cup Final, Headingley 1901 – Batley and Warrington form a scrum in mid-field. Note the spectators on the stand roof.

CHALLENGE CUP FINALS

1896-97 *24 Apr, at Headingley, 13 492*
BATLEY   10 T: Goodall, Munns
     G: Oakland (DG)
ST HELENS   3 T: Traynor

1897-98 *23 Apr, at Headingley, 27 941*
BATLEY   7 T: Goodall
     G: Davies, Goodall
BRADFORD   0

1898-99 *29 Apr, at Fallowfield, 15 762*
OLDHAM   19 T: Williams 2, S Lees, Moffatt,
     J Lees
     G: S Lees, Thomas
HUNSLET   9 T: W Goldthorpe
     G: A Goldthorpe 3

1899-1900 *28 Apr, at Fallowfield, 17 864*
SWINTON   16 T: Davies, R Valentine,
     Lewis, Messer
     G: J Valentine 2
SALFORD   8 T: Pearson, T Williams
     G: Griffiths

1900-01 *27 Apr, at Headingley, 29 569*
BATLEY   6 T: Auty, Davies
WARRINGTON   0

1901-02 *26 Apr, at Rochdale, 15 006*
BROUGHTON RANGERS 25 T: Wilson 3, Hogg, Widdeson
     G: W James 4, Oram
SALFORD   0

1902-03 *25 Apr, at Headingley, 32 507*
HALIFAX   7 T: Bartle
     G: Hadwen 2
SALFORD   0

1903-04 *30 Apr, at Salford, 17 041*
HALIFAX   8 T: Joe Riley, Morley
     G: Hadwen
WARRINGTON   3 T: Davies

1904-05 *29 Apr, at Headingley, 19 638*
WARRINGTON   6 T: Fish 2
HULL KR   0

1905-06 *28 Apr, at Headingley, 15 834*
BRADFORD   5 T: Brear
     G: Laidlaw
SALFORD   0

1906-07 *27 Apr, at Broughton, 18 500*
WARRINGTON   17 T: Isherwood, Hockenhull,
     Fish
     G: Fish 4
OLDHAM   3 T: Avery

1907-08 *25 Apr, at Huddersfield, 18 000*
HUNSLET   14 T: Farrar, Smith
     G: A Goldthorpe 3, Eagers
HULL   0

1908-09 *24 Apr, at Headingley, 23 587*
WAKEFIELD TRINITY   17 T: Bennett 2, Crosland,
     Simpson, Newbould
     G: Metcalfe
HULL   0

1909-10 *16 Apr, at Huddersfield, 19 413*
LEEDS   7 T: Goldthorpe
     G: Young 2
HULL   7 T: Cottrell
     G: Wallace, E Rogers

Replay *18 Apr, at Huddersfield, 11 608*
LEEDS   26 T: Webster, Goldthorpe,
     Topham, Rowe
     G: Young 7
HULL   12 T: Walton, Connell
     G: E Rogers 3

1910-11 *29 Apr, at Salford, 8000*
BROUGHTON RANGERS   4 G: Harris 2
WIGAN   0

1911-12 *27 Apr, at Headingley, 15 371*
DEWSBURY   8 T: Rhodes 2
     G: Neary
OLDHAM   5 T: Cook
     G: Ferguson

1912-13 *26 Apr, at Headingley, 22 754*
HUDDERSFIELD   9 T: Moorhouse 3
WARRINGTON   5 T: Bradshaw
     G: Jolley

1913-14 *18 Apr, at Halifax, 19 000*
HULL   6 T: Harrison, Francis
WAKEFIELD TRINITY   0

1914-15 *1 May, at Oldham, 8000*
HUDDERSFIELD   37 T: Gleeson 2, Wagstaff 2,
     Holland, Rosenfeld,
     Gronow, Rogers,
     Moorhouse
     G: Gronow 5
ST HELENS   3 T: Daniels

1915-16, 1916-17, 1917-18, 1918-19: No competition

1919-20 *10 Apr, at Headingley, 14 000*
HUDDERSFIELD   21 T: Pogson 2, Clark, Todd,
     Habron
     G: Gronow 3
WIGAN   10 T: Hall, Jerram
     G: Jolley 2

1920-21 *30 Apr, at Broughton, 25 000*
LEIGH   13 T: Thomas 2, Parkinson
     G: Clarkson 2
HALIFAX   0

Above *The Broughton Rangers 1911 Challenge Cup-winning team. Captain JL Clampitt (with the ball) led his team to a 4–0 victory over Wigan in the final.*

Below *Challenge Cup winners of 1912, Dewsbury defeated Oldham 8–5 in the final.*

1921–22 *29 Apr, at Headingley, 34 700*
ROCHDALE HORNETS   10 T: Fitton 2
                       G: Paddon 2
HULL   9 T: Kennedy, Batten, Taylor

1922–23 *28 Apr, at Wakefield, 29 335*
LEEDS   28 T: Brittain, Davis, Ashton,
                             Buck, Walmsley, Bowen
                       G: Thompson 5
HULL   3 T: Kennedy

1923–24 *12 Apr, at Rochdale, 41 831*
WIGAN   21 T: Roffey, Price, Ring,
                             Parker, Van Heerden
                       G: Sullivan 3
OLDHAM   4 G: Brough, Knapman

1924–25 *25 Apr, at Headingley, 28 335*
OLDHAM   16 T: Corsi, Davies, Brough,
                             Farrar
                       G: Farrar 2
HULL KR   3 T: JH Wilkinson

1925–26 *1 May, at Rochdale, 27 800*
SWINTON   9 T: Blewer
                       G: Morris 3
OLDHAM   3 T: Corsi

1926–27 *7 May, at Wigan, 33 448*
OLDHAM   26 T: Holliday 3, Rix, Brough,
                             Sloman
                       G: Johnson 2, Brough 2
SWINTON   7 T: Brockbank
                       G: Morris 2

1927–28 *14 Apr, at Wigan, 33 909*
SWINTON   5 T: Brockbank
                       G: J Evans
WARRINGTON   3 T: Seeling

1928–29 *4 May, at Wembley, 41 500*
WIGAN   13 T: Abram, Kinnear, Brown
                       G: Sullivan 2
DEWSBURY   2 G: Davies

1929–30 *3 May, at Wembley, 36 544*
WIDNES   10 T: Ratcliffe, Dennett
                       G: Hoey, Ratcliffe
ST HELENS   3 T: Houghton

1930–31 *2 May, at Wembley, 40 368*
HALIFAX   22 T: Higgins 2, I Davies, Bland
                       G: Adams 4, R Davies
YORK   8 T: H Thomas 2
                       G: Pascoe

1931–32 *9 Apr, at Wigan, 29 000*
LEEDS   11 T: Harris
                       G: Thompson 4
SWINTON   8 G: Hodgson 4

1932–33 *6 May, at Wembley, 41 874*
HUDDERSFIELD   21 T: Richards, Mills, Brindle
                       G: Bowkett 6
WARRINGTON   17 T: Davies 2, Dingsdale
                       G: Holding 4

1933–34 *5 May, at Wembley, 41 280*
HUNSLET   11 T: Morrell, Beverley, Smith
                       G: Tolson
WIDNES   5 T: McDowell
                       G: Ratcliffe

1934–35 *4 May, at Wembley, 39 000*
CASTLEFORD   11 T: Adams, Askin, Cunniffe
                       G: Atkinson
HUDDERSFIELD   8 T: Towill, Fiddes
                       G: Sherwood

1935–36 *18 Apr, at Wembley, 51 250*
LEEDS   18 T: Isaac, F Harris, Parker,
                             E Harris
                       G: Williams 3
WARRINGTON   2 G: Shankland

1936–37 *8 May, at Wembley, 47 699*
WIDNES   18 T: Barber, Shannon, McCue,
                             Silcock
                       G: Topping 3
KEIGHLEY   5 T: Lloyd
                       G: Sherburn

1937–38 *7 May, at Wembley, 51 243*
SALFORD   7 T: Gear
                       G: Risman 2
BARROW   4 G: French, Little

1938–39 *6 May, at Wembley, 55 453*
HALIFAX   20 T: Todd, Smith, Treen, Bevan
                       G: Lockwood 4
SALFORD   3 T: Risman

1939–40: No competition

1940–41 *17 May, at Odsal, 28 500*
LEEDS   19 T: Hey 2, Lawrenson 2,
                           Jenkins
                       G: Eaton 2
HALIFAX   2 G: Meek

1941–42 *6 Jun, at Odsal, 15 250*
LEEDS   15 T: Edwards 2, Morris
                       G: Risman 3
HALIFAX   10 G: Lockwood 5

1942–43 *24 Apr, at Dewsbury, 10 470 FIRST LEG*
DEWSBURY   16 T: Kenny, Seeling, Robinson,
                             Edwards
                       G: Seeling 2
LEEDS   9 T: Eaton
                       G: Eaton 3
26 Apr, at Headingley, 16 000 SECOND LEG
LEEDS   6 G: Walkington, Eaton,
                             Jenkins
DEWSBURY   0
Dewsbury won 16–15 on aggregate

Wembley, 1950 – referee Albert Dobson whistles up as a scrum disintegrates. Double Lance Todd Trophy winner Gerry Helme crouches on the right. His team, Warrington, took the Challenge Cup with a 19–0 victory over local rivals Widnes.

1943-44 *15 Apr, at Wigan, 21 500 FIRST LEG*
WIGAN   3 T: Featherstone
BRADFORD NORTHERN   0
22 Apr, at Odsal, 30 000 SECOND LEG
BRADFORD NORTHERN   8 T: Batten, Whitcombe
         G: Carmichael
WIGAN   0
Bradford Northern won 8–3 on aggregate

1944-45 *28 Apr, at Huddersfield, 9041 FIRST LEG*
HUDDERSFIELD   7 T: Peake
         G: Bawden 2
BRADFORD NORTHERN   4 G: E Ward 2
5 May, at Odsal, 17 500 SECOND LEG
BRADFORD NORTHERN   5 T: Batten
         G: E Ward
HUDDERSFIELD   6 T: Bawden 2
Huddersfield won 13–9 on aggregate

1945-46 *4 May, at Wembley, 54 730*
WAKEFIELD TRINITY   13 T: Stott 2, Croston
         G: Stott 2
WIGAN   12 T: Nordgren 2, Jolley, J Blan

1946-47 *3 May, at Wembley, 77 605*
BRADFORD NORTHERN   8 T: Walters, Foster
         G: E Ward
LEEDS   4 G: Cook 2

1947-48 *1 May, at Wembley, 91 465*
WIGAN   8 T: Hilton, Barton
         G: EH Ward
BRADFORD NORTHERN   3 T: Edwards

1948-49 *7 May, at Wembley, 95 050*
BRADFORD NORTHERN   12 T: Foster, Batten
         G: E Ward 3
HALIFAX   0

1949-50 *6 May, at Wembley, 94 249*
WARRINGTON   19 T: Bath, Knowelden, Ryder
         G: Palin 5
WIDNES   0

1950-51 *5 May, at Wembley, 94 262*
WIGAN   10 T: Gee, Hilton
         G: Gee, Mountford
BARROW   0

1951-52 *19 Apr, at Wembley, 72 093*
WORKINGTON TOWN   18 T: Lawrenson 2, Mudge,
         G Wilson
         G: Risman 3
FEATHERSTONE R   10 T: Evans, Batten
         G: Miller 2

1952-53 *25 Apr, at Wembley, 89 588*
HUDDERSFIELD   15 T: Ramsden 2, Banks
         G: Cooper 2, Devery
ST HELENS   10 T: Llewellyn, Langfield
         G: Langfield 2

1953-54 *24 Apr, at Wembley, 81 777*
WARRINGTON   4 G: Bath 2
HALIFAX   . 4 G: Griffiths 2
Replay *5 May, at Odsal, 102 569*
WARRINGTON   8 T: Challinor, Helme
         G: Bath
HALIFAX   4 G: Griffiths 2

1954-55 *30 Apr, at Wembley, 66 513*
BARROW   21 T: Goodwin, Castle,
         McKeating
         G: Horne 6
WORKINGTON TOWN   12 T: Gibson, Faulder
         G: Paskins 3

1955-56 *28 Apr, at Wembley, 79 341*
ST HELENS   13 T: Llewellyn, Carlton,
         Prescott
         G: Rhodes 2
HALIFAX   2 G: Griffiths

1956-57 *11 May, at Wembley, 76 318*
LEEDS   9 T: Quinn, Hodgkinson,
         Robinson
BARROW   7 T: Jackson
         G: Horne 2

1957-58 *10 May, at Wembley, 66 109*
WIGAN   13 T: Sullivan, Barton, McTigue
         G: Cunliffe 2
WORKINGTON TOWN   9 T: Southward
         G: Southward 3

1958-59 *9 May, at Wembley, 79 811*
WIGAN   30 T: Boston 2, McTigue, Bolton,
         Holden, Sullivan
         G: Griffiths 6
HULL   13 T: Finn
         G: Keegan 5

1959-60 *14 May, at Wembley, 79 773*
WAKEFIELD TRINITY   38 T: Holliday 2, Skene 2,
         Fox 2, Smith, Rollin
         G: Fox 7
HULL   5 T: Cowan
         G: Evans

1960-61 *13 May, at Wembley, 94 672*
ST HELENS   12 T: Murphy, Vollenhoven
         G: Rhodes 3
WIGAN   6 G: Griffiths 3

1961-62 *12 May, at Wembley, 81 263*
WAKEFIELD TRINITY   12 T: Hirst, Fox
         G: Fox 3
HUDDERSFIELD   6 T: Smales, Ramsden

1962-63 *11 May, at Wembley, 84 492*
WAKEFIELD TRINITY   25 T: Coetzer 2, Brooke,
         Sampson, Poynton
         G: Fox 5
WIGAN   10 T: Pitchford, Carlton
         G: Ashton 2

1965 saw one of the game's classic Cup Finals when Wigan beat Hunslet 20–16. Here Wigan full-back Ray Ashby is stopped by Geoff Gunney. Ashby shared the Lance Todd Trophy with Hunslet stand-off Brian Gabbitas, a unique occurrence.

1963-64 *9 May, at Wembley, 84 488*

WIDNES	13	T: Briers, Collier, Myler
		G: Randall 2
HULL KR	5	T: Burwell
		G: Kellett

1964-65 *8 May, at Wembley, 89 016*

WIGAN	20	T: Lake 2, Holden, Gilfedder
		G: Gilfedder 3, Ashton
HUNSLET	16	T: Shelton, Griffiths
		G: Langton 5

1965-66 *21 May, at Wembley, 98 536*

ST HELENS	21	T: Mantle, Bishop, Killeen
		G: Killeen 5, Murphy
WIGAN	2	G: Gilfedder

1966-67 *13 May, at Wembley, 76 290*

FEATHERSTONE	4	17 T: Morgan, Thomas, Smales
		G: Smales 3, Dooler
BARROW		12 T: Watson, Brophy
		G: Delooze 2, Tees

1967-68 *11 May, at Wembley, 87 100*

LEEDS		11 T: Atkinson
		G: Risman 4
WAKEFIELD TRINITY		10 T: Hirst 2
		G: D Fox 2

1968-69 *17 May, at Wembley, 97 939*

CASTLEFORD		11 T: Hardisty, Howe, Hepworth
		G: Redfearn
SALFORD		6 G: Hill 3

65

CURRENT COMPETITIONS

1969–70 *9 May, at Wembley, 95 255*

CASTLEFORD	7	T: Lowndes
		G: Redfearn 2
WIGAN	2	G: Tyrer

1970–71 *15 May, at Wembley, 85 514*

LEIGH	24	T: Dorrington, Eckersley
		G: Ferguson 5, Murphy 2,
		Fiddler, Eckersley
LEEDS	7	T: Wainwright
		G: Holmes 2

1971–72 *13 May, at Wembley, 89 495*

ST HELENS	16	T: Rees, Jones
		G: Coslett 5
LEEDS	13	T: Cookson
		G: Clawson 5

1972–73 *12 May, at Wembley, 72 395*

FEATHERSTONE R	33	T: Newlove 2, Farrar, Smith,
		Hartley
		G: Kellett 8, Nash
BRADFORD NORTHERN	14	T: Redfearn, Fearnley
		G: Tees 4

1973–74 *11 May, at Wembley, 77 400*

WARRINGTON	24	T: Ashcroft, Nicholas
		G: Whitehead 7, Murphy 2
FEATHERSTONE R	9	T: Newlove
		G: Box 3

1974–75 *10 May, at Wembley, 85 098*

WIDNES	14	T: Mills
		G: Dutton 6 (1DG)
WARRINGTON	7	T: Bevan
		G: Whitehead 2

1975–76 *8 May, at Wembley, 89 982*

ST HELENS	20	T: Glynn 2, Heaton,
		Cunningham
		G: Pimblett 5 (2DG)
WIDNES	5	G: Dutton 2, Elwell (DG)

1976–77 *7 May, at Wembley, 80 871*

LEEDS	16	T: Dick, Atkinson, Dyl
		G: Dick 4 (1DG)
WIDNES	7	T: Aspey
		G: Dutton 2

The 1985 final, and Wigan winger John Ferguson scores in his club's classic 28–24 victory over Hull, whose stand-off Fred Ah Kuoi arrives too late.

1977–78 *13 May, at Wembley, 96 000*
LEEDS	14	T: D Smith, Atkinson, Cookson
		G: Ward 2 (2DG), Oulton, Holmes (DG)
ST HELENS	12	T: Liptrot, Francis
		G: Pimblett 3

1978–79 *5 May, at Wembley, 94 218*
WIDNES	12	T: Hughes, Wright
		G: Burke 2, Eckersley (DG), Elwell (DG)
WAKEFIELD TRINITY	3	T: Fletcher

1979–80 *3 May, at Wembley, 95 000*
HULL KR	10	T: Hubbard
		G: Hubbard 3, Millward (DG)
HULL	5	T: Wilby
		G: Lloyd

1980–81 *2 May, at Wembley, 92 496*
WIDNES	18	T: George, Burke, Gregory
		G: Burke 4, Adams (DG)
HULL KR	9	T: Burton G: Hubbard 3

1981–82 *1 May, at Wembley, 92 147*
HULL	14	T: Norton, O'Hara
		G: Lloyd 4
WIDNES	14	T: Cunningham 2, Wright
		G: Burke, Gregory, Elwell (DG)

Replay *19 May, at Elland Road, 41 171*
HULL	18	T: Topliss 2, Kemble, Crooks
		G: Crooks 3
WIDNES	9	T: Wright
		G: Burke 3

1982–83 *7 May, at Wembley, 84 969*
FEATHERSTONE R	14	T: Hobbs 2
		G: Quinn 4
HULL	12	T: Leuluai, Crooks
		G: Crooks 3

1983–84 *5 May, at Wembley, 80 116*
WIDNES	19	T: Lydon 2, O'Loughlin
		G: Burke 3, S O'Neill (DG)
WIGAN	6	T: Hemsley
		G: Whitfield

The goal that made all the difference – Halifax loose-forward John Pendlebury drops a crucial goal in the 1987 final, watched by Mick Scott and Chris Anderson. Halifax beat St Helens 19–18.

1984-85 *4 May, at Wembley, 97 801*
WIGAN 28 T: Ferguson 2, Kenny, Gill,
Edwards
G: Gill 3, Stephenson
HULL 24 T: Leuluai 2, James, Evans,
Divorty
G: Crooks 2

1985-86 *3 May, at Wembley, 82 134*
CASTLEFORD 15 T: R Beardmore, Marchant,
Sandy
G: Ketteridge,
R Beardmore (DG)
HULL KR 14 T: Prohm 2, Lydiat
G: Dorahy

1986-87 *2 May, at Wembley, 91 267*
HALIFAX 19 T: George, Eadie, McCallion
G: Whitfield 3,
Pendlebury (DG)
ST HELENS 18 T: Elia, Loughlin, Round
G: Loughlin 3

1987-88 *30 Apr, at Wembley, 94 273*
WIGAN 32 T: K Iro 2, Bell, Gill, A Iro,
Hanley, Lydon
G: Lydon, Gregory
HALIFAX 12 T: Anderson, James
G: Whitfield 2

1988-89 *29 Apr, at Wembley, 78 000*
WIGAN 27 T: K Iro 2, Hampson, Hanley,
Gregory
G: Lydon 3, Gregory (DG)
ST HELENS 0

1989-90 *28 Apr, at Wembley, 77 729*
WIGAN 36 T: K Iro 2, Preston 2, Betts,
Hanley
G: Lydon 6
WARRINGTON 14 T: Gregory, Lyon
G: Bishop 2, Darbyshire

1990-91 *27 Apr, at Wembley, 75 532*
WIGAN 13 T: Myers, Botica
G: Botica 2, Gregory (DG)
ST HELENS 8 T: Hunte
G: Bishop 2

CHALLENGE CUP HONOURS

Club	Winners	Runners-up
Wigan	12	9
Leeds	10	4
Widnes	7	5
Huddersfield	6	2
St Helens	5	8
Warrington	5	8
Halifax	5	7
Wakefield Trinity	5	3
Bradford Northern	4	4
Castleford	4	–

Club	Winners	Runners-up
Oldham	3	4
Featherstone Rovers	3	2
Swinton	3	2
Batley	3	–
Hull	2	10
Hunslet	2	2
Dewsbury	2	1
Broughton Rangers	2	–
Leigh	2	–
Salford	1	6
Hull KR	1	5
Barrow	1	4
Workington Town	1	2
Rochdale Hornets	1	–
Keighley	–	1
York	–	1

Note – Bradford Northern's record includes two finals as Bradford

CHALLENGE CUP FINAL RECORDS

Most finals	21	Wigan
Most wins	12	Wigan
Most consecutive finals	4	Oldham, Wigan
Most consecutive wins	4	Wigan
Highest score	38	Wakefield T v Hull, 1960
Highest aggregate	52	Wigan 28 Hull 24, 1985
Lowest aggregate	4	Broughton Rangers 4 Wigan 0, 1911
		(In the first leg of the 1944 final only 3 points were scored – Wigan 3 Bradford N 0
Largest crowd	102 569	Halifax v Warrington, 1954 (Replay)
Smallest crowd	8000	Broughton Rangers v Wigan, 1911
	8000	Huddersfield v St Helens, 1915
Highest receipts	£1 610 447	St Helens v Wigan, 1991

PLAYERS' RECORDS IN ONE FINAL

Most tries	3	R Wilson (Broughton R) v Salford, 1902
	3	S Moorhouse (Huddersfield) v Warrington, 1913
	3	T Holliday (Oldham) v Swinton, 1927
Most goals	8	C Kellett (Featherstone R) v Bradford N, 1973
Most points	20	N Fox (Wakefield T) v Hull, 1960

PLAYERS' RECORDS IN ALL FINALS

Most appearances	8	E Batten (Leeds, Bradford N, Featherstone R) 1941, 1943, 1944, 1945, 1947, 1948, 1949, 1952
Most tries	6	K Iro (Wigan) 1988, 1989, 1990
Most goals	15	N Fox (Wakefield T) 1960, 1962, 1963
Most points	39	N Fox (Wakefield T), as above

Kevin Iro, the Wigan centre, performed an unparalleled feat by scoring two tries in each of Wigan's three consecutive Wembley victories in 1988, 1989 and 1990.

ERIC BATTEN

The Cup Final King

Most Rugby League players faithfully state that their two major ambitions are to play for Great Britain and to appear in a Wembley Cup Final. A few achieve them. For most they remain a mirage. Eric Batten was one of those who turned his dreams into reality – repeatedly!

There was little likelihood of Eric Batten failing to be a rugby player. The game ran in his blood. His father was the legendary Billy Batten, probably the most celebrated player in the game before the First World War and one of the first inductees into the Rugby League Hall of Fame in 1988. Two of Eric's uncles were also professionals, as would be two of his own brothers, Bob and Billy junior. Eric's cousin Stanley Smith was one of the great wingers of the pre-war era with Wakefield Trinity and Leeds, and was a British Lion in 1936.

Eric Batten, stocky, swift and strong, was a natural winger who began his professional career with Wakefield Trinity, one of his father's old clubs, in 1933. A transfer to Hunslet in 1936 brought the young flyer his first taste of big-time League as he shared in Hunslet's momentous 8–2 victory over Leeds in the 1938 Championship Final at Elland Road. That year also brought him the first of seven Yorkshire caps and the first of 14 England caps. In 1946 as a Bradford Northern player, Eric emulated his father by earning a Lions tour and winning Test honours.

The most extraordinary achievement of Batten's career, however, was his record of appearing in eight Challenge Cup Finals, four of which were at Wembley. He was fortunate in that a rather haphazard system of 'guesting' for clubs was permitted in the first years of the Second World War, and it was as such a guest player that he made his first Cup Final appearance, in 1941 when he figured on the right wing for Leeds in their 19–2 win over Halifax. His only previous games for the Loiners had been in both legs of the semi-finals against Bradford Northern.

Two years later, as a regular Leeds player, he again won a Cup Final place. The final was contested over two legs, and though Eric missed the first leg against Dewsbury at Crown Flatt when Leeds lost 9–16, he was on the wing for the second leg at Headingley. The only scores were three goals to Leeds, whose 6–0 victory was just not sufficient to pull back Dewsbury's advantage.

In 1943 Eric signed for Bradford Northern, for whom he would make an astonishing five Challenge Cup Final appearances within six years. The first, another two-legged affair in 1944, brought an 8–3 aggregate victory over Wigan after Northern had lost the first leg 0–3. The second leg at Odsal yielded Eric his first Cup Final try. There was another try for Eric in the second leg of the 1945 Cup Final against Huddersfield at Odsal. Huddersfield had won the first leg 7–4 in a blizzard at Fartown and won the second leg 6–5 in equally atrocious conditions.

Peace-time saw Northern establish themselves as a fearsome cup-fighting team. In 1947 Eric Batten and Northern went to Wembley for the first time and defeated arch-rivals Leeds 8–4. They were back at the Empire Stadium in 1948 only to surrender the Cup to Wigan. Then in 1949 Bradford stunned the Rugby League world by reaching Wembley for the third consecutive year. This was Eric's seventh Challenge Cup Final – a record, but one he then shared with his fellow Northern winger, Allan Edwards. Edwards, a Welshman and a 1936 British Lion, played in Cup Finals for Salford (1938, 1939), Leeds (1942), Dewsbury (1943) and Bradford Northern

ERIC BATTEN'S CHALLENGE CUP FINAL APPEARANCES

Year	For		Opponents		Venue
1941	LEEDS	19	HALIFAX	2	Odsal
1943	LEEDS	6	DEWSBURY	0	Headingley*
1944	BRADFORD N	0	WIGAN	3	Wigan**
	BRADFORD N	8	WIGAN	0	Odsal†
1945	BRADFORD N	4	HUDDERSFIELD	7	Huddersfield**
	BRADFORD N	5	HUDDERSFIELD	6	Odsal†
1947	BRADFORD N	8	LEEDS	4	Wembley
1948	BRADFORD N	3	WIGAN	8	Wembley
1949	BRADFORD N	12	HALIFAX	0	Wembley
1952	FEATHERSTONE R	10	WORKINGTON T	18	Wembley

* Second leg. Leeds lost the first leg at Dewsbury 9–16.
** First leg. † Second leg.

Eric Batten leaping over a Leeds tackler.

(1945, 1948 and 1949). Northern's opponents were Halifax and a world record 95 050 crowd saw a dour local derby end 12–0 in Bradford's favour. Batten fractured his shoulder in the early minutes of the game but ignored the handicap to score Bradford's opening try after ten minutes, after following through on a long kick by his captain Ernest Ward.

In 1951–52 Eric Batten left Bradford to become captain-coach at Featherstone Rovers. By the end of the season he had played his record eighth Challenge Cup Final, having taken unfancied Rovers to a first Wembley appearance against Workington Town. A splendid match saw Eric claim a try at the corner to level the scores at 7–7 just after half-time, but Town ran out winners 18–10. Still, four victories in eight Challenge Cup Finals for Eric Batten was good going by any standards.

THE LANCASHIRE CHALLENGE CUP

The Lancashire Challenge Cup Competition was inaugurated in season 1905–06, the first ties being played on 14 October 1905. The original title of the trophy was 'The Lancashire County Rugby Football Challenge Cup'. Apart from wartime seasons, the competition has always been contested in the early months of the season.

LANCASHIRE CUP FINALS

1905-06 *2 Dec, at Broughton, 16 000*
WIGAN	0	
LEIGH	0	

Replay *11 Dec, at Broughton, 10 000*
WIGAN	8	T: Leytham, Jenkins
		G: Mason
LEIGH	0	

1906-07 *1 Dec, at Wigan, 14 048*
BROUGHTON RANGERS	15	T: Flynn, Wilson, Darlison
		G: Harris 2, Flynn
WARRINGTON	6	T: Dickenson, Brooks

1907-08 *30 Nov, at Rochdale, 14 000*
OLDHAM	16	T: Smith, Llewellyn, Ferguson, Oldershaw
		G: Ferguson 2
BROUGHTON RANGERS	9	T: Hogg
		G: Barlow 3

1908-09 *19 Dec, at Broughton, 20 000*
WIGAN	10	T: Thomas, Johnston
		G: Sharrock, Leytham
OLDHAM	9	T: Cook
		G: Wood 3

1909-10 *27 Nov, at Broughton, 14 000*
WIGAN	22	T: Miller 2, Thomas 2, de Francis, Leytham
		G: Leytham 2
LEIGH	5	T: Johnson
		G: Battersby

1910-11 *3 Dec, at Broughton, 14 000*
OLDHAM	4	G: Wood, Ferguson
SWINTON	3	T: Gartrell

1911-12 *2 Dec, at Broughton, 20 000*
ROCHDALE HORNETS	12	T: Jones, Turner
		G: Paddon 2, English
OLDHAM	5	T: GW Smith
		G: GW Smith

1912-13 *11 Dec, at Salford, 6000*
WIGAN	21	T: Bradley 2, Coldrick, Seeling, Todd
		G: Sharrock 3
ROCHDALE HORNETS	5	T: Robinson
		G: Paddon

1913-14 *6 Dec, at Broughton, 18 000*
OLDHAM	5	T: Farnsworth
		G: Wood
WIGAN	0	

1914-15 *5 Dec, at Broughton, 4000*
ROCHDALE HORNETS	3	T: Jones
WIGAN	2	G: J Thomas

1915-16, 1916-17, 1917-18 No competition

1918-19 *10 May, at Salford, 18 617*
ROCHDALE HORNETS	22	T: Carter 2, Woods, Fairhurst, Hopwood, Jones
		G: Jones, Hopwood
OLDHAM	0	

Rochdale Hornets captain George Prudence poses proudly with the Lancashire Challenge Cup in 1914. Hornets defeated Wigan 3–2 in the final.

1919-20 *6 Dec, at Salford, 19 000*
OLDHAM   7 T: Finnerty
           G: Ferguson 2
ROCHDALE HORNETS   0

1920-21 *4 Dec, at Salford, 25 000*
BROUGHTON RANGERS   6 T: Barnes, Price
LEIGH   3 T: Higham

1921-22 *3 Dec, at Broughton, 18 000*
WARRINGTON   7 T: Bradbury
           G: Jolley 2
OLDHAM   5 T: Ferguson
           G: Farrar

1922-23 *25 Nov, at Salford, 15 000*
WIGAN   20 T: Webster 2, Howley, Ring
           G: Sullivan 4
LEIGH   2 G: Clarkson

1923-24 *24 Nov, at Wigan, 25 656*
ST HELENS RECS   17 T: Owen, Pyke, Greenall
           G: Dingsdale 2, Pyke, Owen
SWINTON   0

1924-25 *22 Nov, at Salford, 15 000*
OLDHAM   10 T: Baker, Woodward
           G: Knapman 2
ST HELENS RECS   0

1925-26 *10 Dec, at Broughton, 17 000*
SWINTON   15 T: J Evans, Brockbank,
               B Evans
           G: Morris 3
WIGAN   11 T: Ring 3
           G: Sullivan

1926-27 *20 Nov, at Warrington, 19 439*
ST HELENS   10 T: Ellaby, Fairclough
           G: Lewis 2
ST HELENS RECS   2 G: Pyke

1927-28 *19 Nov, at Oldham, 22 000*
SWINTON   5 T: Cracknell
           G: Morris
WIGAN   2 G: Sullivan

1928-29 *24 Nov, at Warrington, 19 000*
WIGAN   5 T: Brown
           G: Sullivan
WIDNES   4 G: Hoey, Douglas

1929-30 *23 Nov, at Wigan, 21 012*
WARRINGTON   15 T: Kirk, Meredith,
               Blinkhorn
           G: Holding 3
SALFORD   2 G: Dobing

1930-31 *29 Nov, at Swinton, 16 710*
ST HELENS RECS   18 T: Jennion 2, Bailey,
               Mulvanney
           G: Dingsdale 3
WIGAN   3 T: Ring

1931-32 *21 Nov, at Broughton, 26 471*
SALFORD   10 T: Jenkins 2
           G: Southward 2
SWINTON   8 T: Jones, Salmon
           G: Hodgson

1932-33 *19 Nov, at Wigan, 28 500*
WARRINGTON   10 T: Thompson, Davies
           G: Holding 2
ST HELENS   9 T: Fildes
           G: Lewis 3

1933-34 *18 Nov, at Swinton, 9085*
OLDHAM   12 T: Bardsley, Stephens
           G: Rees 3
ST HELENS RECS   0

1934-35 *20 Oct, at Swinton, 33 544*
SALFORD   21 T: Jenkins, Middleton,
               Hudson
           G: Risman 6
WIGAN   12 T: Innes, Bennett
           G: Sullivan 2, H Gee

1935-36 *19 Oct, at Warrington, 16 500*
SALFORD   15 T: Bradbury, Feetham,
               Middleton
           G: Risman 3
WIGAN   7 T: Davies
           G: Sullivan 2

1936-37 *17 Oct, at Warrington, 17 500*
SALFORD   5 T: Osbaldestin
           G: Risman
WIGAN   2 G: Sullivan

1937-38 *23 Oct, at Wigan, 14 000*
WARRINGTON   8 T: Brown 2
           G: Shankland
BARROW   4 G: French 2

1938-39 *22 Oct, at Swinton, 27 940*
WIGAN   10 G: Sullivan 5
SALFORD   7 T: Gear
           G: Risman, Osbaldestin

1939-40 *FIRST LEG 20 Apr, at Widnes, 5500*
WIDNES   4 G: Topping 2
SWINTON   5 T: Garner
           G: Hodgson
SECOND LEG 27 Apr, at Swinton, 8947
SWINTON   16 T: Armitt, Lewis
           G: Hodgson 5
WIDNES   11 T: Rutledge
           G: Topping 2, Shannon, Hoey
After extra time. At full-time the score was Swinton 8
Widnes 9. Swinton won 21-15 on aggregate.

1940-45: No competition

1945-46 *27 Oct, at Warrington, 28 184*
WIDNES   7 T: Reynolds
           G: Hutton 2
WIGAN   3 T: Toohey

1946–47 *26 Oct, at Swinton, 21 618*
WIGAN   9 T: J Blan
                          G: Lawrenson 3
BELLE VUE RANGERS   3 T: Manning

1947–48 *1 Nov, at Warrington, 23 110*
WIGAN   10 T: Ratcliffe, Nordgren
                          G: Ward 2
BELLE VUE RANGERS   7 T: Flanagan
                          G: Thomas 2

1948–49 *13 Nov, at Swinton, 39 015*
WIGAN   14 T: Ward, Ratcliffe
                          G: Ward 4
WARRINGTON   8 T: Bevan, Johnson
                          G: Palin

1949–50 *29 Oct, at Warrington, 35 000*
WIGAN   20 T: Nordgren 4, Hilton, Blan
                          G: Gee
LEIGH   7 T: Cleworth
                          G: Ledgard 2

1950–51 *4 Nov, at Swinton, 42 541*
WIGAN   28 T: Nordgren 2, Slevin, Alty,
                              Roughley, Cunliffe
                          G: Gee 5
WARRINGTON   5 T: Naughton
                          G: Palin

1951–52 *27 Oct, at Swinton, 33 230*
WIGAN   14 T: Nordgren 2, Large, Broom
                          G: Gee
LEIGH   6 T: Harris, Morgan

1952–53 *29 Nov, at Swinton, 34 785*
LEIGH   22 T: Kitchen 2, Chadwick, Allan
                          G: Ledgard 5
ST HELENS   5 T: Gullick
                          G: Langfield

1953–54 *24 Oct, at Swinton, 42 793*
ST HELENS   16 T: Moses, Honey
                          G: Metcalfe 5
WIGAN   8 T: Fleming, Street
                          G: Gee

1954–55 *23 Oct, at Swinton, 25 204*
BARROW   12 T: Goodwin, Parker
                          G: Horne 3
OLDHAM   2 G: Ganley

1955–56 *15 Oct, at Wigan, 26 507*
LEIGH   26 T: Barton, Owen, Gullick,
                              Kindon
                          G: Ledgard 7
WIDNES   9 T: Williamson
                          G: Sale 3

1956–57 *20 Oct, at Wigan, 39 544*
OLDHAM   10 T: Etty, Turner
                          G: Ganley 2
ST HELENS   3 T: Carlton

1957–58 *19 Oct, at Swinton, 42 497*
OLDHAM   13 T: Davies, Ganley, Pitchford
                          G: Ganley 2
WIGAN   8 T: O'Grady, McTigue
                          G: Cunliffe

1958–59 *25 Oct, at Swinton, 38 780*
OLDHAM	12	T: Davies, Kellett
		G: Ganley 2, Kellett
ST HELENS	2	G: Fearis

1959–60 *31 Oct, at Wigan, 39 237*
WARRINGTON	5	T: Bevan
		G: Fraser
ST HELENS	4	G: Rhodes 2

1960–61 *29 Oct, at Wigan, 31 755*
ST HELENS	15	T: Large, Vollenhoven, Rhodes
		G: Rhodes 3
SWINTON	9	T: McGregor
		G: Blan 3

1961–62 *11 Nov, at Wigan, 30 000*
ST HELENS	25	T: Rhodes, Vollenhoven, Large, Murphy, Sullivan
		G: Rhodes 5
SWINTON	9	T: Bretherton
		G: Blan 3

1962–63 *27 Oct, at Wigan, 23 523*
ST HELENS	7	T: Vollenhoven
		G: Coslett 2
SWINTON	4	G: Blan 2

1963–64 *26 Oct, at Swinton, 21 231*
ST HELENS	15	T: Smith, Vollenhoven, Killeen
		G: Coslett 3
LEIGH	4	G: Tyrer 2

1964–65 *24 Oct, at Wigan, 17 383*
ST HELENS	12	T: Benyon, Hicks
		G: Killeen 3
SWINTON	4	G: Gowers 2

1965–66 *29 Oct, at St Helens, 21 360*
WARRINGTON	16	T: Melling 2, Glover, Fisher
		G: Bootle 2
ROCHDALE HORNETS	5	T: Starkey
		G: Starkey

1966–67 *29 Oct, at Swinton, 14 193*
WIGAN	16	T: Clarke, Ashton, Boston, Gilfedder
		G: Gilfedder 2
OLDHAM	13	T: Donovan
		G: Warburton 5

1967–68 *7 Oct, at Wigan, 16 897*
| ST HELENS | 2 | G: Coslett |
| WARRINGTON | 2 | G: Aspinall |

Replay *2 Dec, at Swinton, 7577*
ST HELENS	13	T: Warlow, Chisnall, Jones
		G: Houghton 2
WARRINGTON	10	T: Melling, Gordon
		G: Allen 2

1968–69 *25 Oct, at Wigan, 17 008*
ST HELENS	30	T: Wilson 2, Chisnall, Rees, Williams, Bishop
		G: Coslett 6
OLDHAM	2	G: Briggs

1969–70 *1 Nov, at Wigan, 13 532*
SWINTON	11	T: Philbin
		G: Kenny 4
LEIGH	2	G: Murphy

1970–71 *28 Nov, at Swinton, 10 776*
LEIGH	7	T: Eckersley
		G: Ferguson 2
ST HELENS	4	G: Coslett 2

1971–72 *28 Aug, at St Helens, 6970*
WIGAN	15	T: Francis, Eastham, Ayres
		G: Tyrer 3
WIDNES	8	T: Gaydon, O'Neill
		G: Aspey

1972–73 *21 Oct, at Warrington, 6865*
SALFORD	25	T: Banner, Charlton, Watkins, Eastham, Richards
		G: Watkins 5
SWINTON	11	T: Fleay
		G: Gowers 3, Kenny

Oldham captain Bernard Ganley crosses the Wigan line in the 1957 final for a rare try. Ganley landed over 1000 goals for Oldham and in 1957–58 became the first man to kick 200 goals in a season.

1973-74 *13 Oct, at Warrington, 8012*
WIGAN 19 T: O'Loughlin 2, Wright
G: Gray 4, Ayres
SALFORD 9 T: Watkins
G: Watkins 3

1974-75 *2 Nov, at Wigan, 7403*
WIDNES 6 T: George
G: Dutton, Hughes (DG)
SALFORD 2 G: Fielding

1975-76 *4 Oct, at Wigan, 7566*
WIDNES 16 T: Prescott, George, Aspey
G: Dutton 4 (1DG)
SALFORD 7 T: Richards
G: Watkins 2

1976-77 *30 Oct, at Wigan, 8498*
WIDNES 16 T: George, Wright
G: Dutton 5 (1DG),
Bowden (DG)
WORKINGTON TOWN 11 T: Wilkins
G: MacCorquodale 4

1977-78 *29 Oct, at Warrington, 9548*
WORKINGTON TOWN 16 T: Wilkins, Wright
G: MacCorquodale 4,
Walker 2 (2DG)
WIGAN 13 T: Nulty, Willicombe,
Ashurst
G: Burke, Nulty

1978-79 *7 Oct, at Wigan, 10 020*
WIDNES 15 T: Laughton 2, Wright
G: Burke 3
WORKINGTON TOWN 13 T: Wilkins, L Gorley,
MacCorquodale
G: MacCorquodale 2

1979-80 *8 Dec, at Wigan, 6887*
WIDNES 11 T: Moran, Adams
G: Burke 2, Elwell (DG)
WORKINGTON TOWN 0

1980-81 *4 Oct, at St Helens, 6442*
WARRINGTON 26 T: Martyn, Bevan, Hesford,
Thackray
G: Hesford 7
WIGAN 10 T: Ramsdale, Fairbairn
G: Fairbairn 2

1981-82 *26 Sep, at Wigan, 9011*
LEIGH 8 T: Bilsbury
G: Woods 2, Donlan (DG)
WIDNES 3 T: Bentley

1982-83 *23 Oct, at Wigan, 6462*
WARRINGTON 16 T: Eccles, M Kelly, Fellows,
K Kelly
G: Hesford 2
ST HELENS 0

Right A Salford player runs into trouble in the shape of Widnes forwards Emosi Koloto and Kurt Sorensen in the 1990 final. Widnes scraped home 24–18 to take the trophy for the seventh time.

1983-84 *1 Oct, at Wigan, 7007*
BARROW 12 T: McConnell
G: Ball 4 (1DG), Tickle (DG)
WIDNES 8 T: Lydon
G: Lydon 2

1984-85 *28 Oct, at Wigan, 26 074*
ST HELENS 26 T: Meninga 2, Day, Haggerty
G: Day 5
WIGAN 18 T: Kiss, West, Gill
G: Whitfield 3

1985-86 *13 Oct, at St Helens, 19 202*
WIGAN 34 T: Ella 2, Kiss, Edwards,
Hanley
G: Stephenson 7
WARRINGTON 8 T: Johnson
G: Carbert 2

1986-87 *19 Oct, at St Helens, 20 180*
WIGAN 27 T: Edwards 2, Lydon, Ford
G: Gill 5, Lydon (DG)
OLDHAM 6 T: Bridge
G: Hobbs

1987-88 *11 Oct, at St Helens, 20 237*
WIGAN 28 T: Hanley 2, Gill, West
G: Lydon 5, Stephenson
WARRINGTON 16 T: Forster 2, Gregory
G: Woods 2

1988-89 *23 Oct, at St Helens, 19 154*
WIGAN 22 T: K Iro 2, Shelford, Bell
G: K Iro 3
SALFORD 17 T: Herbert, Bentley, Evans
G: Brown 2, Worrall (DG)

1989-90 *14 Oct, at St Helens, 9895*
WARRINGTON 24 T: Jackson 2, Forster, Ropati
G: Turner 4
OLDHAM 16 T: Irving, Robinson, Lord
G: Platt, Hyde

1990-91 *29 Oct, at Wigan, 7485*
WIDNES 24 T: Currier, Myler, Smith,
Offiah
G: Davies 4
SALFORD 18 T: Williams, Blease, Fell
G: Kerry 3

LANCASHIRE CUP HONOURS

Club	Winners	Runners-up
Wigan	20	14
St Helens	10	7
Oldham	9	9
Warrington	9	6
Widnes	7	6
Salford	5	7
Leigh	4	8
Swinton	4	8
Rochdale Hornets	3	3
Broughton Rangers	2	3
St Helens Recs	2	3
Barrow	2	1
Workington Town	1	3

Note – Broughton Rangers' record includes two losing finals as Belle Vue Rangers.

PLAYERS' RECORDS IN ALL FINALS

Most appearances	10 K Gee (Wigan) 1935, 1938, 1945, 1946, 1947, 1948, 1949, 1950, 1951, 1953
Most tries	9 B Nordgren (Wigan) 1947, 1949, 1950, 1951
Most goals	17 J Sullivan (Wigan) 1922, 1925, 1927, 1928, 1934, 1935, 1936, 1938
Most points	34 J Sullivan (Wigan), as above

LANCASHIRE CUP FINAL RECORDS

Most finals	34	Wigan
Most wins	20	Wigan
Most consecutive finals	7	St Helens, Wigan
Most consecutive wins	6	Wigan
Highest score	34	Wigan v Warrington, 1985
Highest aggregate	44	St Helens 26 Wigan 18, 1984
	44	Wigan 28 Warrington 16, 1987
Lowest aggregate	0	Leigh 0 Wigan 0, 1905
Largest crowd	42 793	St Helens v Wigan, 1953
Smallest crowd	4000	Rochdale H v Wigan, 1914
Highest receipts	£71 879	Salford v Wigan, 1988

PLAYERS' RECORDS IN ONE FINAL

Most tries	4 B Nordgren (Wigan) v Leigh, 1949
Most goals	7 J Ledgard (Leigh) v Widnes, 1955
	7 S Hesford (Warrington) v Wigan, 1980
	7 D Stephenson (Wigan) v Warrington, 1985
Most points	17 S Hesford (Warrington) v Wigan, 1980

THE YORKSHIRE CHALLENGE CUP

The Yorkshire Challenge Cup Competition was inaugurated in season 1905–06, the first tie – Featherstone Rovers v Huddersfield in the preliminary round – being played on 16 September 1905. The original title of the trophy was 'The Yorkshire County Rugby Football Challenge Cup'. Apart from some war-time seasons, the competition has always been contested in the early months of the season.

YORKSHIRE CUP FINALS

1905–06 *2 Dec, at Bradford Park Avenue, 18 500*

HUNSLET	13	T: W Ward
		G: A Goldthorpe 3,
		W Goldthorpe 2
HALIFAX	3	T: Drummond

1906–07 *1 Dec, at Wakefield, 10 500*

BRADFORD	8	T: Brear, Dechan
		G: Laidlaw
HULL KR	5	T: West
		G: Madley

1907–08 *21 Dec, at Headingley, 15 000*

HUNSLET	17	T: Batten, A Goldthorpe, Smith
		G: A Goldthorpe 2, Ward, Eagers
HALIFAX	0	

1908–09 *28 Nov, at Wakefield, 13 000*

HALIFAX	9	T: Hilton
		G: Little 3
HUNSLET	5	T: Randall
		G: A Goldthorpe

1909–10 *27 Nov, at Headingley, 22 000*

HUDDERSFIELD	21	T: Sykes, Rosenfeld, Wrigley, Ainley, Kitchen
		G: Holroyd 2, Wrigley
BATLEY	0	

1910–11 *3 Dec, at Headingley, 19 000*

WAKEFIELD TRINITY	8	T: Simpson, G Taylor
		G: Metcalfe
HUDDERSFIELD	2	G: Wrigley

1911–12 *25 Nov, at Wakefield, 19 000*

HUDDERSFIELD	22	T: Higson, Rosenfeld, Wrigley, Wagstaff, Grey, Moorhouse
		G: Grey 2
HULL KR	10	T: Hughes, McDonald
		G: Carmichael 2

1912–13 *23 Nov, at Headingley, 16 000*

BATLEY	17	T: Tindall 2, Brooksby
		G: Brooksby 2, Garforth, Lyons
HULL	3	T: Rogers

1913–14 *29 Nov, at Halifax, 12 000*

HUDDERSFIELD	19	T: Todd 2, Habron 2, Rosenfeld
		G: Holland 2
BRADFORD NORTHERN	3	T: Wilby

1914–15 *28 Nov, at Headingley, 12 000*

HUDDERSFIELD	31	T: Wagstaff 2, Banks, Rogers, Moorhouse, Todd, Rosenfeld
		G: Holland 5
HULL	0	

1915–16, 1916–17, 1917–18 No competition

1918–19 *17 May, at Headingley, 21 500*

HUDDERSFIELD	14	T: Habron, Gleeson
		G: Gronow 4
DEWSBURY	8	T: Joe Lyman, Sharples
		G: Joe Lyman

1919–20 *29 Nov, at Halifax, 24 935*

HUDDERSFIELD	24	T: Moorhouse 4, Habron, Rosenfeld
		G: Gronow 3
LEEDS	5	T: Whiting
		G: Mirfield

1920–21 *27 Nov, at Headingley, 20 000*

| HULL KR | 2 | G: Bradshaw |
| HULL | 0 | |

1921–22 *26 Nov, at Halifax, 22 001*

LEEDS	11	T: Bacon 2, WH Davies
		G: Walmsley
DEWSBURY	3	T: Joe Lyman

1922–23 *2 Dec, at Headingley, 33 719*

YORK	5	T: Farrar
		G: McEwan
BATLEY	0	

1923-24 *24 Nov, at Headingley, 23 300*
HULL   10 T: Batten, Kennedy
                                 G: Kennedy 2
HUDDERSFIELD   4 G: Gronow, Oliver

1924-25 *22 Nov, at Headingley, 25 546*
WAKEFIELD TRINITY   9 T: Parkin
                                 G: Pollard 2, Parkin
BATLEY   8 T: Davidge, Rees
                                 G: Rees

1925-26 *28 Nov, at Wakefield, 12 616*
DEWSBURY   2 G: Joe Lyman
HUDDERSFIELD   0

1926-27 *1 Dec, at Headingley, 11 300*
HUDDERSFIELD   10 T: Walker, Jones
                                 G: Walmsley 2
WAKEFIELD TRINITY   3 T: Bateson

1927-28 *26 Nov, at Headingley, 21 700*
DEWSBURY   8 T: Coates, Fox
                                 G: Joe Lyman
HULL   2 G: Beardshaw

1928-29 *24 Nov, at Wakefield, 13 000*
LEEDS   5 T: O'Rourke
                                 G: Thompson
FEATHERSTONE R   0

1929-30 *30 Nov, at Headingley, 11 000*
HULL KR   13 T: Dale, Spamer, Rainton
                                 G: Osborne 2
HUNSLET   7 T: Jenkins
                                 G: Traill 2

1930-31 *22 Nov, at Halifax, 17 812*
LEEDS   10 T: O'Rourke, Harris
                                 G: Thompson 2
HUDDERSFIELD   2 G: Bowkett

1931-32 *21 Nov, at Headingley, 27 800*
HUDDERSFIELD   4 G: Bowkett, Stocks
HUNSLET   2 G: Walkington

1932-33 *19 Nov, at Huddersfield, 17 685*
LEEDS   8 T: Moores 2
                                 G: Thompson
WAKEFIELD TRINITY   0

1933-34 *25 Nov, at Headingley, 22 222*
YORK   10 T: Smith, Brown
                                 G: Dingsdale 2
HULL KR   4 G: Carmichael 2

1934-35 *27 Oct, at Dewsbury, 22 598*
LEEDS   5 T: Jubb
                                 G: Brough
WAKEFIELD TRINITY   5 T: Burrows
                                 G: Pollard

Replay *31 Oct, at Huddersfield, 10 500*
LEEDS   2 G: Ralph
WAKEFIELD TRINITY   2 G: Pollard

2nd Replay *7 Nov, at Hunslet, 19.304*
LEEDS   13 T: Smith 3
                                 G: Brough 2
WAKEFIELD TRINITY   0

1935-36 *19 Oct, at Halifax, 14 616*
LEEDS   3 T: Smith
YORK   0

1936-37 *17 Oct, at Headingley, 19 000*
YORK   9 T: Hunt
                                 G: Dingsdale 2, Fender
WAKEFIELD TRINITY   2 G: Oliver

1937-38 *30 Oct, at Wakefield, 22 000*
LEEDS   14 T: Smith 2, Hey, E Harris
                                 G: Eaton
HUDDERSFIELD   8 T: Markham, Mountain
                                 G: Swallow

1938-39 *22 Oct, at Odsal, 28 714*
HUDDERSFIELD   18 T: Markham 3, Madden
                                 G: Fiddes 2, Madden
HULL   10 T: Ellerington, Corner
                                 G: Miller 2

1939-40 *22 Jun, at Odsal, 7077*
FEATHERSTONE R   12 T: Longley, Tennant
                                 G: Sherwood 3
WAKEFIELD TRINITY   9 T: Turner
                                 G: Teall 3

1940-41 *5 Apr, at Huddersfield, 13 316*
BRADFORD NORTHERN   15 T: Foster 2, Best
                                 G: Carmichael 3
DEWSBURY   5 T: Tracey
                                 G: Sullivan

1941-42 *6 Dec, at Huddersfield, 5989*
BRADFORD NORTHERN   24 T: Davies 2, Best, Carter,
                                     Foster, Smith
                                 G: E Ward 2, Carmichael
HALIFAX   0

1942-43 *FIRST LEG 28 Nov, at Dewsbury, 11 000*
DEWSBURY   7 T: Francis
                                 G: Edwards, Seeling
HUDDERSFIELD   0
SECOND LEG 5 Dec, at Huddersfield, 6252
HUDDERSFIELD   2 G: Davies
DEWSBURY   0
Dewsbury won 7–2 on aggregate

1943-44 *FIRST LEG 27 Nov, at Odsal, 10 251*
BRADFORD NORTHERN   5 T: Foster
                                 G: James
KEIGHLEY   2 G: de Lloyd
SECOND LEG 4 Dec, at Keighley, 8993
KEIGHLEY   5 T: Towill
                                 G: de Lloyd
BRADFORD NORTHERN   5 T: E Ward
                                 G: Darlison
Bradford Northern won 10–7 on aggregate

1944-45 *FIRST LEG 2 Dec, at Hunslet, 11 213*
HUNSLET   3   T: Stansfield
HALIFAX   12   T: Meek, Dixon
       G: Lockwood 2, Rule
SECOND LEG 9 Dec, at Halifax, 9800
HALIFAX   2 G: Lockwood
HUNSLET   0
Halifax won 14-3 on aggregate

1945-46 *3 Nov, at Halifax, 24 292*
BRADFORD NORTHERN   5   T: Whitcombe
       G: Carmichael
WAKEFIELD TRINITY   2 G: Stott

1946-47 *2 Nov, at Headingley, 34 300*
WAKEFIELD TRINITY   10   T: Fletcher, Rylance
       G: Perry 2
HULL   0

1947-48 *1 Nov, at Huddersfield, 24 344*
WAKEFIELD TRINITY   7   T: Goodfellow
       G: Stott 2
LEEDS   7   T: Williams
       G: Whitehead 2
Replay *5 Nov, at Odsal, 32 500*
WAKEFIELD TRINITY   8   T: Wilkinson, Bratley
       G: Perry
LEEDS   7   T: Flanagan
       G: Cook, Whitehead

1948-49 *30 Oct, at Headingley, 31 393*
BRADFORD NORTHERN   18   T: Edwards 2, Leake, Foster
       G: Edwards 3
CASTLEFORD   9   T: Foreman
       G: Staines, Langfield, Foreman

1949-50 *29 Oct, at Headingley, 36 000*
BRADFORD NORTHERN   11   T: Davies
       G: E Ward 4
HUDDERSFIELD   4 G: Bawden 2

1950-51 *4 Nov, at Headingley, 28 906*
HUDDERSFIELD   16   T: Pepperell 2
       G: Bowden 5
CASTLEFORD   3   T: Lloyd

1951-52 *27 Oct, at Huddersfield, 25 495*
WAKEFIELD TRINITY   17   T: Robinson, Hughes, Boocker
       G: Hirst 4
KEIGHLEY   3   T: Redman

1952-53 *15 Nov, at Headingley, 14 705*
HUDDERSFIELD   18   T: Cooper 3, Valentine
       G: Devery 3
BATLEY   8   T: Etty, Kenny
       G: Laycock

1953-54 *31 Oct, at Headingley, 22 147*
BRADFORD NORTHERN   7   T: Hawes
       G: Phillips 2
HULL   2 G: Hutton

1954-55 *23 Oct, at Headingley, 25 949*
HALIFAX   22   T: Daniels 2, Ackerley, Pearce
       G: Griffiths 5
HULL   14   T: Conway, Markham
       G: Hutton 4

1955-56 *22 Oct, at Headingley, 23 520*
HALIFAX   10   T: Henderson, Bevan
       G: Griffiths 2
HULL   10   T: Watts, Bowman
       G: Watkinson 2
Replay *2 Nov, at Odsal, 14 000*
HALIFAX   7   T: Daniels
       G: Griffiths 2
HULL   0

1956-57 *20 Oct, at Headingley, 30 942*
WAKEFIELD TRINITY   23   T: Smith 2, Cooper 2, A Mortimer
       G: F Mortimer 4
HUNSLET   5   T: Child
       G: Talbot

1957-58 *19 Oct, at Headingley, 22 531*
HUDDERSFIELD   15   T: Kilroy, Bowman, Smales
       G: Dyson 3
YORK   8   T: Illingworth, Flannery
       G: Yorke

1958-59 *18 Oct, at Odsal, 26 927*
LEEDS   24   T: Hemingway 2, Jones, Simms, Quinn, Stevenson
       G: Jones 3
WAKEFIELD TRINITY   20   T: Metcalfe 3, Rollin
       G: F Mortimer 2, Fox 2

1959-60 *31 Oct, at Headingley, 23 983*
FEATHERSTONE R   15   T: Fox, Woolford, Lambert
       G: Clawson 3
HULL   14   T: Saville, Whiteley
       G: Bateson 4

1960-61 *29 Oct, at Headingley, 17 456*
WAKEFIELD TRINITY   16   T: Fox 2, Smith, Etty
       G: Fox 2
HUDDERSFIELD   10   T: Breen, Lockwood
       G: Dyson 2

1961-62 *11 Nov, at Odsal, 16 329*
WAKEFIELD TRINITY   19   T: Skene, Turner, Smith
       G: Fox 5
LEEDS   9   T: Hemingway
       G: Jones 3

1962-63 *27 Oct, at Headingley, 22 742*
HUNSLET   12   T: Shelton, Baldwinson
       G: Langton 2, Hartley
HULL KR   2 G: Kellett

1963-64 *2 Nov, at Wakefield, 13 238*
HALIFAX   10   T: Jackson, Renilson
       G: James 2
FEATHERSTONE R   0

1964-65 *31 Oct, at Huddersfield, 13 527*
WAKEFIELD TRINITY   18 T: Fox 2, Jones 2
         G: Fox 3
LEEDS   2 G: Dewhurst

1965-66 *16 Oct, at Headingley, 17 522*
BRADFORD NORTHERN   17 T: Williamson 2, Brooke
         G: Clawson 4
HUNSLET   8 T: Lee, Thompson
         G: Langton

1966-67 *15 Oct, at Headingley, 13 241*
HULL KR   25 T: Blackmore, Flanagan,
         Young, Burwell, Moore
         G: Kellett 5
FEATHERSTONE R   12 T: Wrigglesworth, Forsyth
         G: Smales 3

1967-68 *14 Oct, at Headingley, 16 729*
HULL KR   8 T: Burwell, Millward
         G: Kellett
HULL   7 T: Davidson
         G: Maloney, Davidson

1968-69 *19 Oct, at Wakefield, 12 753*
LEEDS   22 T: Smith, Hick, Watson,
         Atkinson
         G: Risman 5
CASTLEFORD   11 T: Hill
         G: Hill 2, Hardisty 2

1969-70 *20 Sep, at Headingley, 11 089*
HULL   12 T: J Macklin, Sullivan
         G: Maloney 2, Brown
FEATHERSTONE R   9 T: Nash
         G: Kellett 3

1970-71 *21 Nov, at Odsal, 6753*
LEEDS   23 T: Smith 2, Atkinson, Dunn,
         Ramsey
         G: Hynes 4
FEATHERSTONE R   7 T: Hartley
         G: Kellett 2

1971-72 *21 Aug, at Wakefield, 5536*
HULL KR   11 T: Longstaff
         G: Millward 4
CASTLEFORD   7 T: Foster
         G: Ackroyd 2

1972-73 *7 Oct, at Odsal, 7806*
LEEDS   36 T: Holmes 3, Dyl 2, Eccles,
         Hardisty, Atkinson
         G: Clawson 5, Hynes
DEWSBURY   9 T: Ashcroft
         G: Agar 3

1973-74 *20 Oct, at Headingley, 7621*
LEEDS   7 T: Langley
         G: Hynes, Marshall
WAKEFIELD TRINITY   2 G: Crook

1974-75 *26 Oct, at Headingley, 5825*
HULL KR   16 T: Watson 2, Dunn,
         Kirkpatrick
         G: Fox 2
WAKEFIELD TRINITY   13 T: Bratt, Hegarty, Smith
         G: Crook 2

1975-76 *15 Nov, at Headingley, 5743*
LEEDS   15 T: Dyl, Cookson
         G: Holmes 5 (1DG)
HULL KR   11 T: Sullivan, Fox
         G: Fox 2, Millward (DG)

1976-77 *16 Oct, at Headingley, 7645*
LEEDS   16 T: Dyl 2, Cookson, Eccles
         G: Marshall 2
FEATHERSTONE R   12 T: Smith, Bray
         G: Quinn 3

1977-78 *15 Oct, at Headingley, 6318*
CASTLEFORD   17 T: Burton 2
         G: Lloyd 5, Burton (DG)
FEATHERSTONE R   7 T: Smith
         G: Quinn, Townend

1978-79 *28 Oct, at Headingley, 10 429*
BRADFORD NORTHERN   18 T: A Redfearn, Gant, Haigh,
         Parker
         G: Fox 3
YORK   8 T: Smith
         G: Banks 2, Hollis (DG)

1979-80 *27 Oct, at Headingley, 9137*
LEEDS   15 T: A Smith 2, D Smith
         G: Dick 3
HALIFAX   6 G: Birts 3

1980-81 *8 Nov, at Huddersfield, 9751*
LEEDS   8 T: A Smith
         G: Dick 3 (1DG)
HULL KR   7 T: McHugh
         G: Hogan 2

1981-82 *3 Oct, at Headingley, 5852*
CASTLEFORD   10 T: Joyner, Hyde
         G: Finch 2
BRADFORD NORTHERN   5 T: Parker
         G: Hanley

1982-83 *2 Oct, at Headingley, 11 888*
HULL   18 T: Rose 2, Evans, Prendiville
         G: Crooks 4 (2DG)
BRADFORD NORTHERN   7 T: Whiteman
         G: Carroll 3 (2DG)

1983-84 *15 Oct, at Elland Road, 14 049*
HULL   13 T: Crane, O'Hara, Proctor
         G: Crane (DG)
CASTLEFORD   2 G: Beardmore

Yorkshire Cup Final, 1980 – Leeds winger John Atkinson, one of only eight men to have scored 400 tries, toes the ball on. Leeds won the Cup for the 16th time with an 8–7 victory over Hull KR.

1984–85 *27 Oct, at Hull City AFC, 25 243*

HULL	29	T:	Kemble 2, Evans, Crooks, Norton
		G:	Schofield 5 (1DG)
HULL KR	12	T:	Robinson, Hall, Fairbairn

1985–86 *27 Oct, at Headingley, 12 686*

HULL KR	22	T:	Miller 2, Clark
		G:	Dorahy 5
CASTLEFORD	18	T:	Marchant 2, R Beardmore
		G:	R Beardmore 2, Diamond

1986–87 *11 Oct, at Headingley, 11 132*

CASTLEFORD	31	T:	K Beardmore 2, Ward, Ketteridge, Atkins
		G:	Ketteridge 5, R Beardmore (DG)
HULL	24	T:	Brand 2, O'Hara 2
		G:	Crooks 4

1987–88 *17 Oct, at Headingley, 10 947*

BRADFORD NORTHERN	12	T:	Fairbank
		G:	Mumby 2, Hobbs 2
CASTLEFORD	12	T:	Plange, Lindner
		G:	Ketteridge 2

Replay *31 Oct, at Elland Road, 8175*

BRADFORD NORTHERN	11	T:	Hill, Heron
		G:	Hobbs 2 (1DG)
CASTLEFORD	2	G:	Ketteridge

1988–89 *16 Oct, at Elland Road, 22 968*

LEEDS	33	T:	Gibson 2, Schofield 2, Medley
		G:	Stephenson 6, Schofield (DG)
CASTLEFORD	12	T:	Boothroyd, Joyner
		G:	Ketteridge 2

1989–90 *5 Nov, at Headingley, 12 055*

BRADFORD NORTHERN	20	T:	Harkin 2, Cordle 2
		G:	Hobbs 2
FEATHERSTONE R	14	T:	Ropati, Smith
		G:	Fox 3

1990–91 *23 Sep, at Elland Road, 11 800*

CASTLEFORD	11	T:	Atkins, Plange
		G:	Crooks, Roebuck (DG)
WAKEFIELD TRINITY	8	T:	Mason
		G:	Harcombe 2

YORKSHIRE CUP HONOURS

Club	Winners	Runners-up
Leeds	17	4
Huddersfield	12	8
Bradford Northern	12	3
Wakefield Trinity	9	10
Hull KR	7	7
Hull	5	12
Halifax	5	4
Castleford	4	8
Hunslet	3	6
Dewsbury	3	4
York	3	3
Featherstone Rovers	2	8
Batley	1	4
Keighley	–	2

Note – Bradford Northern's record includes success as Bradford

YORKSHIRE CUP FINAL RECORDS

Most finals	21	Leeds
Most wins	17	Leeds
Most consecutive finals	4	Huddersfield, Castleford
Most consecutive wins	4	Huddersfield
Highest score	36	Leeds v Dewsbury, 1972
Highest aggregate	55	Castleford 31 Hull 24, 1986
Lowest aggregate	2	Hull KR 2 Hull 0, 1920
	2	Dewsbury 2 Huddersfield 0, 1925
	2	Huddersfield 2 Dewsbury 0, 1942 (2nd leg)
	2	Halifax 2 Hunslet 0, 1944 (2nd leg)
Largest crowd	36 000	Bradford N v Huddersfield, 1949
Smallest crowd	5536	Castleford v Hull KR, 1971
Highest receipts	£83 591	Castleford v Leeds, 1988

PLAYERS' RECORDS IN ONE FINAL

Most tries	4	S Moorhouse (Huddersfield) v Leeds, 1919 (Nov)
Most goals	6	D Stephenson (Leeds) v Castleford, 1988
Most points	14	M Ketteridge (Castleford) v Hull, 1986

Arguably Cumberland's greatest forward, Douglas Clark still holds Huddersfield's appearances record with 485 (1909–29). His 10 appearances in the Yorkshire Cup Final is also a record.

PLAYERS' RECORDS IN ALL FINALS

Most appearances	10	D Clark (Huddersfield) 1909, 1910, 1911, 1913, 1914, 1919 (May), 1919 (Nov), 1923, 1925, 1926
Most tries	6	S Moorhouse (Huddersfield) 1911, 1914, 1919 (Nov)
	6	S Smith (Leeds) 1934, 1935, 1937
	6	A Smith (Leeds) 1968, 1970, 1979, 1980
Most goals	19	N Fox (Wakefield T, Hull KR, Bradford N) 1958, 1960, 1961, 1964, 1974, 1975, 1978
Most points	53	N Fox, as above

THE REGAL TROPHY

The Regal Trophy was inaugurated in 1971–72 as the Player's No.6 Trophy, was renamed the John Player Trophy in 1977–78 and the John Player Special Trophy in 1983–84, before adopting its present title in 1989–90. The competition is run along the same knock-out lines as the Challenge Cup.

REGAL TROPHY FINALS

1971–72 *22 Jan, at Odsal, 7975*

HALIFAX	22	T: Callon, Willicombe, Davies, Kelly
		G: Burton 5
WAKEFIELD TRINITY	11	T: Topliss, Slater, Valentine
		G: Fox

1972–73 *24 Mar, at Huddersfield, 10 102*

LEEDS	12	T: Atkinson 2
		G: Clawson 2, Holmes
SALFORD	7	T: Dixon
		G: Watkins 2

1973–74 *9 Feb, at Wigan, 9347*

WARRINGTON	27	T: Noonan 2, Whitehead, Nicholas, Bevan
		G: Whitehead 6
ROCHDALE HORNETS	16	T: Brelsford 2, Taylor, Brophy
		G: Holliday 2

1974–75 *25 Jan, at Warrington, 5935*

| BRADFORD NORTHERN | 3 | T: Carlton |
| WIDNES | 2 | G: Dutton |

Blackpool Borough produced one of the game's greatest shocks by reaching the final of the John Player Trophy in 1977, but lost to Castleford 15–25. Borough winger Pitman is unable to prevent joint man-of-the-match Gary Stephens from scoring this try.

1975–76 *24 Jan, at Headingley, 9035*
WIDNES   19 T: Jenkins 2, Bowden,
                     Adams
                   G: Dutton 3, Bowden (DG)
HULL   13 T: Crane 2, Hunter
                   G: Boxall 2

1976–77 *22 Jan, at Salford, 4512*
CASTLEFORD   25 T: Burton, Stephens, Wraith,
                     Joyner, Johnson
                   G: Lloyd 5
BLACKPOOL BOROUGH 15 T: Egan, Machen, Allen
                   G: Egan 3

1977–78 *28 Jan, at St Helens, 10258*
WARRINGTON   9 T: Bevan
                   G: Hesford 3
WIDNES   4 G: Woods 2

1978–79 *28 Apr, at St Helens, 10743*
WIDNES   16 T: Hull, Wright
                   G: Burke 3, Elwell 2 (2DG),
                   Adams 2 (2DG)
WARRINGTON   4 G: Hesford 2

1979–80 *6 Jan, at Headingley, 9909*
BRADFORD NORTHERN 6 T: Parker
                   G: Mumby, Stephenson (DG)
WIDNES   0

1980–81 *24 Jan, at Wigan, 12820*
WARRINGTON   12 T: Bevan 2
                   G: Hesford 4 (2DG)
BARROW   5 T: Mason
                   G: Ball

1981–82 *23 Jan, at Headingley, 25245*
HULL   12 T: Wileman
                   G: Crooks 4, Dean (DG)
HULL KR   4 G: Fairbairn 2

1982–83 *22 Jan, at Elland Road, 19553*
WIGAN   15 T: Gill, Juliff
                   G: Whitfield 5 (1DG)
LEEDS   4 G: Dick 2

Regal Trophy Final, 1990 – the crowd and the Halifax players acclaim a try by Richard Milner, but the touch-judge rules no-try. Wigan took the trophy with a 24–12 victory.

1983–84 *14 Jan, at Wigan, 9510*

LEEDS   18 T: Holmes, Dick
       G: Creasser 5

WIDNES   10 T: Lydon, Linton
       G: Burke

1984–85 *26 Jan, at Hull City AFC, 25 326*

HULL KR   12 T: Prohm, Hogan, Clark
HULL   0

1985–86 *11 Jan, at Elland Road, 17 573*

WIGAN   11 T: Ford, Wane
       G: Stephenson, Dowling (DG)

HULL KR   8 T: Laws, Lydiat

1986–87 *10 Jan, at Bolton W AFC, 21 144*

WIGAN   18 T: Gill 2, Goodway, Bell
       G: Gill

WARRINGTON   4 T: Forster

1987–88 *9 Jan, at Wigan, 16 669*

ST HELENS   15 T: Loughlin 2
       G: Loughlin 3, Holding (DG)

LEEDS   14 T: Jackson, Creasser
       G: Creasser 3

1988–89 *7 Jan, at Bolton W AFC, 20 709*

WIGAN   12 T: K Iro, Hanley
       G: Lydon 2

WIDNES   6 T: Wright
       G: Currier

1989–90 *13 Jan, at Headingley, 17 810*

WIGAN   24 T: Hanley 3, Edwards, Goodway
       G: Lydon 2

HALIFAX   12 T: Hill
       G: Holliday 4

1990–91 *12 Jan, at Headingley, 11 154*

WARRINGTON   12 T: Thomas
       G: Lyon 4

BRADFORD NORTHERN   2 G: Hobbs

REGAL TROPHY HONOURS

Club	Winners	Runners-up
Wigan	5	–
Warrington	4	2
Widnes	2	5
Leeds	2	2
Bradford Northern	2	1
Hull	1	2
Hull KR	1	2
Halifax	1	1
Castleford	1	–
St Helens	1	–
Barrow	–	1
Blackpool Borough	–	1
Rochdale Hornets	–	1
Salford	–	1
Wakefield Trinity	–	1

REGAL TROPHY FINAL RECORDS

Most finals	7	Widnes
Most wins	5	Wigan
Most consecutive finals	3	Widnes
Most consecutive wins	2	Wigan (twice)
Highest score	27	Warrington, 1974
Highest aggregate	43	Warrington 27 Rochdale H 16, 1974
Lowest aggregate	5	Bradford N 3 Widnes 2, 1975
Largest crowd	25 326	Hull v Hull KR, 1985
Smallest crowd	4512	Blackpool B v Castleford, 1977
Highest receipts	£94 874	Widnes v Wigan, 1989

PLAYERS' RECORDS IN ONE FINAL

Most tries	3	E Hanley (Wigan) v Halifax, 1990
Most goals	6	D Whitehead (Warrington) v Rochdale H, 1974
Most points	15	D Whitehead (Warrington) v Rochdale H, 1974

PLAYERS' RECORDS IN ALL FINALS

Most appearances	6	M Adams (Widnes) 1975, 1976, 1978, 1979, 1980, 1984
	6	K Elwell (Widnes) 1975, 1976, 1978, 1979, 1980, 1984
	6	E Hughes (Widnes) 1975, 1976, 1978, 1979, 1980, 1984
Most tries	4	J Bevan (Warrington) 1974, 1978, 1981
	4	E Hanley (Wigan) 1989, 1990
Most goals	9	S Hesford (Warrington) 1978, 1979, 1981
Most points	20	D Creasser (Leeds) 1984, 1988

THE RUGBY LEAGUE CHARITY SHIELD

The Rugby League Charity Shield was inaugurated in 1985–86. The Charity Shield is contested by the previous season's Challenge Cup winners and First Division Champions.

CHARITY SHIELD

1985-86 *25 Aug, at Douglas Bowl, Isle of Man, 4066*
WIGAN	34	T: Donlan 2, Gill 2, M Ford
		G: Stephenson 7
HULL KR	6	T: Clark
		G: Lydiat

1986-87 *24 Aug, at Douglas Bowl, Isle of Man, 3276*
HALIFAX	9	T: George, Whitfield
		G: Hague (DG)
CASTLEFORD	8	T: Lord
		G: Ketteridge 2

1987-88 *23 Aug, at Douglas Bowl, Isle of Man, 4804*
WIGAN	44	T: Edwards 2, Bell 2, Hampson 2, Gill
		G: Stephenson 8
HALIFAX	12	T: Dixon, Juliff
		G: Eadie 2

1988-89 *21 Aug, at Douglas Bowl, Isle of Man, 5044*
WIDNES	20	T: Offiah, Wright, McKenzie
		G: Currier 4
WIGAN	14	T: A Iro 2, Lydon
		G: Lydon

1989-90 *27 Aug, at Anfield, Liverpool, 17 263*
WIDNES	27	T: Kebbie, Davies, Offiah, D Hulme
		G: Davies 5, Tait (DG)
WIGAN	22	T: Platt, Lydon, K Iro
		G: Lydon 5

1990-91 *19 Aug, at Swansea AFC, 11 178*
WIDNES*	24	T: Davies 3, Devereux, Offiah
		G: Davies 2
WIGAN	8	T: Botica
		G: Botica 2

*As Wigan had won both the championship and Challenge Cup in 1989–90, the Premiership winners, Widnes, provided their opposition.

The first four Charity Shields were played on the Isle of Man. Halifax (below) celebrate their 9–8 win over Castleford in 1986.

CUP FINALS
MAN-OF-THE-MATCH AWARDS

Most modern Rugby League matches feature player-of-the-match awards. The last couple of decades have seen such awards proliferate to such an extent that they have become almost meaningless. The exceptions are those awards bestowed in Cup Finals of various kinds. The most important of all is the Lance Todd Trophy, which since 1946 has been conferred on the player considered to have been the best player in the Challenge Cup Final. It was not until 1965 that another comparable award, the Harry Sunderland Trophy, was inaugurated for the outstanding performer in the Championship then Premiership Final. Subsequently man-of-the-match awards have been instituted for the finals of the Lancashire Cup, the Yorkshire Cup, the Regal Trophy, the Second Division Premiership and the Charity Shield.

Willie (WTH) Davies, Bradford Northern's stand-off, was the second winner of the Lance Todd Trophy in 1947 when Northern beat Leeds 8–4 in the Challenge Cup Final.

AWARD WINNERS

	Lance Todd Trophy	Harry Sunderland Trophy
1946	W Stott (Wakefield T)	
1947	W Davies (Bradford N)	
1948	F Whitcombe (Bradford N)*	
1949	E Ward (Bradford N)	
1950	G Helme (Warrington)	
1951	C Mountford (Wigan)	
1952	W Ivison (Workington T)	
1953	P Ramsden (Huddersfield)	
1954	G Helme (Warrington)	
1955	J Grundy (Barrow)	
1956	A Prescott (St Helens)	
1957	J Stevenson (Leeds)	
1958	R Thomas (Wigan)	
1959	B McTigue (Wigan)	
1960	T Harris (Hull)*	
1961	R Huddart (St Helens)	
1962	N Fox (Wakefield T)	
1963	H Poynton (Wakefield T)	
1964	F Collier (Widnes)	
1965	R Ashby (Wigan)† B Gabbitas (Hunslet) *†	T Fogerty (Halifax)
1966	L Killeen (St Helens)	A Halsall (St Helens)
1967	C Dooler (Featherstone R)	R Owen (Wakefield T)
1968	D Fox (Wakefield T)*	G Cooper (Wakefield T)
1969	M Reilly (Castleford)	B Risman (Leeds)
1970	W Kirkbride (Castleford)	F Myler (St Helens)
1971	A Murphy (Leigh)	W Ashurst (Wigan)*
1972	K Coslett (St Helens)	T Clawson (Leeds)
1973	S Nash (Featherstone R)	M Stephenson (Dewsbury)
1974	D Whitehead (Warrington)	B Philbin (Warrington)
1975	R Dutton (Widnes)	M Mason (Leeds)
1976	G Pimblett (St Helens)	G Nicholls (St Helens)
1977	S Pitchford (Leeds)	G Pimblett (St Helens)
1978	G Nicholls (St Helens)*	R Haigh (Bradford N)
1979	D Topliss (Wakefield T)*	K Dick (Leeds)
1980	B Lockwood (Hull KR)	M Aspey (Widnes)
1981	M Burke (Widnes)	L Casey (Hull KR)
1982	E Cunningham (Widnes)**	M Burke (Widnes)
1983	D Hobbs (Featherstone R)	A Myler (Widnes)
1984	J Lydon (Widnes)	J Dorahy (Hull KR)
1985	B Kenny (Wigan)	H Pinner (St Helens)
1986	R Beardmore (Castleford)	L Boyd (Warrington)
1987	G Eadie (Halifax)	J Lydon (Wigan)
1988	A Gregory (Wigan)	D Hulme (Widnes)
1989	E Hanley (Wigan)	A Tait (Widnes)
1990	A Gregory (Wigan)	A Tait (Widnes)
1991	D Betts (Wigan)	G Mackey (Hull)

* Member of losing team.
† Joint winners.
** Cunningham won the award in the drawn Wembley final of 1982. His team lost in the replay at Elland Road, when D Topliss (Hull) won the man-of-the-match award.

COUNTY CUP FINALS

The White Rose Trophy has been presented to the man-of-the-match in the Yorkshire Cup Final since 1966. The Lancashire Cup Final's individual award was instituted as the Rugby Leaguer Trophy in 1974. It has undergone several changes of title since then.

Yorkshire Cup Final	Lancashire Cup Final
1966 C Kellett (Hull KR)	
1967 C Davidson (Hull)*	
1968 B Seabourne (Leeds)	
1969 J Brown (Hull)	
1970 S Hynes (Leeds)	
1971 I Markham (Hull KR)	
1972 J Holmes (Leeds)	
1973 K Hepworth (Leeds)	
1974 R Millward (Hull KR)	M Coulman (Salford)*
1975 N Fox (Hull KR)*	D George (Widnes)
1976 L Dyl (Leeds)	D Eckersley (Widnes)
1977 B Burton (Castleford)	A Walker (Workington T)
1978 R Haigh (Bradford N)	A Walker (Workington T)*
1979 A Smith (Leeds)	M Adams (Widnes)
1980 K Dick (Leeds)	A Waller (Warrington)
1981 B Johnson (Castleford)	R Tabern (Leigh)
1982 K Mumby (Bradford N)*	S Hesford (Warrington)
1983 M Crane (Hull)	D Cairns (Barrow)
1984 P Sterling (Hull)	M Meninga (St Helens)
1985 G Miller (Hull KR)	S Ella (Wigan)
1986 K Beardmore (Castleford)	M Ford (Wigan)
1987 P Harkin (Bradford N)**	S Edwards (Wigan)
1988 C Lyons (Leeds)	P Shaw (Salford)*
1989 P Harkin (Bradford N)	R Jackson (Warrington)
1990 T Lazenby (Wakefield T)*	D Fell (Salford)*

* Member of losing team.
** Harkin won the award in the drawn final of 1987. B Hill (Bradford N) won the man-of-the-match award in the replay.

REGAL TROPHY FINAL

1971–72	B Burton (Halifax)
1972–73	K Hepworth (Leeds)
1973–74	K Ashcroft (Warrington)
1974–75	B Seabourne (Bradford N)
1975–76	R Bowden (Widnes)
1976–77	H Allen (Blackpool B)* † G Stephens (Castleford) †
1977–78	S Hesford (Warrington)
1978–79	D Eckersley (Widnes)
1979–80	L Casey (Bradford N)
1980–81	T Martyn (Warrington)
1981–82	T Skerrett (Hull)
1982–83	M Foy (Wigan)
1983–84	M Laurie (Leeds)
1984–85	P Harkin (Hull KR)
1985–86	P Harkin (Hull KR)*
1986–87	A Goodway (Wigan)
1987–88	P Loughlin (St Helens)
1988–89	E Hanley (Wigan)
1989–90	E Hanley (Wigan)
1990–91	W McGinty (Warrington)

* Member of losing team.
† Joint winners.

CHARITY SHIELD

The Jack Bentley Trophy

1985–86	S Edwards (Wigan)
1986–87	C Anderson (Halifax)
1987–88	S Edwards (Wigan)
1988–89	P. McKenzie (Widnes)
1989–90	D Betts (Wigan)*
1990–91	J Davies (Widnes)

* Member of losing team.

SECOND DIVISION PREMIERSHIP FINAL

The Tom Bergin Trophy

1986–87	G Ainsworth (Swinton)
1987–88	D Foy (Oldham)
1988–89	M Aston (Sheffield E)
1989–90	M Ford (Oldham)
1990–91	S Kerry (Salford)

Three of the man-of-the-match awards commemorate outstanding Rugby League journalists – Jack Bentley, Tom Bergin and Harry Sunderland. Sunderland, an Australian, was also tour manager of the 1929, 1933 and 1937 Kangaroos. Lance Todd was a member of the first New Zealand tour team to Britain, joined Wigan and later became manager of Salford.

THE ROSES MATCH

In pre-Northern Union days, the Lancashire-Yorkshire match rivalled even international fixtures for importance. Indeed crowds were often larger for Roses Matches than for international fixtures before 1895. The first Roses Match was played in 1870 and during the quarter century before the Great Schism it was the most prestigious fixture in the north's rugby calendar. The fixture continued to be a highlight of the season following the 1895 breakaway and few seasons have since passed when the Roses Match has not been contested. In 1985 the fixture was first sponsored by Rodstock and subsequently has been unnecessarily dubbed the 'War of the Roses'.

MATCH RESULTS

1895 *7 Dec, at Oldham, 9059*
LANCASHIRE	0	
YORKSHIRE	8	T: Rigg, Hughes
		G: Sharpe

1896 *29 Feb, at Huddersfield, 5300*
YORKSHIRE	3	T: Boothroyd
LANCASHIRE	8	T: Lees, Briers
		G: Lees

1896 *21 Nov, at Oldham, 15 000*
LANCASHIRE	7	T: Valentine
		G: Varley (DG)
YORKSHIRE	3	T: Firth

1897 *20 Nov, at Bradford Park Avenue, 11 000*
YORKSHIRE	7	T: Hambrecht
		G: Cooper 2
LANCASHIRE	6	T: Whitehead, Woodhead

1898 *5 Nov, at Salford 8000*
LANCASHIRE	9	T: Hoskins 2, Traynor
YORKSHIRE	20	T: Rigg, Kemp, Broadley, Robinson
		G: Cooper 4

1899 *4 Nov, at Halifax, 9000*
YORKSHIRE	13	T: Robinson, Parker, Sutcliffe
		G: Parker 2
LANCASHIRE	16	T: Tunney, Davies, Lawton, S Williams
		G: Hadwen, Frater

1900 *3 Nov, at Rochdale, 18 000*
LANCASHIRE	24	T: S Williams 2, T Williams 2, Valentine, Field
		G: Valentine 2, Ferguson
YORKSHIRE	5	T: Franks
		G: Parker

1902 *15 Feb, at The Boulevard, Hull, 12 235*
YORKSHIRE	13	T: Eagers, Grace, Marsden
		G: WP Davies 2
LANCASHIRE	8	T: Wilson 2
		G: W James

1902 *15 Nov, at Salford, 14 286*
LANCASHIRE	13	T: Hogg, Valentine, Fish
		G: W James, Fish
YORKSHIRE	0	

1903 *14 Nov, at Headingley, 11 000*
YORKSHIRE	0	
LANCASHIRE	8	T: Hogg 2
		G: Lomas

1904 *12 Nov, at Oldham, 8500*
LANCASHIRE	5	T: Fish
		G: Fish
YORKSHIRE	14	T: WP Davies 2, Mosby, Marsden
		G: Mosby

1905 *4 Nov, at The Boulevard, Hull, 8000*
YORKSHIRE	0	
LANCASHIRE	8	T: Leytham, Hogg
		G: Leytham

1906 *3 Nov, at Salford, 5000*
LANCASHIRE	19	T: Jenkins 2, White, Leytham, Naylor
		G: Jolley 2
YORKSHIRE	0	

1907 *2 Nov, at Halifax, 7000*
YORKSHIRE	15	T: Stacey 2, Farrar
		G: Hilton 3
LANCASHIRE	11	T: Tyson 2, Butterworth
		G: Hogg

1908 *31 Oct, at Salford, 5000*
LANCASHIRE	13	T: Tyson, Leytham, Ruddick
		G: Leytham 2
YORKSHIRE	0	

1909 *4 Nov, at The Boulevard, Hull, 6000*
YORKSHIRE	27	T: Eccles 3, Devereux 2, Smith, Boylen
		G Place 2, Eccles
LANCASHIRE	14	T: Gallop, Shugars, Miller, Deane
		G: Thomas

1910 *7 Nov, at Wigan, 2000*
LANCASHIRE 17 T: Jenkins 2, Todd, Avery, Anlezark
G: Bolewski
YORKSHIRE 3 T: Jenkinson

1912 *25 Jan, at Halifax, 3199*
YORKSHIRE 12 T: Moorhouse 3, Smith
LANCASHIRE 13 T: Clarkson, Ganley, Bailey
G: Ganley, Harris

1912 *16 Dec, at Oldham, 4000*
LANCASHIRE 8 T: Sharples, Bailey
G: Taylor
YORKSHIRE 20 T: Batten 2, Wagstaff 2, Moorhouse, Moore
G: Carmichael

1913 *10 Dec, at Huddersfield, 3500*
YORKSHIRE 19 T: Tindall 2, Stacey, Poynton, Moore
G: Longstaff 2
LANCASHIRE 11 T: Price, Flanagan, Reid
G: Jolley

1919 *24 Sep, at Broughton, 5000*
LANCASHIRE 15 T: Bowers, Mulvanney, Price
G: Ryder 3
YORKSHIRE 5 T: Stockwell
G: Kennedy

1920 *21 Oct, at the Boulevard, Hull 7000*
YORKSHIRE 18 T: Hardaker 2, Brittain, Harkness
G: Rhodes 3
LANCASHIRE 3 T: Brough

1921 *4 Oct, at Rochdale, 4000*
LANCASHIRE 2 G: Clarkson
YORKSHIRE 5 T: Stockwell
G: Stockwell

1922 *7 Dec, at Craven Park, Hull, 8000*
YORKSHIRE 11 T: Wild, Lyman, Marshall
G: Osbourne
LANCASHIRE 11 T: Owen, Bentham, Price
G: Clarkson

1923 *8 Dec, at Oldham, 8000*
LANCASHIRE 6 T: Darwell, Crooks
YORKSHIRE 5 T: Guerin
G: Pollard

1924 *29 Nov, at Halifax, 6000*
YORKSHIRE 9 T: Denton 2, Hoult
LANCASHIRE 28 T: Carr 2, J Evans 2, Rix Price
G: Dingsdale 3, Brough 2

1925 *12 Dec, at City Road, St Helens, 13 000*
LANCASHIRE 26 T: Rix 3, Carr 2, J Evans
G: Burgess 2, Dingsdale 2
YORKSHIRE 10 T: Denton, Hirst
G: Osbourne 2

1926 *30 Oct, at Wakefield, 9000*
YORKSHIRE 13 T: Parkin 2, Crowther
G: Osbourne 2
LANCASHIRE 18 T: Carr 3, Price
G: Burgess 2, Dingsdale

1927 *29 Oct, at Warrington, 12 000*
LANCASHIRE 35 T: Carr 3, Cowley, Beswick, J Evans, Frodsham
G: Gowers 7
YORKSHIRE 19 T: Bowman 2, Askin, Bateson, Crowther
G: Bateson 2

1928 *3 Nov, at Halifax, 6520*
YORKSHIRE 10 T: Bowman, Lyman
G: Lyman 2
LANCASHIRE 33 T: Carr 2, Ellaby 2, Burgess, Frodsham, Fairclough
G: Gowers 6

1930 *22 Mar, at Rochdale, 4300*
LANCASHIRE 18 T: Butters 2, Kirk, Woods
G: Gowers 3
YORKSHIRE 3 T: Bateman

1930 *18 Oct, at Wakefield, 9000*
YORKSHIRE 25 T: Thompson 2, C Smith, Atkinson, Bateman
G: Pollard 5
LANCASHIRE 15 T: R Smith, Ellaby, Woods
G: Dingsdale 3

1931 *17 Oct, at Warrington, 10 049*
LANCASHIRE 11 T: Ellaby, Woods, Mercer
G: Dingsdale
YORKSHIRE 8 T: Whittaker, Horton
G: Atkinson

1932 *29 Oct, at Wakefield, 4000*
YORKSHIRE 30 T: Aspinall, Walkington, Higson, Dale, Atkinson Pollard, Winter, C Smith
G: Atkinson 2, Pollard
LANCASHIRE 3 T: Martin

1933 *25 Sep, at Oldham, 2000*
LANCASHIRE 12 T: Greenall, Shannon
G: Osbaldestin 2, Beswick
YORKSHIRE 15 T: Brogden, Grainge, Horton
G: Walkington 3

CURRENT COMPETITIONS

1935 *9 Jan, at Headingley, 1500*

YORKSHIRE	5	T: Herbert
		G: Carmichael
LANCASHIRE	5	T: Armitt
		G: Liptrot

Note – Match abandoned because of fog after 44 minutes

1935 *12 Oct, at Widnes, 6700*

LANCASHIRE	16	T: Bennett, Bailey, McCue,
		J Cumberbatch
		G: Belshaw 2
YORKSHIRE	5	T: Sherburn
		G: Sherburn

1936 *21 Oct, at Castleford, 7648*

YORKSHIRE	6	G: Lockwood 3
LANCASHIRE	28	T: Harris 3, Arkwright,
		V Cumberbatch,
		Garvey, Croston,
		J Cumberbatch
		G: Belshaw, Arkwright

1938 *12 Feb, at Rochdale, 3653*

LANCASHIRE	10	T: Winnard, Brown
		G: Belshaw 2
YORKSHIRE	9	T: Morrell
		G: Miller 3

1938 *26 Oct, at Headingley, 3000*

YORKSHIRE	10	T: Morrell, Exley
		G: Miller 2
LANCASHIRE	10	T: Shannon, Arkwright
		G: Belshaw 2

Note – Abandoned because of torrential rain after 70 minutes

1945 *10 Nov, at Swinton, 11 059*

LANCASHIRE	17	T: McCue, Large, Millington,
		Belshaw, Malone
		G: Ryan
YORKSHIRE	16	T: Bratley, Batten,
		Kitching, Rylance
		G: Rylance 2

1946 *9 Nov, at Hunslet, 5000*

YORKSHIRE	13	T: Dockar, Longley, Kitching
		G: Ward, Ledgard
LANCASHIRE	10	T: Johnson, Horne
		G: Stott, Lawrenson

1947 *12 Nov, at Wigan, 6270*

LANCASHIRE	22	T: Ratcliffe 2, Palin 2,
		Johnson, McCormick
		G: Palin 2
YORKSHIRE	10	T: Perry, Fletcher
		G: Ledgard 2

Yorkshire captain Ernest Ward passes out to Albany Longley in the 1946 Roses Match. Ward kicked a goal as Yorkshire won 13–10.

1949 *3 May, at Halifax, 7000*
YORKSHIRE   3 T: Etty
LANCASHIRE   12 T: Kerwick, Slevin
            G: Hutton 3

1949 *5 Oct, at Warrington, 15 000*
LANCASHIRE   22 T: D Naughton, Prescott,
                  A Naughton, Rowe
            G: Gee 5
YORKSHIRE   13 T: Riches 2, Pollard
            G: Ledgard 2

1950 *18 Oct, at Huddersfield, 6547*
YORKSHIRE   23 T: Cracknell 2, Burnell,
                  Wilmot, Metcalfe
            G: Ward 4
LANCASHIRE   15 T: Broome, Knowles,
                  Featherstone
            G: Cunliffe 3

1951 *10 Oct, at Leigh, 11 573*
LANCASHIRE   5 T: Kerwick
            G: Horne
YORKSHIRE   15 T: E Ward 2, L Ward
            G: Ledgard 3

1953 *28 Apr, at The Boulevard, Hull, 8400*
YORKSHIRE   16 T: Riches, Tulloch
            G: Thompson 5
LANCASHIRE   8 T: Stirrup, Silcock
            G: A Blan

1953, *14 Oct, at Leigh, 12 870*
LANCASHIRE   18 T: McCormick, Norburn
            G: Metcalfe 6
YORKSHIRE   10 T: Froggett, Broughton
            G: Ledgard 2

1954 *6 Oct, at Odsal, 8500*
YORKSHIRE   20 T: Mullaney, Robinson
            G: Thompson 7
LANCASHIRE   10 T: Kitchen, Davies
            G: Ganley 2

1955 *26 Sep, at Oldham, 8000*
LANCASHIRE   26 T: O'Grady 3, Blan 2, Davies
            G: Blan 4
YORKSHIRE   10 T: Ledgard, Hollindrake
            G: Ledgard 2

1956 *26 Sep, at The Boulevard, Hull, 8500*
YORKSHIRE   21 T: Gunney 2, D Fox 2,
                  Cracknell
            G: Dyson 3
LANCASHIRE   35 T: O'Grady 3, Davies 2,
                  Bolton 2, Cherrington,
                  Kindon
            G: Fraser 4

1957 *23 Sep, at Widnes, 6200*
LANCASHIRE   11 T: McTigue, Prescott,
                  Gilfedder
            G: Dawson
YORKSHIRE   25 T: Sullivan 2, Whiteley,
                  Snowden, Gunney
            G: Dyson 5

1958 *24 Sep, at Craven Park, Hull, 5000*
YORKSHIRE   35 T: Riley 2, Sullivan 2,
                  Snowden
            G: Yorke 10
LANCASHIRE   19 T: Brennan 2, McIntyre,
                  Kindon, Parkinson
            G: Murphy 2

1958 *29 Oct, at Leigh, 8500*
LANCASHIRE   15 T: Murphy, Ashton, Kindon
            G: Gowers 3
YORKSHIRE   16 T: Sullivan 2
            G: Yorke 5

Note – County Championship Play-off

1959 *11 Nov, at Leigh, 6417*
LANCASHIRE   28 T: Myler 3, Murphy 2,
                  Greenough
            G: Fraser 5
YORKSHIRE   38 T: A Kellett 2, Stevenson 2,
                  Snowden, Ward, N Fox
                  Woolford
            G: N Fox 7

1960 *31 Aug, at Wakefield, 15 054*
YORKSHIRE   20 T: Whiteley 2, A Kellett,
                  Burnett
            G: N Fox 4
LANCASHIRE   21 T: Davies 2, Collier 2,
                  Greenough
            G: Fraser 2, Gilfedder

1961 *9 Oct, at Leigh, 4970*
LANCASHIRE   14 T: Bolton, Noon, Myler,
                  Murphy
            G: Gilfedder
YORKSHIRE   12 T: Waterworth, N Fox
            G: N Fox 3

1962 *26 Sep, at Wakefield, 7956*
YORKSHIRE   22 T: G Smith 2, Shelton, Dyson
            G: N Fox 5
LANCASHIRE   8 T: Collier, Hodgkiss
            G: Gowers

1963 *11 Sep, at St Helens, 11 200*
LANCASHIRE   45 T: Measures 3, Murphy 2,
                  Burgess, Karalius,
                  Stopford, Buckley
            G: Gilfedder 9
YORKSHIRE   20 T: Field, Ward, Hirst, Morgan
            G: Dyson 4.

1964 *23 Sep, at The Boulevard, Hull, 6331*

YORKSHIRE	33	T: Hardisty 3, G Smith 2, Bryant, Hepworth
		G: C Kellett 6
LANCASHIRE	10	T: McCormack, Laughton
		G: Gowers 2

1965 *10 Nov, at Swinton, 5847*

LANCASHIRE	13	T: Tickle, Laughton, Thompson
		G: Gowers, Buckley
YORKSHIRE	16	T: Wriglesworth 2, A Kellett, Brooke
		G: N Fox 2

1966 *21 Sep, at Headingley, 10 528*

YORKSHIRE	17	T: Ramshaw 2, N Fox
		G: N Fox 4
LANCASHIRE	22	T: Glover 2, Aspinall, Bishop
		G: Tyrer 5

1968 *24 Jan, at Widnes, 8932*

LANCASHIRE	23	T: O'Neill 2, Glover, Fletcher, Halliwell
		G: Tyrer 4
YORKSHIRE	17	T: Atkinson, Millward, Ramshaw
		G: N Fox 4

1968 *25 Sep, at Craven Park, Hull, 6656*

YORKSHIRE	10	T: Seabourne, Keegan
		G: Millward 2
LANCASHIRE	5	T: Hesketh
		G: Dutton

1969 *3 Sep, at Salford, 4652*

LANCASHIRE	14	T: Murray, Laughton
		G: Dutton 4
YORKSHIRE	12	T: Lowe, Hepworth
		G: Millward 2, Macklin

1971 *13 Jan, at Castleford, 2000*

YORKSHIRE	32	T: A Smith 2, N Stephenson 2, Hynes, Batten
		G: Jefferson 6, Shoebottom
LANCASHIRE	12	T: Laughton, Davies
		G: Dutton 3

1971 *24 Feb, at Castleford, 4266*

YORKSHIRE	34	T: Slater 2, N Stephenson 2, Jefferson, Jeanes, Irving, Topliss
		G: N Stephenson 3, Hardisty, Jefferson
LANCASHIRE	8	T: Jones, Nicholls
		G: Tyrer

Note – County Championship Play-off

1971 *29 Sep, at Leigh, 5019*

LANCASHIRE	22	T: Welding, Stephens, Clark Kenny
		G: Dutton 5
YORKSHIRE	42	T: Watson, N Stephenson, Halmshaw, Nash, Lamb, Millward, Topliss, Farrar
		G: N Stephenson 5, Millward 4

1972 *11 Oct, at Castleford, 2343*

YORKSHIRE	32	T: Lamb 2, Irving, Worsley, Pickup, D Redfearn
		G: Jefferson 7
LANCASHIRE	18	T: Stephens, Hodgkinson, Hughes, O'Neill
		G: Dutton 2, Walsh

1973 *19 Sep, at Widnes, 3307*

LANCASHIRE	17	T: Benyon, Nicholls, Prescott
		G: Whitehead 3, Fiddler
YORKSHIRE	15	T: A Smith, Atkinson, Davies
		G: Jefferson 3

1974 *25 Sep, at Keighley, 1219*

YORKSHIRE	20	T: Atkinson, Millward, Irving Bates
		G: Marshall 4
LANCASHIRE	14	T: Hesketh, Martyn
		G: Whitehead 4

1974 *16 Oct, at Widnes, 3114*

LANCASHIRE	29	T: Noonan 2, Gill, Wright, Hesketh
		G: Dutton 7
YORKSHIRE	11	T: Atkinson, Roe, Norton
		G: Burton

Note – County Championship Play-off

1975 *20 Dec, at Wigan, 700*

LANCASHIRE	7	T: Turnbull
		G: Dutton 2
YORKSHIRE	17	T: Morgan 2, Atkinson
		G: Holmes 4

1977 *1 Mar, at Castleford, 2740*

YORKSHIRE	18	T: Ward, Rose, N Stephenson, Muscroft
		G: Lloyd 2, Mumby
LANCASHIRE	13	T: Martyn, Hughes
		G: Fairbairn 3, Elwell (DG)

1977 *19 Oct, at Widnes, 5056*

LANCASHIRE	33	T: Woods 2, Aspey, Elwell, Wilkinson, Wright
		G: Pimblett 5, Woods 2, Adams (DG)
YORKSHIRE	8	T: Morgan, Atkinson
		G: Quinn

1978 *27 Sep, at Widnes, 4283*

LANCASHIIRE	23	T: Fielding 2, Cunningham, Bevan, Kelly
		G: Fairbairn 4
YORKSHIRE	7	T: M Smith
		G: Lloyd 2

1979 *12 Sep, at Castleford 2744*

YORKSHIRE	19	T: Branch, Burton, Adams, Raistrick
		G: Box 3, Raistrick (DG)
LANCASHIRE	16	T: Pinner 2, Eckersley
		G: Burke 3, Pinner (DG)

1980 *24 Sep, at Widnes, 1593*

LANCASHIRE	17	T: Bilsbury, Hornby, Holding
		G: Whitfield 4
YORKSHIRE	9	T: Fletcher
		G: Quinn 3

1981 *9 Sep, at Castleford, 1222*

YORKSHIRE	21	T: Joyner 2, Ward, Mumby, Dyl
		G: Finch 3
LANCASHIRE	15	T: Drummond 2, Bentley
		G: Whitfield 3

1982 *26 May, at Leigh, 1738*

LANCASHIRE	21	T: Myler, Stephenson, Burke
		G: Burke 6
YORKSHIRE	22	T: Pryce 3, Dick, K Ward
		G: Dick 4(1DG)

1985 *11 Sep, at Wigan, 6743*

LANCASHIRE	10	T: A Gregory, Eccles
		G: Burke
YORKSHIRE	26	T: Mason 2, Heron, Hobbs, Hyde
		G: Fox 3

1986 *17 Sep, at Headingley, 5983*

YORKSHIRE	26	T: Lyman, Gill, Hanley, Marchant
		G: Hobbs 5
LANCASHIRE	14	T: Stephenson, Basnett
		G: Stephenson 3

1987 *16 Sep, at Wigan, 9748*

LANCASHIRE	10	T: Hampson, Round
		G: Whitfield
YORKSHIRE	16	T: Marchant, Gill, Hanley
		G: Fox, Hobbs

1988 *21 Sep, at Headingley, 8244*

YORKSHIRE	24	T: Marchant, Schofield, Hanley, Gill
		G: Hobbs 4
LANCASHIRE	14	T: Thackray, Dowd, Currier
		G: Loughlin

1989 *20 Sep, at Wigan, 10 182*

LANCASHIRE	12	T: Preston, M Gregory
		G: Loughlin 2
YORKSHIRE	56	T: Steadman 2, Newlove 2, Goodway 2, Schofield, Hobbs, Medley, Fox
		G: Steadman 4, Hobbs 4

ROSES MATCH RECORDS

Victories		Yorkshire 42, Lancashire 41, draws 3
Highest aggregate	68	Lancashire 12, Yorkshire 56, 1989
Lowest aggregate	7	Lancashire 2, Yorkshire 5, 1921

LANCASHIRE RECORDS

Highest score	45–20 at St Helens, 1963
Largest crowd	18,000 at Rochdale, 1900
Smallest crowd	700 at Wigan, 1975
Highest receipts	£34 000 at Wigan, 1989
Most tries – match	3 S Rix 1925, C Carr 1926 and 1927, F Harris 1936, T O'Grady 1955 and 1956, F Myler 1959, J Measures 1963
Most goals – match	9 L Gilfedder, 1963
Most points – match	18 L Gilfedder, 1963
Most tries – career	12 C Carr, 1924–30
Most goals – career	24 R Dutton, 1968–75
Most points – career	48 R Dutton, 1968–75
Most appearances	9 L Fairclough, 1923–31

YORKSHIRE RECORDS

Highest score	56–12 at Wigan, 1989
Largest crowd	15 054 at Wakefield, 1960
Smallest crowd	12 19 at Keighley, 1974
Highest receipts	£27 587 at Headingley, 1988
Most tries – match	3 P Eccles 1909, S Moorhouse 1912, A Hardisty 1964, G Pryce 1982
Most goals – match	10 V Yorke, 1958
Most points – match	20 V Yorke, 1958
Most tries – career	6 J Atkinson, 1968–77
	6 M Sullivan, 1955–61
Most goals – career	29 N Fox, 1959–68
Most points – career	67 N Fox, 1959–68
Most appearances	9 J Atkinson, 1968–77
	9 S Brogden, 1928–38

RESERVE TEAM RUGBY LEAGUE

In recent years reserve team ('A' team) Rugby League has gained a new respectability. Until 1984, reserve team competitions were administered by the Lancashire and Yorkshire County Rugby Leagues before being incorporated into the Rugby League Alliance. The Rugby League Alliance now runs two divisions and its own Alliance Challenge Cup Competition. Winners and runners-up in these competitions are listed below:

THE RUGBY LEAGUE ALLIANCE CHAMPIONSHIP

Year	Winners	Runners-up
1984–85	Hull KR	St Helens
1985–86	Hull	Castleford
1986–87	Wigan	Warrington
1987–88	Leeds	Widnes
1988–89	Wigan	Castleford
1989–90	Hull	Leeds
1990–91	Hull	Hull KR

ALLIANCE SECOND DIVISION CHAMPIONSHIP

Year	Winners	Runners-up
1986–87	Swinton Crusaders	Hunslet
1987–88	Whitehaven	Carlisle
1988–89	Featherstone R	Oldham
1989–90	Wakefield T	Leigh
1990–91	Bradford N	Workington T

ALLIANCE CHALLENGE CUP

Year	Winners	Runners-up
1984–85	Widnes	Salford
1985–86	Swinton Crusaders	Leeds
1986–87	Hull	Hull KR
1987–88	St Helens	Barrow
1988–89	Leeds	St Helens
1989–90	Hull	Bradford N
1990–91	Bradford N	Castleford

Australia's giant second-rower Paul Sironen contributed greatly to their 1990 Ashes series victory. Here he takes on the Widnes defence.

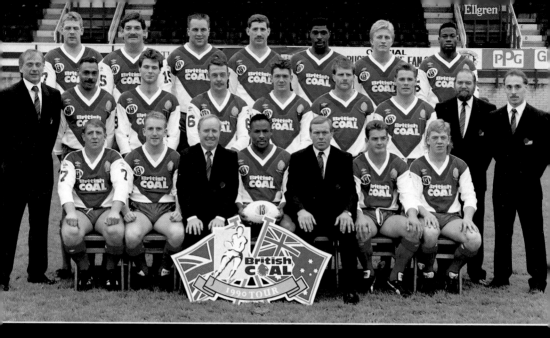

Great Britain's 1990 Ashes squad.
Back row, left to right: Fairbank, Ward, Dannatt, Harrison, R Powell, Betts, Offiah.
Middle: Larder, Gibson, Jackson, Schofield, D Powell, Dixon, Eastwood, Mackenzie, Fevre.
Front: Gregory, Edwards, Lindsay, Hanley, Reilly, Irwin, Hampson.

Australia's 1990 Ashes squad.
Back row: Roach, Ettingshausen, McGaw, Cartwright, Geyer, Carroll, Sironen, Bella, Alexander, Hasler, Hancock.
Middle: Lewis, Hollis, Lyons, Gillespie, Daley, Kevin Walters, Stuart, Shearer, Mackay, Sargent, Lazarus, Gibbs, McRae.
Front: Kerrod Walters, Langer, Johns, Stokes, Elias, Fulton, Meninga, Barnes, Belcher, Lindner, Fittler.

Left *Ellery Hanley, arguably the modern game's greatest player and one of League's top breakers of records, in action for Wigan against the Australians at Central Park.*

Below *Great Britain prop Karl Harrison tackles Australia's captain Mal Meninga in the Old Trafford Test match. Meninga scored a fine last-minute try to clinch the match for Australia.*

Right *Try-machine Martin Offiah joined Widnes in 1987 and had scored 100 tries within 18 months – the fastest century on record in terms of time but not in terms of games played; that record is held by Billy Boston, who reached 100 tries in only 68 games. Offiah took 80.*

Below *One of the game's great contemporary forwards – Mike Gregory, who led the Great Britain Lions to Papua and New Zealand in 1990.*

Above *Sheffield Eagles scrum-half Mark Aston scored a club record 307 points in 1988–89 and joined a select band of players who have played and scored in every game in a season.*

Right *Hull Kingston Rovers' talented centre-cum-stand-off Mike Smith, who has made more appearances for the club than any other player, in action in Rovers' 1984 Premiership Final victory over Castleford.*

Above *Challenge Cup semi-final, 1990, at Central Park. Warrington stand-off Turner and loose-forward Gregory halt an Oldham attack.*

Below Right *Test forward Andy Platt moved from St Helens to Wigan for £140 000 in 1988. Here he is seen scoring for Saints against Wigan in 1985.*

Above *Jonathan Davies scores one of his record three tries for Widnes against Wigan in the 1990 Charity Shield at Swansea.*

Right *Leigh's John Woods releases the ball in a Halifax tackle. Only three players in the history of the game have scored more points than Woods.*

Left *Leeds shook both Rugby League and Rugby Union when they signed the All Black full-back John Gallagher, seen here running the ball against the 1990 Kangaroos.*

Right *New Zealand centre Mark Elia races between Harry Pinner and Barrie Ledger of St Helens in a 1985 Kiwi tour match. Elia later played for Saints, figuring in their 1987 Challenge Cup Final team.*

Above *The World Club Challenge was introduced to Rugby League in 1987, Wigan beating Australian Premiers Manly 8–2 in a gripping encounter. Referee John Holdsworth straightens out the rival packs.*

Left *The Second Division Premiership Final at Old Trafford in 1988, and Featherstone captain Deryck Fox gets the ball away in fine style – but Rovers lost a classic game 26–28 to Oldham.*

Above *Widnes prop Kurt Sorensen in action against Castleford. Sorensen captained Widnes to successive Premierships in 1988, 1989 and 1990.*

Left *Halifax full-back Graham Eadie rushes past Scott Gale (Hull) in the 1988 Challenge Cup semi-final at Headingley. Eadie won the coveted Lance Todd Trophy at Wembley in 1987.*

In pre-Alliance times Lancashire 'A' teams competed for the Lancashire Combination Championship in a league competition and for the Lancashire County Challenge Shield, a knock-out competition which still operates. Post-war winners of these competitions are listed below:

In pre-Alliance times Yorkshire 'A' teams competed for the Yorkshire Senior Competition Championship Shield in a league competition and the Yorkshire Senior Competition Challenge Cup, a knock-out competition which still operates. Post-war winners of these competitions are listed below:

Year	Lancashire Combination Championship	Lancashire County Challenge Shield
1946–47	Widnes	
1947–48	Wigan	
1948–49	St Helens	
1949–50	Wigan	
1950–51	Warrington	
1951–52	Leigh	Wigan
1952–53	St Helens	St Helens
1953–54	St Helens	Leigh
1954–55	Undecided*	St Helens
1955–56	Barrow	Whitehaven
1956–57	St Helens	St Helens
1957–58	St Helens	Wigan
1958–59	Leigh	Wigan
1959–60	Widnes	Widnes
1960–61	Widnes	Widnes
1961–62	Wigan	St Helens
1962–63	Swinton	St Helens
1963–64	Undecided*	Warrington
1964–65	Widnes	Warrington
1965–66	Warrington	Warrington
1966–67	Workington T	Workington T
1967–68	Wigan	Workington T
1968–69	Salford	Salford
1969–70	Wigan	Salford
1970–71	Widnes	Whitehaven
1971–72	Salford	Workington T
1972–73	Salford	Salford
1973–74	Salford	Warrington
1974–75	Warrington	Warrington
1975–76	St Helens	Oldham
1976–77	Wigan	Wigan
1977–78	Widnes	Barrow
1978–79	St Helens	St Helens
1979–80	St Helens	Oldham
1980–81	St Helens	Wigan
1981–82	Warrington	Warrington
1982–83	Widnes	St Helens
1983–84	Warrington	Warrington
1984–85	End of competition	Swinton Crusaders
1985–86		Widnes
1986–87		Widnes
1987–88		Warrington Wizards
1988–89		Wigan
1989–90		Salford
1990–91		Wigan

* The 1954–55 and 1963–64 Combination Championship titles were undecided because the top two teams had played differing numbers of fixtures. No provision had been made for such circumstances.

Year	Yorkshire SCC Shield	Yorkshire SCC Cup
1945–46	Featherstone R	Featherstone R
1946–47	Castleford	Hunslet
1947–48	Hull	Wakefield T
1948–49	Hull	Hull
1949–50	Hull	Hull
1950–51	Hunslet	Castleford
1951–52	Wakefield T	Halifax
1952–53	Leeds	Halifax
1953–54	Halifax	Huddersfield
1954–55	Halifax	Wakefield T
1955–56	Wakefield T	Wakefield T
1956–57	Halifax	Hull KR
1957–58	Halifax	Hull
1958–59	Leeds	Leeds
1959–60	Leeds	Leeds
1960–61	Wakefield T	Dewsbury
1961–62	Featherstone R	Hull KR
1962–63	Castleford	Leeds
1963–64	Halifax	Hull KR
1964–65	Castleford	Hunslet
1965–66	Castleford	Hull
1966–67	Leeds	Leeds
1967–68	Leeds	Leeds
1968–69	Castleford	Leeds
1969–70	Hunslet	Castleford
1970–71	Leeds	Bradford N
1971–72	Featherstone R	Castleford
1972–73	Castleford	Castleford
1973–74	Castleford	Featherstone R
1974–75	Leeds	Leeds
1975–76	Castleford	Castleford
1976–77	Castleford	Huddersfield
1977–78	Castleford	New Hunslet
1978–79	Castleford	Wakefield T
1979–80	Hull KR	Leeds
1980–81	Castleford	Castleford
1981–82	Hull KR	Castleford
1982–83	Hull KR	Castleford
1983–84	Hull KR	Hull
1984–85	End of competition	Castleford
1985–86		Wakefield T
1986–87		Castleford
1987–88		Hull KR
1988–89		Leeds
1989–90		Hull KR
1990–91		Bradford N

DEFUNCT COMPETITIONS: RESULTS HISTORY & RECORDS

THE BBC2 FLOODLIT TROPHY

This competition was inaugurated in the 1965–66 season and ran until 1979–80. Specifically designed for television, the competition was screened on Tuesday evenings during the early part of the season. Only eight clubs competed in the first tournament, a figure which had risen to 20 by 1979. Apart from the first two seasons, the competition was played on a knock-out basis.

FLOODLIT TROPHY FINALS

1965-66 *14 Dec, at St Helens, 11 510*
CASTLEFORD	4	G: Willett 2
ST HELENS	0	

1966-67 *20 Dec, at Castleford, 8986*
CASTLEFORD	7	T: Austin
		G: Willett, Hepworth
SWINTON	2	G: Whitehead

1967-68 *16 Jan, at Headingley, 9716*
CASTLEFORD	8	G: Willett 4
LEIGH	5	T: Tickle
		G: Gilfedder

1968-69 *17 Dec, at Wigan, 13 479*
WIGAN	7	T: C Hill
		G: Tyrer 2
ST HELENS	4	G: Coslett 2

1969-70 *16 Dec, at Wigan, 12 312*
LEIGH	11	T: Tickle
		G: Ferguson 3, Murphy
WIGAN	6	G: Francis 2, D Hill

1970-71 *15 Dec, at Headingley, 7612*
LEEDS	9	T: Hynes
		G: Holmes 2, Hynes
ST HELENS	5	T: Jones
		G: Coslett

1971-72 *14 Dec, at St Helens, 9300*
ST HELENS	8	G: Coslett 4
ROCHDALE HORNETS	2	G: Chamberlain

1972-73 *19 Dec, at Wigan, 4841*
LEIGH	5	T: Lawson
		G: Fiddler
WIDNES	0	

1973-74 *19 Dec, at Widnes, 4422*
BRAMLEY	15	T: Austin, Goodchild, Sampson
		G: Wolford 2, Ward
WIDNES	7	T: Macko
		G: Dutton 2

1974-75 *17 Dec, at Salford, 4473*
SALFORD	0	
WARRINGTON	0	

Replay *28 Jan, at Warrington, 5778*
SALFORD	10	T: Fielding, Richards
		G: Watkins 2
WARRINGTON	5	T: Bevan
		G: Whitehead

1975-76 *16 Dec, at St Helens, 3858*
ST HELENS	22	T: Mathias 2, Benyon, Wilson, Hull
		G: Pimblett 2, Coslett, Heaton (DG)
DEWSBURY	2	G: Stephenson

1976-77 *14 Dec, at Leigh, 5402*
CASTLEFORD	12	T: Burton, Jamie Walsh
		G: Lloyd 3
LEIGH	4	T: Joe Walsh
		G: Ashcroft (DG)

98

St Helens celebrate winning the BBC2 Floodlit Trophy in 1975, having beaten Dewsbury 22–2 in the final. Skipper Kel Coslett holds the trophy.

1977–78 *13 Dec, at Craven Park, Hull, 10 099*

HULL KR	26	T: Dunn 2, Rose, Sullivan, Hartley, Smith
		G: Hall 4
ST HELENS	11	T: Glynn 2, Cunningham
		G: Glynn

1978–79 *12 Dec, at St Helens, 10 250*

WIDNES	13	T: Wright 2, Burke
		G: Burke 2
ST HELENS	7	T: D Chisnall
		G: Pimblett 2

1979–80 *18 Dec, at The Boulevard, Hull, 18 500*

HULL	13	T: Dennison, Birdsall, Evans
		G: Dennison 2
HULL KR	3	T: Hubbard

FLOODLIT TROPHY HONOURS

Club	Winners	Runners-up
Castleford	4	–
St Helens	2	5
Leigh	2	2
Widnes	1	2
Hull KR	1	1
Wigan	1	1
Bramley	1	–
Hull	1	–
Leeds	1	–
Salford	1	–
Dewsbury	–	1
Rochdale Hornets	–	1
Swinton	–	1
Warrington	–	1

FLOODLIT TROPHY FINAL RECORDS

Most finals	7	St Helens
Most wins	4	Castleford
Most consecutive finals	3	Castleford
Most consecutive wins	3	Castleford
Highest score	26	Hull KR v St Helens, 1977
Highest aggregate	37	Hull KR 26 St Helens 11, 1977
Lowest aggregate	0	Salford 0 Warrington 0, 1974
Largest crowd	18 500	Hull v Hull KR, 1979
Smallest crowd	3,858	St Helens v Dewsbury, 1975
Highest receipts	£16 605	Hull v Hull KR, 1979

PLAYERS' RECORDS IN ONE FINAL

Most tries	2	R Mathias (St Helens) v Dewsbury, 1975
	2	G Dunn (Hull KR) v St Helens, 1977
	2	P Glynn (St Helens) v Hull KR, 1977
	2	S Wright (Widnes) v St Helens, 1978
Most goals	4	R Willett (Castleford) v Leigh, 1968 (Jan)
	4	K Coslett (St Helens) v Rochdale H, 1971
	4	D Hall (Hull KR) v St Helens, 1977
Most points	8	R Willett (Castleford) v Leigh, 1968 (Jan)
	8	K Coslett (St Helens) v Rochdale H, 1971
	8	P Glynn (St Helens) v Hull KR, 1977
	8	D Hall (Hull KR) v St Helens, 1977

PLAYERS' RECORD IN ALL FINALS

Most appearances	5	W Benyon (St Helens) 1965, 1968 (Dec), 1970, 1971, 1975
	5	J Mantle (St Helens) 1965, 1968 (Dec) 1970, 1971, 1975
	5	D Laughton (St Helens, Wigan, Widnes) 1965, 1968 (Dec), 1969, 1973, 1978
	5	D Chisnall (Leigh, Warrington, St Helens) 1969, 1974, 1976, 1977, 1978
	5	L Jones (St Helens) 1970 1971, 1975, 1977, 1978
Most tries	2	R Tickle (Leigh) 1968 (Jan), 1969
	2	R Mathias (St Helens) 1975
	2	G Dunn (Hull KR) 1977
	2	P Glynn (St Helens) 1977
	2	S Wright (Widnes) 1978
Most goals	8	K Coslett (St Helens) 1968 (Dec), 1970, 1971, 1975
Most points	16	K Coslett (St Helens), as above

THE NORTHERN RUGBY LEAGUE CHAMPIONSHIP

Between 1906–07 and 1961–62 the Northern Rugby League Championship was decided after a top four play-off. Between 1964–65 and 1972–73 the Championship play-offs were extended to the top 16 clubs.

CHAMPIONSHIP FINALS

1906-07 *20 April, at Huddersfield, 13 200*
HALIFAX	18 T:	Riley, Bartle, Bulmer, Morley
	G:	Little 3
OLDHAM	3 T:	Ferguson

1907-08 *2 May, at Salford, 14 000*
HUNSLET	7 T:	A Goldthorpe
	G:	A Goldthorpe 2
OLDHAM	7 T:	Wright
	G:	White 2

Replay *9 May, at Wakefield, 14 054*
HUNSLET	12 T:	W Goldthorpe 2
	G:	A Goldthorpe 2, Place
OLDHAM	2 G:	White

1908-09 *1 May, at Salford, 12 000*
WIGAN	7 T:	Ramsdale
	G:	Leytham 2
OLDHAM	3 T:	Jardine

1909-10 *23 Apr, at Broughton, 10 850*
OLDHAM	13 T:	Dixon, G Smith, McCabe
	G:	Ferguson, Wood
WIGAN	7 T:	Todd
	G:	Leytham 2

1910-11 *6 May, at Broughton, 15 543*
OLDHAM	20 T:	Lomas 2, White 2
	G:	Lomas 4
WIGAN	7 T:	Leytham
	G:	Thomas, Sharrock

1911-12 *4 May, at Halifax, 15 000*
HUDDERSFIELD	13 T:	Clark, Rosenfeld, Davies
	G:	Longstaff, Grey
WIGAN	5 T:	Bradley
	G:	Thomas

1912-13 *3 May, at Wakefield, 17 000*
HUDDERSFIELD	29 T:	Clark 3, Rosenfeld 2, Grey, Moorhouse
	G:	Holland 4
WIGAN	2 G:	Thomas

1913-14 *25 Apr, at Headingley, 8091*
SALFORD	5 T:	Rees
	G:	Mesley
HUDDERSFIELD	3 T:	Gleeson

1914-15 *24 Apr, at Wakefield, 14 000*
HUDDERSFIELD	35 T:	Gronow 2, Longstaff, Moorhouse, Wagstaff, Clark, Rogers
	G:	Gronow 7
LEEDS	2 G:	Lewis

1915-16, 1916-17, 1917-18, 1918-19: No competition

1919-20 *24 Apr, at Headingley, 12 900*
HULL	3 T:	Batten
HUDDERSFIELD	2 G:	Holland

1920-21 *7 May, at Headingley, 10 000*
HULL	16 T:	Taylor 2, Stone, Devereux
	G:	Kennedy 2
HULL KR	14 T:	Cook, Mulvey
	G:	Gibson 4

1921-22 *6 May, at Broughton, 26 000*
WIGAN	13 T:	Shea
	G:	Sullivan 4, Howley
OLDHAM	2 G:	Farrar

1922-23 *5 May, at Headingley, 14 000*
HULL KR	15 T:	Rees, Cooke, Hoult
	G:	Osborne 3
HUDDERSFIELD	5 T:	Williams
	G:	Gronow

1923-24 *3 May, at Broughton, 13 729*
BATLEY	13 T:	Murray 2, Leeming
	G:	Rees 2
WIGAN	7 T:	Armstrong
	G:	Oakley 2

1924-25 *2 May, at Rochdale, 21 580*
HULL KR	9 T:	Rhoades
	G:	Osborne 3
SWINTON	5 T:	Brockbank
	G:	Brockbank

1925-26 *8 May, at St Helens, 20 000*
WIGAN	22 T:	Ring 3, Howley 2, Van Heerden
	G:	Sullivan 2
WARRINGTON	10 T:	Ryder, Peacock
	G:	Catterall 2

DEFUNCT COMPETITIONS

1926-27 *30 Apr, at Warrington, 24 432*
SWINTON   13 T: B Evans 2, Beswick
    G: Morris 2
ST HELENS RECS   8 T: Innes, Bowen
    G: Dingsdale

1927-28 *5 May, at Oldham, 15 451*
SWINTON   11 T: F Evans, Cracknell, Halsall
    G: Young
FEATHERSTONE R   0

1928-29 *11 May, at Halifax, 25 604*
HUDDERSFIELD   2 G: Brook
LEEDS   0

1929-30 *10 May, at Wakefield, 32 095*
HUDDERSFIELD   2 G: Stocks
LEEDS   2 G: Thompson

Replay *12 May, at Halifax, 18 563*
HUDDERSFIELD   10 T: Parker, Thompson
    G: Stocks 2
LEEDS   0

1930-31 *9 May, at Wigan, 31 000*
SWINTON   14 T: Whittaker, Butters
    G: Hodgson 4
LEEDS   7 T: Grainge
    G: Thompson 2

1931-32 *7 May, at Wakefield, 19 386*
ST HELENS   9 T: Winnard
    G: Lewis 3
HUDDERSFIELD   5 T: Walker
    G: Bowkett

1932-33 *29 Apr, at Wigan, 18 000*
SALFORD   15 T: Brown, Jenkins, Feetham
    G: Risman 3
SWINTON   5 T: Shaw
    G: Scott

1933-34 *28 Apr, at Warrington, 31 565*
WIGAN   15 T: Davies, Targett, Morley
    G: Sullivan 3
SALFORD   3 T: Jenkins

1934-35 *11 May, at Wigan, 27 700*
SWINTON   14 T: Green, Sullivan
    G: Hodgson 4
WARRINGTON   3 T: Dingsdale

1935-36 *9 May, at Huddersfield, 17 276*
HULL   21 T: Oliver 2, Barlow
    G: Oliver 5, Miller
WIDNES   2 G: Jacks

1936-37 *1 May, at Wigan, 31 500*
SALFORD   13 T: Hudson
    G: Risman 5
WARRINGTON   11 T: Cotton
    G: Holding 2, Welsby, Shankland

1937-38 *30 Apr, at Elland Road, 54 112*
HUNSLET   8 T: Winter, O'Sullivan
    G: Walkington
LEEDS   2 G: Tattersfield

1938-39 *13 May, at Maine Road, 69 504*
SALFORD   8 T: Edwards, Kenny
    G: Risman
CASTLEFORD   6 T: Robinson, Brindle

1939-40 *FIRST LEG 18 May, at Swinton, 4800*
SWINTON   13 T: McGurk, Hopkin, Shaw
    G: Hodgson 2
BRADFORD NORTHERN   21 T: Whitcombe, Davies, Harrison, Smith, Brogden
    G: Carmichael 3

SECOND LEG 25 May, at Odsal, 11 271
BRADFORD NORTHERN   16 T: Winnard 2, D Ward, Whitcombe
    G: Carmichael, Whitcombe
SWINTON   9 T: Williams
    G: Hodgson 3
Bradford Northern won 37-22 on aggregate

1940-41 *FIRST LEG 12 Apr, at Wigan, 11 245*
WIGAN   6 T: Jones, Lawrenson
BRADFORD NORTHERN   17 T: Walters 2, Best, Higson, Risman
    G: E Ward

SECOND LEG 14 Apr, at Odsal, 20 205
BRADFORD NORTHERN   28 T: Risman 2, Winnard 2, Moore, Walters
    G: E Ward 5
WIGAN   9 T: Johnson, Aspinall, Bowen
Bradford Northern won 45-15 on aggregate

1941-42 *18 Apr, at Headingley, 18 000*
DEWSBURY   13 T: Hudson, Francis, Kenny
    G: Edwards, Risman
BRADFORD NORTHERN   0

1942-43 *FIRST LEG 15 May, at Dewsbury, 7000*
DEWSBURY   11 T: Francis 2, Royal
    G: Seeling
HALIFAX   3 T: Shannon

SECOND LEG 22 May, at Halifax, 9700
HALIFAX   13 T: McCue 2, Bevan
    G: Lockwood 2
DEWSBURY   22 T: Hudson 2, Morrell, Kenny, Royal, Curran
    G: Walsh 2
Dewsbury won 33-16 on aggregate but the Championship was declared void on 30 July 1943, when Dewsbury were fined £100 for fielding an ineligible player.

Right *Jack Cunliffe holds the Championship trophy aloft after Wigan's 13-6 victory over Bradford Northern in the 1952 Final.*

1943-44 *FIRST LEG 13 May, at Wigan, 14 000*
WIGAN   13 T: K Gee, Featherstone,
                               Lawrenson
                    G: Egan, Lawrenson
DEWSBURY   9 T: Walsh
                    G: Walsh 3

SECOND LEG 20 May, at Dewsbury, 9000
DEWSBURY   5 T: Francis
                    G: Seeling
WIGAN   12 T: Fleming, Egan
                    G: Sullivan 3
Wigan won 25–14 on aggregate

1944-45 *FIRST LEG 19 May, at Halifax, 9426*
HALIFAX   9 T: McCue
                    G: Lockwood 3
BRADFORD NORTHERN 2 G: E Ward

SECOND LEG 21 May, at Odsal, 16 000
BRADFORD NORTHERN 24 T: D Ward 2, Edwards,
                             Marklew, Best,
                             Kitching
                    G: E Ward 3
HALIFAX   11 T: McCue
                    G: Lockwood 4
Bradford Northern won 26–60 on aggregate

1945-46 *18 May, at Maine Road, 67 136*
WIGAN   13 T: Ashcroft 2, Cunliffe
                    G: Nordgren 2
HUDDERSFIELD   4 G: Bawden 2

1946-47 *21 June, at Maine Road, 40 599*
WIGAN   13 T: Bradshaw, Nordgren,
                         Lawrenson
                    G: Ward 2
DEWSBURY   4 G: Ledgard, Holt

1947-48 *8 May, at Maine Road, 69 143*
WARRINGTON   15 T: Pimblett, Powell, Bevan
                    G: Palin 3
BRADFORD NORTHERN 5 T: Case
                    G: E Ward

1948-49 *14 May, at Maine Road, 75 194*
HUDDERSFIELD   13 T: Cooper, Daly, Devery
                    G: Devery 2
WARRINGTON   12 T: Francis, Jackson
                    G: Bath 2, Palin

1949-50 *13 May, at Maine Road, 65 065*
WIGAN   20 T: Nordgren, W Blan,
                       Silcock, Broome
                    G: Ward 4
HUDDERSFIELD   2 G: Bawden

DEFUNCT COMPETITIONS

1950–51 *12 May, at Maine Road, 61 618*
WORKINGTON TOWN   26   T: Gibson 2, Wilson 2,
                                 Lawrenson, Paskins
                                G: Risman 4
WARRINGTON   11   T: Heathwood 2, Jackson
                                G: Bath

1951–52 *10 May, at Huddersfield Town AFC, 48 684*
WIGAN   13   T: Cunliffe, Ryan, Silcock
                                G: Gee 2
BRADFORD NORTHERN   6 G: Phillips 3

1952–53 *9 May, at Maine Road, 51 083*
ST HELENS   24   T: Blakemore 2, Greenall,
                                 Moses, Cale, Metcalfe
                                G: Metcalfe 3
HALIFAX   14   T: Lynch, Wilkinson
                                G   Griffiths 4

1953–54 *8 May, at Maine Road, 36 519*
WARRINGTON   8 G: Bath 4
HALIFAX   7   T: Thorley
                                 G: Griffiths 2

1954–55 *14 May, at Maine Road, 49 434*
WARRINGTON   7   T: Bevan
                                 G: Bath 2
OLDHAM   3   T: Pitchford

1955–56 *12 May, at Maine Road, 36 675*
HULL   10   T: Finn, Harris
                                 G: Hutton 2
HALIFAX   9   T: Palmer, Daniels, Freeman

1956–57 *18 May, at Odsal, 62 199*
OLDHAM   15   T: Etty 2, Ayres
                                 G: Ganley 3
HULL   14   T: Turner, Cowan
                                 G: Hutton 4

1957–58 *17 May, at Odsal, 57 699*
HULL   20   T: Finn, Whiteley, Cooper,
                                 Scott
                                 G: Bateson 4
WORKINGTON TOWN   3   T: Southward

1958–59 *16 May, at Odsal, 52 560*
ST HELENS   44   T: Vollenhoven 3, Murphy 2,
                                 Huddart, Prinsloo,
                                 Smith
                                 G: Rhodes 10
HUNSLET   22   T: Doyle, Poole, Stockdill,
                                 Gunney
                                 G: Langton 5

1959–60 *21 May, at Odsal, 83 190*
WIGAN   27   T: Ashton 2, Boston 2,
                                 Sayer
                                 G: Griffiths 6
WAKEFIELD TRINITY   3   T: Smith

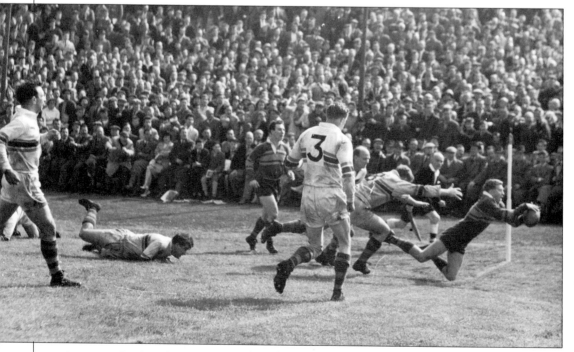

Leeds centre Hallas dives for a try in his side's 25–10 victory over Warrington at Odsal Stadium in the 1961 Championship Final.

1960-61 *20 May, at Odsal, 52 177*

LEEDS	25	T: Hallas 2, Fairbank, Evans, Jones
		G: Jones 5
WARRINGTON	10	T: Challinor 2
		G: Gilfedder 2

1961-62 *19 May, at Odsal, 37 451*

HUDDERSFIELD	14	T: Smales, Wicks
		G: Dyson 4
WAKEFIELD TRINITY	5	T: Fox
		G: Fox

1962-63, 1963-64: No competition

1964-65 *22 May, at Swinton, 20 776*

HALIFAX	15	T: Burnett 2, Jackson
		G: James 3
ST HELENS	7	T: Killeen
		G: Killeen 2

1965-66 *28 May, at Swinton, 30 634*

ST HELENS	35	T: Halsall 3, Killeen 3, A Barrow
		G: Killeen 6, Murphy
HALIFAX	12	T: Baker, Fogerty
		G: Cooper 3

1966-67 *6 May, at Headingley, 20 161*

WAKEFIELD TRINITY	7	T: Owen
		G: N Fox 2
ST HELENS	7	T: Watson
		G: Killeen 2

Replay *10 May, at Swinton, 33 537*

WAKEFIELD TRINITY	21	T: Brooke 2, Owen, Hirst, Poynton
		G: N Fox 3
ST HELENS	9	T: Vollenhoven
		G: Killeen 2, Bishop

1967-68 *4 May, at Headingley, 22 586*

WAKEFIELD TRINITY	17	T: Owen, N Fox, Jeanes
		G: N Fox 2, Poynton, D Fox
HULL KR	10	T: Longstaff, Moore
		G: Millward 2

1968-69 *24 May, at Odsal, 28 442*

LEEDS	16	T: Cowan, Atkinson
		G: Risman 4, Ramsey
CASTLEFORD	14	T: Hardisty, Dickinson
		G: Redfearn 3, Hardisty

1969-70 *16 May, at Odsal, 26 358*

ST HELENS	24	T: Prescott 2, Sayer, Walsh
		G: Coslett 4, Walsh 2
LEEDS	12	T: Smith, Cowan
		G: Holmes 3

1970-71 *22 May, at Swinton, 21 745*

ST HELENS	16	T: Blackwood, Benyon
		G: Coslett 5
WIGAN	12	T: Robinson, Ashurst
		G: Ashurst 2, Tyrer

1971-72 *20 May, at Swinton, 24 055*

LEEDS	9	T: Atkinson
		G: Clawson 3
ST HELENS	5	T: Greenall
		G: Walsh

1972-73 *19 May, at Odsal, 18 889*

DEWSBURY	22	T: M Stephenson 2, Agar, N Stephenson
		G: N Stephenson 5
LEEDS	13	T: Dyl, Eccles, Cookson
		G: Clawson, Hynes

CHAMPIONSHIP FINAL HONOURS

Club	Winners	Runners up
Wigan	10	7
Huddersfield	7	6
St Helens	6	3
Hull	5	1
Swinton	4	3
Salford	4	1
Leeds	3	7
Warrington	3	6
Oldham	3	5
Bradford Northern	3	3
Dewsbury	3	2
Halifax	2	6
Hull KR	2	2
Wakefield Trinity	2	2
Hunslet	2	1
Workington Town	1	1
Batley	1	–
Castleford	–	2
Featherstone Rovers	–	1
St Helens Recs	–	1
Widnes	–	1

Note – Dewsbury's record includes the void Championship victory of 1942–43.

CHAMPIONSHIP FINAL RECORDS

Most finals	17	Wigan
Most wins	10	Wigan
Most consecutive finals	5	Oldham, Wigan
Most consecutive wins		No team has won more than two consecutive Championship Finals. Two consecutive wins have been recorded eleven times, however, Huddersfield being the only club to achieve this twice
Highest score	44	St Helens v Hunslet, 1959
Highest aggregate	66	St Helens 44 Hunslet 22, 1959
Lowest aggregate	2	Huddersfield 2 Leeds 0, 1929
Largest crowd	83 190	Wakefield T v Wigan, 1960
Smallest crowd	4800	Swinton v Bradford N, 1940 (1st leg)
Highest receipts	£14 482	Wakefield T v Wigan, 1960

The 1973 Championship Final, and Dewsbury centre Nigel Stephenson prepares to pass as Les Dyl of Leeds covers. Stephenson scored five goals and a try in his side's 22–13 victory.

PLAYERS' RECORDS IN ONE FINAL

Most tries	3	D Clark (Huddersfield) v Wigan, 1913
	3	J Ring (Wigan) v Warrington, 1926
	3	T Vollenhoven (St Helens) v Hunslet, 1959
	3	A Halsall (St Helens) v Halifax, 1966
	3	L Killeen (St Helens) v Halifax, 1966
Most goals	10	A Rhodes (St Helens) v Hunslet, 1959
Most points	21	L Killeen (St Helens) v Halifax, 1966

PLAYERS' RECORDS IN ALL FINALS

Most appearances	7	A Risman (Salford, Bradford N Dewsbury, Workington T) 1933, 1934, 1937, 1939, 1941, 1942, 1951
Most tries	5	D Clark (Huddersfield) 1912, 1913, 1915
Most goals	14	A Risman (Salford, Bradford N, Dewsbury, Workington T) 1933, 1937, 1939, 1941, 1942, 1951
Most points	37	A Risman, as above

THE LANCASHIRE & YORKSHIRE LEAGUE CHAMPIONSHIPS

From 1895–96 until 1901–02 the senior clubs participated in county leagues known as the Lancashire Senior Competition and the Yorkshire Senior Competition. The winners and runners-up in the competitions were as follows:

	LSC		YSC	
Year	Winners	Runners-up	Winners	Runners-up
1895–96	Runcorn	Oldham	Manningham	Halifax
1896–97	Broughton R	Oldham	Brighouse R	Manningham
1897–98	Oldham	Swinton	Hunslet	Bradford
1898–99	Broughton R	Oldham	Batley	Hull
1899–00	Runcorn	Oldham	Bradford	Batley
1900–01	Oldham	Swinton	Bradford	Halifax
1901–02	Wigan	Widnes	Leeds	Manningham

With the introduction of the Northern Rugby League Championship – a 14-team super league – in 1901–02, the LSC and YSC effectively became regionalised second divisions and were abandoned with the introduction of a full-blown two-division system in 1902–03.

From 1907–08 until 1969–70 Lancashire and Yorkshire League Championships operated within the Rugby League Championship, clubs playing home and away fixtures against all fellow county clubs. Winners and runners-up are listed overleaf:

Warrington 1947–48, winners of the Rugby League Championship and Lancashire League Championship.

	LLC		YLC	
Year	Winners	Runners-up	Winners	Runners-up
1907–08	Oldham	Broughton R	Hunslet	Halifax
1908–09	Wigan	Oldham	Halifax	Batley
1909–10	Oldham	Wigan	Wakefield T	Halifax
1910–11	Wigan	Oldham	Wakefield T	Hunslet
1911–12	Wigan	Oldham	Huddersfield	Hull KR
1912–13	Wigan	Broughton R	Huddersfield	Hull KR
1913–14	Wigan	Salford	Huddersfield	Hull
1914–15	Wigan	Rochdale H	Huddersfield	Leeds
1915–16, 1916–17, 1917–18: No competition				
1918–19	Rochdale H	Leigh	Hull	Leeds
1919–20	Widnes	Rochdale H	Huddersfield	Hull
1920–21	Wigan	Warrington	Halifax	Hull
1921–22	Oldham	Wigan	Huddersfield	Hull
1922–23	Wigan	Swinton	Hull	Huddersfield
1923–24	Wigan	Oldham	Batley	Huddersfield
1924–25	Swinton	Wigan	Hull KR	Leeds
1925–26	Wigan	Swinton	Hull KR	Batley
1926–27	St Helens Recs	Swinton	Hull	Leeds
1927–28	Swinton	St Helens Recs	Leeds	Featherstone R
1928–29	Swinton	Wigan	Huddersfield	Leeds
1929–30	St Helens	Salford	Huddersfield	Leeds
1930–31	Swinton	Wigan	Leeds	Huddersfield
1931–32	St Helens	Salford	Hunslet	Huddersfield
1932–33	Salford	Barrow	Castleford	York
1933–34	Salford	Wigan	Leeds	Hunslet
1934–35	Salford	Swinton	Leeds	Hull
1935–36	Liverpool St	Widnes	Hull	Leeds
1936–37	Salford	Liverpool St	Leeds	Castleford
1937–38	Warrington	Barrow	Leeds	Hunslet
1938–39	Salford	Swinton	Castleford	Leeds
1939–40	Swinton	Salford	Bradford N	Huddersfield
1940–41	Wigan	Warrington	Bradford N	Hull
1941–42, 1942–43, 1943–44, 1944–45: No competition				
1945–46	Wigan	Barrow	Wakefield T	Huddersfield
1946–47	Wigan	Widnes	Dewsbury	Huddersfield
1947–48	Warrington	Wigan	Bradford N	Huddersfield
1948–49	Warrington	Wigan	Huddersfield	Bradford N
1949–50	Wigan	Leigh	Huddersfield	Halifax
1950–51	Warrington	Workington T	Leeds	Halifax
1951–52	Wigan	Warrington	Huddersfield	Bradford N
1952–53	St Helens	Leigh	Halifax	Huddersfield
1953–54	Warrington	St Helens	Halifax	Hull
1954–55	Warrington	Oldham	Leeds	Halifax
1955–56	Warrington	St Helens	Halifax	Hull
1956–57	Oldham	Barrow	Leeds	Hull
1957–58	Oldham	St Helens	Halifax	Hull
1958–59	Wigan	St Helens	Wakefield T	Hunslet
1959–60	St Helens	Wigan	Wakefield T	Hull
1960–61	Swinton	St Helens	Leeds	Wakefield T
1961–62	Wigan	Workington T	Wakefield T	Featherstone R
1962–63	Workington T	Widnes	Hull KR	Huddersfield
1963–64	St Helens	Swinton	Halifax	Castleford
1964–65	St Helens	Warrington	Castleford	Halifax
1965–66	St Helens	Swinton	Wakefield T	Castleford
1966–67	St Helens	Workington T	Leeds	Hull KR
1967–68	Warrington	St Helens	Leeds	Hull KR
1968–69	St Helens	Wigan	Leeds	Castleford
1969–70	Wigan	Salford	Leeds	Castleford

Note – In 1962–63 and 1963–64 the Lancashire League Championship was replaced by the Western Division Championship and the Yorkshire League Championship was replaced by the Eastern Division Championship. Each team played eight fixtures and a top four play-off ensued with Championship Finals played on neutral grounds. The actual trophies played for were the Lancashire and Yorkshire League Championship Cups.

WESTERN DIVISION FINALS

1962–63 *10 Nov, at Wigan, 13 588*
WORKINGTON TOWN	9	T: Pretorius
		G: Lowden 3
WIDNES	9	T: Thompson
		G: Randall 3

Replay *14 Nov, at Wigan, 7584*
WORKINGTON TOWN	10	T: Glastonbury, Pretorius
		G: Lowden 2
WIDNES	0	

1963–64 *16 May, at Wigan, 17 363*
ST HELENS	10	T: Northey, French
		G: Coslett 2
SWINTON	7	T: Stopford
		G: Blan 2

EASTERN DIVISION FINALS

1962–63 *10 Nov, at Headingley, 6751*
HULL KR	13	T: Paul 2, Harris
		G: Kellett 2
HUDDERSFIELD	10	T: Haywood, Smales
		G: Dyson 2

1963–64 *23 May, at Huddersfield, 10 798*
HALIFAX	20	T: Jackson 2, Robinson, Dixon
		G: James 4
CASTLEFORD	12	T: Howe, Dickinson
		G: Clark 3

LANCASHIRE LEAGUE CHAMPIONSHIP HONOURS

Club	Champions	Runners-up
Wigan	18	10
St Helens	9	6
Warrington	8	4
Swinton	6	7
Oldham	5	5
Salford	5	5
Widnes	1	3
Workington Town	1	3
Rochdale Hornets	1	2
Liverpool Stanley	1	1
St Helens Recs	1	1
Barrow	–	4
Leigh	–	3
Broughton Rangers	–	2

YORKSHIRE LEAGUE CHAMPIONSHIP HONOURS

Club	Champions	Runners-up
Leeds	14	8
Huddersfield	11	10
Halifax	7	6
Wakefield Trinity	7	1
Hull	4	11
Castleford	3	5
Hull KR	3	4
Bradford Northern	3	2
Hunslet	2	4
Batley	1	2
Dewsbury	1	–
Featherstone Rovers	–	2
York	–	1

'ONE-SEASON WONDERS'

From time to time Rugby League has introduced competitions which have failed to capture public interest and have quickly been discarded. On other occasions they have been used as convenient trials for rule changes. Four of these competitions have lasted only one season.

1955–56 ITV FLOODLIT COMPETITION

Eight clubs participated in this competition, all the games taking place at London soccer grounds.

FINAL *16 Nov, at Loftus Road, 3500*
WARRINGTON   43 T: Bevan 2, McFarlane 2,
                                 Bath 2, Fraser, Helme,
                                 A Naughton
                           G: Bath 8
LEIGH   18 T: Dickens, Gibson, Holden,
                                 Wilson
                           G: Ledgard 3

1964–65 BOTTOM 14 COMPETITION

Ten of the bottom 14 clubs accepted invitations to compete in this end-of-season tournament in which two differing play-the-ball experiments were tested.

FINAL *18 May, at Doncaster, 2450*
HUDDERSFIELD   13 T: Hagan, Senior, Valentine
                           G: Curry 2
DONCASTER   3 T: Roberts

1973–74 CAPTAIN MORGAN TROPHY

First round winners in the Lancashire and Yorkshire Cups participated in this sponsored tournament.

FINAL *26 Jan, at Salford, 5259*
WARRINGTON   4 G: Whitehead 2
FEATHERSTONE R   0

1973–74 CLUB CHAMPIONSHIP

Almost all the clubs in the Rugby League were eligible (through participation in an inordinately complicated merit table) to be included in this end-of season knock-out competition. It was designed primarily to replace the top 16 play-offs.

FINAL *18 May at Wigan, 18 040*
WARRINGTON   13 T: M Philbin, Brady, Noonan
                           G: Whitehead 2
ST HELENS   12 T: Wilson 2
                           G: Coslett 3

INDIVIDUAL RECORDS IN RUGBY LEAGUE

400 APPEARANCES FOR A CLUB

774	J Sullivan	Wigan	1921–46	561+15	M Aspey	Widnes	1964–80
626	J Ferguson	Oldham	1899–1923	559	K Gee	Wigan	1935–54
620	B Bevan	Warrington	1945–62	530	E Ashcroft	Wigan	1942–58
605	H Wilkinson	Wakefield T	1930–49	528+15	P Gordon	Warrington	1963–81
604+17	J Holmes	Leeds	1968–89	525	J Miller	Warrington	1926–46
593+8	K Gowers	Swinton	1954–73	519+12	K Coslett	St Helens	1962–76
587+4	K Elwell	Widnes	1969–86	513+4	W Benyon	St Helens	1962–77
581+22	J Joyner	Castleford	1973–91	512+6	J Atkinson	Leeds	1966–82
573+4	K Mumby	Bradford N	1973–90	512	W Briers	St Helens	1895–1912
572	J Walkington	Hunslet	1927–48	504	F Dawson	Hunslet	1922–37
569+10	G Gunney	Hunslet	1951–73	503	A Worrall	Leigh	1920–38
562+12	N Fox	Wakefield T	1956–74	501	E Rogers	Hull	1906–25

Halifax scrum-half Stan Kielty, who played 481 games for the club, in action against Huddersfield in the 1952 Yorkshire Cup semi-final.

Total	Player	Club	Years
500	J Lewthwaite	Barrow	1943–57
497+27	E Chisnall	St Helens	1967–82
496+2	M Richards	Salford	1969–83
493	L White	Hunslet	1928–46
491	D Greenall	St Helens	1946–59
489	S Walker	Runcorn	1895–1911
487+10	E Ashton	Wigan	1955–69
487	H Day	Salford	1931–48
486+2	W Boston	Wigan	1953–68
485	D Clark	Huddersfield	1909–29
482+6	E Hughes	Widnes	1969–84
481+8	M Smith	Hull KR	1975–91
481	G Carmichael	Bradford N	1934–50
481	S Kielty	Halifax	1946–58
476+8	L Jones	St Helens	1967–81
476	G Aspey	Widnes	1896–1915
473	M Hodgson	Swinton	1927–40
468+11	A Smith	Leeds	1962–83
468+6	K Senior	Huddersfield	1962–79
467	H Crowther	Hunslet	1919–34
467	A Fiddes	Huddersfield	1933–47
466	J Spamer	Hull KR	1926–40
464	W Burgess	Barrow	1919–33
464	B Evans	Swinton	1920–36
464	J Read	Oldham	1926–40
463+4	A Buckley	Swinton	1960–74
463	H Millington	Widnes	1928–46
462	W Horne	Barrow	1943–59
460+3	G Kemel	Widnes	1951–68
460	A Goldthorpe	Hunslet	1895–1910
459	M Scott	Hull	1949–63
457	G Parkinson	Swinton	1952–66
456	W Gowers	Rochdale H	1922–46
454+6	M Murphy	Oldham	1966–82
454	J Lyman	Dewsbury	1913–31
453	F Webster	Leeds	1902–20
451	H Bowman	Hull	1921–34
451	M Exley	Wakefield T	1929–47
450	W Reid	Widnes	1909–27
449	W Hargreaves	York	1952–65
448	A Blan	Swinton	1949–64
447	J Cunliffe	Wigan	1939–60
444	T Harris	Hull	1950–62
443+9	C Hesketh	Salford	1967–79
443	W Horton	Wakefield T	1924–38
443	W Thomas	Salford	1903–21
442+40	D Ward	Leeds	1971–86
442	J Brough	Leeds	1925–44
442	G Helme	Warrington	1945–57
441+22	M Coulman	Salford	1968–83
441	P Norburn	Swinton	1950–64
440	J Denton	Featherstone R	1921–34
440*	H Wilson	Hunslet	1898–1913
439	E Slevin	Huddersfield	1951–63
439	J Tranter	Warrington	1911–28
438	W Cunliffe	Warrington	1914–30
438	N Silcock	Widnes	1923–38
437+8	M Elliott	Oldham	1962–79
437+1	K Holliday	Wakefield T	1952–66
436	H Wagstaff	Huddersfield	1906–25
435	E Barraclough	Featherstone R	1921–34
434	W Williams	Salford	1927–39
433	T Foster	Bradford N	1938–55
432	L Osbourne	Hull KR	1920–32
431+5	C Clarke	Wigan	1963–78
431	A Atkinson	Castleford	1926–42
431	W Thornton	Hunslet	1928–46
428	G Lewis	St Helens	1922–36
427	A Risman	Salford	1929–46
426+1	K Taylor	Oldham	1963–77
426	H Goodfellow	Wakefield T	1934–50
426	J Oliver	Hull	1928–45
426	H Place	Hunslet	1901–20
422+13	J Mantle	St Helens	1965–76
422	B McTigue	Wigan	1951–66
421	W Davies	Batley	1897–1912
421	G Ruddick	Broughton R	1900–15
420+14	R Batten	Leeds	1963–76
419+14	L Dyl	Leeds	1970–85
419	J Riley	Halifax	1901–15
418	T Rees	Oldham	1928–44
418	J Wright	Swinton	1928–45
417	J McKeown	Whitehaven	1948–61
417	R Schofield	Rochdale H	1901–15
417	P Topping	Widnes	1927–40
417	J Whiteley	Hull	1950–65
416	H Gifford	Barrow	1901–22
415+4	P Charlton	Workington T	1961–80
415	S Owen	Leigh	1951–64
415	E Williams	Leeds	1925–39
414	G Langhorn	Halifax	1898–1913
413+5	T Lowe	Dewsbury	1962–75
413	J Maloney	Liverpool St †	1926–45
413	I Watts	Hull	1945–59
411	B Hudson	Salford	1928–46
411	D John	Salford	1905–22
410+10	D Topliss	Wakefield T	1968–88
410+3	P Flanagan	Hull KR	1960–74
410*	W Goldthorpe	Hunslet	1895–1908
409+9	C Dixon	Salford	1968–80
409	T Vollenhoven	St Helens	1957–68
408	J Feetham	Salford	1929–47
407	A Boardman	Warrington	1898–1914
406+4	J Wolford	Bramley	1962–76
405+2	D Close	Huddersfield	1958–71
405+2	D Watkins	Salford	1967–79
405	J Heaton	Rochdale H	1919–31
405	A Prescott	St Helens	1948–60
402+14	M Adams	Widnes	1971–84
402+6	M Collins	Leigh	1963–75
401	E Caswell	Hull	1919–31
400+7	R Millward	Hull KR	1966–80
400+1	A Hardisty	Castleford	1958–71

† Maloney's figures include games for Wigan Highfield and London Highfield, the direct precursors of Liverpool Stanley.

* Goldthorpe's and Wilson's totals are probably incomplete as some early Hunslet records are unavailable.

200 TRIES FOR A CLUB

740	B Bevan	Warrington	1945–62
478	W Boston	Wigan	1953–68
420	L Cooper	Huddersfield	1947–55
393	E Harris	Leeds	1930–39
392	T Vollenhoven	St Helens	1957–68
368	J Ring	Wigan	1922–31
366	A Rosenfeld	Huddersfield	1909–21
352	J Lewthwaite	Barrow	1943–57
340	J Atkinson	Leeds	1966–82
312	B Nordgren	Wigan	1946–55
297	M Richards	Salford	1969–83
290	J Freeman	Halifax	1954–67
285	L Jones	St Helens	1967–81
284	A Smith	Leeds	1962–83
282	B Hudson	Salford	1928–46
282	E Mills	Huddersfield	1927–35
281	F Castle	Barrow	1949–60
280	A Ellaby	St Helens	1926–39
274	I Southward	Workington T	1952–68
272	N Fox	Wakefield T	1956–74
261	J McLean	Bradford N	1950–56
258	J Leytham	Wigan	1903–12
255	R Markham	Huddersfield	1933–39
253	K Fielding	Salford	1973–83
250	C Sullivan	Hull	1961–85

241	E Ashcroft	Wigan	1942–58
241	D Redfearn	Bradford N	1970–88
240	S Moorhouse	Huddersfield	1909–22
238	S Llewellyn	St Helens	1947–58
234	M Aspey	Widnes	1964–80
231	E Ashton	Wigan	1955–69
228	A Turnbull	Leeds	1948–56
223	J Morley	Wigan	1932–40
217	R Mathias	St Helens	1972–83
215	A Daniels	Halifax	1945–57
215	J Fish	Warrington	1898–1911
212	K Senior	Huddersfield	1962–79
211	P Henderson	Huddersfield	1950–57
211	W Kitchen	Huddersfield	1900–13
210	J Lomas	Salford	1901–23
207	R Millward	Hull KR	1966–80
206	A Hardisty	Castleford	1958–71
204	J Maloney	Liverpool Stanley †	1926–45
201	J Bevan	Warrington	1973–86
200	A Fiddes	Huddersfield	1933–47
200	E Hughes	Widnes	1969–84

† Maloney's figures include tries scored for Wigan Highfield and London Highfield, the direct precursors of Liverpool Stanley.

Nine Huddersfield players have scored 200 or more tries for the club, a record no other club can match. Australian winger Ray Markham rattled up 255 tries in only six years (1933–39).

MICK MARTYN

League's Highest-Scoring Forward

In its earliest days, rugby discounted tries and only goals had value. Once tries became the prime object of the game, it was considered that obtaining them should be left to the backs, while forwards should primarily concern themselves with providing the ball for the backs. There have always been exceptions, of course, and British Rugby League's biggest exception was mighty Mick Martyn, the game's most prolific try-scoring forward.

The game has nurtured exceptionally fast, try-hungry forwards both before and since Mick Martyn cut defences to shreds in the 1950s and 1960s. Bob Taylor, the Hull second-rower who bagged 164 tries for Hull in the post-1920 period, was one truly amazing exception to the 'forwards-are-not-supposed-to-score-tries' dictum, whilst fellow Boulevarder Johnny Whiteley, a classic loose-forward, scored almost as many tries in the 1950s and 1960s. Salford loose-forward Jack Feetham in pre-war days and Hull KR's devastating second-rower of the seventies Phil Lowe are two others who spring readily to mind in the forward try-scoring stakes along with Leeds' Bob Haigh, Salford's Mike Coulman, Warrington's Bob Eccles and a good many more.

None, however, can quite match the record of Mick Martyn, a local boy who became a local hero in Leigh where he played out his entire career. Mick signed for Leigh in November 1952, aged 16. His first team debut, at loose-forward, was delayed until 25 September 1954 when Leigh won

13–11 at Dewsbury. He had to wait a further six months for his next game and it was not until 26 March 1955 against Widnes that he registered the first of his record 213 tries.

Once he got the taste for tries there was, almost literally, no stopping him. Supremely fit,

MICK MARTYN's SCORING RECORD

For Leigh

Season	Games	Tries
1954–55	10	3
1955–56	29	21
1956–57	35	16
1957–58	35	24
1958–59	27	28
1959–60	15	10
1960–61	32	22
1961–62	13	5
1962–63	30	19
1963–64	41	22
1964–65	12	3
1965–66	39	13
1966–67	8+1	3
1967–68	2	–
TOTALS	**328+1**	**189**

1958 Lions

		Tries
18 May	Southern Division	0
4 Jun	Riverina	2
14 Jun	Australia	0
16 Jun	Brisbane	0
22 Jun	Central Queensland	2
25 Jun	Wide Bay	1
28 Jun	Far North Queensland	4
29 Jun	North Queensland	3
9 Jul	Toowoomba	0
13 Jul	NSW North Coast	2
28 Jul	Taranaki	1
2 Aug	Canterbury	2
3 Aug	West Coast	1
5 Aug	North Island	4
11 Aug	Auckland	0
24 Aug	Perth	1
TOTAL	**(16 Games)**	**23**

	Games	Tries
Lancashire	4	1
1959 GB v Australia	1	0
Representative	3	0
CAREER TOTALS	**352+1**	**213 Tries**

enthusiastic and loyal, Martyn quickly established himself as one of the great forwards of his era. His speed in the second-row was extraordinary, his determination legendary. Given a glimmer of an opening Martyn would be through in a flash. If there was no opening he had the strength to create one and his surging, twisting, bumping runs were enough to disconcert any defence. He played in a good pack – Stan Owen, Walt Tabern and Bill Robinson constituted as strong a front-row as any – but 14½ stones of mighty Mick Martyn, head invariably skull-capped, was the sight spectators came to see.

His tearaway, all-action style forced Martyn into Alan Prescott's 1958 Great Britain touring party. Although Martyn only played in the first Australian Test, he wrote his name into the annals of Lions' history on the tour with a series of storming displays which yielded him a record 23 tries in only 16 appearances. No Lions forward before or since has claimed as many.

On his return to England he was no less effective, scoring 28 tries in only 27 games for Leigh in 1958–59. In January and February of 1959 Mick scored tries in 11 consecutive games for Leigh – a record for a forward in British Rugby League. During that run he scored the 100th try of his career when he grabbed Leigh's only try in an 11–7 victory over Oldham on 14 February 1959. The following season he scored his 100th try for Leigh, and by 1963 he had passed the Leigh club record of 149 tries held by winger Bill Kindon.

Although affected by injuries in the second half of his career, Mick Martyn maintained his remarkable try rate and on 9 October 1965 the second of two tries in a 20–12 defeat of Whitehaven at Hilton Park gave him a unique double century of touchdowns. His final tally of 213 tries in 353 games was worthy of a first-rate winger.

The game's most prolific try-scoring forward, Mick Martyn, in his familiar head-gear. Here he is in Lancashire kit alongside Leigh team-mate Walt Tabern.

500 GOALS FOR A CLUB

2317	J Sullivan	Wigan	1921–46
1836	N Fox	Wakefield T	1956–74
1639	K Coslett	St Helens	1962–76
1365	B Ganley	Oldham	1951–61
1244	L Jones	Leeds	1952–64
1241	D Watkins	Salford	1967–79
1210	S Quinn	Featherstone R	1976–88
1192	C Kellett	Hull KR	1956–67
1159	S Hesford	Warrington	1975–85
1083	R Dutton	Widnes	1966–78
1060	V Yorke	York	1954–67
1050	J McKeown	Whitehaven	1948–61
1044	W Langton	Hunslet	1955–66
1043	J Ledgard	Leigh	1948–58
1028	R James	Halifax	1961–71
970	K Gowers	Swinton	1954–73
967	B Jefferson	Keighley	1965–77
958	F Dyson	Huddersfield	1949–63
926	J Wilson	Bramley	1953–64
904	J Woods	Leigh	1976–90
875	A Lunn	Castleford	1951–63
863	N Stephenson	Dewsbury	1968–86
862	M Hodgson	Swinton	1927–40
862	J Thompson	Leeds	1923–33
845	D Noble	Doncaster	1974–89
834	W Holding	Warrington	1928–40
817	H Lockwood	Halifax	1934–46
813	C Tyrer	Wigan	1967–74
812	H Bath	Warrington	1948–57
809	I MacCorquodale	Workington T	1972–80
789	A Risman	Salford	1929–46
778	K Mumby	Bradford N	1973–90
745	A Blan	Swinton	1949–64
743	G Lloyd	Castleford	1970–78
741	W Gowers	Rochdale H	1922–46
741	W Horne	Barrow	1943–59
734	D Whitehead	Warrington	1969–79
727	A Carmichael	Hull KR	1903–18
717	A Risman	Workington T	1946–54
713	L Osbourne	Hull KR	1920–32
710	M Burke	Widnes	1978–86
691	A Goldthorpe	Hunslet	1895–1910
687	J Oliver	Hull	1928–45
677	P Loughlin	St Helens	1984–91
674	J Maloney	Hull	1965–73
673	B Gronow	Huddersfield	1910–28
663	F Griffiths	Wigan	1957–62
661	J Phillips	Bradford N	1950–56
660	T Rees	Oldham	1928–44
654	C Pollard	Wakefield T	1919–31
631	C Hutton	Hull	1951–57
611	B Risman	Leeds	1966–70
607	R Millward	Hull KR	1966–80
594	G Fairbairn	Wigan	1974–81
577	J Walkington	Hunslet	1927–48
573	G Fairbairn	Hull KR	1981–90
566	M Parrish	Oldham	1980–86
558	F Miller	Hull	1933–49
557	C Kellett	Featherstone R	1968–74
556	H Cook	Leeds	1947–53
554	J Holmes	Leeds	1968–89
542	P Bateson	Hull	1957–62

541	W Burgess	Barrow	1919–33
540	J Ferguson	Oldham	1899–1923
539	E Ward	Bradford N	1936–53
535	G Owen	Halifax	1956–61
533	E Rogers	Hull	1906–25
527	R Beardmore	Castleford	1979–89

523	J Kennedy	Hull	1915–26
515	J Bawden	Huddersfield	1943–52
508	I Ball	Barrow	1978–84
508	K Gee	Wigan	1935–54
503	D Fox	Featherstone R	1953–65

Hull KR full-back George Fairbairn evades Castleford centre Gary Hyde in the 1984 Premiership Final. With over 500 goals for both Wigan and Hull KR, Fairbairn is one of only three men to have scored 500 goals for two clubs.

1000 POINTS FOR A CLUB

4883	J Sullivan	Wigan	1921–46	1382	J Lyman	Dewsbury	1913–31
4488	N Fox	Wakefield T	1956–74	1381	G Pimblett	St Helens	1970–79
3413	K Coslett	St Helens	1962–76	1375	E Rogers	Hull	1906–25
2920	L Jones	Leeds	1952–64	1344	L Cooper	Huddersfield	1947–55
2907	D Watkins	Salford	1967–79	1341	T Rees	Oldham	1928–44
2775	B Ganley	Oldham	1951–61	1334	C Hutton	Hull	1951–57
2656	S Quinn	Featherstone R	1976–88	1321	G Fairbairn	Hull KR	1981–90
2489	C Kellett	Hull KR	1956–67	1308	J Leytham	Wigan	1903–12
2416	S Hesford	Warrington	1975–85	1303	J Bawden	Huddersfield	1943–52
2288	B Bevan	Warrington	1945–62	1297	W Davies	Batley	1897–1912
2272	J Woods	Leigh	1976–90	1282	P Larder	Oldham	1968–80
2202	W Langton	Hunslet	1955–66	1282	B Risman	Leeds	1966–70
2195	R Dutton	Widnes	1966–78	1267	G Fairbairn	Wigan	1974–81
2194	J Ledgard	Leigh	1948–58	1266	J Ferguson	Oldham	1899–1923
2191	R James	Halifax	1961–71	1259	J Walkington	Hunslet	1927–48
2133	J McKeown	Whitehaven	1948–61	1256	I Ball	Barrow	1978–84
2116	B Jefferson	Keighley	1965–77	1256	M Parrish	Oldham	1980–86
2105	K Gowers	Swinton	1954–73	1250	J Kennedy	Hull	1915–26
2082	N Stephenson	Dewsbury	1968–86	1244	W Burgess	Barrow	1919–33
2072	F Dyson	Huddersfield	1949–63	1211	E Harris	Leeds	1930–39
2007	A Risman	Salford	1929–46	1202	J Thomas	Wigan	1904–20
1930	A Rhodes	St Helens	1954–69	1182	F Miller	Hull	1933–49
1903	J Wilson	Bramley	1953–64	1178	K Gee	Wigan	1935–54
1894	H Bath	Warrington	1948–57	1176	T Vollenhoven	St Helens	1957–68
1890	C Tyrer	Wigan	1967–74	1169	H Cook	Leeds	1947–53
1883	J Thompson	Leeds	1923–33	1169	J Fish	Warrington	1898–1911
1870	A Lunn	Castleford	1951–63	1161	L Killeen	St Helens	1962–67
1842	J Oliver	Hull	1928–45	1159	C Kellett	Featherstone R	1968–74
1841	M Hodgson	Swinton	1927–40	1154	B Nordgren	Wigan	1946–55
1831	G Lewis	St Helens	1922–36	1141	J Denton	Featherstone R	1921–34
1818	W Horne	Barrow	1943–59	1140	L Gilfedder	Warrington	1951–63
1818	K Mumby	Bradford N	1973–90	1131	E Ward	Wigan	1938–53
1800	I MacCorquodale	Workington T	1972–80	1123	H Box	Featherstone R	1970–80
1741	D Noble	Doncaster	1974–89	1112	J Ring	Wigan	1922–31
1715	A Blan	Swinton	1949–64	1105	W Guerin	Hunslet	1911–28
1686	W Holding	Warrington	1928–40	1102	A Rosenfeld	Huddersfield	1909–21
1652	H Lockwood	Halifax	1934–46	1099	P Bateson	Hull	1957–62
1631	M Burke	Widnes	1978–87	1098	J Lewthwaite	Barrow	1943–57
1616	G Lloyd	Castleford	1969–78	1097	T Clawson	Featherstone R	1957–78
1589	E Ashton	Wigan	1955–69	1096	E Fraser	Warrington	1951–64
1586	B Gronow	Huddersfield	1910–28	1095	J Hoey	Widnes	1922–35
1570	J Lomas	Salford	1901–23	1087	E Davies	Salford	1947–55
1558	P Loughlin	St Helens	1984–91	1086	P Devery	Huddersfield	1947–54
1555	J Holmes	Leeds	1968–89	1082	G Owen	Halifax	1956–61
1547	A Goldthorpe	Hunslet	1895–1910	1073	C Johnson	Leigh	1984–90
1531	A Risman	Workington T	1946–54	1067	T Winnard	Bradford N	1933–44
1516	D Whitehead	Warrington	1969–79	1061	K Dick	Leeds	1975–86
1497	W Gowers	Rochdale H	1922–46	1056	H Dawson	Widnes	1951–62
1492	D Fox	Featherstone R	1953–65	1029	D Creasser	Leeds	1983–91
1492	L Osbourne	Hull KR	1920–32	1029	S Tickle	Barrow	1978–89
1490	A Carmichael	Hull KR	1903–18	1028	F Davies	Huddersfield	1963–76
1463	J Phillips	Bradford N	1950–56	1025	K Fielding	Salford	1973–83
1462	J Maloney	Hull	1965–73	1020	J Atkinson	Leeds	1966–82
1455	F Griffiths	Wigan	1957–62	1000	J Fennell	Featherstone R	1952–65
1448	W Boston	Wigan	1953–68				
1434	C Pollard	Wakefield T	1919–31				
1432	I Southward	Workington T	1952–68				
1425	E Ward	Bradford N	1936–53				
1397	R Beardmore	Castleford	1979–89				

600 APPEARANCES IN A CAREER *All first-class club and representative games included*

928	J Sullivan	Wigan	1921–46
873	A Risman	Salford, Workington T, Batley	1929–54
800+28	N Fox	Wakefield T, Bradford N, Hull KR, York, Bramley, Huddersfield	1956–79
718+9	P Charlton	Workington T, Salford, Blackpool B,	1961–81
713+25	C Dixon	Halifax, Salford, Hull KR	1961–81
690+1	E Ashcroft	Wigan, Huddersfield, Warrington	1942–62
688	B Bevan	Warrington, Blackpool B	1945–64
682	J Ferguson	Oldham	1899–1923
679	J Oliver	Huddersfield, Batley, Hull, Hull KR	1923–45
665	G Carmichael	Hull KR, Bradford N	1929–50
659+24	J Wolford	Bramley, Bradford N, Dewsbury, Hunslet	1962–85
651	J Miller	Warrington, Leigh	1926–47
650+22	J Grayshon	Dewsbury, Bradford N, Leeds, Featherstone R	1970–91
648+43	G Idle	Bramley, Wakefield T, Bradford N, Hunslet, Rochdale H, Sheffield E, Doncaster	1969–91
638+25	J Holmes	Leeds	1968–89
638	S Brogden	Bradford N, Huddersfield, Leeds, Hull, Rochdale H, Salford, Whitehaven	1927–48
637+5	K Mumby	Bradford N, Sheffield E	1973–91
637	K Gee	Wigan	1935–54
634+28	M Aspey	Widnes, Fulham, Wigan, Salford	1964–83
634+8	K Gowers	Swinton	1954–73
633+28	J Joyner	Castleford	1973–91
630	E Batten	Wakefield T, Hunslet, Bradford N, Featherstone R	1933–54
629+11	C Sullivan	Hull, Hull KR, Oldham, Doncaster	1961–85
622	H Wilkinson	Wakefield T	1930–49
620+8	W Benyon	St Helens, Warrington	1962–81
618+13	F Myler	Widnes, St Helens, Rochdale H	1955–73
615+10	G Gunney	Hunslet	1951–73
613+9	T Clawson	Featherstone R, Bradford N, Hull KR, Leeds, Oldham, York, Wakefield T, Huddersfield, Hull	1957–80

Above *Only eight men have played more games than Joe Oliver, one of the finest centres of the inter-war period. Here he poses with the Yorkshire League and Championship cups to which he led Hull in 1935–36.*

611+6	J Atkinson	Leeds, Carlisle	1966–83
611+5	K Elwell	Widnes, Barrow	1969–86
607	A Ackerley	Workington T, Halifax, Hull KR	1946–62
606	L Higson	Wakefield T, Leeds, Bradford N	1927–48
605	C Halliday	Halifax, Huddersfield Keighley	1923–39

Overleaf *Terry Clawson served nine clubs and played over 600 games in a 23-year career (1957–80). An astute forward and a fine goal-kicker, he is pictured in action for Featherstone Rovers in 1978.*

250 TRIES IN A CAREER *All first-class club and representative games included*

796	B Bevan	Warrington, Blackpool B	1945–64
571	W Boston	Wigan, Blackpool B	1953–70
446	A Ellaby	St Helens, Wigan	1926–39
443	E Batten	Wakefield T, Hunslet, Bradford N, Featherstone R	1933–54
441	L Cooper	Huddersfield	1947–55
415	J Ring	Wigan, Rochdale H	1922–33
406	C Sullivan	Hull, Hull KR, Oldham, Doncaster	1961–85
401	J Atkinson	Leeds, Carlisle	1966–83
399	E Harris	Leeds	1930–39
395	T Vollenhoven	St Helens	1957–68
386	A Rosenfeld	Huddersfield, Wakefield T, Bradford N	1909–24
383	J Lewthwaite	Barrow	1943–57
374	I Southward	Workington T, Oldham Whitehaven	1952–69
372	B Hudson	Salford	1928–46
358	N Fox	Wakefield T, Bradford N, Hull KR, York, Bramley, Huddersfield	1956–79
342	M Sullivan	Huddersfield, Wigan, St Helens, York Dewsbury	1952–66
321	J Lawrenson	Wigan, Workington T, Swinton	1939–54
319	E Ashton	Wigan	1955–69
319	E Hanley	Bradford N, Wigan	1978–91
314	J Leytham	Lancaster, Wigan	1901–12
312	B Nordgren	Wigan	1946–55
311	A Smith	Leeds	1962–83
310	J Lomas	Bramley, Salford, Oldham, York	1900–23
304	A Hardisty	Castleford, Leeds	1958–74
302	M Richards	Salford	1969–83
297	F Castle	Barrow	1949–60
294	A Edwards	Salford, Bradford N	1935–49
293	E Ashcroft	Wigan, Huddersfield, Warrington	1942–61
291	J Freeman	Halifax	1954–67
286	L Jones	St Helens	1967–81
284	K Fielding	Salford	1973–83
283	E Mills	Huddersfield	1927–35
279	R Millward	Castleford, Hull KR	1964–80
276	S Brogden	Bradford N, Huddersfield Leeds, Hull, Rochdale H, Salford, Whitehaven	1927–48
276	S Moorhouse	Huddersfield, Bradford N	1909–24
275	A Murphy	St Helens, Leigh, Warrington	1956–75
270	S Wright	Wigan, Widnes	1969–87
268	A Daniels	Halifax, Bradford N	1945–59
267	T O'Grady	Oldham, Wigan, Warrington	1951–62
266	D Topliss	Wakefield T, Hull, Oldham	1968–88
265	F Carlton	St Helens, Wigan	1953–65
263	J McLean	Bradford N	1950–56
261	A Davies	Oldham, Wigan, Wakefield T, Salford	1950–65
257	M Aspey	Widnes, Fulham, Wigan, Salford	1964–83
257	R Markham	Huddersfield	1933–39
257	S Smith	Wakefield T, Leeds	1927–39

Above *The inimitable Wigan winger Billy Boston falls to a tackle by the St Helens pair Cliff Watson and John Mantle in the 1966 Challenge Cup Final. Only Brian Bevan has bettered Boston's tally of 571 tries (1953–70).*

BRIAN BEVAN

League's Most Lethal Try-Scorer

Brian Bevan's try-scoring feats in British and world Rugby League almost beggar description. Arguments will always rage as to who was the greatest winger the game has known. Proponents of genii such as Tom Van Vollenhoven, Lionel Cooper, Billy Boston, Alf Ellaby, Albert Rosenfeld, Johnny Ring, Mick Sullivan, Eric Harris and comparative moderns John Atkinson and Clive Sullivan would all present valid arguments as to why their man was the best. Other names would also enter the lists – Billy Batten, Jim Leytham, Jack Fish, Attie Van Heerden, Alan Edwards, Barney Hudson, Stanley Smith, Brian Nordgren, Jack McLean, Johnny Freeman, Keith Fielding and Martin Offiah, to mention but a few. Wingers have always been the idols of the crowds and have come in all shapes and sizes. To nominate the greatest inevitably invites debate about different circumstances, different styles, different everything!

One winger, however, arguably emerges pre-eminent when all the comparisons have been made. Through sheer volume of tries, which after all are a winger's *raison d'être*, Brian Bevan must be regarded as the deadliest winger in history. Sydney-born Bevan never played Test rugby. He never even played first-grade Sydney Rugby League, although he was a member of the Eastern Suburbs club prior to joining the Royal Australian Navy in 1942. It was English Rugby League's supreme good fortune that

Left *Brian Bevan pursued by Dave Valentine, 1948.*

naval service brought Bevan to England in the winter of 1945–46. Leeds and Hunslet both declined to give the 21-year-old Bevan a trial, but Warrington displayed more sense and after a game for the reserves he was given his first-class debut against Oldham on 17 November 1945 on the right wing.

Nineteen years later he retired, having gathered no fewer than 796 tries for Warrington, Blackpool Borough, Other Nationalities and various representative XIIIs. Bevan's insatiable lust for tries and success in claiming them are clearly reflected in the bare fact that his nearest challenger in the try-scoring stakes, Wigan's Billy Boston, fell over 200 tries short of Bev's total.

Bevan was certainly extraordinary. He did not look athletic or robust, yet he clearly was. He often took the field with his joints swathed in bandages and was reputedly a heavy smoker. Many were unimpressed by his defence. None of that mattered, for he did the business – his business was scoring tries and he did it in the grand manner. Devilishly quick, he would often touch down after length of the field runs and frequently scored in the opposite corner from where he started. His acceleration was obviously God-given and his eccentric running simply baffled opponents. He was a nightmare for opposing wingers, who could rarely anticipate his intentions. It appeared that Bevan could run backwards faster than some players could forwards.

Bevan took the English game by storm. Within four years of his arrival at Warrington he had overhauled the legendary Jack Fish's club record of 215 tries, which had taken Fish 13 years

(1898–1911) to amass. In 1952–53 he set a club record for a season of 66 tries, the fourth time he had broken the club record. The 1953–54 season saw him become the highest try-scorer in the game's history when he passed the 446 tries mark set by the great English Test winger Alf Ellaby (1926–39), whilst 1955 brought him his 500th try.

The great man continued to play for Warrington until 1962, clocking up 740 tries in 620 games for the club as he helped them to lift two Challenge Cups, three Championships, a Lancashire Cup and six Lancashire League Championships. Although never appearing in a Test for his country, Bevan did win international honours in Britain, appearing 16 times (29 tries) for the celebrated Other Nationalities team against England, France and Wales. His career ended in 1964 after two seasons with Blackpool Borough.

BRIAN BEVAN'S TRY-SCORING RECORD

Year	Tries	Position in Try Chart
1945–46	0	–
1946–47	48	1
1947–48	57	1
1948–49	56	2
1949–50	33	5
1950–51	68	1
1951–52	51	4
1952–53	72	1
1953–54	67	1
1954–55	63	2
1955–56	57	2
1956–57	17	–
1957–58	46	3
1958–59	54	2
1959–60	40	3
1960–61	35	4
1961–62	15	–
1962–63	10	–
1963–64	7	–
TOTAL	796	

750 GOALS IN A CAREER *All first-class club and representative games included*

2867	J Sullivan	Wigan	1921–46
2575	N Fox	Wakefield T, Bradford N, Hull KR York, Bramley, Huddersfield	1956–79
1768	C Kellett	Hull KR, Featherstone R	1956–74
1698	K Coslett	St Helens, Rochdale H	1962–79
1677	A Risman	Salford, Workington T Batley	1929–54
1578	S Quinn	York, Featherstone R	1970–88
1560	J Ledgard	Dewsbury, Leigh	1944–61
1499	J Woods	Leigh, Bradford N, Warrington, Rochdale H	1976–90
1478	L Jones	Leeds	1952–64
1398	B Ganley	Oldham	1951–61
1376	R Dutton	Widnes, Whitehaven	1966–81
1342	D Watkins	Salford, Swinton, Cardiff C	1967–83
1306	G Fairbairn	Wigan, Hull KR	1974–90
1272	C Tyrer	Leigh, Wigan, Barrow, Hull KR	1962–78
1189	F Dyson	Huddersfield, Oldham	1949–65
1179	T Clawson	Featherstone R, Bradford N, Hull KR Leeds, Oldham, York, Wakefield T, Huddersfield, Hull	1957–80
1169	S Hesford	Warrington, Huddersfield	1975–86
1154	D Whitehead	Swinton, Oldham, Warrington	1964–79
1127	G Lloyd	Castleford, Hull	1970–83
1092	J McKeown	Whitehaven	1948–61
1081	V Yorke	York	1954–67
1075	K Gowers	Swinton	1954–73
1044	W Langton	Hunslet	1955–66
1030	R James	Halifax	1961–71
1016	I MacCorquodale	Salford, Workington T, Fulham, Blackpool B, Rochdale H	1970–82

Right *Iain MacCorquodale scored 1800 points for Workington Town (1972–80) and kicked a club record 11 goals against Blackpool Borough in 1973. He is pictured here in his days as a Fulham player.*

Left *Oldham full-back Frank Dyson grabs Hull KR winger Graham Paul in a 1964 Challenge Cup semi-final replay at Fartown. Dyson's career with Huddersfield and Oldham (1949–65) yielded 1189 goals.*

998	B Jefferson	Keighley	1965–77
998	J Maloney	Hull, York, Dewsbury, Rochdale H	1965–78
995	M Hodgson	Swinton	1927–42
975	W Holding	Warrington, Workington T	1928–46
963	N Stephenson	Dewsbury, Bradford N, Carlisle, Wakefield T, York, Huddersfield	1968–89
954	L Gilfedder	Warrington, Wigan, Leigh	1951–68
934	J Wilson	Dewsbury, Bramley	1952–64
921	J Thompson	Leeds	1923–33
899	J Phillips	Bradford N, Keighley	1950–59
895	D Marshall	Hunslet, Leeds, Hull	1966–78
894	A Rhodes	St Helens, Leigh, Swinton	1955–69
890	G Owen	Halifax, Keighley	1956–65
886	B Risman	Leigh, Leeds	1961–70
875	A Lunn	Castleford	1951–63
862	E Ward	Bradford N, Castleford, Batley	1936–56
856	H Lockwood	Huddersfield, Halifax	1932–46

854	D Noble	Doncaster, Wakefield T, Hull	1974–89
854	C Whitfield	Salford, Wigan, Halifax, Rochdale H	1979–81
849	G Langfield	Castleford, St Helens, Hull, Bramley	1946–58
849	G Lewis	St Helens	1922–36
848	M Burke	Widnes, Oldham, Keighley	1978–90
843	J Oliver	Huddersfield, Batley, Hull, Hull KR	1923–45
832	H Bath	Barrow, Warrington	1947–57
826	B Gronow	Huddersfield, Batley, Featherstone R	1910–29
810	K Mumby	Bradford N, Sheffield E	1973–91
808	W Gowers	Rochdale H, St Helens	1922–46
808	F Miller	Hull, Featherstone R	1933–52
803	W Horne	Barrow	1942–59
801	C Hutton	Widnes, Hull	1945–57
761	T Griffiths	Hunslet, Doncaster, Halifax, Dewsbury	1946–56

JIM SULLIVAN

Rugby's Greatest Goal-Kicker

In simple terms, Jim Sullivan was the finest full-back and goal-kicker the Rugby League game has ever seen. It is conceivable that his loss at only 17 years of age was Welsh Rugby Union's gravest ever to the professional game. Indeed, many deem him the greatest rugby player of either code in any period. His scoring feats alone indicate a player of rare quality, and he was unquestionably the dominating figure of English Rugby League during the 1920s and 1930s.

Sullivan was born in Cardiff on 2 December 1903, and by the age of 16 he was full-back in Cardiff's First XV. On 28 December 1920 he played for the Barbarians at Newport only 26 days after his 17th birthday, the youngest Barbarian in history. A little while later he was a Welsh trialist, but Wigan recognised his colossal talent and signed him for £750 on 18 June 1921. That was a huge amount at the time, especially for one so young, but it was perhaps the bargain of the century. He made his debut for Wigan on 27 August 1921 and played his last game in the cherry and white against Batley on 23 February 1946. In the intervening years he broke record after record.

Jim's kicking was truly prodigious. He could place, punt and drop-kick vast distances with almost unerring accuracy. His positional play was excellent and he was a resolute tackler. He was also a master tactician and for a full-back in that era was a prolific try-scorer. His scoring feats were staggering. For Wigan alone in 774

appearances, a club record, he scored 2317 goals, 83 tries and 4883 points. In all first-class matches (928) he aggregated 2687 goals, 96 tries and 6022 points. No other player in the history of the sport has made so many appearances or landed so many goals, and only Neil Fox has scored more points.

Perhaps the most telling statistic relating to Jim Sullivan is the fact that between 1921–22 and 1938–39 he never failed to kick at least 100 goals per season, a feat which has never been remotely paralleled and is eloquent testimony indeed to his unsurpassed consistency of performance. In that period he failed only twice, in 1927–28 and 1929–30, to top the goal-kicking charts.

Jim still holds the Rugby League record for kicking most goals in a first-class fixture – 22 for Wigan against Flimby & Fothergill in a first round Challenge Cup tie in 1925, a game Wigan won 116–0. In 1922–23 he broke Ben Gronow's (Huddersfield) records for most goals and points in a season by claiming 161 goals and 349 points. He extended these records to 194 goals and 406 points in 1933–34.

For many years he was an inspirational captain of Wigan and had the distinction of leading the cherry and whites to a 13–2 victory over Dewsbury in the game's first Wembley final in 1929, when he also scored the first points at the stadium. In all he played in 17 major cup finals, including a Yorkshire Cup Final whilst guesting for Dewsbury in 1944.

Jim Sullivan's feats as an

international player remain unchallenged. No one has played as many international matches – he played a record 26 games for Wales, 25 Tests for Great Britain, six games for Other Nationalities and three for England for a total of 60. His international career yielded 160 goals and 3 tries for a total of 329 points. He toured Australasia in 1924, 1928 and 1932, in the latter year as captain of the Lions, but turned down a record fourth tour in 1936.

When his playing days were over, 'Sully' became a master-coach, leading his beloved

JIM SULLIVAN'S GOAL-KICKING CAREER

Season	Goals	Position in Goal Chart
1921–22	100	1
1922–23	161	1
1923–24	158	1
1924–25	138	1
1925–26	131	1
1926–27	148	1
1927–28	104	2
1928–29	107	1
1929–30	110	2
1930–31	133	1
1931–32	117	1
1932–33	146	1
1933–34	194	1
1934–35	165	1
1935–36	117	1
1936–37	117	1
1937–38	135	1
1938–39	124	1
1939–40	66	5
1940–41	40	7
1941–42	49	3
1942–43	49	2
1943–44	7	–
1944–45	0	–
1945–46	5	–
1924 Tour	84	
1928 Tour	52	
1932 Tour	110	
TOTAL	2867	

Wigan to continuous success between 1946 and 1952. He then moved to St Helens where he coached with equal distinc-tion, taking Saints to a Challenge Cup victory for the first time in 1956 and two Championships, in 1953 and 1959. When the Rugby League created its Hall of Fame in 1988, no-one dreamed of opposing the election of Jim Sullivan.

1500 POINTS IN A CAREER *All first-class club and representative games included*

6220	N Fox	Wakefield T, Bradford N, Hull KR, York, Bramley, Huddersfield	1956–79
6022	J Sullivan	Wigan	1921–46
4050	A Risman	Salford, Workington T, Batley	1929–54
3765	J Woods	Leigh, Bradford N, Warrington, Rochdale H	1976–90
3686	C Kellett	Hull KR, Featherstone R	1956–74
3545	K Coslett	St Helens, Rochdale H	1962–79
3445	L Jones	Leeds	1952–64
3438	S Quinn	York, Featherstone R	1970–88
3279	J Ledgard	Dewsbury, Leigh	1944–61
3117	D Watkins	Salford, Swinton, Cardiff C,	1967–82
2902	C Tyrer	Leigh, Wigan, Barrow, Hull KR	1962–78
2894	G Fairbairn	Wigan, Hull KR	1974–90
2844	B Ganley	Oldham	1951–61
2786	R Dutton	Widnes, Whitehaven	1966–81

2574	T Clawson	Featherstone R, Bradford N, Hull KR, Leeds, Oldham, York, Wakefield T Huddersfield, Hull	1957–80
2561	F Dyson	Huddersfield, Oldham	1949–65
2492	N Stephenson	Dewsbury, Bradford N, Carlisle, Wakefield T, York, Huddersfield	1968–89
2456	B Bevan	Warrington, Blackpool B	1945–64
2446	G Lloyd	Castleford, Hull	1970–83
2439	S Hesford	Warrington, Huddersfield	1975–86
2432	D Whitehead	Swinton, Oldham, Warrington	1964–79
2343	J Oliver	Huddersfield, Batley, Hull, Hull KR	1923–45
2334	J Lomas	Bramley, Salford, Oldham, York	1900–23
2315	L Gilfedder	Warrington, Wigan, Leigh	1951–68
2315	K Gowers	Swinton	1954–73
2283	R Millward	Castleford, Hull KR	1964–80
2241	I MacCorquodale	Salford, Workington T, Fulham, Blackpool B, Rochdale H	1970–82
2217	J McKeown	Whitehaven	1948–61
2202	W Langton	Hunslet	1955–66
2201	V Yorke	York	1954–67
2195	R James	Halifax	1961–71
2184	B Jefferson	Keighley	1965–77
2178	A Rhodes	St Helens, Leigh, Swinton	1955–69
2177	E Ward	Bradford N, Castleford, Batley	1936–56
2171	J Maloney	Hull, York, Dewsbury, Rochdale H	1965–78
2146	M Hodgson	Swinton	1927–42
2092	C Whitfield	Salford, Wigan, Halifax, Rochdale H	1979–91
2043	J Thompson	Leeds	1923–33
2002	W Horne	Barrow	1942–59
1992	G Langfield	Castleford, St Helens, Hull, Bramley	1946–58
1987	J Phillips	Bradford N, Keighley	1950–59
1971	W Holding	Warrington, Workington T	1928–46
1965	M Burke	Widnes, Oldham, Keighley	1978–90
1958	H Bath	Barrow, Warrington	1947–57
1934	B Risman	Leigh, Leeds	1961–70
1925	J Wilson	Dewsbury, Bramley	1952–64
1919	E Ashton	Wigan	1955–69
1911	K Mumby	Bradford N, Sheffield E	1973–91
1910	B Gronow	Huddersfield, Batley, Featherstone R	1910–29
1886	D Marshall	Hunslet, Leeds, Hull	1966–78
1870	A Lunn	Castleford	1951–63
1836	G Lewis	St Helens	1922–36

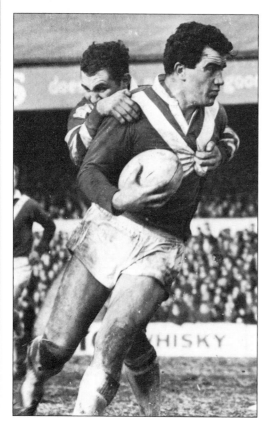

Laurie Gilfedder, scorer of 2315 points (1951–68) for Warrington, Wigan and Leigh.

Mick Burke, a versatile performer in most back positions, scored 1965 points, mostly for Widnes, in a career which has also incorporated spells with Oldham and Keighley.

1830	I Southward	Workington T, Oldham, Whitehaven	1952–69
1800	T Hollindrake	Keighley, Hull, Bramley	1953–70
1798	G Owen	Halifax, Keighley	1956–65
1764	D Noble	Doncaster, Wakefield T, Hull	1974–89
1751	D Fox	Featherstone R, Wakefield T, Batley	1953–71
1733	H Lockwood	Huddersfield, Halifax	1932–46
1727	W Boston	Wigan, Blackpool B	1953–68
1722	C Hutton	Widnes, Hull	1945–57
1716	P Loughlin	St Helens	1984–91
1691	F Miller	Hull, Featherstone R	1933–52
1647	J Holmes	Leeds	1968–89
1631	W Gowers	Rochdale H, St Helens	1922–46
1579	M Parrish	Hunslet, Oldham	1978–86
1579	E Tees	Barrow, Wigan, Rochdale H, Bradford N	1963–73
1577	D Hobbs	Featherstone R, Oldham, Bradford N	1978–91
1564	T Griffiths	Hunslet, Doncaster, Halifax, Dewsbury	1946–56
1553	G Steadman	York, Featherstone R, Castleford	1982–91
1550	J Leytham	Lancaster, Wigan	1901–12
1532	A Carmichael	Hull KR	1903–18
1532	L Osbourne	Hull KR	1920–32
1513	G Carmichael	Hull KR, Bradford N	1929–50

A try for Halifax centre Colin Whitfield at Featherstone. Since his debut in 1979 he has scored over 2000 points for Salford, Wigan, Halifax and Rochdale Hornets.

NEIL FOX

The Points Machine

When Neil Fox made his debut for Wakefield Trinity a few weeks short of his 17th birthday, few could have imagined that he would still be playing 23 years later having scored more points than anyone in the history of the game – he did not score in this first appearance, at Keighley on 10 April 1956, and Trinity lost 5–9. Thereafter, however, Neil's life in Rugby League simply rained caps, cups, medals and points on him.

Neil Fox was one of the most physically powerful centres the game has known, at 6ft 0in and around 15 stones at his peak. Moreover he had the proverbial footballer's brain, sense of

timing and the inclination and capacity to be in the right place at the right time. His tally of 358 tries is testimony to his prowess in the try-scoring sphere, for only the great wingers have ever claimed more. His general play alone would have made him one of history's 'greats', but in addition he had a siege-gun left boot which enabled him to kick his way permanently into the record books, his 2575 goals being second only to Jim Sullivan's 2867.

Neil began his record-breaking in the 1957–58 season, when he rewrote the Wakefield Trinity record book with 344 points from 32 tries and 124 goals, shattering the marks set only the previous season by Test full-back Frank Mortimer. The following two seasons saw him twice hit the 370-points mark for Trinity, and in 1961–62 he established new records of 163 goals and 407 points, which still stand. In all games that season Fox totalled 456 points, a figure at that time second only to Lewis Jones' world record of 496 points.

It was not until 1967 that Neil managed to break Trinity's record for goals in a match (11), although he had previously equalled it. On 26 August 1967 he finally smashed the barrier by landing a dozen goals against Batley. Three tries were thrown in by the rampant centre as he rattled up 33 points that day, another Trinity record which still endures.

Fox's career with Wakefield coincided with the club's finest era. He was a member of three Challenge Cup-winning teams at Wembley, winning the Lance Todd Trophy in 1962 when his

three drop goals and a try were largely instrumental in defeating Huddersfield 12–6. In 1960 he had scored a Cup Final record 20 points in the 38–5 annihilation of Hull, and five goals in a 25–10 victory over Wigan in 1963 brought his tally of Wembley points to a record 38. In 1966–67 and 1967–68 he was a key figure in Wakefield's only Championship-winning seasons.

After a brief spell with Bradford Northern in 1969–70, Neil Fox finally ended his Trinity career on 10 March 1974, when his seven points helped defeat Hull KR 10–7. He was almost 35 and his career at Wakefield had yielded 4488 points (272 tries, 1836 goals), but his playing days were far from over. Five more years were to pass before he was to play his last first-class fixture, aged 40. In the meantime he saw service with Hull KR, York, Bramley, Huddersfield and Bradford Northern, where his career finally ended on 19 August 1979 with Fox kicking a couple of goals in a 22–7 Yorkshire Cup victory at Huddersfield.

Neil's later years saw him make the transition from swashbuckling centre to the pack, where he became a wily, ballhandling back-rower. He clocked up his 6000th point on 4 December 1977 at Doncaster when he kicked the first of three goals for Huddersfield in a 31–8 victory. A month later on 2 January 1978. the second of four goals against Oldham in a 22–15 success at Fartown nudged Fox past Jim Sullivan's record of 6022 points and left him as the most prolific Rugby League scorer in history.

NEIL FOX'S POINTS SCORING RECORD

Season	Tries	Goals	Points
1955–56	0	6	12
1956–57	10	54	138
1957–58	32	124	344
1958–59	28	148	380
1959–60	37	171	453
1960–61	20	94	248
1961–62	30	183	456
1962–63	14	125	292
1963–64	21	125	313
1964–65	13	121	281
1965–66	11	98	229
1966–67	16	144	336
1967–68	18	98	250
1968–69	9	95	217
1969–70	5	17	49
1970–71	12	110	256
1971–72	6	84	186
1972–73	8	138	300
1973–74	8	62	148
1974–75	14	146†	333
1975–76	4	102†	215
1976–77	6	79†	175
1977–78	9	95†	216
1978–79	4	50	112
1979–80	0	2	4
1962 Tour	23	104	277
TOTALS	**358**	**2575**	**6220**

† Includes one one-point drop goal

PLAYERS WHO HAVE SCORED IN EVERY GAME IN A SEASON

Before 1970, scoring in every club match in a season was one of the rarest accomplishments in the Rugby League record books. Only two players had managed the feat in the first three-quarters of a century of the sport's development. Since then, however, 12 further instances have been recorded. Two players have achieved the distinction twice – David Watkins, in consecutive seasons with Salford, and Mick Parrish, the only player to have done it with two clubs.

Season	Player	Position	Apps	Tries	Goals	Points
1932–33	Jim Hoey (Widnes)	Second-rower	41	21	84	231
1958–59	Billy Langton (Hunslet)	Full-back	44	6	181	380
1970–71	Stuart Ferguson (Leigh)	Full-back/winger	48	8	166	356
1972–73	David Watkins (Salford)	Centre	47	17	221	493
1973–74	David Watkins (Salford)	Centre	45	24	182	436
1977–78	John Woods (Leigh)	Centre	34	16	140	328
1979–80	Mick Parrish (Hunslet)	Centre	36	4	95	202
1979–80	Steve Quinn (Featherstone R)	Centre/stand-off	31	17	161+2DG	375
1980–81	John Gorton (Swinton)	Full-back	31	2	92+1DG	191
1981–82	Mick Parrish (Oldham)	Centre	39	17	164	379
1984–85	Peter Wood (Runcorn H)	Full-back	33	4	98+28DG	240
1986–87	David Noble (Doncaster)	Second-rower/prop	33	6	112+2DG	250
1988–89	Mark Aston (Sheffield E)	Scrum-half/stand-off	36	6	135+13DG	307
1989–90	Mike Fletcher (Hull KR)	Centre	35	13	199	450

DG = Drop goals

Steve Quinn played and scored in all Featherstone Rovers' games in 1979–80.

300 TRIES & 300 GOALS

Player	Club	Tries	Goals
Eric Ashton (1955–69)	Wigan	319	481
Neil Fox (1956–79)	Wakefield T, Bradford N, Hull KR, York, Bramley, Huddersfield	358	2575
Jim Leytham (1901–12)	Lancaster, Wigan	314	304
James Lomas (1900–23)	Bramley, Salford, Oldham, York	310	702
Ike Southward (1952–69)	Workington T, Oldham, Whitehaven	374	354

200 TRIES & 200 GOALS

Player	Club	Tries	Goals
Jack Fish (1898–1911)	Warrington	244	282
Terry Hollindrake (1953–70)	Keighley, Hull, Bramley	214	579
Roger Millward (1964–80)	Castleford, Hull KR	279	728
Johnny Lawrenson (1939–54)	Wigan, Workington T, Swinton	321	236
Joe Oliver (1923–45)	Huddersfield, Batley, Hull Hull KR	219	843
Gus Risman (1929–54)	Salford, Workington T, Batley	232	1677
Nigel Stephenson (1968–89)	Dewsbury, Bradford N, Carlisle, Wakefield T, York, Huddersfield	206	963
John Woods (1976–90)	Leigh, Bradford N, Warrington, Rochdale H	227	1499
Garry Schofield (1983–91)	Hull, Leeds	230	270

Alex Murphy, the most free-scoring scrum-half in history. His 37 tries in 1958–59 remains a record for a number 7.

HIGHEST SCORERS IN A SEASON – BY PLAYING POSITION

Tries

Position		Player	Season
Full-back	33	Paul Charlton (Salford)	1972–73
Winger	76	Albert Rosenfeld (Huddersfield)*	1911–12
Centre	48	Steve Halliwell (Leigh)*	1985–86
Stand-off	51	Ellery Hanley (Bradford N)*	1984–85
Scrum-half	37	Alex Murphy (St Helens)	1958–59
Prop	25	Mick Morgan (Carlisle)	1981–82
	25	Tommy David (Cardiff C)*	1982–83
Hooker	21	Len McIntyre (Barrow)	1958–59
Second-rower	40	Bob Haigh (Leeds)	1970–71
Loose-forward	30	Billy Blan (Wigan)*	1949–50
	30	Ellery Hanley (Wigan)*	1986–87

Goals

Position		Player	Season
Full-back	219	Bernard Ganley (Oldham)	1957–58
Winger	157	Sean Day (St Helens)	1984–85
Centre	216	David Watkins (Salford)*	1972–73
Stand-off	152	Peter Metcalfe (St Helens)*	1953–54
	152	John Woods (Warrington)	1987–88
Scrum-half	155	Steve Kerry (Salford)*	1990–91
Prop	148	Vic Yorke (York)	1957–58
Hooker	114	Colin Maskill (Leeds)	1989–90
Second-rower	165	Harry Bath (Warrington)*	1952–53
Loose-forward	202	Kel Coslett (St Helens)*	1971–72

* Indicates player also scored tries or goals from other positions. These are not included in the totals above.

DAVID WATKINS

221 Goals In A Season

David Watkins came into Rugby League in October 1967 as arguably the most celebrated Rugby Union player of the era. Salford had reportedly splashed out £16 000 in signing fees and contract incentives to gain his services. The cost was immense, a record for a signing from either code. In the final analysis, Watkins was a snip at the price – although the little ex-captain of Wales was no instant success as a League player.

Watkins was already 26 when he joined Salford, having graduated through the Cwmcelyn Youth team and Newport to the

Welsh XV. As a wickedly quick fly-half, he won 21 Welsh caps and toured Australasia with the 1966 British Lions, skippering them in two Tests against New Zealand. Consequently there was not much more for him to achieve as a Union player.

As a stand-off in Rugby League, Watkins was not destined for greatness, although he spent his first three years struggling with the position before finding his niche as a centre, despite his lack of size. Nor had he any pedigree as a place-kicker. In Union he had been a match-winning dropper of goals, but in over 200 games for Newport had only place-kicked a dozen goals.

In 1970–71 Salford handed David the goal-kicking job, as much in hope, perhaps, as expectation. The results were astounding. By the close of the season he had booted 155 goals and smashed Gus Risman's club records for goals and points. His style was novel, as he was a round-the-corner-kicker, the vast majority of kickers at that time being traditional toe-enders. Watkins was not the first round-the-corner kicker – the great Barrovian stand-off Willie Horne a generation earlier had been a master of the art, and even earlier York's full-back Tommy Dingsdale had amused crowds by taking the circuitous approach to goal-kicking – but he undoubtedly led the vanguard of this modern kicking vogue.

In 1971–72, the little Welshman with the big right boot belted over 192 goals for Salford, who were now one of the game's glamour clubs, and he was kicking like an automaton. The 1972–73 season would, however, eclipse all that he had achieved so far. On 17 November 1972 David kicked four goals in an 11–16 defeat at Warrington, his last success

bringing him his 100th goal of the season. No one has kicked a quicker century – it had taken 18 games. Only Oldham's Test full-back Bernard Ganley (1957–58) and Featherstone's Steve Quinn (1979–80) have ever emulated Watkins' performance. By the turn of the year he had amassed a staggering 158 goals in 28 games and Salford had won the Lancashire Cup and reached the John Player Trophy Final.

On 6 April 1973 he passed the 200 mark with four goals in a 17–7 beating of Widnes at the Willows. Only Bernard Ganley and Watkins' fellow Welshman Kel Coslett (St Helens, 1971–72) had ever scored a double-century of goals, and although his rate of scoring was slowing, Watkins was beginning to approach Ganley's world record of 219 goals in a season (1957–58). Going into the final league

match of the season, his total stood at 216 as Salford played host to Wigan. Salford won 15–3 and Watkins landed three goals to equal Ganley's record.

There were still the Championship play-offs to negotiate and Salford seemed to have an easy first round tie at home to Rochdale. David Watkins needed only one goal to take Ganley's record and only eight points to pass Lewis Jones' world record 496 points in a season. Few would bet against the prolific little centre achieving both. Sure enough, two goals gave him the goal-kicking record – but Hornets' surprise 14–10 victory left Watkins three points short of Jones' mark and no further chance to overhaul it. Ganley's goals record had gone, however, and almost 20 years later no other player has threatened David Watkins' phenomenal performance of 1972–73.

DAVID WATKINS' RECORD GOAL-KICKING SEASON

1972	Match		Goals	1973	Match		Goals
19 Aug	Leeds	H	5	3 Jan	Bradford N	H	6
23 Aug	Featherstone R	A	3	7 Jan	Rochdale H	A	2
26 Aug	Whitehaven	A	4	12 Jan	Featherstone R	H	4
28 Aug	Swinton	H	1	28 Jan	Featherston R	A	4 CC
1 Sep	Oldham	H	10 LC	2 Feb	Whitehaven	H	4
9 Sep	Leeds	A	2	11 Feb	Barrow	A	5
15 Sep	Rochdale H	H	11 LC	23 Feb	St Helens	H	3
17 Sep	Leigh	A	6	7 Mar	Widnes	A	3
24 Sep	Barrow	A	4 JP	9 Mar	Dewsbury	H	3
29 Sep	Huyton	H	10	16 Mar	St Helens	A	2
3 Oct	Oldham	A	4 FT	24 Mar	Leeds	†	2 JP
6 Oct	Wigan	A	4 LC	30 Mar	Warrington	H	1
8 Oct	Blackpool B	A	5	6 Apr	Widnes	H	4
13 Oct	Blackpool B	H	8	13 Apr	Oldham	H	3
21 Oct	Swinton	*	5 LC	15 Apr	Dewsbury	A	2
5 Nov	Huyton	A	8	17 Apr	Wigan	A	3
10 Nov	Rochdale H	H	6	20 Apr	Swinton	A	7
17 Nov	Warrington	A	4	23 Apr	Wigan	H	3
19 Nov	New Zealanders	H	10	29 Apr	Rochdale H	H	2 PO
24 Nov	Dewsbury	H	4 JP				
26 Nov	Workington T	H	6				
1 Dec	Barrow	H	9	* At Warrington			
10 Dec	Bradford N	H	9 JP	LC Lancashire Cup			
13 Dec	Oldham	A	4	JP John Player Trophy			
15 Dec	Leigh	H	3	FT BBC2 Floodlit Trophy			
24 Dec	Bradford N	A	5	† At Huddersfield			
26 Dec	Workington T	A	3	CC Challenge Cup			
30 Dec	Hull KR	A	5 JP	PO Championship Play-off			

INDIVIDUAL RECORDS

MOST TRIES IN A MATCH

11	G West	Hull K R	v Brookland Rovers	4 Mar 1905
10	L Cooper	Huddersfield	v Keighley	17 Nov 1951
9	R Markham	Huddersfield	v Featherstone R	21 Sep 1935
8	D Thomas	Dewsbury	v Liverpool City	13 Apr 1907
8	A Rosenfeld	Huddersfield	v Wakefield T	26 Dec 1911
8	F Webster*	Leeds	v Coventry	12 Apr 1913
8	L Cooper	Huddersfield	v Yorkshire Amateurs	11 Sep 1948
8	K Williams	Halifax	v Dewsbury	9 Nov 1957
7	J Sedgewick	Bramley	v Normanton	16 Apr 1906
7	J Dechan	Bradford	v Bramley	13 Oct 1906
7	J Miller	Oldham	v Barry	31 Oct 1908
7	A Rosenfeld	Huddersfield	v Swinton Park	28 Feb 1914
7	C Blinkhorn	Australians	v Bramley	9 Nov 1921
7	J Ring	Wigan	v Flimby & Fothergill	14 Feb 1925
7	J Ring	Wigan	v Salford	13 Apr 1925
7	A Walker	Huddersfield	v Bramley	1 Jan 1927
7	J Ring	Wigan	v Pemberton Rovers	12 Feb 1927
7	G Dennis	Hunslet	v Bradford N	20 Jan 1934
7	E Harris	Leeds	v Acton & Willesden	20 Apr 1936
7	J Lewthwaite	Great Britain	v Mackay	2 Jul 1946
7	G Ratcliffe	Wigan	v Liverpool Stanley	23 Aug 1947
7	G Clark	Dewsbury	v Yorkshire Amateurs	13 Sep 1947
7	B Bevan	Warrington	v Leigh	29 Mar 1948
7	L Cooper	Huddersfield	v Yorkshire Amateurs	16 Sep 1948
7	J Hilton	Great Britain	v Western Australia	14 May 1950
7	L Cooper	Huddersfield	v Hull K R	20 Sep 1952
7	B Bevan	Warrington	v Bramley	22 Apr 1953
7	W Boston	Wigan	v Dewsbury	20 Aug 1955
7	I Southward	Workington T	v Blackpool B	17 Sep 1955
7	M Sullivan	Great Britain	v Western Australia	9 Jun 1957
7	M Sullivan	Great Britain	v Perth	24 Aug 1958
7	F Smith	Wakefield T	v Keighley	25 Apr 1959
7	W Boston	Wigan	v Salford	30 Apr 1962
7	C Sullivan	Hull	v Doncaster	15 Apr 1968
7	K Slater	Wakefield T	v Hunslet	6 Feb 1971
7	G Vigo	Wigan	v St Helens	21 Aug 1976

* Fred Webster is the only forward to appear on this list

MOST GOALS IN A MATCH

22	J Sullivan	Wigan	v Flimby & Fothergill	14 Feb 1925
18	M Holland	Huddersfield	v Swinton Park	28 Feb 1914
17	E Ward	Great Britain	v Mackay	2 Jul 1946
17	G Lloyd	Castleford	v Millom	16 Sep 1973
16	P Loughlin	St Helens	v Carlisle	14 Sep 1986
15	A Wood	Great Britain	v South Australia	23 May 1914
15	J Ledgard	Great Britain	v Wide Bay	28 Jun 1950
15	L Jones	Great Britain	v Southern NSW	21 Aug 1954
15	E Fraser	Great Britain	v North Queensland	29 Jun 1958
15	M Stacey	Leigh	v Doncaster	28 Mar 1976
14	A Carmichael	Hull K R	v Merthyr Tydfil	8 Oct 1910
14	J Kennedy	Hull	v Rochdale H	7 Apr 1921
14	H Palin	Warrington	v Liverpool Stanley	13 Sep 1950
14	J Phillips	Bradford N	v Batley	6 Sep 1952
14	B Ganley	Oldham	v Liverpool City	4 Apr 1959
14	B Burton	Halifax	v Hunslet	27 Aug 1972
14	G Lloyd	Hull	v Oldham	10 Sep 1978
14	C Johnson	Leigh	v Keighley	30 Apr 1986
14	S Turner	Rochdale H	v Runcorn H	5 Nov 1989

14	M Fletcher	Hull KR	v Whitehaven	18 Mar 1990
14	C Armstrong	Hull KR	v Nottingham City	19 Aug 1990
13	W Jacques	Hull	v Elland	1 Apr 1899
13	G Lewis	St Helens	v Wardley	16 Feb 1924
13	A Risman	Salford	v Bramley	5 Apr 1933
13	A Risman	Salford	v Broughton R	18 May 1940
13	J Sullivan	Wigan	v Batley	23 Jan 1943
13	L Jones	Leeds	v Blackpool B	19 Aug 1957
13	F Dyson	Huddersfield	v Batley	31 Aug 1957
13	P Fearis	St Helens	v Barrow	14 Feb 1959
13	L Gilfedder	Wigan	v Blackpool B	26 Oct 1963
13	D Watkins	Salford	v Keighley	7 Jan 1972
13	J Woods	Leigh	v Blackpool B	11 Sep 1977
13	G Pimblett	St Helens	v Bramley	5 Mar 1978
13	S Rule	Salford	v Doncaster	4 Sep 1981
13	M Ketteridge	Castleford	v Huddersfield	18 Sep 1988
13	M Knapper	Featherstone R	v Keighley	17 Sep 1989
13	A Platt	Halifax	v Runcorn H	14 Oct 1990

Sammy (Geoff) Lloyd was one of the game's deadliest kickers in the 1970s. One of his most spectacular performances came against amateurs Millom in a 1973 John Player Trophy match when he collected 17 goals and 43 points for Castleford. Here he kicks for goal for Hull at Wembley in 1982.

INDIVIDUAL RECORDS

MOST POINTS IN A MATCH

53	G West	Hull KR	v Brookland R	4 Mar	1905
44	J Sullivan	Wigan	v Flimby & Fothergill	14 Feb	1925
43	G Lloyd	Castleford	v Millom	16 Sep	1973
40	P Loughlin	St Helens	v Carlisle	14 Sep	1986
39	J Lomas	Salford	v Liverpool City	2 Feb	1907
39	M Holland	Huddersfield	v Swinton Park	28 Feb	1914
38	J Woods	Leigh	v Blackpool B	11 Sep	1977
38	R Beardmore	Castleford	v Barrow	22 Mar	1987
36	J Kennedy	Hull	v Keighley	29 Jan	1921
36	M Stacey	Leigh	v Doncaster	28 Mar	1976
36	J Woods	Bradford N	v Swinton	13 Oct	1985
36	G Steadman	Castleford	v Salford	1 Apr	1990
35	J Bawden	Huddersfield	v Swinton	20 Apr	1946
34	E Ward	Bradford N	v Liverpool Stanley	20 Oct	1945
34	E Ward	Great Britain	v Mackay	2 Jul	1946
34	J Wood	Leigh	v York	4 Oct	1947
34	L Cooper	Huddersfield	v Keighley	17 Nov	1951
34	R Beardmore	Castleford	v Leeds	2 Oct	1983
34	M Ketteridge	Castleford	v Huddersfield	18 Sep	1988
34	A Currier	Widnes	v Featherstone R	25 Sep	1988
34	K Iro	Wigan	v Runcorn H	13 Nov	1988
34	J Davies	Widnes	v Whitehaven	26 Aug	1990
33	G Thomas	Warrington	v St Helens	12 Apr	1909
33	A Wood	Great Britain	v South Australia	23 May	1914
33	E Ward	Great Britain	v Western Australia	14 May	1950
33	J Ledgard	Great Britain	v Wide Bay	28 Jun	1950
33	I Southward	Workington T	v Blackpool B	17 Sep	1955
33	N Fox	Wakefield T	v Batley	26 Aug	1967
32	W Harris	Broughton R	v Liverpool City	22 Sep	1906
32	A Risman	Salford	v Bramley	5 Apr	1933
32	A Risman	Salford	v Broughton R	18 May	1940
32	F Dyson	Huddersfield	v Batley	31 Aug	1957
32	N Fox	Great Britain	v Northern NSW	22 Jul	1962
32	C Johnson	Leigh	v Keighley	30 Apr	1986
32	R Rafferty	Sheffield E	v Fulham	21 Sep	1986
32	S Turner	Rochdale H	v Runcorn H	5 Nov	1989
32	G Steadman	Castleford	v Rochdale H	3 Mar	1991
31	J Lomas	Salford	v Goole	29 Mar	1902
31	J Phillips	Bradford N	v Batley	6 Sep	1952
31	L Jones	Leeds	v Bradford N	22 Aug	1956
31	N Fox	Wakefield T	v Batley	4 Apr	1958
31	L Jones	British XIII	v French XIII	20 Jul	1957
31	E Fraser	Great Britain	v Central Queensland	22 Jun	1958
31	B Burton	Halifax	v Hunslet	27 Aug	1972
31	R Millward	Hull KR	v Hunslet	28 Aug	1972
31	I MacCorquodale	Workington T	v Blackpool B	6 Jan	1973
31	G Lloyd	Hull	v Oldham	10 Sep	1978

PROGRESSION OF MATCH SCORING RECORDS

Tries

3	B Pollard	Bradford	v Rochdale H	28 Sep	1985
4	J Hurst	Oldham	v Wakefield T	7 Oct	1895
4	T Martin	Oldham	v Leigh	31 Oct	1896
4	J Butterworth	Runcorn	v Morecambe	13 Feb	1897
5	W Hannah	Hunslet	v Broughton Rec	20 Mar	1897
5	D Traynor	St Helens	v Lees	20 Mar	1897
5	H West	Runcorn	v Warrington Loco	20 Mar	1897
6	F Miles	Salford	v Lees	5 Mar	1898
6	E Bone	Salford	v Goole	29 Mar	1902
6	J Dechan	Bradford	v Widnes	7 Jan	1905
11	G West	Hull KR	v Brookland R	4 Mar	1905

Goals

5	S Lees	Oldham	v Morecambe	16 Jan	1897
8	W Jacques	St Helens	v Lees	20 Mar	1897
8	W Rigg	Rochdale H	v Waterhead H	20 Mar	1897
9	W Phillips	Salford	v Luddendenfoot	18 Mar	1899
10	J Nelson	Broughton R	v Rothwell	18 Mar	1899
13	W Jacques	Hull	v Elland	1 Apr	1899
14	A Carmichael	Hull KR	v Merthyr Tydfil	8 Oct	1910
18	M Holland	Huddersfield	v Swinton Park	28 Feb	1914
22	J Sullivan	Wigan	v Flimby & Fothergill	14 Feb	1925

Points

13	B Sharpe	Liversedge	v St Helens	25 Apr	1896
14	B Sharpe	Liversedge	v Leeds Parish Church	14 Nov	1896
17	R Lockwood	Wakefield T	v Liversedge	12 Dec	1896
19	W Jacques	St Helens	v Lees	20 Mar	1897
19	W Rigg	Rochdale H	v Waterhead H	20 Mar	1897
19	O Badger	Swinton	v Rochdale H	1 Oct	1898
23	J Nelson	Broughton R	v Rothwell	18 Mar	1899
27	W Phillips	Salford	v Luddendenfoot	18 Mar	1899
29	W Jacques	Hull	v Elland	1 Apr	1899
29	J Fish	Warrington	v Goole	24 Mar	1900
31	J Lomas	Salford	v Goole	29 Mar	1902
53	G West	Hull KR	v Brookland R	4 Mar	1905

MOST TRIES IN A SEASON – The Top Hundred

All first-class and representative games included

80	A Rosenfeld	Huddersfield	1913–14		48	S Moorhouse	Huddersfield	1914–15
78	A Rosenfeld	Huddersfield	1911–12		48	J Morley	Wigan	1932–33
72	B Bevan	Warrington	1952–53		48	B Bevan	Warrington	1946–47
71	L Cooper	Huddersfield	1951–52		48	J Freeman	Halifax	1956–57
68	B Bevan	Warrington	1950–51		47	S Williams	Oldham	1900–01
67	B Bevan	Warrington	1953–54		47	T Gleeson	Huddersfield	1913–14
66	L Cooper	Huddersfield	1954–55		47	E Harris	Leeds	1934–35
63	J Ring	Wigan	1925–26		47	R Cracknell	Huddersfield	1951–52
63	E Harris	Leeds	1935–36		47	B Nordgren	Wigan	1952–53
63	J McLean	Bradford N	1951–52		47	I Southward	Workington T	1957–58
63	B Bevan	Warrington	1954–55		47	W Boston	Wigan	1959–60
63	E Hanley	Wigan	1986–87		47	G Austin	Hull KR and Halifax	1990–91
62	T Vollenhoven	St Helens	1958–59		46	L Cooper	Huddersfield	1949–50
61	J McLean	Bradford N	1955–56		46	P Henderson	Huddersfield	1952–53
60	L Cooper	Huddersfield	1948–49		46	B Bevan	Warrington	1957–58
60	L Cooper	Huddersfield	1954–55		46	T Vollenhoven	St Helens	1961–62
60	W Boston	Wigan	1956–57		45	R Brown	Salford	1933–34
60	M Offiah	Widnes	1988–89		45	J Morley	Wigan	1933–34
59	L Cooper	Huddersfield	1950–51		45	E Harris	Leeds	1937–38
59	J McLean	Bradford N	1952–53		45	P Henderson	Huddersfield	1954–55
59	T Vollenhoven	St Helens	1960–61		45	M Davies	Bradford N	1957–58
58	E Harris	Leeds	1930–31		45	J Stopford	Swinton	1963–64
57	E Harris	Leeds	1932–33		45	G Prohm	Hull KR	1984–85
57	B Bevan	Warrington	1947–48		45	M Offiah	Widnes	1989–90
57	B Nordgren	Wigan	1949–50		44	J Leytham	Wigan	1907–08
57	B Bevan	Warrington	1955–56		44	W Curran	Wigan	1914–15
56	A Rosenfeld	Huddersfield	1912–13		44	L Brown	Wigan	1928–29
56	A Rosenfeld	Huddersfield	1914–15		44	E Mills	Huddersfield	1928–29
56	B Bevan	Warrington	1948–49		44	R Hardgrave	St Helens	1931–32
55	A Ellaby	St Helens	1926–27		44	W Rosenberg	Leeds	1960–61
55	E Hanley	Bradford N	1984–85		44	M Offiah	Widnes	1987–88
54	S Moorhouse	Huddersfield	1911–12		43	S Moorhouse	Huddersfield	1912–13
54	J Ring	Wigan	1924–25		43	A Ellaby	St Helens	1930–31
54	B Bevan	Warrington	1958–59		43	R Markham	Huddersfield	1933–34
54	W Boston	Wigan	1958–59		43	J Etty	Oldham	1956–57
54	T Vollenhoven	St Helens	1959–60		43	W Boston	Wigan	1957–58
53	R Markham	Huddersfield	1935–36		43	T Lake	Wigan	1963–64
52	J Harrison	Hull	1914–15		42	E Harris	Leeds	1931–32
52	F Castle	Barrow	1951–52		42	B Nordgren	Wigan	1950–51
52	J McLean	Bradford N	1953–54		42	A Turnbull	Leeds	1954–55
51	J Lewthwaite	Barrow	1956–57		42	F Carlton	St Helens	1955–56
51	B Bevan	Warrington	1951–52		42	G Dunn	Hull KR	1974–75
51	W Boston	Wigan	1961–62					
50	E Mills	Huddersfield	1931–32					
50	L Cooper	Huddersfield	1952–53					
50	M Sullivan	Huddersfield and Wigan	1957–58					
49	J Miller	Wigan	1908–09					
49	W Williams	Halifax	1908–09					
49	R Farrar	Oldham	1921–22					
49	J Ring	Wigan	1923–24					
49	J Ring	Wigan	1926–27					
49	J Morley	Wigan	1934–35					
49	G Ratcliffe	Wigan	1947–48					
49	J Lawrenson	Workington T	1951–52					
49	W Boston	Wigan	1955–56					
49	K Fielding	Salford	1973–74					
49	S Halliwell	Leigh	1985–86					
49	M Offiah	Widnes	1990–91					
48	J Leytham	Wigan	1909–10					

MOST GOALS IN A SEASON – The Top Hundred

All first-class club and representative games included

221	D Watkins	Salford	1972–73		154	B Risman	Leeds	1967–68
219	B Ganley	Oldham	1957–58		153	H Bath	Warrington	1953–54
214	K Coslett	St Helens	1971–72		153	P Metcalfe	St Helens	1953–54
199	M Fletcher	Hull KR	1989–90		152	G Pimblett	St Helens	1976–77
194	J Sullivan	Wigan	1933–34		152	S Quinn	Featherstone R	1976–77
194	L Jones	Leeds	1956–57		152	J Woods	Warrington	1987–88
193	K Coslett	St Helens	1970–71		150	C Kellett	Hull KR	1964–65
193	D Watkins	Salford	1971–72		149	H Palin	Warrington	1948–49
190	B Ganley	Oldham	1958–59		149	G Langfield	St Helens	1952–53
190	L Hopkins	Workington T	1981–82		149	J McKeown	Whitehaven	1956–57
190	P Loughlin	St Helens	1986–87		149	N Stephenson	Dewsbury	1972–73
189	B Ganley	Oldham	1956–57		149	G Lloyd	Castleford	1975–76
183	N Fox	Wakefield T	1961–62		149	G Pimblett	St Helens	1975–76
183	F Griffiths	Wigan	1961–62		149	J Woods	Leigh	1977–78
183	D Watkins	Salford	1973–74		148	B Gronow	Huddersfield	1919–20
181	W Langton	Hunslet	1958–59		148	J Sullivan	Wigan	1926–27
178	J Ledgard	Leigh	1954–55		148	F Dyson	Huddersfield	1956–57
178	G Pimblett	St Helens	1977–78		148	V Yorke	York	1957–58
177	S Kerry	Salford	1990–91		148	N Fox	Wakefield T	1958–59
176	F Griffiths	Wigan	1958–59		148	L Killeen	St Helens	1966–67
175	D Watkins	Salford	1975–76		148	R Dutton	Widnes	1975–76
173	E Tees	Bradford N	1971–72		148	M Aston	Sheffield E	1988–89
173	C Johnson	Leigh	1985–86		147	T Griffiths	Halifax	1955–56
172	G Lloyd	Hull	1978–79		147	S Hesford	Warrington	1980–81
171	N Fox	Wakefield T	1959–60		146	J Sullivan	Wigan	1932–33
171	A Rhodes	St Helens	1959–60		146	N Fox	Hull KR	1974–75
170	H Bath	Warrington	1952–53		146	G Fairbairn	Wigan	1975–76
170	S Hesford	Warrington	1978–79		145	P Devery	Huddersfield	1952–53
169	B Ganley	Oldham	1959–60		145	A Rhodes	St Helens	1956–57
168	D Whitehead	Warrington	1973–74		145	G Owen	Halifax	1959–60
168	G Fairbairn	Hull KR	1981–82		145	A Rhodes	St Helens	1960–61
167	C Tyrer	Wigan	1969–70		145	C Kellett	Hull KR	1966–67
166	C Hutton	Hull	1956–57		145	P Loughlin	St Helens	1989–90
166	S Ferguson	Leigh	1970–71		144	N Fox	Wakefield T	1966–67
165	J Sullivan	Wigan	1934–35		143	J Phillips	Bradford N	1953–54
165	P Fearis	St Helens	1958–59		143	T Price	Bradford N	1968–69
165	B Risman	Leeds	1968–69		142	C Kellett	Hull KR	1962–63
165	B Jefferson	Keighley	1973–74		142	R Beardmore	Castleford	1983–84
164	M Parrish	Oldham	1981–82		142	S Hesford	Warrington	1983–84
163	B Risman	Leeds	1966–67		141	E Ward	Wigan	1947–48
163	G Lloyd	Castleford	1976–77		141	J Ledgard	Leigh	1951–52
163	S Quinn	Featherstone R	1979–80		141	L Killeen	St Helens	1964–65
162	K Coslett	St Helens	1972–73		141	C Tyrer	Wigan	1970–71
161	J Sullivan	Wigan	1922–23		141	G Fairbairn	Hull KR	1984–85
161	P Bateson	Hull	1959–60					
161	K Coslett	St Helens	1969–70					
160	E Tees	Bradford N	1972–73					
159	J Holmes	Leeds	1970–71					
158	J Sullivan	Wigan	1923–24					
158	K Coslett	St Helens	1968–69					
158	S Hesford	Warrington	1977–78					
158	J Woods	Leigh	1981–82					
157	S Day	St Helens	1984–85					
156	K Coslett	St Helens	1962–63					
155	E Ward	Wigan	1948–49					
155	H Cook	Leeds	1950–51					
155	J Ledgard	Leigh	1955–56					
155	D Watkins	Salford	1970–71					
154	H Bath	Warrington	1955–56					

ALBERT ROSENFELD

80 Tries In A Season

Albert Aaron Rosenfeld set a record back in 1913–14 which has survived the ravages of time and seems unlikely to be broken in the foreseeable future. He scored 80 tries for Huddersfield in that season before the Great War sickened and devastated Europe. Huddersfield in that period had produced a team against which all other teams aspiring to greatness have since been measured. Harold Wagstaff's 'Team of All the Talents', the legendary Claret and Golds, had been recruited from all corners of the rugby-playing world. They were so entrancing in their style of play, and so successful in gathering trophies, that even three-quarters of a century after their heyday they are still regarded as perhaps the finest of all Rugby League teams.

Rosenfeld had come from Australia to join Huddersfield in 1909. His first taste of the Northern Union (Rugby League) game in England had come the previous year when he had been a member of the first Kangaroo touring team, for whom he had scored five tries in 15 games. He had made his name in Australia as a five-eighth (stand-off), appearing in that position in all three Tests against New Zealand prior to the 1908 tour. Although it was to be as a devastatingly clinical winger that 'Rozzy' was to be lionised in Huddersfield, the Fartown club initially used him in the centre.

In his second season in England (1910–11) Huddersfield decided that his talents would be best employed on the wing. At barely 5ft 6in and 12 stones, Rosenfeld was no giant and centre was probably too physically demanding for the little Australian. On the wing, however, he was in his element – a perfect running machine at the end of a sublime back-line – and the tries came at a rare rate. Thirty-five in his first season on the flank was a quick dividend, but the following season saw him shatter all the records when he ran in 78 tries, including eight against Wakefield Trinity on Boxing Day. Only Dai Thomas of Dewsbury had ever scored as many tries in a league fixture. In all he scored three or more tries in 11 games. In the last four seasons before the Great War brought competitive football to a close, little Abe scored well over 250 tries and topped the try-scoring lists without fail.

By 1913–14 Huddersfield

had become well-nigh unbeatable. A powerful and unselfish pack included titans such as Ben Gronow, Douglas Clark, Jack Chilcott, Fred Longstaff, Aaron Lee, Willie Higson and Arthur Swinden. Behind them, Welsh halves Jim Davies and Johnny Rogers provided the ammunition for a three-quarter line which has probably never been bettered at club level. Harold Wagstaff and Stanley Moorhouse – both locals – formed the left-wing pairing, whilst on the right, Rosenfeld's centre was Tommy Gleeson, a fiery fellow Australian.

Rosenfeld had scored a dozen tries in his first four games in 1913 and soon afterwards hit a purple patch in which he scored in 14 consecutive matches, a record which was not beaten until Leeds' Eric Harris, also an Australian, scored in 17 consecutive games in 1935–36. In

those 14 games Rosenfeld bagged 33 tries, including one in Huddersfield's 19–3 victory over Bradford Northern in the Yorkshire Cup Final at Halifax.

By the beginning of 1914 Rosenfeld's try tally was 47 from a mere 22 games and at that rate he was odds-on to break his own record. Five tries against Bramley and seven against amateurs Swinton Park in a record 119–2 victory in the Challenge Cup gave him a glimpse of the record, which he duly equalled with a hat-trick in a 28–0 home win over Keighley on 25 March 1914. Three days later at Fartown a solitary try in a 29–5 drubbing of Hull Kingston broke the old record, and the 80th followed in a 5–8 defeat at Bradford on 30 March. It is said that records are made to be broken. Rozzy's may well be the exception that proves the rule.

ALBERT ROSENFELD'S RECORD TRY-SCORING SEASON

1913			Tries	1914			Tries
6 Sep	York	A	4	1 Jan	St Helens	A	0
8 Sep	Warrington	H	2	3 Jan	Warrington	A	0
13 Sep	Leeds	H	5	10 Jan	York	H	3
20 Sep	Halifax	A	1	17 Jan	Keighley	A	2
27 Sep	Batley	A	0	24 Jan	Dewsbury	H	1
4 Oct	Oldham	H	2	31 Jan	Batley	H	0
11 Oct	Rochdale H	A	0	7 Feb	Oldham	A	0
18 Oct	Bramley	H	2 YC	14 Feb	Bramley	H	5
25 Oct	Dewsbury	A	4	21 Feb	Wigan	H	3
1 Nov	Halifax	A	2 YC	28 Feb	Swinton Park	H	7 CC
8 Nov	Wigan	A	1	7 Mar	Wakefield T	A	2
15 Nov	Dewsbury	H	3 YC	14 Mar	Hull KR	A	2 CC
19 Nov	Bradford N	H	3	18 Mar	Bramley	A	3
22 Nov	Leeds	A	3	21 Mar	Widnes	H	0 CC
29 Nov	Bradford N	*	1 YC	25 Mar	Keighley	H	3
3 Dec	Halifax	H	3	28 Mar	Hull KR	H	1
6 Dec	Hunslet	A	2	30 Mar	Bradford N	A	1
13 Dec	Rochdale H	H	3	4 Apr	Hull	†	0 CC
20 Dec	Hull KR	A	2	11 Apr	Hull	H	DNP
25 Dec	Hull	A	1	13 Apr	St Helens	H	0
26 Dec	Wakefield T	H	3	20 Apr	Hull	H	DNP PO
27 Dec	Hunslet	H	0	25 Apr	Salford	†	0 PO

* At Halifax	CC Challenge Cup
YC Yorkshire Cup	PO Championship Play-off
† At Headingley	DNP Did not play

MOST POINTS IN A SEASON – The Top Hundred

All first-class club and representative games included

496	L Jones	Leeds	1956–57		341	B Ganley	Oldham	1959–60
493	D Watkins	Salford	1972–73		341	G Lloyd	Castleford	1976–77
476	D Watkins	Salford	1971–72		338	A Rhodes	St Helens	1960–61
456	N Fox	Wakefield T	1961–62		337	J Ledgard	Leigh	1955–56
453	B Ganley	Oldham	1957–58		336	L Killeen	St Helens	1965–66
453	N Fox	Wakefield T	1959–60		336	N Fox	Wakefield T	1966–67
452	K Coslett	St Helens	1971–72		334	S Hesford	Warrington	1977–78
450	M Fletcher	Hull KR	1989–90		334	R Beardmore	Castleford	1983–84
446	L Hopkins	Workington T	1981–82		333	N Fox	Hull KR	1974–75
438	D Watkins	Salford	1973–74		332	B Gronow	Huddersfield	1919–20
427	S Kerry	Salford	1990–91		332	B Risman	Leeds	1967–68
424	P Loughlin	St Helens	1986–87		331	N Stephenson	Dewsbury	1970–71
406	J Sullivan	Wigan	1933–34		330	J Holmes	Leeds	1970–71
400	C Johnson	Leigh	1985–86		330	K Coslett	St Helens	1972–73
399	A Rhodes	St Helens	1959–60		329	E Tees	Bradford N	1972–73
395	K Coslett	St Helens	1970–71		328	P Bateson	Hull	1959–60
394	F Griffiths	Wigan	1958–59		328	M Stacey	Leigh	1975–76
390	F Griffiths	Wigan	1961–62		328	S Quinn	Featherstone R	1976–77
385	C Tyrer	Wigan	1969–70		326	D Stephenson	Wigan	1985–86
385	D Watkins	Salford	1975–76		325	K Coslett	St Helens	1969–70
384	B Ganley	Oldham	1956–57		324	F Botica	Wigan	1990–91
383	B Ganley	Oldham	1958–59		322	H Palin	Warrington	1948–49
381	G Pimblett	St Helens	1977–78		322	H Cook	Leeds	1950–51
380	N Fox	Wakefield T	1958–59		322	G Langfield	St Helens	1952–53
380	W Langton	Hunslet	1958–59		322	K Coslett	St Helens	1968–69
379	H Bath	Warrington	1952–53		321	K Coslett	St Helens	1962–63
379	M Parrish	Oldham	1981–82		320	J Sullivan	Wigan	1926–27
376	N Stephenson	Dewsbury	1972–73		320	L Jones	Leeds	1957–58
375	S Quinn	Featherstone R	1979–80		319	J Sullivan	Wigan	1923–24
374	J Ledgard	Leigh	1954–55		319	S Lowden	Salford and Workington T	1959–60
373	G Lloyd	Hull	1978–79					
372	J Woods	Leigh	1981–82		318	H Bath	Warrington	1953–54
369	P Metcalfe	St Helens	1953–54		318	G Steadman	York	1984–85
369	G Fairbairn	Hull KR	1981–82		316	G Lloyd	Castleford	1975–76
366	S Hubbard	Hull KR	1979–80		316	M Burke	Widnes	1978–79
365	A Rhodes	St Helens	1956–57		316	G Fairbairn	Hull KR	1984–85
364	E Tees	Bradford N	1971–72		315	C Tyrer	Wigan	1968–69
362	S Day	St Helens	1984–85		313	W Horne	Barrow	1951–52
361	E Ward	Wigan	1948–49		313	N Fox	Wakefield T	1963–64
360	L Killeen	St Helens	1964–65		313	G Pimblett	St Helens	1976–77
358	D Watkins	Salford	1970–71		312	E Ward	Wigan	1947–48
358	J Woods	Leigh	1977–78		312	C Tyrer	Wigan	1970–71
358	P Loughlin	St Helens	1989–90		311	F Dyson	Huddersfield	1956–57
356	S Ferguson	Leigh	1970–71		311	G Pimblett	St Helens	1975–76
355	J Woods	Leigh	1983–84		310	J Phillips	Bradford N	1953–54
354	B Jefferson	Keighley	1973–74		310	S Hesford	Warrington	1980–81
353	L Killeen	St Helens	1966–67					
351	J Woods	Warrington	1987–88					
350	H Bath	Warrington	1955–56					
349	J Sullivan	Wigan	1922–23					
348	J Sullivan	Wigan	1934–35					
347	B Risman	Leeds	1966–67					
345	B Risman	Leeds	1968–69					
345	D Whitehead	Warrington	1973–74					
344	N Fox	Wakefield T	1957–58					
342	S Hesford	Warrington	1978–79					
342	J Davies	Widnes	1990–91					
341	P Devery	Huddersfield	1952–53					

PROGRESSION OF SCORING RECORDS FOR A SEASON

Tries

28	J Hurst	Oldham	1895–96
30	J Hoskins	Salford	1897–98
39	S Williams	Oldham	1898–99
47	S Williams	Oldham	1900–01
49	J Miller	Wigan	1908–09
49	W Williams	Halifax	1908–09
78	A Rosenfeld	Huddersfield	1911–12
80	A Rosenfeld	Huddersfield	1913–14

Goals

35	G Lorimer	Manningham	1895–96
66	A Goldthorpe	Hunslet	1897–98
67	A Goldthorpe	Hunslet	1898–99
75	W James	Broughton R	1901–02
86	J Lomas	Salford	1906–07
101	A Goldthorpe	Hunslet	1907–08
129	A Carmichael	Hull KR	1910–11
131	M Holland	Huddersfield	1913–14
140	B Gronow	Huddersfield	1914–15
148	B Gronow	Huddersfield	1919–20

161	J Sullivan	Wigan	1922–23
194	J Sullivan	Wigan	1933–34
194	L Jones	Leeds	1956–57
219	B Ganley	Oldham	1957–58
221	D Watkins	Salford	1972–73

Points

106	F Cooper	Bradford	1895–96
106	G Lorimer	Manningham	1895–96
112	A Rigg	Halifax	1896–97
135	A Goldthorpe	Hunslet	1897–98
169	W Jacques	Hull	1898–99
172	J Lomas	Salford	1901–02
222	J Lomas	Salford	1903–04
280	J Lomas	Salford	1906–07
292	B Gronow	Huddersfield	1914–15
332	B Gronow	Huddersfield	1919–20
349	J Sullivan	Wigan	1922–23
406	J Sullivan	Wigan	1933–34
496	L Jones	Leeds	1956–57

Welsh forward Ben Gronow (Huddersfield) twice broke the record for most goals in a season, in 1914–15 and 1919–20. In the latter season he became the first player to break the 300-point barrier.

THE LEADING SCORERS – SEASON BY SEASON

Tries	Goals	Points
1895–96		
28 J Hurst (Oldham)	35 G Lorimer (Manningham)	106 F Cooper (Bradford)
20 A Boothroyd (Huddersfield)	34 F Cooper (Bradford)	106 G Lorimer (Manningham)
18 A Rigg (Halifax)	28 S Lees (Oldham)	94 J Hurst (Oldham)
1896–97		
19 W Hannah (Hunslet)	26 A Goldthorpe (Hunslet)	112 A Rigg (Halifax)
18 A Rigg (Halifax)	26 B Sharpe (Liversedge)	85 A Goldthorpe (Hunslet)
17 D Traynor (St Helens)	24 A Rigg (Halifax)	81 B Sharpe (Liversedge)
1897–98		
30 J Hoskins (Salford)	66 A Goldthorpe (Hunslet)	135 A Goldthorpe (Hunslet)
29 T Williams (Salford)	37 F Cooper (Bradford)	107 T Williams (Salford)
21 J Hurst (Oldham)	30 S Lees (Oldham)	98 F Cooper (Bradford)
1898–99		
39 S Williams (Oldham)	67 A Goldthorpe (Hunslet)	169 W Jacques (Hull)
31 T Davies (Oldham)	65 W Jacques (Hull)	161 A Goldthorpe (Hunslet)
24 T Jackson (Broughton R)	40 F Cooper (Bradford)	120 WP Davies (Batley)
24 C Lempriere (Hull)		
1899–1900		
36 S Williams (Oldham)	39 F Cooper (Bradford)	108 S Williams (Oldham)
27 T Davies (Oldham)	31 J Metcalfe (Wakefield T)	107 WP Davies (Batley)
26 J Lewis (Swinton)	30 A Goldthorpe (Hunslet)	105 F Cooper (Bradford)
	30 F Lorriman (Huddersfield)	
1900–01		
47 S Williams (Oldham)	44 A Goldthorpe (Hunslet)	141 S Williams (Oldham)
28 L Deere (Huddersfield)	39 W James (Broughton R)	134 J Fish (Warrington)
24 J Fish (Warrington)	38 WP Davies (Batley)	115 F Cooper (Bradford)
24 B Pollard (Bradford)	38 A Starks (Hull KR)	
1901–02		
38 R Wilson (Broughton R)	75 W James (Broughton R)	172 J Lomas (Salford)
29 J Barr (Wigan)	53 J Lomas (Salford)	159 W James (Broughton R)
23 A Hogg (Broughton R)	53 J Metcalfe (Wakefield T)	115 J Fish (Warrington)
1902–03		
25 W Evans (Leeds)	48 A Goldthorpe (Hunslet)	136 WP Davies (Batley)
22 J Jenkins (Leeds)	47 WP Davies (Batley)	119 F Blincow (Rochdale H)
21 T Gartrell (Millom)	46 F Blincow (Rochdale H)	108 J Lomas (Salford)
1903–04		
34 A Hogg (Broughton R)	66 J Lomas (Salford)	222 J Lomas (Salford)
30 J Lomas (Salford)	44 P Mosby (Bradford)	149 J Fish (Warrington)
25 J Fish (Warrington)	37 J Fish (Warrington)	112 P Mosby (Bradford)
1904–05		
31 J Dechan (Bradford)	47 J Ferguson (Oldham)	146 J Lomas (Salford)
28 G West (Hull KR)	43 J Lomas (Salford)	122 W Harris (Broughton R)
22 W Harris (Broughton R)	42 A Goldthorpe (Hunslet)	106 G West (Hull KR)
22 J Leytham (Wigan)		
1905–06		
40 J Leytham (Wigan)	50 J Ferguson (Oldham)	160 J Leytham (Wigan)
31 A Hogg (Broughton R)	49 A Goldthorpe (Hunslet)	138 J Lomas (Salford)
28 R Wilson (Broughton R)	45 J Mason (Wigan)	115 W Harris (Broughton R)
1906–07		
40 P Eccles (Halifax)	86 J Lomas (Salford)	280 J Lomas (Salford)
40 D Thomas (Dewsbury)	83 W Harris (Broughton R)	250 W Harris (Broughton R)
36 J Lomas (Salford)	75 R Walker (Keighley)	203 J Leytham (Wigan)
1907–08		
44 J Leytham (Wigan)	101 A Goldthorpe (Hunslet)	217 A Goldthorpe (Hunslet)
31 D Thomas (Dewsbury/Halifax)	81 A Carmichael (Hull KR)	196 J Leytham (Wigan)
30 J Fish (Warrington)	61 J Ferguson (Oldham)	165 A Carmichael (Hull KR)
1908–09		
49 J Miller (Wigan)	88 J Lomas (Salford)	272 J Lomas (Salford)
49 W Williams (Halifax)	78 A Carmichael (Hull KR)	267 J Leytham (Wigan)
39 J Leytham (Wigan)	76 W Little (Halifax)	185 E Rogers (Hull)

Tries

1909–10
48 J Leytham (Wigan)
37 G Smith (Oldham)
33 J Flanagan (St Helens)

1910–11
41 W Kitchen (Huddersfield)
40 J Miller (Wigan)
38 A Rosenfeld (Huddersfield)

1911–12
78 A Rosenfeld (Huddersfeld)
54 S Moorhouse (Huddersfield)
28 W Batten (Hunslet)

1912–13
56 A Rosenfeld (Huddersfield)
43 S Moorhouse (Huddersfield)
37 L Bradley (Wigan)
37 W Rhodes (Dewsbury)

1913–14
80 A Rosenfeld (Huddersfield)
47 T Gleeson (Huddersfield)
39 L Bradley (Wigan)

1914–15
56 A Rosenfeld (Huddersfield)
52 J Harrison (Hull)
48 S Moorhouse (Huddersfield)

1915–16, 1916–17, 1917–18
No official games played

Goals

78 A Carmichael (Hull KR)
63 E Rogers (Hull)
57 J Lomas (Salford)

129 A Carmichael (Hull KR)
62 A Wood (Oldham)
61 J Metcalfe (Wakefield T)

127 A Carmichael (Hull KR)
96 T Grey (Huddersfield)
72 E Rogers (Hull)

94 A Carmichael (Hull KR)
84 J Thomas (Wigan)
50 E Rogers (Hull)

131 M Holland (Huddersfield)
83 J Thomas (Wigan)
71 E Rogers (Hull)

140 B Gronow (Huddersfield)
100 E Rogers (Hull)
77 J Thomas (Wigan)

Points

234 J Leytham (Wigan)
192 J Lomas (Salford)
183 E Rogers (Hull)

261 A Carmichael (Hull KR)
181 J Leytham (Wigan)
157 E Rogers (Hull)

254 A Carmichael (Hull KR)
234 A Rosenfeld (Huddersfield)
219 T Grey (Huddersfield)

198 J Thomas (Wigan)
191 A Carmichael (Hull KR)
168 A Rosenfeld (Huddersfield)

268 M Holland (Huddersfield)
240 A Rosenfeld (Huddersfield)
190 J Thomas (Wigan)

292 B Gronow (Huddersfield)
203 E Rogers (Hull)
179 T Barton (St Helens)

Hull centre Jim Kennedy who topped the leading goals and points lists in 1918–19 and 1920–21. Kennedy captained Hull to consecutive Championships in 1919–20 and 1920–21.

INDIVIDUAL RECORDS

Tries	Goals	Points

1918–19
Official games January–May only

Tries	Goals	Points
25 A Francis (Hull)	54 J Kennedy (Hull)	135 J Kennedy (Hull)
17 W Batten (Hull)	29 W Bradshaw (Hull KR)	75 A Francis (Hull)
15 J Holdsworth (Hull)	20 J Matthews (Widnes)	67 W Bradshaw (Hull KR)
15 F Williams (Halifax)	20 F Mirfield (Leeds)	

1919–20

39 S Moorhouse (Huddersfield)	148 B Gronow (Huddersfield)	332 B Gronow (Huddersfield)
38 A Francis (Hull)	86 J Kennedy (Hull)	217 J Kennedy (Hull)
31 A Rosenfeld (Huddersfield)	45 A Brough (Barrow)	123 A Brough (Barrow)
31 J Wallace (Barrow)	45 J Ferguson (Oldham)	

1920–21

41 W Stone (Hull)	108 J Kennedy (Hull)	264 J Kennedy (Hull)
22 J Brittain (Leeds)	65 W Rhodes (Dewsbury)	143 B Gronow (Huddersfield)
21 B Williams (Batley)	62 C Garforth (Halifax)	141 W Stone (Hull)

1921–22

49 R Farrar (Oldham)	100 J Sullivan (Wigan)	211 R Farrar (Oldham)
28 J Bacon (Leeds)	83 B Gronow (Huddersfield)	203 J Sullivan (Wigan)
24 C Stacey (Halifax)	76 J Kennedy (Hull)	193 B Gronow (Huddersfield)

1922–23

41 J Ring (Wigan)	161 J Sullivan (Wigan)	349 J Sullivan (Wigan)
30 H Buck (Leeds)	102 L Osborne (Hull KR)	222 L Osborne (Hull KR)
29 R Taylor (Hull)	100 B Gronow (Huddersfield)	221 B Gronow (Huddersfield)

1923–24

49 J Ring (Wigan)	158 J Sullivan (Wigan)	319 J Sullivan (Wigan)
39 A Van Heerden (Wigan)	80 L Osborne (Hull KR)	210 A Brough (Oldham)
31 J Corsi (Oldham)	75 G Lewis (St Helens)	164 B Gronow (Huddersfield)
		164 J Thompson (Leeds)

1924–25

54 J Ring (Wigan)	138 J Sullivan (Wigan)	282 J Sullivan (Wigan)
37 G Austin (Hull KR)	74 L Osborne (Hull KR)	182 H Rees (Batley)
31 A Van Heerden (Wigan)	64 G Lewis (St Helens)	172 A Brough (Oldham)

1925–26

63 J Ring (Wigan)	131 J Sullivan (Wigan)	274 J Sullivan (Wigan)
36 R Taylor (Hull)	92 H Morris (Swinton)	198 J Thompson (Leeds)
30 A Murdison (Halifax)	87 J Thompson (Leeds)	193 H Morris (Swinton)

1926–27

55 A Ellaby (St Helens)	148 J Sullivan	320 J Sullivan (Wigan)
49 J Ring (Wigan)	109 G Lewis (St Helens)	233 G Lewis (St Helens)
34 J Wilson (St Helens Recs)	99 T Dingsdale (St Helens Recs)	207 T Dingsdale (St Helens Recs)

1927–28

37 A Ellaby (St Helens)	106 J Thompson (Leeds)	233 J Thompson (Leeds)
31 E Mills (Huddersfield)	104 J Sullivan (Wigan)	217 J Sullivan (Wigan)
28 E Bateson (Wakefield T)	74 C Pollard (Wakefield T)	197 A Johnson (Oldham)
28 F Evans (Swinton)		

1928–29

44 L Brown (Wigan)	107 J Sullivan (Wigan)	226 J Sullivan (Wigan)
44 E Mills (Huddersfield)	77 L Osborne (Hull KR)	184 T Blinkhorn (Wigan Highfield and Warrington)
38 A Ellaby (St Helens)	75 J Thompson (Leeds)	176 J Lyman (Dewsbury)

1929–30

39 A Ellaby (St Helens)	111 J Thompson (Leeds)	243 J Thompson (Leeds)
35 L Brown (Wigan)	110 J Sullivan (Wigan)	226 J Sullivan (Wigan)
34 J Woods (Barrow)	89 W Holding (Warrington)	178 W Holding (Warrington)

1930–31

58 E Harris (Leeds)	133 J Sullivan (Wigan)	278 J Sullivan (Wigan)
43 A Ellaby (St Helens)	112 J Thompson (Leeds)	239 J Thompson (Leeds)
39 E Mills (Huddersfield)	108 W Holding (Warrington)	219 W Holding (Warrington)

1931–32

50 E Mills (Huddersfield)	117 J Sullivan (Wigan)	249 J Sullivan (Wigan)
44 R Hardgrave (St Helens)	113 J Walkington (Hunslet)	239 M Hodgson (Swinton)
42 E Harris (Leeds)	109 M Hodgson (Swinton)	226 J Walkington (Hunslet)

Tries	Goals	Points
1932-33		
57 E Harris (Leeds)	146 J Sullivan (Wigan)	307 J Sullivan (Wigan)
48 J Morley (Wigan)	134 W Holding (Warrington)	274 W Holding (Warrington)
35 R Hardgrave (St Helens)	100 A Risman (Salford)	248 A Risman (Salford)
1933-34		
45 R Brown (Salford)	194 J Sullivan (Wigan)	406 J Sullivan (Wigan)
45 J Morley (Wigan)	118 A Risman (Salford)	287 A Risman (Salford)
43 R Markham (Huddersfield)	116 W Holding (Warrington)	252 J Oliver (Hull)
1934-35		
49 J Morley (Wigan)	165 J Sullivan (Wigan)	348 J Sullivan (Wigan)
47 E Harris (Leeds)	93 E Pollard (Wakefield T)	228 J Oliver (Hull)
45 R Markham (Huddersfield)	89 A Risman (Salford)	219 J Sherburn (Keighley)
1935-36		
63 E Harris (Leeds)	117 J Sullivan (Wigan)	246 J Sullivan (Wigan)
53 R Markham (Huddersfield)	99 G Lewis (Castleford)	244 J Oliver (Hull)
38 A Ellaby (Wigan)	95 H Lockwood (Halifax)	243 A Risman (Salford)
1936-37		
40 E Harris (Leeds)	117 J Sullivan (Wigan)	257 T Winnard (Bradford N)
33 A Pimblett (St Helens Recs)	108 E Pollard (Leeds)	252 J Sullivan (Wigan)
32 D Madden (Huddersfield)	97 T Dingsdale (York)	249 E Pollard (Leeds)
1937-38		
45 E Harris (Leeds)	135 J Sullivan (Wigan)	285 J Sullivan (Wigan)
32 D Madden (Huddersfield)	119 H Lockwood (Halifax)	247 A Risman (Salford)
31 R Markham (Huddersfield)	98 A Risman (Salford)	241 H Lockwood (Halifax)
1938-39		
39 R Markham (Huddersfield)	124 J Sullivan (Wigan)	267 A Risman (Salford)
36 I Davies (Warrington)	111 S Lee (Wakefield T)	260 J Sullivan (Wigan)
34 A Edwards (Salford)	105 A Risman (Salford)	222 S Lee (Wakefield T)
1939-40		
38 E Batten (Hunslet)	98 M Hodgson (Swinton)	211 M Hodgson (Swinton)
25 E Walters (Bradford N)	82 A Risman (Salford)	197 A Risman (Salford)
24 A Bowers (Hull)	81 H Lockwood (Halifax)	162 H Lockwood (Halifax)
1940-41		
35 E Walters (Bradford N)	70 H Lockwood (Halifax)	176 W Belshaw (Warrington)
24 W Best (Bradford N)	55 W Belshaw (Warrington)	143 H Lockwood (Halifax)
24 J Bevan (Halifax)	44 F Walker (Castleford)	126 W Davies (Huddersfield)
24 W Dockar (Hull)	44 W Thompson (Hunslet)	
1941-42		
30 R Francis (Dewsbury)	91 H Lockwood (Halifax)	185 H Lockwood (Halifax)
26 O Peake (Huddersfield)	49 W Stott (Oldham)	127 J Lawrenson (Wigan)
25 J Lawrenson (Wigan)	49 J Sullivan (Wigan)	122 W Stott (Oldham)
1942-43		
23 E Batten (Leeds)	65 H Lockwood (Halifax)	136 H Lockwood (Halifax)
19 A Edwards (Dewsbury)	49 J Sullivan (Wigan)	110 J Sullivan (Wigan)
19 R Francis (Dewsbury)	47 W Thompson (Leeds)	99 C Seeling (Dewsbury)
19 B Hudson (Dewsbury)		
1943-44		
21 J Lawrenson (Wigan)	58 W Horne (Barrow)	146 W Horne (Barrow)
18 B Knowelden (Barrow)	47 W Davies (Huddersfield)	111 J Lawrenson (Wigan)
18 J Thurling (Hunslet)	45 C Eaton (Leeds)	106 W Davies (Huddersfield)
1944-45		
41 E Batten (Bradford N)	51 W Stott (Wakefield T)	129 W Stott (Wakefield T)
28 W Best (Bradford N)	44 E Ward (Bradford N)	123 E Batten (Bradford N)
23 J Perry (Wakefield T)	43 D Clarkson (Hunslet)	103 E Ward (Bradford N)
1945-46		
35 E Batten (Bradford N)	89 J Ledgard (Dewsbury)	239 J Bawden (Huddersfield)
32 W Best (Bradford N and Leeds)	85 J Bawden (Huddersfield)	194 W Stott (Wakefield T)
30 J Taylor (Wigan)	76 W Stott (Wakefield T)	190 J Ledgard (Dewsbury)
1946-47		
48 B Bevan (Warrington)	103 F Miller (Hull)	246 J Bawden (Huddersfield)
34 E Ashcroft (Wigan)	93 J Bawden (Huddersfield)	215 F Miller (Hull)
34 E Walters (Bradford N)	85 J Ledgard (Dewsbury)	212 B Bevan (Warrington)

Tries

1947-48
57 B Bevan (Warrington)
49 G Ratcliffe (Wigan)
37 L Cooper (Huddersfield)

1948-49
60 L Cooper (Huddersfield)
56 B Bevan (Warrington)
36 G Ratcliffe (Wigan)

1949-50
57 B Nordgren (Wigan)
46 L Cooper (Huddersfield)
36 A Daniels (Halifax)

1950-51
68 B Bevan (Warrington)
59 L Cooper (Huddersfield)
42 B Nordgren (Wigan)

1951-52
71 L Cooper (Huddersfield)
63 J McLean (Bradford N)
52 F Castle (Barrow)

1952-53
72 B Bevan (Warrington)
59 J McLean (Bradford N)
50 L Cooper (Huddersfield)

1953-54
67 B Bevan (Warrington)
52 J McLean (Bradford N)
41 A Turnbull (Leeds)

1954-55
66 L Cooper (Huddersfield)
63 B Bevan (Warrington)
45 P Henderson (Huddersfield)

1955-56
61 J McLean (Bradford N)
57 B Bevan (Warrington)
49 W Boston (Wigan)

1956-57
60 W Boston (Wigan)
51 J Lewthwaite (Barrow)
48 J Freeman (Halifax)

1957-58
50 M Sullivan (Huddersfield and Wigan)
47 I Southward (Workington T)
46 B Bevan (Warrington)

1958-59
62 T Vollenhoven (St Helens)
54 B Bevan (Warrington)
54 W Boston (Wigan)

1959-60
54 T Vollenhoven (St Helens)
47 W Boston (Wigan)
40 B Bevan (Warrington)

1960-61
59 T Vollenhoven (St Helens)
44 W Rosenberg (Leeds)
37 W Boston (Wigan)

1961-62
51 W Boston (Wigan)
46 T Vollenhoven (St Helens)
38 F Carlton (Wigan)

Goals

141 E Ward (Wigan)
102 J Bawden (Huddersfield)
96 A Risman (Workington T)

155 E Ward (Wigan)
149 H Palin (Warrington)
103 J Bawden (Huddersfield)

133 K Gee (Wigan)
133 H Palin (Warrington)
115 H Cook (Leeds)

155 H Cook (Leeds)
112 J Perry (Batley)
108 A Risman (Workington T)

141 J Ledgard (Leigh)
137 W Horne (Barrow)
130 J Phillips (Bradford N)

170 H Bath (Warrington)
149 G Langfield (St Helens)
145 P Devery (Huddersfield)

153 P Metcalfe (St Helens)
153 H Bath (Warrington)
143 J Phillips (Bradford N)

178 J Ledgard (Leigh)
120 H Bath (Warrington)
110 C Hutton (Hull)

155 J Ledgard (Leigh)
154 H Bath (Warrington)
147 T Griffiths (Halifax)

194 L Jones (Leeds)
189 B Ganley (Oldham)
166 C Hutton (Hull)

219 B Ganley (Oldham)
148 V Yorke (York)
139 L Jones (Leeds)

190 B Ganley (Oldham)
181 W Langton (Hunslet)
176 F Griffiths (Wigan)

171 N Fox (Wakefield T)
171 A Rhodes (St Helens)
169 B Ganley (Oldham)

145 A Rhodes (St Helens)
130 G Owen (Halifax)
128 A Blan (Swinton)
128 F Griffiths (Wigan)

183 N Fox (Wakefield T)
183 F Griffiths (Wigan)
133 J Wilson (Bramley)

Points

312 E Ward (Wigan)
261 J Bawden (Huddersfield)
206 H Palin (Warrington)

361 E Ward (Wigan)
322 H Palin (Warrington)
221 J Bawden (Huddersfield)

290 H Palin (Warrington)
281 K Gee (Wigan)
245 H Cook (Leeds)

322 H Cook (Leeds)
281 J Perry (Batley)
237 A Risman (Workington T)

313 W Horne (Barrow)
305 J Phillips (Bradford N)
297 J Ledgard (Leigh)

379 H Bath (Warrington)
341 P Devery (Huddersfield)
322 G Langfield (St Helens)

369 P Metcalfe (St Helens)
318 H Bath (Warrington)
310 J Phillips (Bradford N)

374 J Ledgard (Leigh)
264 H Bath (Warrington)
247 L Jones (Leeds)

350 H Bath (Warrington)
337 J Ledgard (Leigh)
306 A Rhodes (St Helens)

496 L Jones (Leeds)
384 B Ganley (Oldham)
365 A Rhodes (St Helens)

453 B Ganley (Oldham)
344 N Fox (Wakefield T)
320 L Jones (Leeds)

394 F Griffiths (Wigan)
383 B Ganley (Oldham)
380 N Fox (Wakefield T)
380 W Langton (Hunslet)

453 N Fox (Wakefield T)
399 A Rhodes (St Helens)
341 B Ganley (Oldham)

338 A Rhodes (St Helens)
283 A Blan (Swinton)
274 F Griffiths (Wigan)

456 N Fox (Wakefield T)
390 F Griffiths (Wigan)
274 G Sims (Oldham)

Tries	Goals	Points
1962–63		
41 R Glastonbury (Workington T)	156 K Coslett (St Helens)	321 K Coslett (St Helens)
37 W Burgess (Barrow)	142 C Kellett (Hull KR)	292 N Fox (Wakefield T)
36 G Paul (Hull KR) 36 G Smith (York)	134 W Langton (Hunslet)	290 C Kellett (Hull KR)
1963–64		
45 J Stopford (Swinton)	138 K Coslett (St Helens)	313 N Fox (Wakefield T)
43 T Lake (Wigan)	135 F Dyson (Oldham)	301 D Fox (Featherstone R)
36 K Howe (Castleford)	131 D Fox (Featherstone R)	291 K Coslett (St Helens)
1964–65		
40 T Lake (Wigan)	150 C Kellett (Hull KR)	360 L Killeen (St Helens)
28 J Freeman (Halifax)	141 L Killeen (St Helens)	306 C Kellett (Hull KR)
27 J Griffiths (Hunslet)	132 W Langton (Hunslet)	281 N Fox (Wakefield T)
1965–66		
32 L Killeen (St Helens)	120 L Killeen (St Helens)	336 L Killeen (St Helens)
32 T Lake (Wigan)	119 B Curry (Huddersfield)	256 B Curry (Huddersfield)
25 W Burgess (Barrow)	117 C Kellett (Hull KR)	243 C Kellett (Hull KR)
25 G Wriglesworth (Leeds)	117 J Winton (Oldham)	
1966–67		
34 K Howe (Castleford)	163 B Risman (Leeds)	353 L Killeen (St Helens)
34 C Young (Hull KR)	148 L Killeen (St Helens)	347 B Risman (Leeds)
30 C Sullivan (Hull)	145 C Kellett (Hull KR)	336 N Fox (Wakefield T)
1967–68		
38 R Millward (Hull KR)	154 B Risman (Leeds)	332 B Risman (Leeds)
34 J Atkinson (Leeds)	120 J Maloney (Hull)	298 C Tyrer (Wigan)
33 W Francis (Wigan)	119 C Tyrer (Wigan)	255 J Maloney (Hull)
1968–69		
40 W Francis (Wigan)	165 B Risman (Leeds)	345 B Risman (Leeds)
37 W Burgess (Barrow and Salford)	158 K Coslett (St Helens)	322 K Coslett (St Helens)
26 W Briggs (Oldham)	143 T Price (Bradford N)	315 C Tyrer (Wigan)
26 S Hynes (Leeds)		
1969–70		
38 J Atkinson (Leeds)	167 C Tyrer (Wigan)	385 C Tyrer (Wigan)
36 F Wilson (St Helens)	161 K Coslett (St Helens)	325 K Coslett (St Helens)
34 A Smith (Leeds)	126 R Dutton (Widnes)	302 R Millward (Hull KR)
1970–71		
40 R Haigh (Leeds)	193 K Coslett (St Helens)	395 K Coslett (St Helens)
40 L Jones (St Helens)	166 S Ferguson (Leigh)	358 D Watkins (Salford)
36 J Atkinson (Leeds)	159 J Holmes (Leeds)	356 S Ferguson (Leigh)
1971–72		
36 J Atkinson (Leeds)	214 K Coslett (St Helens)	476 D Watkins (Salford)
36 M Lamb (Bradford N)	193 D Watkins (Salford)	452 K Coslett (St Helens)
35 D Redfearn (Bradford N)	173 E Tees (Bradford N)	364 E Tees (Bradford N)
35 M Richards (Salford)		
1972–73		
39 J Atkinson (Leeds)	221 D Watkins (Salford)	493 D Watkins (Salford)
38 M Richards (Salford)	162 K Coslett (St Helens)	376 N Stephenson (Dewsbury)
33 P Charlton (Salford)	160 E Tees (Bradford N)	330 K Coslett (St Helens)
1973–74		
49 K Fielding (Salford)	183 D Watkins (Salford)	438 D Watkins (Salford)
40 R Mathias (St Helens)	168 D Whitehead (Warrington)	354 B Jefferson (Keighley)
38 D Smith (Wakefield T)	165 B Jefferson (Keighley)	345 D Whitehead (Warrington)
1974–75		
42 G Dunn (Hull KR)	146 N Fox (Hull KR)	333 N Fox (Hull KR)
35 K Fielding (Salford)	129 K Coslett (St Helens)	264 K Coslett (St Helens)
31 J Bevan (Warrington)	122 R Dutton (Widnes)	263 K Fielding (Salford)
1975–76		
37 M Richards (Salford)	175 D Watkins (Salford)	385 D Watkins (Salford)
33 K Fielding (Salford)	149 G Lloyd (Castleford)	328 M Stacey (Leigh)
31 L Jones (St Helens)	149 G Pimblett (St Helens)	316 G Lloyd (Castleford)
1976–77		
31 S Wright (Widnes)	163 G Lloyd (Castleford)	341 G Lloyd (Castleford)
29 B Burton (Castleford)	152 G Pimblett (St Helens)	328 S Quinn (Featherstone R)
28 D Smith (Leeds)	152 S Quinn (Featherstone R)	313 G Pimblett (St Helens)

BOB HAIGH

40-Try Forward

The introduction of limited tackles in 1966 upset the balance of nature in Rugby League. The natural order decreed that wingers scored more tries than any other players and always finished at the top of the try-scoring chart. That something had changed was evident at the close of the 1967–68 season when Hull KR's will-o'-the-wisp stand-off Roger Millward topped the chart with 38 tries. For a For a non-winger to lead the try-chase would have been unthinkable under the old unlimited tackle regime, but the plain truth after 1966 was that there was no longer time to get the ball to the wingers.

If a stand-off topping the lists was disconcerting to the traditionalists, the events of 1970–71 were positively mind-boggling. A forward had the temerity to outscore all the best backs in the game.

Bob Haigh had begun his professional career with Wakefield Trinity in 1962. By the time he left Trinity for Leeds in April 1970 he had already achieved most things to which League players aspire, having played for Yorkshire, England and Great Britain. He had shared in Wakefield's Championship victories of 1967 and 1968, won Yorkshire Cup and Yorkshire League Championship medals and appeared at Wembley, albeit as a loser in the 'Watersplash Final' of 1968. His pedigree as a try-scoring second-rower was already well established when Trinity accepted a club record £6000 fee from Leeds, but no-one was prepared for Bob's amazing performances in 1970–71.

Leeds in this period were a superbly entertaining and successful team, one of the few who had really come to terms with the new limited-tackles game. They still relied heavily on star three-quarters such as Smith, Hynes, Cowan, Dyl and Atkinson to run in the tries, but also knew the value of swift, athletic forwards in the modern game. Bob Haigh, a great cover tackler, had the pace and power to puncture defences. Just as importantly he had the presence of mind to follow loose-forward Ray Batten about the field. Where Batten went, tries usually followed as the loose-forward's sleight of hand and precision passes opened the path to the line.

Haigh scored tries in the first four games of the season including a hat-trick in a 35–3 drubbing of Widnes at Headingley. It was a flying start, but the next 11 games only yielded him three tries. A second hat-trick against Featherstone on 10 October seemed small beer against his selection for Great Britain's World Cup squad. Bob played in Britain's 27–17 victory over New Zealand at Swinton as hot favourites Britain qualified for the final against Australia at Headingley on 8 November. Britain crashed 7–12 in a stormy encounter, but Bob Haigh only played as a 79th-minute substitute for Ray Dutton.

Leeds, however, were playing brilliantly and Haigh was in the second row in their 23–7 Yorkshire Cup Final triumph over Featherstone at Odsal on 21 November and received a second winners' medal on 15 December when Leeds took the

BBC2 Floodlit Trophy after defeating St Helens 9–5 at Headingley. By the turn of the year he had scored 18 tries, but better was to come. January added another nine to his tally including four at Fartown as Huddersfield were dispatched 30–8. Suddenly he was at the top of the scoring charts alongside his own team-mate John Atkinson and other top-rate wings such as Les Jones and Clive Sullivan. The Rugby League world woke up to the realisation that for the first time a forward might just finish as the game's leading scorer.

A 4–0 victory over St Helens in a second round Challenge Cup tie on 20 February halted a scoring run of seven games for Haigh but catapulted the Loiners on course for a Wembley Final against Leigh in May. On 20 March two tries against Hull KR took Haigh past Billy Blan's total of 34 tries for Wigan in 1949–50, and only Hull's Bob Taylor, with 36 tries in 1925–26, stood between Bob Haigh and a new record.

He duly equalled the record with a touchdown in a 32–0 home win over Bramley on 9 April, then three days later he took the record with a 37th try in a 25–2 beating of Batley at Headingley. A brace of tries in a 37–22 Championship quarter-final victory against Salford brought his final tally to 40 tries for the season, level with St Helens' winger Les Jones, and left Bob Haigh as the first forward in the game's history to finish top try-scorer.

Bob Haigh throws off a Bramley defender in a 1971 Challenge Cup tie.

BOB HAIGH'S SCORING RECORD IN 1970-71

1970	Opponents		Tries
22 Aug	Featherstone R	A	1
26 Aug	Widnes	H	3
29 Aug	Wakefield T	A	1 YC
1 Sep	Hull KR	A	1
12 Sep	Swinton	H	1
23 Sep	Halifax	H	1
3 Oct	Wigan	A	1
10 Oct	Featherstone R	H	3
28 Nov	Hull	H	2
5 Dec	Warrington	H	1
12 Dec	Whitehaven	A	2
19 Dec	Bradford N	H	1

1971	Opponents		Tries
2 Jan	Leigh	H	1
9 Jan	Huddersfield	A	4
16 Jan	St Helens	H	1
23 Jan	Oldham	H	1 CC
29 Jan	Salford	A	2
10 Feb	Hull	A	1
13 Feb	Whitehaven	H	2
27 Feb	Salford	H	2
13 Mar	Widnes	A	1
20 Mar	Hull KR	H	2
9 Apr	Bramley	H	1
12 Apr	Batley	H	1
24 Apr	Batley	H	1 PO
1 May	Salford	H	2 PO

YC Yorkshire Cup
CC Challenge Cup
PO Championship Play-off

Bob Haigh played in 51 games in 1970-71 – 47 for Leeds, 3 for Great Britain and 1 for Yorkshire.

INDIVIDUAL RECORDS

Tries

1977–78
33 S Wright (Widnes)
31 K Fielding (Salford)
30 J Bevan (Warrington)
30 E Cunningham (St Helens)
30 S Fenton (Castleford)

1978–79
35 S Hartley (Hull KR)
28 S Wright (Widnes)
25 D Barends (Bradford N)
25 P Lowe (Hull KR)
25 P Prendiville (Hull)

1979–80
30 K Fielding (Salford)
30 S Hubbard (Hull KR)
29 G Munro (Oldham)

1980–81
35 J Crossley (York)
28 T Richardson (Castleford)
25 S Hubbard (Hull KR)

1981–82
31 J Jones (Workington T)
26 R Ashton (Oldham)
26 J Basnett (Widnes)
26 D Drummond (Leigh)

1982–83
37 R Eccles (Warrington)
28 S Evans (Hull)
27 J Crossley (Fulham)

1983–84
38 G Schofield (Hull)
28 G King (Hunslet)
28 J Lydon (Widnes)

1984–85
55 E Hanley (Bradford N)
45 G Prohm (Hull KR)
34 H Gill (Wigan)

1985–86
48 S Halliwell (Leigh)
38 E Hanley (Wigan)
34 P Lister (Bramley)

1986–87
63 E Hanley (Wigan)
37 G Schofield (Hull)
32 H Gill (Wigan)

1987–88
44 M Offiah (Widnes)
36 E Hanley (Wigan)
25 G Schofield (Leeds)

1988–89
60 M Offiah (Widnes)
34 B Ledger (Leigh)
32 D Bate (Swinton)

1989–90
45 M Offiah (Widnes)
38 G Austin (Hull KR)
35 A Sullivan (Hull KR)

1990–91
49 M Offiah (Widnes)
47 G Austin (Hull KR, Halifax)
31 A Hadley (Salford)
31 M Wood (Halifax)

Goals

1977–78
178 G Pimblett (St Helens)
158 S Hesford (Warrington)
149 J Woods (Leigh)

1978–79
172 G Lloyd (Hull)
170 S Hesford (Warrington)
140 M Burke (Widnes)

1979–80
163 S Quinn (Featherstone R)
138 S Hubbard (Hull KR)
134 S Rule (Salford)

1980–81
147 S Hesford (Warrington)
123 S Quinn (Featherstone R)
112 S Diamond (Wakefield T)

1981–82
190 L Hopkins (Workington T)
168 G Fairbairn (Hull KR)
164 M Parrish (Oldham)

1982–83
136 S Diamond (Fulham)
121 E Fitzsimons (Hunslet)
120 L Crooks (Hull)

1983–84
142 R Beardmore (Castleford)
142 S Hesford (Warrington)
140 L Hallett (Cardiff C)

1984–85
157 S Day (St Helens)
141 G Fairbairn (Hull KR)
126 P Wood (Runcorn H)

1985–86
173 C Johnson (Leigh)
128 D Stephenson (Wigan)
118 D Noble (Doncaster)

1986–87
190 P Loughlin (St Helens)
117 P Bishop (Warrington)
114 D Noble (Doncaster)

1987–88
152 J Woods (Warrington)
128 S Quinn (Featherstone R)
116 K Harcombe (Wakefield T)

1988–89
148 M Aston (Sheffield E)
129 M Ketteridge (Castleford)
118 D Hobbs (Bradford N)

1989–90
199 M Fletcher (Hull KR)
145 P Loughlin (St Helens)
126 D Platt (Oldham)

1990–91
177 S Kerry (Salford)
126 F Botica (Wigan)
119 P Eastwood (Hull)

Points

1977–78
381 G Pimblett (St Helens)
358 J Woods (Leigh)
334 S Hesford (Warrington)

1978–79
373 G Lloyd (Hull)
342 S Hesford (Warrington)
316 M Burke (Widnes)

1979–80
375 S Quinn (Featherstone R)
366 S Hubbard (Hull KR)
308 I Ball (Barrow)

1980–81
310 S Hesford (Warrington)
293 S Hubbard (Hull KR)
258 I Ball (Barrow)

1981–82
446 L Hopkins (Workington T)
379 M Parrish (Oldham)
372 J Woods (Leigh)

1982–83
308 S Diamond (Fulham)
276 R Beardmore (Castleford)
270 L Crooks (Hull)

1983–84
355 J Woods (Leigh)
334 R Beardmore (Castleford)
305 S Hesford (Warrington)

1984–85
362 S Day (St Helens)
318 G Steadman (York)
316 G Fairbairn (Hull KR)

1985–86
400 C Johnson (Leigh)
326 D Stephenson (Wigan)
247 J Woods (Bradford N)

1986–87
424 P Loughlin (St Helens)
298 C Whitfield (Halifax)
276 H Gill (Wigan)

1987–88
351 J Woods (Warrington)
299 S Quinn (Featherstone R)
260 P Loughlin (St Helens)

1988–89
307 M Aston (Sheffield E)
289 A Currier (Widnes)
279 C Johnson (Leigh)

1989–90
450 M Fletcher (Hull KR)
358 P Loughlin (St Helens)
290 P Eastwood (Hull)

1990–91
427 S Kerry (Salford)
342 J Davies (Widnes)
324 F Botica (Wigan)

MISCELLANY

Harold Edmondson – Rugby League's youngest first-class debutant.

YOUNGEST PLAYER

Harold Edmondson (born 16 Nov 1903) was only 15 years and 81 days old when he played stand-off for Bramley in a try-scoring debut against Bradford Northern on 1 Feb 1919.

OLDEST PLAYER

Joe Ferguson (born 25 Feb 1879) was 44 years and 48 days old when he played in Oldham's pack at St Helens on 14 Apr 1923.

YOUNGEST PLAYER IN A WEMBLEY CUP FINAL

Shaun Edwards (born 17 Oct 1966) was 17 years and 201 days old when he played full-back for Wigan against Widnes on 5 May 1984.

OLDEST PLAYER IN A WEMBLEY CUP FINAL

Gus Risman (born 21 Mar 1911) was 41 years and 29 days old when he played full-back for Workington Town against Featherstone Rovers on 19 Apr 1952. Risman was captain of his team.

LONGEST FIRST-CLASS CAREER

Gus Risman (Salford, Workington Town, Batley) played for 25 years and 4 months after making his debut for Salford against Barrow on 31 Aug 1929.

MOST CONSECUTIVE APPEARANCES

Widnes hooker **Keith Elwell** played 239 consecutive games for his club between 7 May 1977 and 5 Sep 1982. Elwell also played in the next two games as substitute and started a third game against Hull (26 Sep 1982) before missing Widnes' game against Halifax on 3 Oct 1982, thereby arguably extending his record to 242 games.

MOST CONSECUTIVE TRY-SCORING GAMES

Leeds winger **Eric Harris** scored tries in 17 consecutive club games between 7 Dec 1935 and 29 Feb 1936.

MOST CONSECUTIVE GOAL-SCORING GAMES

Salford centre **David Watkins** kicked goals in 92 consecutive club games between 19 Aug 1972 and 25 Apr 1974.

MOST CENTURIES OF GOALS

Wigan full-back **Jim Sullivan** kicked 100 or more goals in a season 18 times. He achieved this feat in consecutive seasons from 1921–22 to 1938–39 inclusive. He also kicked over 100 goals on the 1932 Lions tour of Australasia.

MOST HALF-CENTURIES OF TRIES

Warrington winger **Brian Bevan** scored 50 or more tries in a season nine times, the first in 1947–48, the last in 1958–59.

MOST ONE-POINT DROP GOALS IN A MATCH

Three players have dropped five one-point goals in a match, as follows:
Danny Wilson, Swinton v Hunslet, 6 Nov 1983
Peter Wood, Runcorn H v Batley, 21 Oct 1984
Paul Bishop, Warrington v Wigan, 11 May 1986

MOST ONE-POINT DROP GOALS IN A SEASON

Lyn Hallett, Cardiff City full-back, scored 29 in 1983–84.

MOST ONE-POINT DROP GOALS IN A CAREER

Norman Turley scored 96 between 1974 and 1991 for Warrington, Runcorn H, Swinton, Blackpool B, Rochdale H, Barrow, Workington T, Trafford B and Whitehaven.

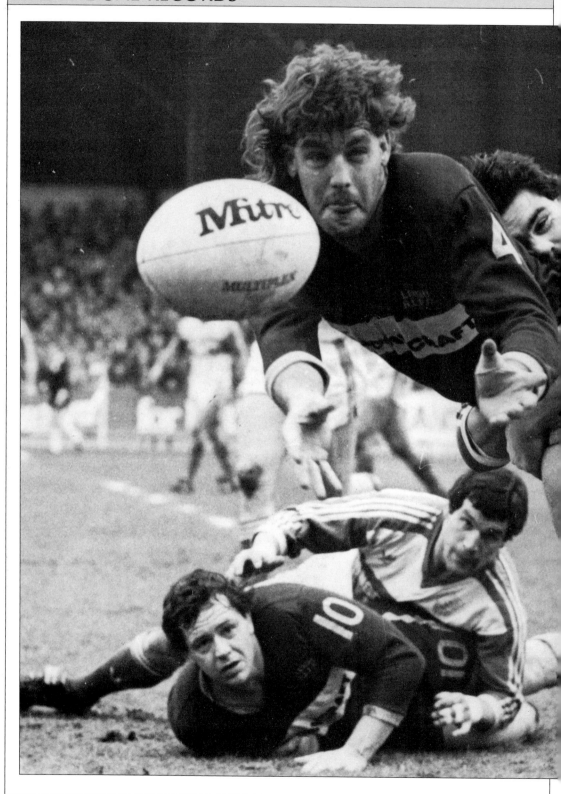

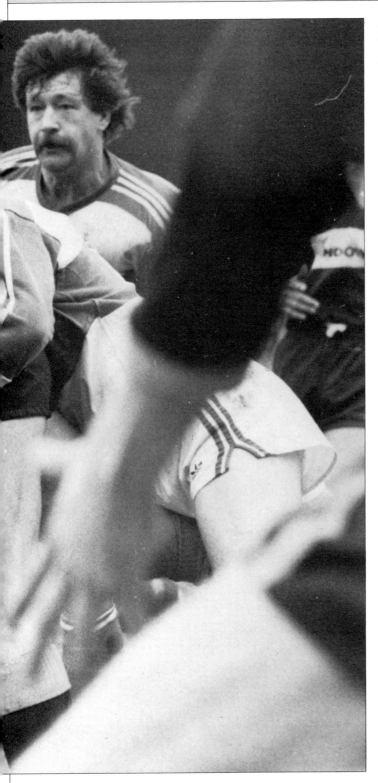

Leigh's Steve Halliwell scored a British record 48 tries from centre-three-quarter in 1985–86. Here he unloads in a Hull KR tackle.

OTHER RUGBY LEAGUE RECORDS

HIGHEST ATTENDANCE

102 569 spectators attended the Challenge Cup Final replay at Odsal Stadium between Halifax and Warrington on 5 May 1954.

HIGHEST LEAGUE ATTENDANCE

47 477, Wigan v St Helens, 27 Mar 1959.

HIGHEST SCORING DRAW

Huddersfield 32 Keighley 32, 17 Apr 1986
Hunslet 32 Swinton 32, 20 Sep 1987

MOST POINTS BY LOSING TEAM

40 Hunslet 40 Barrow 41, 9 Sep 1984

100% WINNING SEASON

Hull won all 26 of their Second Division fixtures in 1978–79.

100% LOSING SEASON

Runcorn Highfield lost all 28 of their Second Division fixtures in 1989–90. They also lost all three cup-ties played.

MOST CONSECUTIVE WINS (ALL GAMES)

29 Wigan, 15 Feb–11 Oct 1987 inclusive.

MOST CONSECUTIVE WINS (LEAGUE)

31 Wigan, 28 Feb 1970–5 Feb 1971 inclusive.

MOST GAMES WITHOUT DEFEAT

44 Huddersfield, 17 Oct 1914–23 Aug 1919 inclusive. This achievement encompassed the last 39 games of 1914–15 (including one abandoned game), the four first-class fixtures Huddersfield played in 1918–19 and the first game of 1919–20.

LONGEST LOSING RUN

Runcorn Highfield lost 61 consecutive first-class fixtures between 29 Jan 1989 and 27 Jan 1991, including 55 league matches. Runcorn also hold the record for the longest sequence without a victory – 75 games between 30 Oct 1988 and 17 Feb 1991 inclusive.

HIGHEST SCORES IN FIRST-CLASS RUGBY LEAGUE

119–2	Huddersfield v Swinton Park	28 Feb 1914	CC
116–0	Wigan v Flimby & Fothergill	14 Feb 1925	CC
112–0	St Helens v Carlisle	14 Sep 1986	LC
102–0	Leeds v Coventry	12 Apr 1913	L
101–0	Great Britain v South Australia	23 May 1914	T
100–6	Hull KR v Nottingham*	19 Aug 1990	YC
94–0	Great Britain v Mackay	2 Jul 1946	T
94–12	Castleford v Huddersfield	18 Sep 1988	YC
92–7	Australians v Bramley	9 Nov 1921	T
92–2	Leigh v Keighley	30 Apr 1986	SD
92–2	Wigan v Runcorn H	13 Nov 1988	JP
92–0	Rochdale H v Runcorn H	5 Nov 1989	SD
92–10	Hull KR v Whitehaven	18 Mar 1990	SD
90–0	Leeds v Barrow	11 Feb 1990	FD
88–0	Great Britain v Central Queensland	25 Jun 1950	T
88–5	Castleford v Millom	16 Sep 1973	JP
88–2	Leigh v Runcorn H	15 Jan 1989	SD
87–4	Great Britain v Western Australia	14 May 1950	T
86–0	Hull v Elland	1 Apr 1899	CC
86–18	Featherstone R v Keighley	17 Sep 1989	YC
84–20	Great Britain v Wide Bay-Burnett	1 Jul 1962	T
83–3	Barrow v Maryport	19 Feb 1938	CC
82–0	Widnes v Dewsbury	30 Nov 1986	JP
82–8	Halifax v Runcorn H	14 Oct 1990	SD
81–14	Great Britain v Bay of Plenty	7 Aug 1962	T
80–7	Hull v Keighley	29 Jan 1921	L
80–8	Barrow v Kent Invicta	8 Apr 1984	SD
80–8	Sheffield E v Wigan St Patricks	13 Nov 1988	JP

CC	Challenge Cup	FD	First Division
LC	Lancashire Cup	SD	Second Division
YC	Yorkshire Cup	JP	John Player Trophy
T	Tour Match	L	League Match (single division era)
*	Highest away score by a club side		

GREAT BRITAIN: TEST MATCH RESULTS

GREAT BRITAIN v AUSTRALIA

TEST MATCH RESULTS

1908 *12 Dec, at Park Royal, London, 2000*
GREAT BRITAIN   22 T: Batten 2, Thomas, Brooks, Tyson, Robinson
    G: Brooks 2
AUSTRALIA   22 T: Devereaux 3, Butler
    G: Messenger 5

1909 *23 Jan, at Newcastle, 22 000*
GREAT BRITAIN   15 T: Thomas, Lomas, Tyson
    G: Lomas 3
AUSTRALIA   5 T: Messenger
    G: Messenger

1909 *15 Feb, at Villa Park, Birmingham, 9000*
GREAT BRITAIN   6 T: Thomas, Tyson
AUSTRALIA   5 T: Frawley
    G: Devereaux

1910 *18 Jun, at Sydney, 42 000*
GREAT BRITAIN   27 T: Jukes 3, Leytham 2, Thomas, Batten
    G: Lomas, Thomas, Leytham
AUSTRALIA   20 T: Hickey, Messenger, Woodhead, Barnett
    G: Messenger 4

1910 *2 Jul, at Brisbane, 18 000*
GREAT BRITAIN   22 T: Leytham 4, Thomas, Kershaw
    G: Lomas 2
AUSTRALIA   17 T: Barnett, Messenger, McKivat, Craig, Tubman
    G: Hickey

1911 *8 Nov, at Newcastle, 6500*
GREAT BRITAIN   10 T: Davies 2
    G: Thomas 2
AUSTRALIA   19 T: V Farnsworth 2, Cann, Francis, Hallett
    G: Francis 2

1911 *16 Dec, at Edinburgh, 6000*
GREAT BRITAIN   11 T: Wagstaff 2, Lomas
    G: Wood
AUSTRALIA   11 T: Frawley, McKivat, Russell
    G: Francis

1912 *1 Jan, at Villa Park, Birmingham, 4000*
GREAT BRITAIN   8 T: Lomas, Clark
    G: Wood
AUSTRALIA   33 T: Berecry 2, McKivat 2, Frawley 2, McCue 2, V Farnsworth
    G: Frawley 2, Gilbert

1914 *27 Jun, at Sydney, 40 000*
GREAT BRITAIN   23 T: Moorhouse 2, Clark, Holland, Robinson
    G: Longstaff 2, Robinson 2
AUSTRALIA   5 T: Norman
    G: Bolewski

1914 *29 Jun, at Sydney, 55 000*
GREAT BRITAIN   7 T: Coldrick
    G: Rogers 2
AUSTRALIA   12 T: Fraser, Burge
    G: Messenger 3

1914 *4 Jul, at Sydney, 34 420*
GREAT BRITAIN   14 T: Davies, Johnson
    G: Wood 4
AUSTRALIA   6 T: Deane, Messenger

1920 *26 Jun, at Brisbane, 28 000*
GREAT BRITAIN   4 G: Gronow 2
AUSTRALIA   8 T: Fraser, Burge
    G: Horder

1920 *3 Jul, at Sydney, 40 000*
GREAT BRITAIN   8 T: Johnson, Gallagher
    G: Gronow
AUSTRALIA   21 T: Potter, V Farnsworth, Horder, Vest, Gilbert
    G: Fraser, Horder, Burge

1920 *10 Jul, at Sydney, 32 000*
GREAT BRITAIN   23   T: Hilton 2, Stone 2, Bacon
       G: Rogers 3, Stone
AUSTRALIA   13   T: Gray, Burge, Thompson
       G: Burge 2

1921 *1 Oct, at Headingley, 32 000*
GREAT BRITAIN   6   T: Stone, Stockwell
AUSTRALIA   5   T: Blinkhorn
       G: Craig

1921 *5 Nov, at The Boulevard, Hull, 21 504*
GREAT BRITAIN   2   G: Rogers
AUSTRALIA   16   T: Blinkhorn 2, Vest, Horder
       G: Thompson 2

1922 *14 Jan, at Salford, 21 000*
GREAT BRITAIN   6   T: Hilton, Gallagher
AUSTRALIA   0

1924 *23 Jun, at Sydney, 50 005*
GREAT BRITAIN   22   T: Parkin 2, Price, Rix
       G: Sullivan 5
AUSTRALIA   3   T: Aynsley

1924 *28 Jun, at Sydney, 33 842*
GREAT BRITAIN   5   T: Parkin
       G: Sullivan
AUSTRALIA   3   T: Aynsley

1924 *12 Jul, at Brisbane, 36 000*
GREAT BRITAIN   11   T: F Evans 2, Parkin
       G: Sullivan
AUSTRALIA   21   T: Paten, Armbruster,
          Oxford
       G: Aynsley 2, Thompson 2,
          Oxford, Craig

1928 *23 Jun, at Brisbane, 39 200*
GREAT BRITAIN   15   T: Fairclough, Horton,
          Ellaby
       G: Sullivan 3
AUSTRALIA   12   T: Armbruster, Aynsley
       G: Craig, Aynsley,
          Freestone

1928 *14 Jul, at Sydney, 44 548*
GREAT BRITAIN   8   T: Parkin, Ellaby
       G: Sullivan
AUSTRALIA   0

1928 *21 Jul, at Sydney, 37 380*
GREAT BRITAIN   14   T: Fairclough 2
       G: Sullivan 4
AUSTRALIA   21   T: Wearing 2, Pearce
       G: Craig 3, Wearing 3

1929 *5 Oct, at Craven Park, Hull, 20 000*
GREAT BRITAIN   8   T: Middleton, Feetham
       G: Thompson
AUSTRALIA   31   T: Shankland 2, Treweeke,
          Prigg, Bishop, Weissel,
          Spencer
       G: Weissel 5

1929 *9 Nov, at Headingley, 31 402*
GREAT BRITAIN   9   T: Atkinson
       G: Sullivan 3
AUSTRALIA   3   T: Shankland

1930 *4 Jan, at Swinton, 34 709*
GREAT BRITAIN   0
AUSTRALIA   0

1930 *15 Jan, at Rochdale, 16 743*
GREAT BRITAIN   3   T: Smith
AUSTRALIA   0

1932 *6 Jun, at Sydney, 70 204*
GREAT BRITAIN   8   T: Ellaby, Atkinson
       G: Sullivan
AUSTRALIA   6   G: Weissel 3

1932 *18 Jun, at Brisbane, 26 574*
GREAT BRITAIN   6   T: Smith, Pollard
AUSTRALIA   15   T: Gee 2, Wilson
       G: Weissel 2, S Pearce

1932 *16 Jul, at Sydney, 50 053*
GREAT BRITAIN   18   T: Smith 3, Brogden
       G: Sullivan 3
AUSTRALIA   13   T: O'Connor
       G: Weissel 5

1933 *7 Oct, at Belle Vue, Manchester, 34 000*
GREAT BRITAIN   4   G: Sullivan 2
AUSTRALIA   0

1933 *11 Nov, at Headingley, 29 618*
GREAT BRITAIN   7   T: Woods
       G: Sullivan 2
AUSTRALIA   5   T: Brown
       G: Brown

1933 *16 Dec, at Swinton, 10 990*
GREAT BRITAIN   19   T: Hudson, Feetham, Smith
       G: Sullivan 5
AUSTRALIA   16   T: Hey, Prigg
       G: Brown 5

1936 *29 Jun, at Sydney, 63 920*
GREAT BRITAIN   8   T: Beverley 2
       G: Hodgson
AUSTRALIA   24   T: Brown 2, Ridley, Pearce
       G: Brown 4, Beaton 2

1936 *4 Jul, at Brisbane, 29 486*
GREAT BRITAIN   12   T: Edwards 2
       G: Risman 2, Hodgson
AUSTRALIA   7   T: Crippin
       G: Beaton, Brown

1936 *18 Jul, at Sydney, 53 546*
GREAT BRITAIN   12   T: Hudson, Brogden
       G: Hodgson 3
AUSTRALIA   7   T: Hey
       G: Brown 2

1937 *16 Oct, at Headingley, 31 949*
GREAT BRITAIN   5   T: Jenkins
                 G: Hodgson
AUSTRALIA   4   G: Beaton 2

1937 *13 Nov, at Swinton, 31 724*
GREAT BRITAIN   13   T: Edwards 2, Hudson
                 G: Risman 2
AUSTRALIA   3   T: Dawson

1937 *18 Dec, at Huddersfield, 9093*
GREAT BRITAIN   3   T: Hudson
AUSTRALIA   13   T: Norval, Reardon, Narvo
                 G: Beaton 2

1946 *17 Jun, at Sydney, 64 527*
GREAT BRITAIN   8   T: Horne, Whitcombe
                 G: Risman
AUSTRALIA   8   T: Cooper, Bailey
                 G: Jorgenson

1946 *6 Jul, at Brisbane, 40 500*
GREAT BRITAIN   14   T: Bassett 3, Johnson
                 G: E Ward
AUSTRALIA   5   T: Cooper
                 G: Jorgenson

1946 *20 Jul, at Sydney, 35 294*
GREAT BRITAIN   20   T: Bassett 2, Curran, Owens
                 G: Risman 3, EH Ward
AUSTRALIA   7   T: Kennedy
                 G: Jorgenson 2

1948 *9 Oct, at Headingley, 36 529*
GREAT BRITAIN   23   T: Foster 2, McCormick 2,
                      Pimblett 2, Valentine
                 G: E Ward
AUSTRALIA   21   T: McMahon 2, Hall,
                      Froome, Graves
                 G: Graves 3

1948 *6 Nov, at Swinton, 36 354*
GREAT BRITAIN   16   T: Pimblett 2, Lawrenson 2
                 G: E Ward 2
AUSTRALIA   7   T: Horrigan
                 G: Graves 2

1949 *29 Jan, at Odsal, 42 000*
GREAT BRITAIN   23   T: Curran 2, E Ward,
                      McCormick, Williams
                 G: E Ward 4
AUSTRALIA   9   T: Lulham, de Belin, Hall

1950 *12 Jun, at Sydney, 47 215*
GREAT BRITAIN   6   T: Hilton 2
AUSTRALIA   4   G: Pidding 2

1950 *1 Jul, at Brisbane, 35 000*
GREAT BRITAIN   3   T: Danby
AUSTRALIA   15   T: Graves, Cowie, Holman
                 G: Graves, Churchill,
                      Holland

1950 *22 Jul, at Sydney, 47 178*
GREAT BRITAIN   2   G: E Ward
AUSTRALIA   5   T: Roberts
                 G: Churchill

1952 *4 Oct, at Headingley, 34 505*
GREAT BRITAIN   19   T: Castle, Ryder, Daniels
                 G: Horne 5
AUSTRALIA   6   G: Pidding 3

1952 *8 Nov, at Swinton, 32 421*
GREAT BRITAIN   21   T: Castle 2, Greenall 2,
                      E Ward
                 G: E Ward 2, Horne
AUSTRALIA   5   T: Geelan
                 G: Carlson

1952 *13 Dec, at Odsal, 30 509*
GREAT BRITAIN   7   T: Horne
                 G: Evans 2
AUSTRALIA   27   T: Ryan 2, Pidding, Holman,
                      Davies
                 G: Pidding 6

1954 *12 Jun, at Sydney, 65 884*
GREAT BRITAIN   12   T: Silcock, Jackson
                 G: Jones 3
AUSTRALIA   37   T: McCaffery 2, Provan,
                      O'Shea, Hall, Pidding,
                      Carlson
                 G: Pidding 8

1954 *3 Jul, at Brisbane, 46 355*
GREAT BRITAIN   38   T: Boston 2, Jackson,
                      Helme, Pawsey,
                      Williams
                 G: Jones 10
AUSTRALIA   21   T: Carlson 2, Provan, Hall,
                      Holman
                 G: Pidding 3

1954 *17 Jul, at Sydney, 67 577*
GREAT BRITAIN   16   T: Williams 2, Ashcroft,
                      Valentine
                 G: Jones 2
AUSTRALIA   20   T: Watson, Diversi, Wells,
                      Pidding
                 G: Pidding 4

1956 *17 Nov, at Wigan, 22 473*
GREAT BRITAIN   21   T: Boston 2, Grundy,
                      Davies, Sullivan
                 G: Mortimer 3
AUSTRALIA   10   T: Moir, Poole
                 G: Holman 2

1956 *1 Dec, at Odsal, 23 634*
GREAT BRITAIN   9   T: Stevenson
                 G: Mortimer 3
AUSTRALIA   22   T: Holman, Banks, Davies,
                      Bull
                 G: Clifford 5

1956 *15 Dec, at Swinton, 17 542*
GREAT BRITAIN   19 T: Little, Turner, Gunney,
                               Sullivan, Boston
                        G: Davies 2
AUSTRALIA   0

1958 *14 Jun, at Sydney, 68 777*
GREAT BRITAIN   8 T: Bolton, Southward
                        G: Southward
AUSTRALIA   25 T: O'Shea, Mossop,
                               Carlson, Kite, Provan
                        G: Clifford 5

1958 *5 Jul, at Brisbane, 32 965*
GREAT BRITAIN   25 T: Southward 2, Murphy,
                               Sullivan, Challinor
                        G: Fraser 5
AUSTRALIA   18 T: Marsh, Holman, Carlson,
                               Dimond
                        G: Clifford 3

1958 *19 Jul, at Sydney, 68 720*
GREAT BRITAIN   40 T: Sullivan 3, Southward,
                               Whiteley, Terry,
                               Murphy, Davies
                        G: Fraser 8
AUSTRALIA   17 T: Holman, Provan, Hawick
                        G: Clifford 4

1959 *17 Oct, at Swinton, 35 224*
GREAT BRITAIN   14 T: Boston, Turner
                        G: Fraser 4
AUSTRALIA   22 T: Gasnier 3, Wells
                        G: Barnes 5

1959 *21 Nov, at Headingley, 30 184*
GREAT BRITAIN   11 T: Robinson, Fox, Whiteley
                        G: Fox
AUSTRALIA   10 T: Carlson 2
                        G: Barnes, Carlson

1959 *12 Dec, at Wigan, 26 089*
GREAT BRITAIN   18 T: Fox, Southward
                        G: Fox 6
AUSTRALIA   12 T: Raper, Carlson
                        G: Barnes 3

1962 *9 Jun, at Sydney, 69 990*
GREAT BRITAIN   31 T: Sullivan 2, Ashton 2,
                               Turner, Huddart,
                               Boston
                        G: Fox 5
AUSTRALIA   12 T: Irvine, Gasnier
                        G: Parish 3

1962 *30 Jun, at Brisbane, 34 760*
GREAT BRITAIN   17 T: Boston 2, Murphy
                        G: Fox 3, Ashton
AUSTRALIA   10 T: Irvine, Summons
                        G: Barnes 2

1962 *14 Jul, at Sydney, 42 104*
GREAT BRITAIN   17 T: Ashton, Murphy, Fox
                        G: Fox 4
AUSTRALIA   18 T: Irvine 2, Summons, Drake
                        G: Irvine 3

1963 *16 Oct, at Wembley, 13 946*
GREAT BRITAIN   2 G: N Fox
AUSTRALIA   28 T: Gasnier 3, Langlands,
                               Irvine, K Thornett
                        G: Langlands 5

1963 *9 Nov, at Swinton, 30 833*
GREAT BRITAIN   12 T: Stopford, Measures
                        G: N Fox 3
AUSTRALIA   50 T: Irvine 3, Gasnier 2,
                               Langlands 2, Dimond
                               2, Kelly, R Thornett,
                               Harrison
                        G: Langlands 7

1963 *30 Nov, at Headingley, 20 497*
GREAT BRITAIN   16 T: Ward, Stopford, D Fox,
                               Smith
                        G: D Fox 2
AUSTRALIA   5 T: Irvine
                        G: Langlands

1966 *25 Jun, at Sydney, 57 962*
GREAT BRITAIN   17 T: Watson, Hardisty,
                               Burgess
                        G: Keegan 3, Bishop
AUSTRALIA   13 T: Banks
                        G: Barnes 5

1966 *16 Jul, at Brisbane, 45 057*
GREAT BRITAIN   4 G: Keegan 2
AUSTRALIA   6 G: Barnes 3

1966 *23 Jul, at Sydney, 63 503*
GREAT BRITAIN   14 T: Hardisty 2
                        G: Gowers 4
AUSTRALIA   19 T: Irvine 3, King, Lynch
                        G: Johns 2

1967 *21 Oct, at Headingley, 22 293*
GREAT BRITAIN   16 T: Young, Millward
                        G: Millward 3, Bishop,
                               Holliday
AUSTRALIA   11 T: Langlands
                        G: Langlands 4

1967 *3 Nov, at White City, London, 17 445*
GREAT BRITAIN   11 T: Bishop
                        G: Fox 3, Bishop
AUSTRALIA   17 T: Langlands, King, Coote
                        G: Langlands 4

1967 *9 Dec, at Swinton, 13 615*
GREAT BRITAIN   3 T: Price
AUSTRALIA   11 T: Coote, Branson, King
                        G: Langlands

Jeff Stevenson and Keith Barnes lead out the teams in the 1959 Ashes decider at Wigan. Scrum-half Stevenson is the only York player to captain Great Britain in Test matches.

1970 *6 Jun, at Brisbane, 42 807*
GREAT BRITAIN   15 T: Watson, Flanagan, Laughton
    G: Price 3
AUSTRALIA   37 T: Morgan 2, King 2, McDonald
    G: Langlands 9, Hawthorne 2

1970 *20 Jun, at Sydney, 60 962*
GREAT BRITAIN   28 T: Millward 2, Atkinson, Fisher
    G: Millward 7, Hynes
AUSTRALIA   7 T: King
    G: McDonald, Hawthorne

1970 *4 Jul, at Sydney, 61 258*
GREAT BRITAIN   21 T: Atkinson 2, Hynes, Millward, Hartley
    G: Millward 3
AUSTRALIA   17 T: McCarthy
    G: McKean 7

1973 *3 Nov, at Wembley, 9874*
GREAT BRITAIN   21 T: Lowe 2, Clarke, Lockwood
    G: Clawson 4, Nash (DG)
AUSTRALIA   12 T: Branighan, Fulton
    G: Langlands 3

1973 *24 Nov, at Headingley, 16 674*
GREAT BRITAIN   6 G: Clawson 3
AUSTRALIA   14 T: McCarthy
    G: Eadie 5, Fulton (DG)

1973 *1 Dec, at Warrington, 10 019*
GREAT BRITAIN   5 T: Millward
    G: Millward
AUSTRALIA   15 T Maddison 2, Fulton, Starling, Walters

1974 *15 Jun, at Brisbane, 30 280*
GREAT BRITAIN   6 G: Clawson 2, Watkins
AUSTRALIA   12 T: Orr
    G: Langlands 4, Fulton (DG)

1974 *6 Jul, at Sydney, 48 006*
GREAT BRITAIN   16 T: Chisnall, Dixon, Gill
    G: Gray 4 (1DG)
AUSTRALIA   11 T: Fulton, Lang, Coote
    G: Cronin

1974 *20 Jul, at Sydney, 55 505*
GREAT BRITAIN   18 T: Dyl, Richards
    G: Gray 6
AUSTRALIA   22 T: Williamson, McCarthy, Langlands, Coote
    G: Langlands 5

Australian second-rower John Cartwright moves to block hooker Lee Jackson's progress during Britain's epic 19–12 First Test victory at Wembley in 1990.

1978 *21 Oct, at Wigan, 17 644*
GREAT BRITAIN   9   T: Bevan
   G: Fairbairn 3
AUSTRALIA   15   T: Boustead, Fulton
   G: Cronin 4, Fulton (DG)

1978 *5 Nov, at Odsal, 26 447*
GREAT BRITAIN   18   T: Wright 2
   G: Fairbairn 6
AUSTRALIA   14   T: Price, Rogers
   G: Cronin 2, Rogers 2

1978 *18 Nov, at Headingley, 29 627*
GREAT BRITAIN   6   T: Millward, Bevan
AUSTRALIA   23   T: Peponis, Boyd, Gerard,
   Raudonikis
   G: Cronin 5, Fulton (DG)

1979 *16 Jun, at Brisbane, 23 051*
GREAT BRITAIN   0
AUSTRALIA   35   T: Boustead 2, Price 2,
   Corowa
   G: Cronin 10

1979 *30 Jun, at Sydney, 26 837*
GREAT BRITAIN   16   T: Joyner, Hughes
   G: Woods 5
AUSTRALIA   24   T: Cronin 2, Rogers, Reddy
   G: Cronin 6

1979 *14 Jul, at Sydney, 16 854*
GREAT BRITAIN   2   G: Fairbairn
AUSTRALIA   28   T: Eadie, Price, Boyd,
   Reddy
   G: Cronin 8

1982 *30 Oct, at Boothferry Park, Hull, 26 771*
GREAT BRITAIN   4   G: Crooks 2
AUSTRALIA   40   T: Meninga, Boyd, Grothe,
   Price, Boustead,
   Kenny, Pearce, Reddy
   G: Meninga 8

1982 *20 Nov, at Wigan, 23 216*
GREAT BRITAIN   6   G: Mumby 3
AUSTRALIA   27   T: Price, Sterling, Grothe,
   Meninga, Rogers
   G: Meninga 6

1982 *28 Nov, at Headingley, 17 318*
GREAT BRITAIN   8   T: Evans
   G: Crooks 3 (1DG)
AUSTRALIA   32   T: Ribot, Krilich, Boustead,
   Rogers, Pearce, Kenny
   G: Meninga 7

1984 *9 Jun, at Sydney, 30 190*
GREAT BRITAIN   8   T: Schofield
   G: Burke 2
AUSTRALIA   25   T: Lewis, Price, Boustead,
   Murray
   G: Conlon 4, Lewis (DG)

1984 *26 Jun, at Brisbane, 26 534*
GREAT BRITAIN   6   T: Schofield
   G: Burke
AUSTRALIA   18   T: Grothe, Pearce, Meninga,
   G: Meninga 3

1984 *7 Jul, at Sydney, 18 756*
GREAT BRITAIN   7   T: Hanley
   G: Burke, Holding (DG)
AUSTRALIA   20   T: Grothe, Conescu, Jack
   G: Meninga 4

1986 *25 Oct, at Old Trafford, 50 583*
GREAT BRITAIN   16   T: Schofield 2, Lydon
   G: Crooks, Gill
AUSTRALIA   38   T: Miles 3, O'Connor 3, Jack
   G: O'Connor 5

1986 *8 Nov, at Elland Road, 30 808*
GREAT BRITAIN   4   T: Schofield
AUSTRALIA   34   T: Jack 2, Lindner,
   O'Connor, Lewis,
   Kenny
   G: O'Connor 5

1986 *22 Nov*, at Wigan, 20 169*
GREAT BRITAIN   15   T: Schofield 2
   G: Lydon 2, Gill, Schofield
   (DG)
AUSTRALIA   24   T: Lindner, Shearer, Lewis,
   Miles
   G: O'Connor 4

1988 *11 Jun, at Sydney, 24 202*
GREAT BRITAIN   6   T: Hanley
   G: Loughlin
AUSTRALIA   17   T: Jackson 2, Backo
   G: O'Connor 2, Lewis (DG)

1988 *28 Jun, at Brisbane, 27 103*
GREAT BRITAIN   14   T: Offiah, Ford
   G: Loughlin 3
AUSTRALIA   34   T: Lewis, Pearce, Backo,
   O'Connor,
   Ettingshausen, Jackson
   G: O'Connor 5

1988 *9 Jul*, at Sydney, 15 994*
GREAT BRITAIN   26   T: Gill 2, Offiah, Ford,
   M Gregory
   G: Loughlin 3
AUSTRALIA   12   T: Lewis, Backo
   G: O'Connor 2

1990 *27 Oct, at Wembley, 54 569*
GREAT BRITAIN   19   T: Eastwood 2, Offiah
   G: Eastwood 3, Schofield
   (DG)
AUSTRALIA   12   T: Meninga, McGaw
   G: Meninga 2

1990 *10 Nov, at Old Trafford, 46 615*

GREAT BRITAIN	10	T:	Dixon, Loughlin
		G:	Eastwood
AUSTRALIA	14	T:	Shearer, Lyons, Meninga
		G:	Meninga

1990 *24 Nov*, at Elland Road, 32 500*

GREAT BRITAIN	0		
AUSTRALIA	14	T:	Ettingshausen, Meninga, Elias
		G:	Meninga

* World Cup Match

GREAT BRITAIN v NEW ZEALAND

TEST MATCH RESULTS

1908 *25 Jan, at Headingley, 8182*

GREAT BRITAIN	14	T:	Robinson 2, Leytham, Llewellyn
		G:	Jolley
NEW ZEALAND	6	T:	Turtill, R Wynyard

1908 *8 Feb, at Chelsea, 14 000*

GREAT BRITAIN	6	T:	Eccles, Leytham
NEW ZEALAND	18	T:	Johnston 2, Smith, Todd
		G:	Messenger 3

1908 *15 Feb, at Cheltenham, 4013*

GREAT BRITAIN	5	T:	Jolley
		G:	White
NEW ZEALAND	8	T:	Messenger, Johnston
		G:	Wrigley

1910 *30 Jul, at Auckland, 16 000*

GREAT BRITAIN	52	T:	Avery 3, Kershaw 2, Jenkins 2, Leytham 2, Lomas, Smith, Thomas
		G:	Lomas 6, Thomas, Sharrock
NEW ZEALAND	20	T:	Seagar, McDonald, Hughes, Buckland
		G:	Jackson 4

1914 *1 Aug, at Auckland, 15 000*

GREAT BRITAIN	16	T:	Moorhouse 2, Davies, Johnson
		G:	Wood 2
NEW ZEALAND	13	T:	Wilson 2, Banks
		G:	Ifwerson 2

1920 *31 Jul, at Auckland, 34 000*

GREAT BRITAIN	31	T:	Parkin 3, Stone 3, Bacon
		G:	Gronow 5
NEW ZEALAND	7	T:	Scott
		G:	Davidson, Ifwerson

1920 *7 Aug, at Christchurch, 10 000*

GREAT BRITAIN	19	T:	Stone 2, Hilton, Parkin, Bacon
		G:	Gronow 2
NEW ZEALAND	3	T:	Guiney

1920 *14 Aug, at Wellington, 4000*

GREAT BRITAIN	11	T:	Clark, Bacon, Bowers
		G:	Gronow
NEW ZEALAND	10	T:	Walters, Ifwerson
		G:	Ifwerson 2

1924 *2 Aug, at Auckland, 22 000*

GREAT BRITAIN	8	T:	Bentham, Thompson
		G:	Thompson
NEW ZEALAND	16	T:	Stewart, Gilroy, Wetherill, Herring
		G:	Delgrosso 2

1924 *6 Aug, at Wellington, 6000*

GREAT BRITAIN	11	T:	Carr, Rix, Howley
		G:	Thompson
NEW ZEALAND	13	T:	O'Brien, Mullins, Brisbane
		G:	Dufty 2

1924 *9 Aug, at Dunedin, 14 000*

GREAT BRITAIN	31	T:	Brough 2, Price, F Evans, Howley, Carr, Hurcombe
		G:	Sullivan 5
NEW ZEALAND	18	T:	Brisbane, Delgrosso, Herring, O'Brien
		G:	Dufty 3

1926 *2 Oct, at Wigan, 14 500*

GREAT BRITAIN	28	T:	Taylor 2, Carr, Rix, Gallagher, J Evans
		G:	Sullivan 5
NEW ZEALAND	20	T:	Avery, Brisbane, Mason, Davidson
		G:	Mouat 4

The Great Britain team which defeated New Zealand 21–11 at Hull in 1926.

1926 *13 Nov, at The Boulevard, Hull, 7000*
GREAT BRITAIN   21 T: Thomas 2, Wallace, Fildes,
                                          Fairclough
                              G: Sullivan 3
NEW ZEALAND   11 T: Peterson, Avery, Brown
                              G: Gregory

1927 *15 Jan, at Headingley, 6000*
GREAT BRITAIN   32 T: Carr 3, Bacon 2, Bowman,
                                          J Evans, Rees
                              G: Sullivan 4
NEW ZEALAND   17 T: Delgrosso, Herring,
                                          Avery
                              G: Dufty 4

1928 *4 Aug, at Auckland, 28 000*
GREAT BRITAIN   13 T: Fairclough, Oliver, Ellaby
                              G: Sullivan 2
NEW ZEALAND   17 T: Scott 2, List
                              G: Delgrosso 3, Dufty

1928 *18 Aug, at Dunedin, 12 000*
GREAT BRITAIN   13 T: Ellaby, Bowen, Rees
                              G: Sullivan 2
NEW ZEALAND   5 T: Scott
                              G: Dufty

1928 *25 Aug, at Christchurch, 21 000*
GREAT BRITAIN   6 T: Fairclough, Askin
NEW ZEALAND   5 T: O'Brien
                              G: Dufty

1932 *30 Jul, at Auckland, 25 000*
GREAT BRITAIN   24 T: Ellaby 2, Atkinson 2,
                                          Feetham, Smith
                              G: Sullivan 3
NEW ZEALAND   9 T: Cooke
                              G: Laing 3

1932 *13 Aug, at Christchurch, 5000*
GREAT BRITAIN   25 T: Atkinson 2, Horton,
                                          Smith, Brogden
                              G: Sullivan 5
NEW ZEALAND   14 T: List 2
                              G: Amos 4

1932 *20 Aug, at Auckland, 6500*
GREAT BRITAIN   20 T: Hudson 2, Fildes, Smith
                              G: Sullivan 4
NEW ZEALAND   18 T: Brisbane 2, Abbott,
                                          Cooke
                              G: Watene 3

1936 *8 Aug, at Auckland, 25 000*
GREAT BRITAIN   10 T: Edwards, Jenkins
                              G: Hodgson 2
NEW ZEALAND   8 G: Watene 3, Trevarthan

1936 *15 Aug, at Auckland, 17 000*
GREAT BRITAIN   23 T: Arkwright 2, Edwards,
                                          Miller, Hudson
                              G: Risman 4
NEW ZEALAND   11 T: Cootes
                              G: Watene 4

1946 *10 Aug, at Auckland, 10 000*
GREAT BRITAIN   8 T: E Ward, Batten
   G: E Ward
NEW ZEALAND   13 T: Graham
   G: Clarke 5

1947 *4 Oct, at Headingley, 28 445*
GREAT BRITAIN   11 T: Gwyther, Aston, Johnson
   G: EH Ward
NEW ZEALAND   10 T: McGregor, Forrest
   G: Clarke 2

1947 *8 Nov, at Swinton, 29 031*
GREAT BRITAIN   7 T: Jenkins
   G: Ledgard 2
NEW ZEALAND   10 T: Forrest, Newton
   G: Clarke 2

1947 *20 Dec, at Odsal, 42 685*
GREAT BRITAIN   25 T: Francis 2, Palin 2, Gee
   G: E Ward 4, Horne
NEW ZEALAND   9 T: McGregor
   G: Clarke 3

1950 *29 Jul, at Christchurch, 10 000*
GREAT BRITAIN   10 T: Pollard, Williams
   G: E Ward 2
NEW ZEALAND   16 T: Hardwick, Barchard
   G: White 5

1950 *12 Aug, at Auckland, 20 000*
GREAT BRITAIN   13 T: Featherstone, E Ward, Ryan
   G: E Ward 2
NEW ZEALAND   20 T: Haig 2, Hough, M Robertson
   G: White 2, Haig, Davidson

1951 *6 Oct, at Odsal, 37 475*
GREAT BRITAIN   21 T: Wilson 3, Greenall, Cracknell
   G: Gee 3
NEW ZEALAND   15 T: Johnson, M Robertson, Eastlake
   G: White 3

1951 *10 Nov, at Swinton, 29 938*
GREAT BRITAIN   20 T: McKeating, Wilson, Cracknell, Traill
   G: Ledgard 4
NEW ZEALAND   19 T: B Robertson 2, Eastlake, Forrest, McBride
   G: White 2

1951 *15 Dec, at Headingley, 18 649*
GREAT BRITAIN   16 T: Turnbull 2, Wilson, Blan
   G: E Ward 2
NEW ZEALAND   12 T: Edwards 2, Mulcare, Hough

1954 *24 Jul, at Auckland, 22 097*
GREAT BRITAIN   27 T: Boston 4, Ashcroft 2, Harris
   G: Jones 3
NEW ZEALAND   7 T: Bond
   G: Haig, White

1954 *31 Jul, at Greymouth, 4240*
GREAT BRITAIN   14 T: O'Grady, Wilkinson
   G: Jones 4
NEW ZEALAND   20 T: Butterfield, Mulcare
   G: White 7

1954 *14 Aug, at Auckland, 6186*
GREAT BRITAIN   12 T: O'Grady, Price
   G: Jones 3
NEW ZEALAND   6 G: White 3

1955 *8 Oct, at Swinton, 21 937*
GREAT BRITAIN   25 T: Sullivan 2, Boston, Grundy, Wilkinson
   G: Jones 5
NEW ZEALAND   6 T: B Robertson, Maxwell

1955 *12 Nov, at Odsal, 24 443*
GREAT BRITAIN   27 T: Sullivan 3, Wilkinson, Prescott, Watts, Stevenson
   G: Jones 3
NEW ZEALAND   12 T: Roberts, Menzies
   G: Haggie 3

1955 *17 Dec, at Headingley, 10 438*
GREAT BRITAIN   13 T: Sullivan, Brown, Jones
   G: Jones 2
NEW ZEALAND   28 T: Blanchard, Roberts, Percy, Bakalich, Maxwell, Butterfield
   G: Creedy 5

1958 *26 Jul, at Auckland, 25 000*
GREAT BRITAIN   10 T: Sullivan, Jackson
   G: Fraser 2
NEW ZEALAND   15 T: Percy 2, Hadfield
   G: Eastlake 3

1958 *9 Aug, at Auckland, 25 000*
GREAT BRITAIN   32 T: Sullivan 3, Ashton 2, Murphy
   G: Fraser 7
NEW ZEALAND   15 T: Percy, Hadfield, Roberts
   G: Eastlake 3

1961 *30 Sep, at Headingley, 16 540*
GREAT BRITAIN   11 T: Boston 2, Murphy
   G: Rhodes
NEW ZEALAND   29 T: Edwards, Hadfield, Reidy, M Cooke, Hammond
   G: Fagan 7

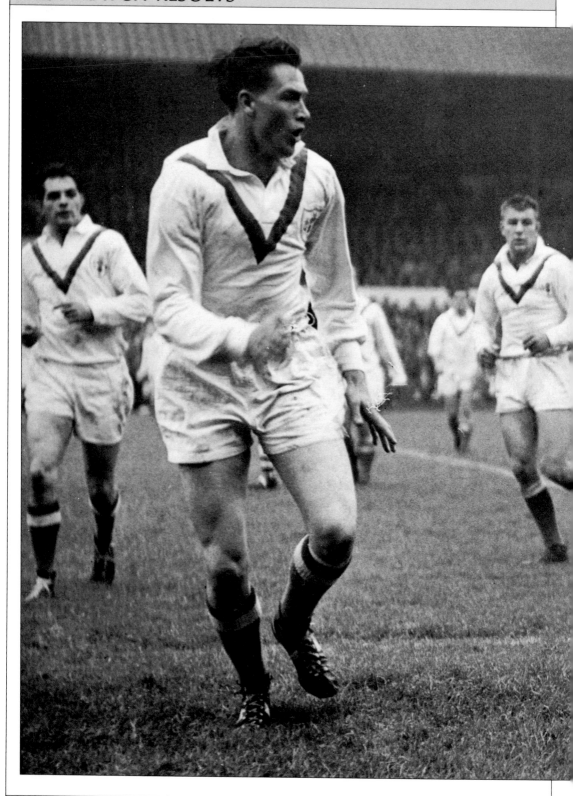

1961 *21 Oct, at Odsal, 19 980*

GREAT BRITAIN	23	T: Sullivan 2, Evans, Bolton, Ashton
		G: Fox 4
NEW ZEALAND	10	T: Bailey 2
		G: Fagan 2

1961 *4 Nov, at Swinton, 22 536*

GREAT BRITAIN	35	T: Sullivan 2, Herbert, Murphy, Ashton, Dagnall, Fraser
		G: Fox 7
NEW ZEALAND	19	T: Hadfield 2, Edwards
		G: R Cooke 5

1962 *28 Jul, at Auckland, 14 976*

GREAT BRITAIN	0	
NEW ZEALAND	19	T: Reidy 2, Ackland, Bond, Edwards
		G: Smith, Denton

1962 *11 Aug, at Auckland, 16 411*

GREAT BRITAIN	8	T: Small, Fox
		G: Gilfedder
NEW ZEALAND	27	T: Bailey 2, Reidy, Emery, Denton
		G: Fagan 6

1965 *25 Sep, at Swinton, 8541*

GREAT BRITAIN	7	T: Renilson
		G: Holliday 2
NEW ZEALAND	2	G: Tait

1965 *23 Oct, at Odsal, 15 740*

GREAT BRITAIN	15	T: Burgess, Shelton, Stopford
		G: Holliday 3
NEW ZEALAND	9	T: W Schultz
		G: Fagan 3

1965 *6 Nov, at Wigan, 7919*

GREAT BRITAIN	9	T: Burgess
		G: Gowers 3
NEW ZEALAND	9	T: Tait
		G: Fagan 3

1966 *6 Aug, at Auckland, 14 494*

GREAT BRITAIN	25	T: Brooke, Clarke, Myler, Burgess, Watson
		G: Gowers 5
NEW ZEALAND	8	T: Christian, Mincham
		G: Kennedy

1966 *20 Aug, at Auckland, 10 657*

GREAT BRITAIN	22	T: Brooke 2, Burgess, Aspinall
		G: Gowers 5
NEW ZEALAND	14	G: Wiggs 7

1970 *11 Jul, at Auckland, 15 948*

GREAT BRITAIN	19	T: Laughton 2, Millward, Hynes, Atkinson
		G: Hynes 2
NEW ZEALAND	15	T: P Orchard
		G: Ladner 6

1970 *19 Jul, at Christchurch, 8600*

GREAT BRITAIN	23	T: Millward 2, Laughton, Myler, Reilly
		G: Dutton 4
NEW ZEALAND	9	T: Christian
		G: Ladner 3

1970 *25 Jul, at Auckland, 13 137*

GREAT BRITAIN	33	T: Lowe 2, Watson, Smith, Hesketh, Hepworth, Hynes
		G: Dutton 5, Millward
NEW ZEALAND	16	T: Bailey, R Orchard
		G: Ladner 5

1971 *25 Sep, at Salford, 3764*

GREAT BRITAIN	13	T: Benyon, Ashurst, Hesketh
		G: Whitehead 2
NEW ZEALAND	18	T: Williams, Whittaker, P Orchard, R Orchard
		G: Tatana 3

1971 *16 Oct, at Castleford, 4108*

GREAT BRITAIN	14	T: Coulman, Walsh, Millward, Sullivan
		G: Watkins
NEW ZEALAND	17	T: P Orchard 2, Tatana
		G: Tatana 4

1971 *6 Nov, at Headingley, 5479*

GREAT BRITAIN	12	T: Atkinson 2
		G: Holmes 4 (2DG)
NEW ZEALAND	3	T: Greengrass

1974 *27 Jul, at Auckland, 10 466*

GREAT BRITAIN	8	T: Nash, Bevan
		G: Clawson
NEW ZEALAND	13	T: Stirling
		G: Collicoat 5

1974 *4 Aug, at Christchurch, 6316*

GREAT BRITAIN	17	T: Dyl, Redfearn, Hesketh
		G: Gray 4
NEW ZEALAND	8	G: Collicoat 4

1974 *10 Aug, at Auckland, 11 574*

GREAT BRITAIN	20	T: Bevan 2, Hesketh, Dyl
		G: Gray 4
NEW ZEALAND	0	

Previous page *Great Britain skipper Eric Ashton moves to tackle New Zealand half-back Billy Snowden at Headingley in 1961. Ashton is one of a handful of players who have scored over 300 tries and 300 goals.*

1979 *21 Jul, at Auckland, 9000*
GREAT BRITAIN   16   T: Smith, Evans, Fairbairn, Hughes
    G: Fairbairn 2
NEW ZEALAND   8   T: Uluave, Ah Kuoi
    G: Collicoat

1979 *5 Aug, at Christchurch, 8500*
GREAT BRITAIN   22   T: Evans, Casey, Hughes, Grayshon
    G: Fairbairn 5
NEW ZEALAND   7   T: Filipaina
    G: Filipaina 2

1979 *11 Aug, at Auckland, 7000*
GREAT BRITAIN   11   T: Stephens, Smith, Hughes
    G: Fairbairn
NEW ZEALAND   18   T: Fisher, O'Hara, Graham, Leuluai
    G: Filipaina 3

1980 *18 Oct, at Wigan, 7031*
GREAT BRITAIN   14   T: Camilleri, M Smith
    G: Fairbairn 4
NEW ZEALAND   14   T: Ah Kuoi, Coll
    G: G Smith 4

1980 *2 Nov, at Odsal, 10 946*
GREAT BRITAIN   8   G: Fairbairn 4
NEW ZEALAND   12   T: O'Donnell, O'Hara
    G: G Smith 3

1980 *15 Nov, at Headingley, 8210*
GREAT BRITAIN   10   T: Drummond 2
    G: Burke 2
NEW ZEALAND   2   G: G Smith

1984 *14 Jul, at Auckland, 10 238*
GREAT BRITAIN   0
NEW ZEALAND   12   T: Leuluai, Ah Kuoi
    G: Filipaina 2

1984 *22 Jul, at Christchurch, 3824*
GREAT BRITAIN   12   T: Hanley, Myler
    G: Burke 2
NEW ZEALAND   28   T: O'Hara 2, Leuluai, Ah Kuoi, Bell
    G: Filipaina 4

1984 *28 Jul, at Auckland, 7967*
GREAT BRITAIN   16   T: Hanley, Mumby
    G: Burke 4
NEW ZEALAND   32   T: Leuluai 2, Friend 2, O'Hara
    G: Filipaina 6

1985 *19 Oct, at Headingley, 12 591*
GREAT BRITAIN   22   T: Goodway, Hanley, Lydon
    G: Burke 3, Lydon 2
NEW ZEALAND   24   T: O'Hara, Bell, Graham, K Sorensen, Leuluai
    G: Filipaina 2

1985 *2 Nov, at Wigan, 15 506*
GREAT BRITAIN   25   T: Schofield 4
    G: Lydon 4, Pinner (DG)
NEW ZEALAND   8   T: Bell
    G: Filipaina 2

1985 *9 Nov*, at Elland Road, 22 209*
GREAT BRITAIN   6   G: Crooks 3
NEW ZEALAND   6   T: Graham
    G: D Sorensen

1988 *17 Jul, at Christchurch, 8525*
GREAT BRITAIN   10   T: Loughlin, D Hulme
    G: Loughlin
NEW ZEALAND   12   T: Freeman 2
    G: Brown 2

1989 *21 Oct, at Old Trafford, 18 273*
GREAT BRITAIN   16   T: Ford, Tait, Offiah
    G: Loughlin 2
NEW ZEALAND   24   T: Goulding, McGahan, K Shelford, Freeman, K Iro
    G: Sherlock 2

1989 *28 Oct, at Elland Road, 13 073*
GREAT BRITAIN   26   T: Goodway 2, Edwards, Offiah
    G: Loughlin 5
NEW ZEALAND   6   T: McGahan
    G: Sherlock

1989 *11 Nov*, at Wigan, 20 346*
GREAT BRITAIN   10   T: Offiah, Tait
    G: Loughlin
NEW ZEALAND   6   T: K Shelford
    G: K Shelford

1990 *24 Jun, at Palmerston North, 8073*
GREAT BRITAIN   11   T: Davies, Gibson
    G: Davies, Schofield (DG)
NEW ZEALAND   10   T: Panapa, K Iro
    G: Brown

1990 *8 Jul, at Auckland, 7843*
GREAT BRITAIN   16   T: Schofield, Betts, Offiah
    G: Davies 2
NEW ZEALAND   14   T: M Horo
    G: Ridge 5

1990 *15 Jul*, at Christchurch, 3133*
GREAT BRITAIN   18   T: Schofield, R Powell, Offiah
    G: Davies 3
NEW ZEALAND   21   T: Kemp, Nikau
    G: Ridge 6, McGahan (DG)

* World Cup Match

GREAT BRITAIN v FRANCE

TEST MATCH RESULTS

1957 *26 Jan, at Headingley, 20 221*
GREAT BRITAIN   45 T: Turner 2, Sullivan, Bolton,
    Little, Boston, Jones,
    Gunney, Prescott
    G: Jones 9
FRANCE   12 T: Merquey, Duple
    G: Benausse 3

1957 *3 Mar, at Toulouse, 16 000*
GREAT BRITAIN   19 T: Jones, Prescott, Boston
    G: Jones 5
FRANCE   19 T: Merquey 2, Benausse
    G: Rives 3, Benausse 2

1957 *10 Apr, at St Helens, 20 928*
GREAT BRITAIN   29 T: Sullivan 2, Moses, Jones,
    Price
    G: Jones 7
FRANCE   14 T: Merquey, Tonus
    G: Benausse 3, Rouqueyrol

1957 *3 Nov, at Toulouse, 15 762*
GREAT BRITAIN   25 T: Sullivan 2, Ganley,
    Davies, Turner
    G: Ganley 5
FRANCE   14 T: Jimenez 2, Ayme, Voron
    G: Rives

1957 *23 Nov, at Wigan, 19 152*
GREAT BRITAIN   44 T: Bolton 3, Davies, Turner,
    Sullivan, Boston,
    Stevenson
    G: Ganley 10
FRANCE   15 T: Parent, Contrastin,
    Medus
    G: A Lacaze 3

1958 *2 Mar, at Grenoble, 20 000*
GREAT BRITAIN   23 T: Boston, Turner, Sullivan,
    Prescott, Stevenson
    G: Ganley 4
FRANCE   9 T: Contrastin
    G: A Lacaze 3

1959 *14 Mar, at Headingley, 21 948*
GREAT BRITAIN   50 T: Murphy 4, Sullivan 3,
    Vines, Ashton, Harris,
    Davies, Bolton
    G: Fraser 7
FRANCE   15 T: Carrere, Fages, Gruppi
    G: Rives 3

1959 *5 Apr, at Grenoble, 9000*
GREAT BRITAIN   15 T: Fox 2, McTigue
    G: Fraser 3
FRANCE   24 T: Savonne 2, Benausse 2,
    Gruppi, Bonnet
    G: Benausse 3

1960 *6 Mar, at Toulouse, 15 308*
GREAT BRITAIN   18 T: Fox 2, Ashton, Sullivan
    G: Fox 3
FRANCE   20 T: Quaglio 2, Bescos,
    Jimenez
    G: P Lacaze 4

The French cover descends on Great Britain scrum-half Alex Murphy at Grenoble in 1959. France won the Test 24–15, a rarity in Anglo-French Test matches.

1960 *26 Mar, at St Helens, 13 165*
GREAT BRITAIN	17 T:	Bolton, Sullivan, Fox
	G:	Fox 4
FRANCE	17 T:	Jimenez, Eramouspe, Verge
	G:	P Lacaze 4

1960 *11 Dec, at Bordeaux, 5127*
GREAT BRITAIN	21 T:	Fox 2, J Shaw, Myler, Murphy
	G:	Fox 2, Fraser
FRANCE	10 T:	Foussat 2
	G:	A Lacaze 2

1961 *28 Jan, at St Helens, 14 804*
GREAT BRITAIN	27 T:	Murphy 2, B Shaw, Stopford, Boston
	G:	Fraser 6
FRANCE	8 T:	Quaglio, Foussat
	G:	P Lacaze

1962 *17 Feb, at Wigan, 17 277*
GREAT BRITAIN	15 T:	Sullivan, Huddart, Ashton
	G:	Fox 3
FRANCE	20 T:	Benausse 2, Mantoulan, Dubon
	G:	Benausse 4

1962 *11 Mar, at Perpignan, 12 500*
GREAT BRITAIN	13 T:	Herbert, Ashton, Sullivan
	G:	Fox 2
FRANCE	23 T:	Verge 2, Dubon
	G:	Benausse 5, Carrere 2

1962 *2 Dec, at Perpignan, 12 500*
GREAT BRITAIN	12 T:	Ashton, Fox
	G:	Fox 3
FRANCE	17 T:	Mantoulan, Carrere, Bourreil
	G:	Benausse 4

1963 *3 Apr, at Wigan, 19 487*
GREAT BRITAIN	42 T:	Smales 2, Stopford 2, Bolton, Fox, Boston, Ashton
	G:	Fox 9
FRANCE	4 G:	P Lacaze 2

1964 *8 Mar, at Perpignan, 4326*
GREAT BRITAIN	11 T:	Shelton 2, Buckley
	G:	Gowers
FRANCE	5 T:	Verge
	G:	Villeneuve

TEST MATCH RESULTS

1964 *18 Mar, at Leigh, 4750*
GREAT BRITAIN   39   T: Hardisty 2, Jordan, Parker, Dixon, Smith, Fox
         G: Fox 9
FRANCE   0

1964 *6 Dec, at Perpignan, 7150*
GREAT BRITAIN   8   T: Hardisty, Jones
         G: Gowers
FRANCE   18   T: Bruzy 2
         G: P Lacaze 4, Courtine 2

1965 *23 Jan, at Swinton, 9959*
GREAT BRITAIN   17   T: Jones
         G: Fox 7
FRANCE   7   T: Bruzy
         G: P Lacaze 2

1966 *16 Jan, at Perpignan, 7255*
GREAT BRITAIN   13   T: Murphy, Jones, Stopford
         G: Fox 2
FRANCE   18   T: Lecompte, Marty
         G: P Lacaze 6

1966 *5 Mar, at Wigan, 14 004*
GREAT BRITAIN   4   G: Gowers 2
FRANCE   8   G: P Lacaze 2, Courtine, Mantoulan

1967 *22 Jan, at Carcassonne, 10 650*
GREAT BRITAIN   16   T: Sullivan 2, Hardisty 2
         G: Fox 2
FRANCE   13   T: Ferren
         G: P Lacaze 5

1967 *4 Mar, at Wigan, 7448*
GREAT BRITAIN   13   T: Keegan, Hardisty, Robinson
         G: Fox 2
FRANCE   23   T: Clar, Marracq, Lecompte
         G: P Lacaze 7

1968 *11 Feb, at Paris, 5500*
GREAT BRITAIN   22   T: Risman 2, Millward, Burwell
         G: Risman 5
FRANCE   13   T: Pellerin 2, Sabatie
         G: Mantoulan 2

1968 *2 Mar, at Odsal, 13 992*
GREAT BRITAIN   19   T: Burwell 2, Young, Millward, Morgan
         G: Risman 2
FRANCE   8   T: Mazard, Pellerin
         G: Capdouze

1968 *30 Nov, at St Helens, 6207*
GREAT BRITAIN   34   T: Burgess 3, Gemmell 2, Ashcroft, Burwell, Dixon
         G: Fox 5
FRANCE   10   T: Cabero, Calle
         G: Chabert 2

1969 *2 Feb, at Toulouse, 7536*
GREAT BRITAIN   9   T: Dixon
         G: Fox 3
FRANCE   13   T: De Nadai, Mantoulan, Bonnery
         G: Capdouze 2

1971 *7 Feb, at Toulouse, 14 960*
GREAT BRITAIN   8   T: Smith, Jeanes
         G: Whitehead
FRANCE   16   T: Bonal, Marsolan
         G: Capdouze 5

1971 *17 Mar, at St Helens, 7783*
GREAT BRITAIN   24   T: Millward 2, Whitehead, Benyon, Thompson, Smith
         G: Whitehead 3
FRANCE   2   G: Pere

1972 *6 Feb, at Toulouse, 11 508*
GREAT BRITAIN   10   T: Sullivan, Benyon
         G: Holmes 2
FRANCE   9   T: Ruiz
         G: Capdouze 4 (2DG)

1972 *12 Mar, at Odsal, 7313*
GREAT BRITAIN   45   T: Ashurst 2, Sullivan, Benyon, Charlton, Holmes, Atkinson, Lowe, Stephenson, Walsh, Jeanes
         G: Holmes 6
FRANCE   10   T: Pierre, Marsolan
         G: Capdouze 2

1974 *20 Jan, at Grenoble, 4100*
GREAT BRITAIN   24   T: Fielding 3, Laughton, Gill, Willicombe
         G: Clawson 3
FRANCE   5   T: Molinier
         G: Pierre

1974 *17 Feb, at Wigan, 9108*
GREAT BRITAIN   29   T: Charlton 2, Redfearn 2, Laughton, Willicombe, Gray
         G: Clawson 2, Gray, Watkins
FRANCE   0

1981 *6 Dec, at The Boulevard, Hull, 13 173*
GREAT BRITAIN   37   T: Gill 3, Drummond 2, Woods, Hartley
         G: Woods 7, Fairbairn
FRANCE   0

1981 *20 Dec, at Marseilles, 6500*
GREAT BRITAIN   2   G: Woods
FRANCE   19   T: Solal 2, Kaminski, Scicchitano
         G: Perez 3, Laville (DG)

Toulouse, 1972 – Britain's second-rower Bill Ashurst breaks the French defence with winger Clive Sullivan rushing to support.

TEST MATCH RESULTS

1983 *20 Feb, at Carcassonne, 3862*

GREAT BRITAIN	20	T:	Joyner, Lydon, Noble, Goodway
		G:	Lydon 3, Burke
FRANCE	5	T:	Bernard
		G:	Imbert

1983 *6 Mar, at The Boulevard, Hull, 6055*

GREAT BRITAIN	17	T:	Duane, Smith, A Gregory
		G:	Mumby 4
FRANCE	5	T:	Solal
		G:	Baloup

1984 *29 Jan, at Avignon, 4000*

GREAT BRITAIN	12	T:	Goodway, Foy
		G:	Crooks 2
FRANCE	0		

1984 *17 Feb, at Headingley, 7646*

| GREAT BRITAIN | 10 | G: | Hobbs 5 |
| FRANCE | 0 | | |

1985 *1 Mar, at Headingley, 6491*

GREAT BRITAIN	50	T:	Hanley 2, Fox 2, Gill, Gribbin, Watkinson, Divorty
		G:	Creasser 8, Fox
FRANCE	4	T:	Macalli

1985 *17 Mar, at Perpignan, 5000*

GREAT BRITAIN	16	T:	Ford 2, Foy
		G:	Creasser, Divorty
FRANCE	24	T:	Couston 3, Fourquet
		G:	Pallares 4

1986 *16 Feb*, at Avignon, 4000*

GREAT BRITAIN	10	T:	Hanley
		G:	Crooks 3
FRANCE	10	T:	Dumas
		G:	Dumas 3

1986 *1 Mar, at Wigan, 8112*

GREAT BRITAIN	24	T:	Schofield, Drummond, James, Marchant
		G:	Crooks 2, Schofield 2
FRANCE	10	T:	Couston 2
		G:	Dumas

1987 *24 Jan*, at Headingley, 6567*

GREAT BRITAIN	52	T:	Edwards 2, M Gregory 2, Hanley 2, Goodway, Lydon, Forster
		G:	Lydon 8
FRANCE	4	G:	Perez 2

1987 *8 Feb, at Carcassonne, 1968*

GREAT BRITAIN	20	T:	Beardmore, Gill, Hanley
		G:	Lydon 4
FRANCE	10	T:	Espugna
		G:	Perez 3

1988 *24 Jan, at Avignon, 6500*

GREAT BRITAIN	28	T:	Schofield 2, Hanley, Offiah, Drummond
		G:	Loughlin 3, Creasser
FRANCE	14	T:	Ratier, Verdes
		G:	Dumas 3

1988 *6 Feb, at Headingley, 7007*

GREAT BRITAIN	30	T:	Hanley 2, A Gregory, Schofield, Plange
		G:	Schofield 5
FRANCE	12	T:	Pons, Khedimi
		G:	Bourrel 2

1989 *21 Jan, at Wigan, 8266*

GREAT BRITAIN	26	T:	Offiah, Ford, Lydon, Hanley, Edwards
		G:	Loughlin 3
FRANCE	10	T:	Moliner, Dumas
		G:	Fraisse

1989 *5 Feb, at Avignon, 6500*

GREAT BRITAIN	30	T:	Ford 2, Tait, Edwards, Hanley, Williams
		G:	Lydon 3
FRANCE	8	T:	Ratier, Dumas

1990 *18 Mar, at Perpignan, 6000*

GREAT BRITAIN	8	T:	Offiah
		G:	Schofield 2
FRANCE	4	T:	Pons

1990 *7 Apr, at Headingley, 6554*

GREAT BRITAIN	18	T:	Cordle, Tait, Offiah
		G:	Steadman 3
FRANCE	25	T:	Pons, Rabot, Divet
		G:	Fraisse 5, Dumas 2 (1DG)

1991 *27 Jan*, at Perpignan, 5500*

GREAT BRITAIN	45	T:	Offiah 2, Edwards 2, Schofield 2, Betts, Platt
		G:	Eastwood 6, Schofield (DG)
FRANCE	10	T:	Auroy, Fraisse
		G:	Tisseyre

1991 *16 Feb, at Headingley, 5284*

GREAT BRITAIN	60	T:	Offiah 5, Schofield 3, Eastwood, Edwards, Hampson
		G:	Eastwood 8
FRANCE	4	T:	Pons

* World Cup Match

GREAT BRITAIN v PAPUA NEW GUINEA

TEST MATCH RESULTS

1984 *5 Aug, at Mount Hagen, 7510*

GREAT BRITAIN	38	T: Drummond 2, Burke, Mumby, Rayne, Hanley, Hobbs
		G: Burke 5
PAPUA NEW GUINEA	20	T: Tolik, Noifa, Jekis, Taumaku
		G: Numapo 2

1987 *24 Oct*, at Wigan, 9121*

GREAT BRITAIN	42	T: Edwards 2, Ford, Hanley, Medley, Lydon, A Gregory
		G: Stephenson 7
PAPUA NEW GUINEA	0	

1988 *22 May*, at Port Moresby, 12 107*

GREAT BRITAIN	42	T: Schofield 2, Gill 2, Medley, M Gregory, Stephenson
		G: Loughlin 7
PAPUA NEW GUINEA	22	T: Kovae 2, Krewanty, Rop
		G: Numapo 3

1990 *27 May, at Goroka, 10 500*

GREAT BRITAIN	18	T: Eastwood, Davies, Goulding
		G: Davies 3
PAPUA NEW GUINEA	20	T: Evei, Haru
		G: Numapo 6 (1DG), Haru (DG)

1990 *2 Jun*, at Port Moresby, 8000*

GREAT BRITAIN	40	T: Gibson 2, Eastwood, Goulding, Dixon, D Powell, Schofield
		G: Davies 6
PAPUA NEW GUINEA	8	T: Ongogo
		G: Numapo 2

* World Cup Match

Dario Kovae, a two-try Kumul against Great Britain in 1988.

INCOMING TOURS

AUSTRALIANS TO GREAT BRITAIN

The first Australian tour of Great Britain took place in 1908–09, since which time there have been 17 Kangaroo tours. From 1937–38 onwards the tours have included French sections. The records below, however, apply only to games played in Britain.

Season	Captain	P	W	D	L	Points For-Agn	Test Series
1908–09	D Lutge	45	17	6	22	513–474	*GB2 A0
1911–12	C McKivat	35	28	2	5	619–281	*GB0 A2
1921–22	L Cubitt	36	27	0	9	763–248	GB2 A1
1929–30	T Gorman	35	24	2	9	710–347	*GB2 A1
1933–34	F McMillan	37	27	0	10	754–295	GB3 A0
1937–38	W Prigg	25	13	1	11	293–232	GB2 A1
1948–49	C Maxwell	27	15	0	12	348–275	GB3 A0
1952–53	C Churchill	27	23	1	3	816–248	GB2 A1
1956–57	K Kearney	19	10	0	9	335–296	GB2 A1
1959–60	K Barnes	24	15	0	9	495–390	GB2 A1
1963–64	A Summons	22..	16	1	5	379–201	GB1 A2
1967–68	R Gasnier	20	12	1	7	293–196	GB1 A2
1973–74	G Langlands	16	14	0	2	364–141	GB1 A2
1978–79	R Fulton	16	13	0	3	375–117	GB1 A2
1982–83	M Krilich	15	15	0	0	423–80	GB0 A3
1986–87	W Lewis	13	13	0	0	452–105	GB0 A3
1990–91	M Meninga	13	12	0	1	347–121	GB1 A2

* Great Britain and Australia also played a drawn Test

NEW ZEALANDERS TO GREAT BRITAIN

The first New Zealand tour of Great Britain took place in 1907–08 when AH Baskerville brought over the 'All Golds'. There have since been 12 Kiwi tours, the 1939 tour being restricted to only two games because of the outbreak of war. Since 1947 the tours have included French sections. The records below, however, apply only to games played in Britain.

Season	Captain	P	W	D	L	Points For-Agn	Test Series
1907–08	HR Wright	35	19	2	14	414–294	GB1 NZ2
1926–27	H Avery	34	17	0	17	562–554	GB3 NZ0
1939–40	R King	2	2	0	0	41–13	
1947–48	PA Smith	27	16	1	10	391–240	GB2 NZ1
1951–52	MW Robertson	28	18	0	10	482–348	GB3 NZ0
1955–56	TO Baxter	26	13	2	11	445–418	GB2 NZ1
1961–62	RD Hammond	20	8	0	12	320–328	GB2 NZ1
1965–66	WL Snowden	23	13	1	9	274–259	*GB2 NZ0
1971–72	RF Christian	20	10	0	10	319–300	GB1 NZ2
1980–81	M Graham	14	7	1	6	202–143	*GB1 NZ1
1985–86	M Graham	12	8	1	3	249–153	*GB1 NZ1
1989–90	H McGahan	12	8	0	4	300–183	GB2 NZ1

*Great Britain and New Zealand also played a drawn Test

PAPUA NEW GUINEANS TO GREAT BRITAIN

The Kumuls have made one tour to Great Britain as a fully fledged member of the International Board. A Kumul tour was undertaken in 1979–80, but only games against amateur sides were staged.

Season	Captain	P	W	D	L	Points For-Agn	Test Series
1987–88	B Numapo	8*	3	1	4	90–163	GB1 PNG0

* Includes a fixture against a BARLA XIII

OTHER INTERNATIONAL MATCHES

The first International match was a 12-a-side fixture between England and Other Nationalities at Central Park, Wigan on 5 April 1904. In the intervening three-quarters of a century International fixtures, as distinct from Tests, have been staged somewhat haphazardly, sometimes as part of a European tournament, sometimes as merely isolated representative matches. The games listed below are official Internationals for which caps were awarded.

ENGLAND v WALES

Year		Venue					
1908	20 Apr	Tonypandy	Wales	35	18	England
1908	28 Dec	Broughton	England	31	7	Wales
1909	4 Dec	Wakefield	England	19	13	Wales
1910	9 Apr	Ebbw Vale	Wales	39	18	England
1910	10 Dec	Coventry	England	39	13	Wales
1911	1 Apr	Ebbw Vale	Wales	8	27	England
1912	20 Jan	Oldham	England	31	5	Wales
1913	15 Feb	Plymouth	England	40	16	Wales
1914	14 Feb	St Helens	England	16	12	Wales
1921	19 Jan	Headingley	England	35	9	Wales
1922	11 Dec	Herne Hill	England	12	7	Wales
1923	7 Feb	Wigan	England	2	13	Wales
1923	1 Oct	Huddersfield	England	18	11	Wales
1925	7 Feb	Workington	England	27	22	Wales
1925	30 Sep	Wigan	England	18	14	Wales
1926	12 Apr	Pontypridd	Wales	22	30	England
1927	6 Apr	Broughton	England	11	8	Wales
1928	11 Jan	Wigan	England	20	12	Wales
1928	14 Nov	Cardiff	Wales	15	39	England
1931	18 Mar	Huddersfield	England	23	18	Wales
1932	27 Jan	Salford	England	19	2	Wales
1932	30 Nov	Headingley	England	14	13	Wales
1935	10 Apr	Liverpool	England	24	11	Wales
1936	1 Feb	Craven Park, Hull	England	14	17	Wales
1936	7 Nov	Pontypridd	Wales	3	2	England
1938	29 Jan	Odsal	England	6	7	Wales
1938	5 Nov	Llanelli	Wales	17	9	England
1939	23 Dec	Odsal	England	3	16	Wales
1940	9 Nov	Oldham	England	8	5	Wales
1941	18 Oct	Odsal	England	9	9	Wales
1943	27 Feb	Wigan	England	15	9	Wales
1944	26 Feb	Wigan	England	9	9	Wales
1945	10 Mar	Wigan	England	18	8	Wales
1945	24 Nov	Swansea	Wales	11	3	England
1946	12 Oct	Swinton	England	10	13	Wales
1946	16 Nov	Swansea	Wales	5	19	England
1947	20 Sep	Wigan	England	8	10	Wales
1947	6 Dec	Swansea	Wales	7	18	England
1948	22 Sep	Wigan	England	11	5	Wales
1949	5 Feb	Swansea	Wales	14	10	England
1950	1 Mar	Wigan	England	11	6	Wales
1950	14 Oct	Abertillery	Wales	4	22	England
1951	19 Sep	St Helens	England	35	11	Wales
1952	17 Sep	Wigan	England	19	8	Wales
1953	16 Sep	St Helens	England	24	5	Wales
1968	7 Nov	Salford	England	17	24	Wales

Left *England v Wales at St Helens in 1953. Welsh centre Don Gullick sends out a pass to winger Arthur Daniels as England's Alan Davies challenges.*

Year		Venue					
1969	18 Oct	Headingley	England	40	23	Wales
1970	24 Feb	Headingley	England	26	7	Wales
1975	25 Feb	Salford	England	12	8	Wales
1975*	10 Jun	Brisbane	England	7	12	Wales
1975*	20 Sep	Warrington	England	22	16	Wales
1977	29 Jan	Headingley	England	2	6	Wales
1978	28 May	St Helens	England	60	13	Wales
1979	16 Mar	Widnes	England	15	7	Wales
1980	29 Feb	Craven Park, Hull	England	26	9	Wales
1981	18 Mar	Craven Park, Hull	England	17	4	Wales
1981	8 Nov	Cardiff	Wales	15	20	England
1984	14 Oct	Ebbw Vale	Wales	9	28	England

* World Championship   England 41 victories, Wales 15. Draws: 2

ENGLAND v FRANCE

Year		Venue					
1934	15 Apr	Paris	France	21	32	England
1935	28 Mar	Paris	France	15	15	England
1936	16 Feb	Paris	France	7	25	England
1937	10 Apr	Halifax	England	23	9	France
1938	20 Mar	Paris	France	15	17	England
1939	25 Feb	St Helens	England	9	23	France
1946	23 Feb	Swinton	England	16	6	France
1946	8 Dec	Bordeaux	France	0	3	England
1947	17 May	Headingley	England	5	2	France
1947	25 Oct	Huddersfield	England	20	15	France
1948	11 Apr	Marseilles	France	10	25	England
1948	28 Nov	Bordeaux	France	5	12	England
1949	12 Mar	Wembley	England	5	12	France
1949	4 Dec	Bordeaux	France	5	13	England
1950	11 Nov	Headingley	England	14	9	France
1951	25 Nov	Marseilles	France	42	13	England
1953	11 Apr	Paris	France	13	15	England
1953	7 Nov	Odsal	England	7	5	France
1956	10 May	Lyons	France	23	9	England
1962	17 Nov	Headingley	England	18	6	France
1969	25 Oct	Wigan	England	11	11	France
1970	15 Mar	Toulouse	France	14	9	England
1975	19 Jan	Perpignan	France	9	11	England
1975*	16 Mar	Headingley	England	20	2	France
1975*	11 Oct	Bordeaux	France	2	48	England
1977	20 Mar	Carcassonne	France	28	15	England
1978	5 Mar	Toulouse	France	11	13	England
1979	24 Mar	Warrington	England	12	6	France
1980	16 Mar	Narbonne	France	2	4	England
1981	21 Feb	Headingley	England	1	5	France

* World Championship   England 21 victories, France 7. Draws: 2

ENGLAND v OTHER NATIONALITIES

Year		Venue				
1904	5 Apr	Wigan	England	3	9	Other Nats
1905	2 Jan	Bradford PA	England	26	11	Other Nats
1906	1 Jan	Wigan	England	3	3	Other Nats
1921	5 Feb	Workington	England	33	16	Other Nats
1924	15 Oct	Headingley	England	17	23	Other Nats
1926	4 Feb	Whitehaven	England	37	11	Other Nats
1929	20 Mar	Headingley	England	27	20	Other Nats
1930	7 Apr	Halifax	England	19	35	Other Nats
1930	1 Oct	St Helens	England	31	18	Other Nats
1933	30 Mar	Workington	England	34	27	Other Nats
1949	19 Sep	Workington	England	7	13	Other Nats
1951	11 Apr	Wigan	England	10	35	Other Nats
1952	23 Apr	Wigan	England	31	18	Other Nats
1952	18 Oct	Huddersfield	England	12	31	Other Nats
1953	28 Nov	Wigan	England	30	22	Other Nats
1955	12 Sep	Wigan	England	16	33	Other Nats

England 8 victories, Other Nationalities 7. Draws: 1

ENGLAND v AUSTRALIA

Year		Venue				
1909	2 Jan	Huddersfield	England	14	9	Australia
1909	3 Feb	Glasgow	England	17	17	Australia
1909	3 Mar	Everton	England	14	7	Australia
1911	18 Oct	Fulham	England	6	11	Australia
1911	6 Dec	Notts County	England	5	3	Australia
1921	10 Oct	Highbury	England	5	4	Australia
1933	31 Dec	Paris	England	13	63	Australia
1934	13 Jan	Gateshead	England	19	14	Australia
1975*	28 Jun	Sydney	Australia	10	10	England
1975*	1 Nov	Wigan	England	16	13	Australia

* World Championship   England 6 victories, Australia 2. Draws: 2

ENGLAND v NEW ZEALAND

Year		Venue				
1908	11 Jan	Wigan	England	18	16	New Zealand
1975*	21 Jun	Auckland	New Zealand	17	17	England
1975*	25 Oct	Odsal	England	27	12	New Zealand

* World Championship   England 2 victories, New Zealand 0. Draws: 1

WALES v FRANCE

Year		Venue				
1935	1 Jan	Bordeaux	France	18	11	Wales
1935	23 Nov	Llanelli	Wales	41	7	France
1936	6 Dec	Paris	France	3	9	Wales
1938	2 Apr	Llanelli	Wales	18	2	France
1939	16 Apr	Bordeaux	France	16	10	Wales
1946	24 Mar	Bordeaux	France	19	7	Wales
1947	18 Jan	Marseilles	France	14	5	Wales
1947	12 Apr	Swansea	Wales	17	15	France
1947	23 Nov	Bordeaux	France	29	21	Wales
1948	20 Mar	Swansea	Wales	12	20	France
1948	23 Oct	Swansea	Wales	9	12	France
1949	10 Apr	Marseilles	France	11	0	Wales
1949	12 Nov	Swansea	Wales	16	8	France
1951	15 Apr	Marseilles	France	28	13	Wales
1952	6 Apr	Bordeaux	France	20	12	Wales

Year		Venue					
1952	25 Oct	Headingley	Wales	22	16	France
1953	13 Dec	Marseilles	France	23	22	Wales
1969	9 Mar	Paris	France	17	13	Wales
1969	23 Oct	Salford	Wales	2	8	France
1970	25 Jan	Perpignan	France	11	15	Wales
1975	16 Feb	Swansea	Wales	21	8	France
1975*	2 Mar	Toulouse	France	14	7	Wales
1975*	6 Nov	Salford	Wales	23	2	France
1977	20 Feb	Toulouse	France	13	2	Wales
1978	15 Jan	Widnes	Wales	29	7	France
1979	4 Feb	Narbonne	France	15	8	Wales
1980	26 Jan	Widnes	Wales	7	21	France
1981	31 Jan	Narbonne	France	23	5	Wales

* World Championship   Wales 10 victories, France 18. Draws: 0

WALES v OTHER NATIONALITIES

Year		Venue					
1949	22 Oct	Abertillery	Wales	5	6	Other Nats
1951	31 Mar	Swansea	Wales	21	27	Other Nats
1951	1 Dec	Abertillery	Wales	11	22	Other Nats
1953	15 Apr	Warrington	Wales	18	16	Other Nats
1953	7 Oct	Odsal	Wales	5	30	Other Nats

Wales 1 victory, Other Nationalities 4. Draws: 0

WALES v AUSTRALIA

Year		Venue					
1911	7 Oct	Ebbw Vale	Wales	20	28	Australia
1921	10 Dec	Pontypridd	Wales	16	21	Australia
1930	18 Jan	Wembley	Wales	10	26	Australia
1933	30 Dec	Wembley	Wales	19	51	Australia
1948	20 Nov	Swansea	Wales	5	12	Australia
1975*	14 Jun	Sydney	Australia	30	13	Wales
1975*	19 Oct	Swansea	Wales	6	18	Australia
1978	15 Oct	Swansea	Wales	3	8	Australia
1982	24 Oct	Cardiff	Wales	7	37	Australia

* World Championship   Wales 0 victories, Australia 9. Draws: 0

WALES v NEW ZEALAND

Year		Venue					
1908	1 Jan	Aberdare	Wales	9	8	New Zealand
1926	4 Dec	Pontypridd	Wales	34	8	New Zealand
1947	18 Oct	Swansea	Wales	20	28	New Zealand
1951	7 Dec	Odsal	Wales	3	15	New Zealand
1975*	28 Jun	Auckland	New Zealand	13	8	Wales
1975*	2 Nov	Swansea	Wales	25	24	New Zealand

* World Championship   Wales 3 victories, New Zealand 3. Draws: 0

BRITISH INTERNATIONAL RECORDS

GREAT BRITAIN – PLAYING SUMMARY

TESTS AGAINST

Country	P	W	D	L	F	A
Australia	105	51	4	50	1313	1605
France	54	37	3	14	1275	597
New Zealand	77	47	3	27	1293	1009
Papua New Guinea	5	4	0	1	180	70
Totals	241	139	10	92	4061	3281

WORLD CUP MATCHES 1954–77 AGAINST

Country	P	W	D	L	F	A
Australia	10	4	1	5	126	151
France	8	6	1	1	129	52
New Zealand	7	6	0	1	218	105
Totals	25	16	2	7	473	308
Grand Totals	266	155	12	99	4534	3589

MATCH RECORDS

Highest score v Australia	40–17	at Sydney	19 Jul 1958
Highest score v France	60–4	at Headingley	16 Feb 1991
Highest score v New Zealand	53–19	at Pau	4 Nov 1972
Highest score v Papua New Guinea	42–0	at Wigan	24 Oct 1987
	42–22	at Port Moresby	22 May 1988
Highest score by Australia	50–12	at Swinton	9 Nov 1963
Highest score by France	25–18	at Headingley	7 Apr 1990
Highest score by New Zealand	32–16	at Auckland	28 Jul 1984
Highest score by Papua New Guinea	22–42	at Port Moresby	22 May 1988

LOWEST MATCH AGGREGATES

v Australia	0–0	at Swinton	4 Jan 1930
v France	6–0	at Castleford	28 Oct 1970
v New Zealand	7–2	at Swinton	25 Sep 1965
v Papua New Guinea	18–20	at Goroka	27 May 1990

ATTENDANCE RECORDS

In Britain:

v Australia	54 569	at Wembley	27 Oct 1990
v France	22 923	at Swinton	1 Oct 1960
v New Zealand	42 685	at Odsal	20 Dec 1947
v Papua New Guinea	9 121	at Wigan	24 Oct 1987

Abroad:

v Australia	70 204	at Sydney	6 Jun 1932
v France	37 471	at Toulouse	7 Nov 1954
v New Zealand	34 000	at Auckland	31 Jul 1920
v Papua New Guinea	12 107	at Port Moresby	22 May 1988

INDIVIDUAL RECORDS

MOST TRIES FOR GREAT BRITAIN IN A MATCH

v Australia	4	J Leytham	at Brisbane	2 Jul	1910
v France	5	M Offiah	at Headingley	16 Feb	1991
v New Zealand	4	W Boston	at Auckland	24 Jul	1954
	4	G Schofield	at Wigan	2 Nov	1985
v Papua New Guinea	2	By five players			

MOST GOALS FOR GREAT BRITAIN IN A MATCH

v Australia	10	L Jones	at Brisbane	3 Jul	1954
v France	10	B Ganley	at Wigan	23 Nov	1957
v New Zealand	10	J Holmes	at Pau	4 Nov	1972
v Papua New Guinea	7	D Stephenson	at Wigan	24 Oct	1987
	7	P Loughlin	at Port Moresby	22 May	1988

MOST POINTS FOR GREAT BRITAIN IN A MATCH

v Australia	20	L Jones	at Brisbane	3 Jul	1954
	20	R Millward	at Sydney	20 Jun	1970
v France	21	L Jones	at Headingley	26 Jan	1957
	21	N Fox	at Wigan	3 Apr	1963
	21	N Fox	at Leigh	18 Mar	1964
v New Zealand	26	J Holmes	at Pau	4 Nov	1972
v Papua New Guinea	14	M Burke	at Mount Hagen	5 Aug	1984
	14	D Stephenson	at Wigan	24 Oct	1987
	14	P Loughlin	at Port Moresby	22 May	1988

MOST TRIES AGAINST GREAT BRITAIN IN A MATCH

For Australia	3	By eight players			
For France	3	D Couston	at Perpignan	17 Mar	1985
For New Zealand	2	No player has scored more than two			
For Papua New Guinea	2	D Kovae	at Port Moresby	22 May	1988

MOST GOALS AGAINST GREAT BRITAIN IN A MATCH

For Australia	10	M Cronin	at Brisbane	16 Jun	1979
For France	7	P Lacaze	at Wigan	4 Mar	1967
For New Zealand	7	D White	at Greymouth	31 Jul	1954
	7	W Sorensen	at Sydney	25 Jun	1957
	7	J Fagan	at Headingley	30 Sep	1961
	7	E Wiggs	at Auckland	20 Aug	1966
For Papua New Guinea	6	B Numapo	at Goroka	27 May	1990

BRITISH INTERNATIONAL RECORDS

MOST POINTS AGAINST GREAT BRITAIN IN A MATCH

For Australia	22	M O'Connor	at Old Trafford	25 Oct 1986
For France	14	G Benausse	at Wigan	17 Feb 1962
	14	P Lacaze	at Wigan	4 Mar 1967
For New Zealand	14	D White	at Greymouth	31 Jul 1954
	14	W Sorensen	at Sydney	25 Jun 1957
	14	J Fagan	at Headingley	30 Sep 1961
	14	E Wiggs	at Auckland	20 Aug 1966
For Papua New Guinea	11	B Numapo	at Goroka	27 May 1990

LEADING GREAT BRITAIN CAP WINNERS

Tests and World Cup matches

46	Mick Sullivan (Huddersfield, Wigan, St Helens, York)	1954–63
34*	Ellery Hanley (Bradford N, Wigan)	1984–91
31	Billy Boston (Wigan)	1954–63
31	Garry Schofield (Hull, Leeds)	1984–91
30*	Cliff Watson (St Helens)	1963–71
29	Neil Fox (Wakefield T)	1959–69
29	George Nicholls (Widnes, St Helens)	1969–79
29*	Roger Millward (Castleford, Hull KR)	1966–78
28	Alan Prescott (St Helens)	1951–58
27	Phil Jackson (Barrow)	1954–58
27	Alex Murphy (St Helens, Warrington)	1958–71
26	Eric Ashton (Wigan)	1957–63
26	John Atkinson (Leeds)	1968–80
25	Tommy Harris (Hull)	1954–60
25	Brian McTigue (Wigan)	1958–63
25	Jim Sullivan (Wigan)	1924–33
25*	Andy Gregory (Widnes, Warrington, Wigan)	1981–90
24	Des Drummond (Leigh, Warrington)	1980–88
24	Frank Myler (Widnes, St Helens)	1960–70
24	Steve Nash (Featherstone R, Salford)	1971–82
24	Derek Turner (Oldham, Wakefield T)	1956–62
24†	Joe Lydon (Widnes, Wigan)	1983–90
23	Dave Bolton (Wigan)	1957–63
23	Andy Goodway (Oldham, Wigan)	1983–90
23†	Chris Hesketh (Salford)	1970–74
21*	Jimmy Thompson (Featherstone R, Bradford N)	1970–78
20	Alan Davies (Oldham)	1955–60
20	Ernest Ward (Bradford N)	1946–52
20*	Mike Gregory (Warrington)	1987–90
20§	John Holmes (Leeds)	1971–82

* Includes one game as playing substitute
† Includes two games as playing substitute
§ Includes six games as playing substitute

191

MICK SULLIVAN

Top Test Match Player

Traditionally the Test match has been the most demanding, gruelling and searching way of proving a Rugby League player's mettle. A small minority of professional players attain Test status and a great many are found wanting when thrust into the Test cauldron. An endless list of players have seen their Test careers grind to a halt after a single cap, for it requires a special type of player to survive and flourish at the very top level of the game. Invariably the truly gifted man makes it, and often

the truly gritty player makes it. Mick Sullivan was both gifted and gritty. His 46 Tests for Great Britain were ample testimony to his grit and durability, while his 41 Test tries are an accurate measure of his gifts as an attacking, resourceful winger. Both remain all-time Test records over quarter of a century after Mick pulled on his last Test jersey in 1963.

Sullivan signed for Huddersfield from Shawcross Boys Club on 29 May 1952 as an 11 stone, 18-year-old right-winger. He

was quick, direct and decisive. Mick Sullivan did not mess about, and though he was always comparatively light, his defence was notoriously hard and he seemed to glory in his notoriety. Once the selectors had marked him down as Test material in 1954, he was a permanent fixture in Britain's red, white and blue.

His introduction to the Great Britain team followed in the wake of a disappointing tour of Australia and New Zealand by the 1954 Lions. The first World

Cup was scheduled for the autumn of 1954 in France. Most of the Lions declined invitations to participate and Mick was one of the youngbloods selected to salvage British pride across the Channel. The squad, under Scottish loose-forward Dave Valentine, was given the proverbial snowball-in-Hell's chance. Hell must have frozen over, for Great Britain beat Australia 28–13, with Sullivan making his debut at centre, New Zealand 26–6 and drew 13–13 with France before taking the World cup after a superb 16–12 victory over the French in a Paris play-off.

Mick Sullivan played in all four games and would not miss a Test or World Cup game for the next seven years. The vast majority of his games were as a left-winger, but he was a good enough footballer to be used as both a centre and a scrum-half, the latter against New Zealand in 1962 when injuries had crippled a brilliant Lions team in Australia.

Sullivan toured Australasia in 1958, when he set a tour record of 38 tries, and in 1962. On both tours he played in all the Tests and shared in Ashes victories. He also appeared in three World Cup series, from two of which Great Britain emerged victorious. His try in the final match of the 1960 World Cup when Britain downed Australia 10–3 on a mud-heap at Odsal was crucial to his team's success.

In 1957 Mick had moved from Fartown to Wigan for a world record £9500 and it was on his home ground, Central Park, in the Ashes decider on 12 December 1959 that he became Great Britain's most capped Test player, his 29th appearance removing his former Lions captain and team-mate Alan Prescott from the top spot. Great Britain won the Ashes with a hard-fought 18–12 triumph, the

series being notable for Sullivan's failure to register a solitary try!

Mick Sullivan would go on as a Test star for four more years, set another world transfer record with his £11 000 move to St Helens in 1961, win all the honours in the game and spend

his latter playing days with York and Dewsbury, apart from taking in a spell with rebel Australian club Junee. Whatever his successes in club football, Mick Sullivan will always primarily be remembered for his teak-tough displays on Britain's left wing – the ultimate Test player.

MICK SULLIVAN'S TEST APPEARANCES & TRIES

Date	Opponents	Venue	Tries
31 Oct 1954*	Australia	Lyons	0
7 Nov 1954*	France	Toulouse	0
11 Nov 1954*	New Zealand	Bordeaux	0
13 Nov 1954*	France	Paris	0
8 Oct 1955	New Zealand	Swinton	2
12 Nov 1955	New Zealand	Odsal	3
17 Dec 1955	New Zealand	Headingley	1
17 Nov 1956	Australia	Wigan	1
1 Dec 1956	Australia	Odsal	0
15 Dec 1956	Australia	Swinton	1
26 Jan 1957	France	Headingley	1
3 Mar 1957	France	Toulouse	0
10 Apr 1957	France	St Helens	2
15 Jun 1957*	France	Sydney	2
17 Jun 1957*	Australia	Sydney	0
25 Jun 1957*	New Zealand	Sydney	1
3 Nov 1957	France	Toulouse	2
23 Nov 1957	France	Wigan	1
2 Mar 1958	France	Grenoble	1
14 Jun 1958	Australia	Sydney	0
5 Jul 1958	Australia	Brisbane	1
19 Jul 1958	Australia	Sydney	3
26 Jul 1958	New Zealand	Auckland	1
9 Aug 1958	New Zealand	Auckland	3
14 Mar 1959	France	Headingley	3
5 Apr 1959	France	Grenoble	0
17 Oct 1959	Australia	Swinton	0
21 Nov 1959	Australia	Headingley	0
12 Dec 1959	Australia	Wigan	0
6 Mar 1960	France	Toulouse	1
26 Mar 1960	France	St Helens	1
24 Sep 1960*	New Zealand	Odsal	0
1 Oct 1960*	France	Swinton	1
8 Oct 1960*	Australia	Odsal	1
11 Dec 1960	France	Bordeaux	0
28 Jan 1961	France	St Helens	0
21 Oct 1961	New Zealand	Odsal	2
4 Nov 1961	New Zealand	Swinton	2
17 Feb 1962	France	Wigan	1
11 Mar 1962	France	Perpignan	1
9 Jun 1962	Australia	Sydney	2
30 Jun 1962	Australia	Brisbane	0
14 Jul 1962	Australia	Sydney	0
28 Jul 1962	New Zealand	Auckland	0
2 Dec 1962	France	Perpignan	0
9 Nov 1963	Australia	Swinton	0
Totals	46 Tests		41

* World Cup

LEADING GREAT BRITAIN TRY-SCORERS

Tests and World Cup matches

41	Mick Sullivan (Huddersfield, Wigan, St Helens, York)	1954–63
25	Garry Schofield (Hull, Leeds)	1984–91
24	Billy Boston (Wigan)	1954–63
19	Martin Offiah (Widnes)	1988–91
18	Ellery Hanley (Bradford N, Wigan)	1984–91
17	Roger Millward (Castleford, Hull KR)	1966–78
16	Alex Murphy (St Helens, Warrington)	1958–71
14	Eric Ashton (Wigan)	1957–63
14	Neil Fox (Wakefield T)	1959–69
13	Clive Sullivan (Hull)	1967–73
12	John Atkinson (Leeds)	1968–80
10	Jim Leytham (Wigan)	1908–10

LEADING GREAT BRITAIN GOAL-KICKERS

Tests and World Cup matches

93	Neil Fox (Wakefield T)	1959–69
66	Lewis Jones (Leeds)	1954–57
64	Jim Sullivan (Wigan)	1924–33
53	Eric Fraser (Warrington)	1958–61
44	George Fairbairn (Wigan, Hull KR)	1977–82
29	Paul Loughlin (St Helens)	1988–91
26	Joe Lydon (Widnes, Wigan)	1983–90
25	Terry Clawson (Featherstone R, Leeds, Oldham)	1962–74
22	Ray Dutton (Widnes)	1970
22	John Holmes (Leeds)	1971–82
22	Ernest Ward (Bradford N)	1946–52
21	Mick Burke (Widnes)	1980–86
21	Ken Gowers (Swinton)	1962–66

LEADING GREAT BRITAIN POINTS-SCORERS

Tests and World Cup matches

228	Neil Fox (Wakefield T)	1959–69
147	Lewis Jones (Leeds)	1954–57
128	Jim Sullivan (Wigan)	1924–33
123	Mick Sullivan (Huddersfield, Wigan, St Helens, York)	1954–63
122	Garry Schofield (Hull, Leeds)	1984–91
109	Eric Fraser (Warrington)	1958–61
91	George Fairbairn (Wigan, Hull KR)	1977–82
81	Roger Millward (Castleford, Hull KR)	1966–78
76	Martin Offiah (Widnes)	1988–91
75	Joe Lydon (Widnes, Wigan)	1983–90
72	Billy Boston (Wigan)	1954–63
72	Ellery Hanley (Bradford N, Wigan)	1984–91
66	Paul Loughlin (St Helens)	1988–91
56	Ernest Ward (Bradford N)	1946–52
56	Paul Eastwood (Hull)	1990–91
51	John Holmes (Leeds)	1971–82
50	Terry Clawson (Featherstone R, Leeds, Oldham)	1962–74

MOST CONSECUTIVE TESTS FOR GREAT BRITAIN

Winger **Mick Sullivan** appeared in 36 consecutive tests between 1954 and 1961.

GREAT BRITAIN CAPTAINS

Since the first Test match against New Zealand in 1908, 59 players have been awarded the Great Britain captaincy. The number of matches as captain for each is as follows:

19 Ellery Hanley (Bradford N, Wigan)

17 Alan Prescott (St Helens)

15 Eric Ashton (Wigan), Jim Sullivan (Wigan)

11 Jonty Parkin (Wakefield T)

10 Roger Millward (Hull KR), Harold Wagstaff (Huddersfield)

9 Frank Myler (St Helens), Gus Risman (Salford), Clive Sullivan (Hull), Ernest Ward (Bradford N)

8 Brian Noble (Bradford N), Mike Gregory (Warrington)

7 James Lomas (Salford, Oldham)

6 Chris Hesketh (Salford), Tommy Smales (Huddersfield, Bradford N)

5 Doug Laughton (Wigan, Widnes), George Nicholls (St Helens), Dickie Williams (Leeds, Hunslet)

4 Eric Fraser (Warrington), Harry Pinner (St Helens), Jeff Stevenson (York), Dave Valentine (Huddersfield), David Watkinson (Hull KR)

3 Ernie Ashcroft (Wigan), Len Casey (Hull KR), Brian Edgar (Workington T), Neil Fox (Wakefield T), Bill Holliday (Hull KR), Willie Horne (Barrow), Alex Murphy (St Helens), Bev Risman (Leeds), Harry Taylor (Hull)

2 Tommy Bishop (St Helens), George Fairbairn (Wigan), Frank Gallagher (Batley), Jeff Grayshon (Bradford N), Alan Hardisty (Castleford), Phil Jackson (Barrow), Harry Poole (Leeds), Gwyn Thomas (Huddersfield), Derek Turner (Wakefield T), Johnny Whiteley (Hull)

1 Arthur Atkinson (Castleford), Jim Brough (Leeds), Jack Cunliffe (Wigan), Shaun Edwards (Wigan), Joe Egan (Wigan), Les Fairclough (St Helens), Andy Goodway (Oldham), Syd Hynes (Leeds), Bert Jenkins (Wigan), Tommy McCue (Widnes), Keith Mumby (Bradford N), Steve Nash (Salford), Johnny Thomas (Wigan), David Topliss (Hull), David Ward (Leeds), Ted Ward (Wigan).

OLDEST GREAT BRITAIN PLAYER

Leeds' **Jeff Grayshon** (born 4 Mar 1949) was 36 years 8 months and 5 days old when he propped for Great Britain in a 6–6 draw with New Zealand at Elland Road on 9 Nov 1985.

YOUNGEST GREAT BRITAIN PLAYER

Featherstone Rovers' centre **Paul Newlove** (born 10 Aug 1971) was 18 years 72 days old when he made his Test debut against New Zealand in a 16–24 loss at Old Trafford on 21 Oct 1989.

LONGEST TEST CAREER FOR GREAT BRITAIN

Gus Risman (Salford) enjoyed a Test career lasting 14 years and 4 days. Risman made his Test debut as a stand-off in an 18–13 victory over Australia at Sydney on 16 Jul 1932. His last Test, as a centre on 20 Jul 1946, saw Great Britain defeat Australia 20–7 at Sydney.

Great Britain centre Paul Loughlin swerves away from New Zealand second-rower Kurt Sorensen at Old Trafford in 1989. Loughlin is one of the contemporary game's best goal-kickers, having landed over 700 goals since his debut for St Helens in 1984.

Above *Bill Burgess senior, one of Barrow's most famous forwards, played in 16 Tests (1924–29). His son, Bill junior (***left***) played in 13 Tests (1962–68) whilst a Barrow player and one whilst with Salford.*

GREAT BRITAIN TOURISTS

The most coveted of representative honours for British players is selection for a Lions tour of Australasia. Lions tours began in 1910 when the great Salford centre James Lomas led a 26-strong party to victory in both Australia and New Zealand. Since then, 19 Lions tours have taken place, usually within a four-year cycle. Until 1990 all tours took in both Australia and New Zealand. Tradition was broken with the 1990 tour which took the Lions only to New Zealand and Papua New Guinea. Papua New Guinea has been included on the tours of 1984, 1988 and 1990.

TOUR SUMMARIES

Year	Captain	P	W	D	L	Points For–Agn			Test series			
1910	J Lomas	18	13	1	4	527–294	GB2	A0	GB1	NZ0		
1914	H Wagstaff	18	15	0	3	535–196	GB2	A1	GB1	NZ0		
1920	H Wagstaff	25	21	0	4	738–332	GB1	A2	GB3	NZ0		
1924	J Parkin	27	21	0	6	738–375	GB2	A1	GB1	NZ2		
1928	J Parkin	24	18	1	5	558–291	GB2	A1	GB2	NZ1		
1932	J Sullivan	26	23	1	2	782–259	GB2	A1	GB3	NZ0		
1936	J Brough	25	22	0	3	611–260	GB2	A1	GB2	NZ0		
1946	A Risman	27	21	1	5	783–276	*GB2	A0	GB0	NZ1		
1950	E Ward	25	19	0	6	764–266	GB1	A2	GB0	NZ2		
1954	R Williams	32 †	21	1	9	919–532	GB1	A2	GB2	NZ1		
1958	A Prescott	30	27	1	2	1196–486	GB2	A1	GB1	NZ1		
1962	E Ashton	30	24	0	6	998–464	GB2	A1	GB0	NZ2		
1966	H Poole	30	21	0	9	771–385	GB1	A2	GB2	NZ0		
1970	F Myler	24	22	1	1	753–288	GB2	A1	GB3	NZ0		
1974	C Hesketh	28	21	0	7	675–313	GB1	A2	GB2	NZ1		
1979	D Laughton	27	21	1	5	559–322	GB0	A3	GB2	NZ1		
1984	B Noble	24	16	0	8	616–400	GB0	A3	GB0	NZ3	GB1	PNG0
1988	E Hanley	18	11	0	7	456–341	GB1	A2	GB0	NZ1	GB1	PNG0
1990	M Gregory	15	10	0	5	351–221			GB2	NZ1	GB1	PNG1

* Great Britain and Australia also played a drawn Test
† Includes one abandoned game

TOUR RECORDS

Most games	32	1954
Fewest games	15	1990
Most wins	27	1958
Most losses	9	1966
Fewest wins	10	1990
Fewest losses	1	1970
Most points	1196	1958
Fewest points	351	1990
Most points conceded	532	1954
Fewest points conceded	196	1914

Highest score in Australia	101–0	v South Australia	1914
Highest score in New Zealand	81–14	v Bay of Plenty	1962
Highest score in Papua New Guinea	50–4	v Islands Zone	1990
Highest against in Australia	6–42	v New South Wales	1920
Highest against in New Zealand	13–46	v Auckland	1962
Highest against in Papua New Guinea	42–22	v Papua New Guinea	1988

Above *Tour hopefuls, 1954 – the White team which drew 17–17 with the Red team in a Tour Trial at Headingley.*

Below *The pioneer Lions team to Australia and New Zealand in 1910.*

J. RILEY,   F. H. SHUGARS,   D. MURRAY (*Trainer*),   E. CURZON,   F. WEBSTER.
W. JUKES,   F. BOYLEN,   H. KERSHAW,   J. LEYTHAM,   J. SHARROCK.
W. WINSTANLEY,   J. THOMAS,   T. H. NEWBOULD,   W. WARD,   B. JENKINS,   R. RAMSDALE.
MR. J. CLIFFORD (*Joint Manager*),   F. FARRAR,   J. DAVIES,   J. H. HOUGHTON (*Joint Manager*),   J. LOMAS,   W. BATTEN,   G. PELL
F. SMITH.

INDIVIDUAL RECORDS

MOST TOURS

3	J Parkin	1920, 1924, 1928
3	J Sullivan	1924, 1928, 1932
3	J Thompson	1924, 1928, 1932
3	A Risman	1932, 1936, 1946
3	B Edgar	1958, 1962, 1966
3	R Millward	1970, 1974, 1979
3	J Joyner	1979, 1984, 1988*
3	G Schofield	1984, 1988, 1990

* Replacement

MOST APPEARANCES

24	R Huddart	1958
24	R Huddart and L Gilfedder	1962

SCORING RECORDS

Most tries	38	M Sullivan	1958
Most goals	127	L Jones	1954
Most points	278	L Jones	1954

RECORDS FOR ONE GAME

Most tries in a game	7	J Lewthwaite	v Mackay	1946
	7	J Hilton	v Western Australia	1950
	7	M Sullivan	v Perth	1958
Most goals in a game	17	E Ward	v Mackay	1946
Most points in a game	34	E Ward	v Mackay	1946

RECORD AGGREGATES

Highest aggregate appearances	53	J Sullivan 1924, 1928, 1932
Highest aggregate tries	58	W Boston 1954, 1962
Highest aggregate goals	246	J Sullivan 1924, 1928, 1932
Highest aggregate points	504	J Sullivan 1924, 1928, 1932

OLDEST AND YOUNGEST

Youngest Lion – Bobby Goulding (born 2 Feb 1972) was 18 when he toured in 1990.

Oldest Lion – Alf Wood (born 27 Nov 1883) was 36 when he toured in 1920.

BROTHERS WHO HAVE TOURED

B Evans	1928, 1932	J Evans	1928
C Pollard	1924	E Pollard	1932
M Martyn	1958	T Martyn	1979
D Fox	1962	N Fox	1962
D Chisnall	1970	E Chisnall	1974
A Bates	1974	J Bates	1974
D Redfearn	1974	A Redfearn	1979
D Hulme	1988	P Hulme	1988

FATHERS AND SONS WHO HAVE TOURED

W Batten	1910	E Batten	1946
W Burgess	1924, 1928	W Burgess	1966
C Pollard	1924	R Pollard	1950
W Gowers	1928	K Gowers	1966
N Silcock	1932, 1936	D Silcock	1954
C Clarke	1966	P Clarke	1990
C Sullivan	1970	A Sullivan	1990

Above *Ken Gowers emulated his father, Walter, by becoming a British Lion. Ken toured in 1966, Walter in 1928. Both were goal-kicking full-backs.*

Left *18-year-old Wigan scrum-half Bobby Goulding became Britain's youngest Lion on the 1990 tour of Papua and New Zealand.*

ROGER MILLWARD

Six Tours Down-Under

The summit of a Rugby League player's aspirations at international level is a Lions tour to Australasia. As the cycle in which tours occur has usually been of a four-yearly order, selection depends to a large extent on producing top form in a particular year. Many great players have never acquired Lions status, injury or loss of form at the crucial time being their Nemesis. Eight immortals have made three Australasian tours. One of this select company was Roger Millward, who made his three Lions tours in 1970, 1974 and 1979.

Millward did not merely make a trio of tours, however. He doubled that number by playing in World Cup series in Australasia in 1968, 1975 and 1977. No other player has approached Millward's achievement. Yet Millward did not fit the stereotype bruiser needed to match muscle with the giants of antipodean Rugby League – not at all. Roger, inevitably dubbed 'The Dodger', stood 5ft 4ins, weighed barely 10 stone and looked like a cherub. He played like the devil, however, and tortured the best defences world rugby could raise.

Originally a spring-heeled stand-off who developed into a masterful scrum-half, Roger had all the gifts. Hare-quick,

slippery, intelligent and always in the right place at the right time, he had an appetite for tackling which belied his frame. A fine goal-kicker and an extraordinary try-poacher, Millward ultimately became a highly respected captain and a man whose sportsmanship was beyond reproach.

His first taste of Australasia was as a member of Great Britain's 1968 World Cup squad. Unfortunately Britain did not perform up to expectations, losing to Australia at Sydney and disastrously to France at Auckland before salvaging a little pride with a 38–14 hammering of New Zealand at Sydney. Roger played in all three games and went on to play in every other tour fixture.

Two years later the little maestro was a lynch-pin of the last Lions team to win the Ashes. After missing the First Test at Brisbane, which Britain lost 15–37, Roger gave one of the performances of his life in the Second Test at Sydney; 7 goals and two tries were his record contribution to Britain's 28–7 triumph, and in the deciding Test on the same ground nine points from the tiny titan were a crucial contribution to a 21–17 victory. Britain won all three Tests in New Zealand with Millward figuring in the scoring in

each. The 1970 tour yielded him a century of points.

Millward was one of Britain's major hopes for success on the 1974 Lions tour and the team did astonishingly well to only lose the Ashes 1–2. It was not the best of tours for Roger, yet he played in all the Ashes games and was one of the heroes of the Second Test when Britain squared the series with a 16–11 victory. A patched-up team meant a place on the wing for Millward.

In 1975 the World Championship was played in both hemispheres and Great Britain was split into England and Wales. Millward skippered England against Wales at Brisbane, and against Australia at Sydney when a creditable 10–10 draw was achieved. In the final analysis, defeat in the Welsh match cost England the World Championship.

Millward was back in 1977 as captain of the Great Britain World Cup squad which went desperately close to winning the trophy. In the preliminary games he scored tries against France, New Zealand and Australia as Britain qualified for a place against the Aussies in the final at Sydney, only for his team to lose agonisingly and controversially 12–13.

By 1979 Millward was almost 32 but the selectors chose him for yet another tour. This time Great Britain lost the Ashes 0–3 but beat New Zealand 2–1. Roger was destined not even to see New Zealand as he was invalided home after making only three appearances in Australia, a sad end to a marvellous international career.

ROGER MILLWARD'S AUSTRALASIAN TOURS

		App	T	G	Pts
1968	GREAT BRITAIN WORLD CUP	6+1	4	2	16
1970	LIONS	14+1	18	23	100
1974	LIONS	10+2	8	18	60
1975	ENGLAND WORLD CHAMPIONSHIP*	6	2	0	6
1977	GREAT BRITAIN WORLD CUP*	7+1	4	0	12
1979	LIONS	3	0	4	8

* Captain

LIONS TOURS – THE TOP PERFORMERS

Year	Most games	Most tries	Most goals
1910	14 F Webster	14 B Jenkins	53 J Lomas
	14 W Winstanley		
1914	13 WA Davies	19 S Moorhouse	47 A Wood
	13 H Wagstaff		
1920	19 H Hilton	24 W Stone	65 B Gronow
1924	22 W Burgess	23 J Ring	84 J Sullivan
1928	19 W Rees	20 A Ellaby	52 J Sullivan
1932	21 J Sullivan	21 A Ellaby	110 J Sullivan
1936	18 M Hodgson	21 A Edwards	65 M Hodgson
1946	19 F Whitcome	25 J Lewthwaite	43 E Ward
1950	18 T Danby	34 T Danby	52 E Ward
1954	22 T McKinney	36 W Boston	127 L Jones
1958	24 R Huddart	38 M Sullivan	110 E Fraser
1962	24 L Gilfedder	22 W Boston	85 N Fox
	24 R Huddart		
1966	22 D Robinson	24 B Jones	67 K Gowers
1970	18 J Atkinson	19 S Hynes	51 T Price
1974	21 J Thompson	18 D Redfearn	53 J Gray
1979	19 S Evans	16 S Evans	68 J Woods
1984	17 D Drummond	12 E Hanley	36 M Burke
1988	14 R Powell	19 M Offiah	43 P Loughlin
1990	14 R Powell	9 P Eastwood	34 J Davies

Note – records relating to appearances on the tours of 1914, 1920 and 1924 have never been fully authenticated.

GREAT BRITAIN LIONS 1910–90

Player	Club	Tour(s)	Player	Club	Tour(s)
Ackerley A	Halifax	1958	Bevan J	Warrington	1974
Adams L	Leeds	1932	Beverley H	Hunslet	1936
Adams M	Widnes	1979, 1984	Bibb C	Featherstone R	1990
Archer H	Workington T	1958	Bishop D	Hull KR	1990
Arkwright J	Warrington	1936	Bishop T	St Helens	1966
Armitt T	Swinton	1936	Bolton D	Wigan	1958, 1962
Ashcroft E	Wigan	1950, 1954	Boston W	Wigan	1954, 1962
Ashcroft K	Warrington	1974	Bowden J	Huddersfield	1954
Ashton E	Wigan	1958, 1962	Bowen F	St Helens Recs	1928
Ashton R	Oldham	1984	Bowers J	Rochdale H	1920
Askin T	Featherstone R	1928	Bowman H	Hull	1924, 1928
Aspinall W	Warrington	1966	Boylen F	Hull	1910
Atkinson A	Castleford	1932, 1936	Bradshaw T	Wigan	1950
Atkinson J	Leeds	1970, 1974	Bridges J	Featherstone R	1974
Avery A	Oldham	1910	Briggs B	Huddersfield	1954
Bacon J	Leeds	1920, 1924	Brogden S	Huddersfield	1932
Barends D	Bradford N	1979		Leeds	1936
Bartholomew J	Huddersfield	1910	Brooke I	Bradford N	1966
Basnett J	Widnes	1984	Brough A	Oldham	1924
Bassett A	Halifax	1946	Brough J	Leeds	1928, 1936
Bates A	Dewsbury	1974	Bryant W	Castleford	1966
Bates J	Dewsbury	1974	Buckley A	Swinton	1966
Batten E	Bradford N	1946	Burgess W	Barrow	1924, 1928
Batten W	Hunslet	1910	Burgess W	Barrow	1966
Beardmore K	Castleford	1984, 1988	Burke J	Wakefield T	1979
Belshaw W	Liverpool Stanley	1936	Burke M	Widnes	1984
Bennett J	Rochdale H	1924	Burnell A	Hunslet	1954
Bentham N	Wigan Highfield	1928	Burton C	Hull KR	1984
Bentham W	Broughton R	1924	Butler J	Rochdale H	1974
Betts D	Wigan	1990	Butters F	Swinton	1932

Player	Club	Tour(s)
Cahill E	Rochdale H	1954
Carlton F	St Helens	1958
	Wigan	1962
Carr C	Barrow	1924
Cartwright J	Leigh	1920
Case B	Wigan	1984, 1988
Casey L	Bradford N	1979
Castle F	Barrow	1954
Challinor J	Warrington	1958
Charlton P	Salford	1974
Chilcott J	Huddersfield	1914
Chisnall D	Leigh	1970
Chisnall E	St Helens	1974
Clampitt J	Broughton R	1914
Clark D	Huddersfield	1914, 1920
Clark G	Hull KR	1984
Clarke C	Wigan	1966
Clarke P	Wigan	1990
Clawson T	Oldham	1974
Coldrick P	Wigan	1914
Cooper G	Featherstone R	1962
Crewdson G	Keighley	1966
Crooks L	Hull	1984
	Leeds	1988
Cunliffe J	Wigan	1950, 1954
Cunliffe W	Warrington	1920, 1924
Curran G	Salford	1946
Currier A	Widnes	1988
Curzon E	Salford	1910
Danby T	Salford	1950
Daniels A	Halifax	1950
Darwell J	Leigh	1924
Davies A	Oldham	1958
Davies E	Oldham	1920
Davies EG	Wigan	1936
Davies I	Halifax	1932
Davies J	Huddersfield	1910
Davies JD	Widnes	1990
Davies WA	Leeds	1914
Davies WTH	Bradford N	1946
Dermott M	Wigan	1990
Devereux J	Widnes	1990
Dingsdale W	Warrington	1932
Dixon C	Salford	1974
Dixon P	Halifax	1988
	Leeds	1990
Dolan O	St Helens Recs	1928
Donlan S	Leigh	1984
Dooler C	Featherstone R	1966
Doyle J	Barrow	1920
Drummond D	Leigh	1984
Duane R	Warrington	1984
Dutton R	Widnes	1970
Dyl L	Leeds	1974
Eastwood P	Hull	1990
Eckersley D	St Helens	1974
Edgar B	Workington T	1958, 1962, 1966
Edwards A	Salford	1936
Edwards D	Castleford	1970
Edwards S	Wigan	1988
Egan J	Wigan	1946, 1950
Ellaby A	St Helens	1928, 1932

Player	Club	Tour(s)
Ellerington H	Hull	1936
England K	Castleford	1990
Evans B	Swinton	1928, 1932
Evans F	Swinton	1924
Evans J	Swinton	1928
Evans R	Wigan	1962
Evans S	Featherstone R	1979
Exley G	Wakefield T	1936
Eyres R	Widnes	1988
Fairbairn G	Wigan	1979
Fairbank K	Bradford N	1988, 1990
Fairclough L	St Helens	1928
Farrar F	Hunslet	1910
Featherstone J	Warrington	1950
Feetham J	Salford	1932
Fender N	York	1932
Field H	York	1936
Fildes A	St Helens Recs	1928
	St Helens	1932
Fisher A	Bradford N	1970
Flanagan P	Hull KR	1966, 1970
Flanagan T	Oldham	1984
Fogerty T	Halifax	1966
Ford M	Oldham	1988
Ford P	Bradford N	1988
Foster T	Bradford N	1946
Fox D	Featherstone R	1962
Fox JD	Featherstone R	1990
Fox N	Wakefield T	1962
Foy D	Oldham	1984
Francis A	Hull	1914
Fraser E	Warrington	1958, 1962
Frodsham A	St Helens	1928
Gallagher F	Dewsbury	1920
	Batley	1924
Gee K	Wigan	1946, 1950
Gibson C	Leeds	1988, 1990
Gilfedder L	Warrington	1962
Gill H	Wigan	1988
Gill K	Salford	1974
Glynn P	St Helens	1979
Goodway A	Oldham	1984
Goodwin D	Barrow	1958
Goulding R	Wigan	1990
Gowers K	Swinton	1966
Gowers W	Rochdale H	1928
Gray J	Wigan	1974
Grayshon J	Bradford N	1979
Greenall D	St Helens	1954
Gregory A	Widnes	1984
	Wigan	1988
Gregory M	Warrington	1988, 1990
Gronow B	Huddersfield	1920, 1924
Groves P	St Helens	1988
Guerin W	Hunslet	1914
Gunney G	Hunslet	1954
Gwynne E	Hull	1928
Gwyther E	Belle Vue R	1950
Haggerty R	St Helens	1988
Halfpenny B	St Helens	1928
Hall W	Oldham	1914

1950 British Lions – Ernie Ashcroft (Wigan), Ken Gee (Wigan), Dickie Williams (Leeds) and Ken Traill (Bradford Northern).

Player	Club	Tour(s)
Hanley E	Bradford N	1984
	Wigan	1988
Hardisty A	Castleford	1966, 1970
Harris F	Leeds	1936
Harris T	Hull	1954, 1958
Hartley D	Castleford	1970
Helm T	Oldham	1910
Helme G	Warrington	1954
Henderson J	Workington T	1954
Hepworth K	Castleford	1970
Herbert N	Workington T	1962
Hesketh C	Salford	1970, 1974
Higgins F	Widnes	1950
Hilton H	Oldham	1920
Hilton J	Wigan	1950
Hobbs D	Featherstone R	1984
Hodgson M	Swinton	1932, 1936
Hogan P	Hull KR	1979
Holding N	St Helens	1984
Holland D	Oldham	1914
Holmes J	Leeds	1979
Horne W	Barrow	1946, 1950
Horton W	Wakefield T	1928, 1932
Howley T	Wigan	1924
Huddart R	Whitehaven	1958
	St Helens	1962
Hudson B	Salford	1932, 1936
Hughes E	Widnes	1979
Hughes F	Barrow	1946
Hulme D	Widnes	1988
Hulme P	Widnes	1988
Hurcombe D	Wigan	1920, 1924
Hynes S	Leeds	1970
Irving R	Oldham	1970
Irwin S	Castleford	1990
Jackson K	Oldham	1958
Jackson L	Hull	1990
Jackson P	Barrow	1954, 1958
James M	St Helens	1979
Jarman W	Leeds	1914
Jenkins B	Wigan	1910, 1914
Jenkins D	Leeds	1946
Jenkins E	Salford	1936
Jenkins T	Ebbw Vale	1910
Johnson A	Widnes	1914, 1920
Johnson AE	Warrington	1946
Jones B	Wakefield T	1966
Jones E	Rochdale H	1920
Jones H	Keighley	1936
Jones J	Barrow	1946
Jones L	Leeds	1954
Joyner J	Castleford	1979, 1984, 1988
Jukes W	Hunslet	1910
Karalius V	St Helens	1958
Keegan A	Hull	1966
Kershaw H	Wakefield T	1910
Kitching J	Bradford N	1946
Knapman E	Oldham	1924
Knowelden B	Barrow	1946
Laughton D	Wigan	1970
	Widnes	1979
Ledgard J	Leigh	1950

Two of the main driving forces in the outstanding Hull team of the early 1980s, Steve Norton and David Topliss. Both were Great Britain tourists in 1979, Norton having also been a 1974 Lion.

Player	Club	Tour(s)	Player	Club	Tour(s)
Lewthwaite J	Barrow	1946	Pollard E	Leeds	1932
Leytham J	Wigan	1910	Pollard R	Dewsbury	1950
Liptrot G	St Helens	1979	Poole H	Leeds	1966
Lloyd R	Halifax	1920	Powell D	Sheffield E	1990
Lockwood B	Hull KR	1979	Powell R	Leeds	1988, 1990
Lomas J	Salford	1910	Poynton H	Wakefield T	1962
Longstaff F	Huddersfield	1914	Prescott A	St Helens	1954, 1958
Loughlin P	St Helens	1988	Price G	Wakefield T	1990
Lowe J	Leeds	1932	Price J	Wigan	1924
Lowe P	Hull KR	1970	Price R	Warrington	1954
Lucas I	Wigan	1990	Price T	Bradford N	1970
Lydon J	Widnes	1984	Proctor W	Hull	1984
	Wigan	1990	Prosser S	Halifax	1914
Lyon D	Warrington	1990	Ramsdale R	Wigan	1910, 1914
Mantle J	St Helens	1966	Ramsey W	Hunslet	1966
Martyn M	Leigh	1958		Bradford N	1974
Martyn T	Warrington	1979	Ratcliffe G	Wigan	1950
Mathias R	St Helens	1979	Rayne Keith	Leeds	1984
McCue T	Widnes	1936, 1946	Redfearn A	Bradford N	1979
McKinney T	Salford	1954	Redfearn D	Bradford N	1974
McTigue B	Wigan	1958, 1962	Rees D	Halifax	1924
Medley P	Leeds	1988	Rees G	Leeds	1920
Miller J	Warrington	1936	Rees W	Swinton	1928
Mills J	Widnes	1974, 1979	Reid W	Widnes	1920
Millward R	Hull KR	1970, 1974, 1979	Reilly M	Castleford	1970
Milnes A	Halifax	1920	Richards M	Salford	1974
Mooney W	Leigh	1924	Riley J	Halifax	1910
Moorhouse S	Huddersfield	1914	Ring J	Wigan	1924
Morley J	Wigan	1936	Risman A	Salford	1932, 1936, 1946
Moses G	St Helens	1958	Rix S	Oldham	1924
Mumby K	Bradford N	1979, 1984	Roberts K	Halifax	1966
Murphy A	St Helens	1958, 1962	Robinson D	Swinton	1966
Murphy H	Wakefield T	1946, 1950		Wigan	1970
Myler A	Widnes	1984	Robinson G	Wakefield T	1932
Myler E	Widnes	1966	Robinson J	Rochdale H	1914
	St Helens	1970	Rogers J	Huddersfield	1914, 1920
Nash S	Featherstone R	1974	Roman W	Rochdale H	1914
	Salford	1979	Rose P	Hull KR	1974
Naughton D	Widnes	1950	Rosser M	Leeds	1928
Newbould T	Wakefield T	1910	Round G	Wakefield T	1962
Nicholls G	St Helens	1974, 1979	Ruddick G	Broughton R	1910
Nicholson R	Huddersfield	1946	Ryan M	Wigan	1946, 1950
Noble B	Bradford N	1984	Ryan R	Warrington	1950
Noble K	Huddersfield	1962	Sayer W	Wigan	1962
Norton S	Castleford	1974	Schofield G	Hull	1984
	Hull	1979		Leeds	1988, 1990
Offiah M	Widnes	1988, 1990	Seabourne B	Leeds	1970
O'Garra J	Widnes	1914	Sharrock J	Wigan	1910
O'Grady T	Oldham	1954	Shaw J	Halifax	1962
Oliver J	Batley	1928	Shelton G	Hunslet	1966
O'Neill M	Widnes	1984	Shoebottom M	Leeds	1970
Osmond F	Swinton	1950	Shugars F	Warrington	1910
Owens I	Leeds	1946	Silcock D	Wigan	1954
Parkin J	Wakefield T	1920, 1924, 1928	Silcock N	Widnes	1932, 1936
Pawsey C	Leigh	1954	Simpson R	Bradford N	1990
Pepperell A	Workington T	1950	Skelhorne A	Warrington	1920
Phillips D	Oldham	1946	Skerrett K	Bradford N	1990
	Belle Vue R	1950	Skerrett T	Wakefield T	1979
Pinner H	St Helens	1984	Sloman R	Oldham	1924, 1928
Pitchford F	Oldham	1958	Smales I	Featherstone R	1990
Platt A	St Helens	1988	Smales J	Hunslet	1914
Pollard C	Wakefield T	1924	Small P	Castleford	1962

Oldham full-back Alf Wood toured Australasia in 1914 and 1920. On the latter tour he was aged 36 – the oldest Lion in history.

Player	Club	Tour(s)
Smith A	Leeds	1970
Smith F	Hunslet	1910, 1914
Smith M	Hull KR	1979, 1984
Smith S	Leeds	1932, 1936
Southward I	Workington T	1958, 1962
Stacey C	Halifax	1920
Steadman G	Castleford	1990
Stephens G	Castleford	1979
Stephenson D	Leeds	1988
Stockwell S	Leeds	1920
Stone C	Hull	1979
Stone W	Hull	1920
Stopford J	Swinton	1966
Street H	Dewsbury	1950
Sullivan A	Hull KR	1990
Sullivan C	Hull	1970
Sullivan J	Wigan	1924, 1928, 1932
Sullivan M	Wigan	1958
	St Helens	1962
Tait A	Widnes	1990
Taylor J	Hull KR	1962
Terry A	St Helens	1958
Thomas G	Wigan	1914
	Huddersfield	1920
Thomas J	Wigan	1910
Thompson J	Featherstone R	1970, 1974
Thompson JF	Leeds	1924, 1928, 1932
Topliss D	Wakefield T	1979
Traill K	Bradford N	1950, 1954
Troup L	Barrow	1936
Turnbull A	Leeds	1954
Turner D	Wakefield T	1962
Valentine D	Huddersfield	1954
Waddell H	Oldham	1988
Wagstaff H	Huddersfield	1914, 1920
Ward D	Leeds	1979

Player	Club	Tour(s)
Ward E	Bradford N	1946, 1950
Ward EH	Wigan	1946
Ward J	Salford	1970
Ward K	Castleford	1988
Ward W	Leeds	1910
Watkins D	Salford	1974
Watkins W	Salford	1936
Watkinson D	Hull KR	1979
Watson C	St Helens	1966, 1970
Webster F	Leeds	1910
Whitcombe F	Bradford N	1946
White L	York	1946
White LL	Hunslet	1932
Whiteley J	Hull	1958
Whitty S	Hull	1924
Wilkinson I	Halifax	1988
Wilkinson J	Halifax	1954
	Wakefield T	1962
Williams F	Halifax	1914
Williams R	Leeds	1950
	Hunslet	1954
Williams W	Salford	1928, 1932
Willicombe D	Wigan	1974
Winstanley W	Leigh	1910
Wood A	Oldham	1914, 1920
Woods H	Liverpool Stanley	1936
Woods J	Leigh	1979
Woods JT	Barrow	1932
Wookey W	Workington T	1958
Worrall M	Oldham	1984
Wright D	Widnes	1988
Wright J	Swinton	1932
Wriglesworth G	Leeds	1966
Young F	Leeds	1910
Young H	Bradford N	1928

CLUB REPRESENTATION OF LIONS

There have been 518 places on the 19 Lions tours. Eight players have made three tours, and a further 84 have toured twice. Club representation has been as follows:

64	Wigan	14	Hunslet
49	Leeds	13	Featherstone R
36	St Helens	11	Leigh
34	Widnes	10	Workington T
28	Bradford N	8	Rochdale H
27	Oldham	5	Broughton R/Belle Vue R
25	Salford	5	Dewsbury
24	Warrington	3	St Helens Recs
22	Wakefield T	3	York
21	Castleford	2	Batley
20	Huddersfield	2	Keighley
20	Hull	2	Liverpool Stanley
17	Barrow	1	Ebbw Vale
17	Halifax	1	Sheffield E
17	Hull KR	1	Whitehaven
15	Swinton	1	Wigan Highfield

Note – Tom Helm (1910), the Oldham forward, and Anthony Sullivan (1990), the Hull KR winger, are the only Lions never to have played on tour, both having been injured before the first tour match.

Largest tour contingent from a club – 8, Wigan 1950

THE WORLD CUP

The first World Cup competition was staged in France in 1954 – Great Britain were its first winners. The competition has subsequently been staged at irregular intervals and taken a number of different forms. The competitions of 1954, 1957, 1960, 1968, 1970, 1972 and 1977 were played over a period of a few weeks, each nation meeting the other three, with the team finishing top of the table winning the World Cup or the top two playing off in a final. The World Championship of 1975 differed in that Great Britain was split into England and Wales and each nation played all the others at home and abroad, the competition stretching from March until November. The two most recent World Cup competitions have been spread over several years. The current World Cup has been running since July 1989, whilst the last completed competition ran from July 1985 until July 1988. Games in the modern World Cup are specially designated games from within Test series, usually the last Test. Under this formula, a play-off between the top two nations decides the World Cup winners.

Great Britain v New Zealand at Bordeaux in the 1954 World Cup. Winger David Rose bends to tackle Kiwi prop Bill McLennan in Britain's 26–6 victory.

1954

In France
WINNERS:
GREAT BRITAIN

MATCH RESULTS

30 Oct *at Paris, 13 240*
FRANCE   22 T: Contrastin, Delaye,
                                Crespo, Audoubert
                     G: Puig Aubert 5
NEW ZEALAND   13 T: Edwards, Eastlake, McKay
                     G: Bond 2

31 Oct *at Lyons, 10 250*
AUSTRALIA   13 T: Wells 2, Kearney
                     G: Pidding 2
GREAT BRITAIN   28 T: Jackson 2, Brown 2,
                                Kitchen, Rose
                     G: Ledgard 5

7 Nov *at Toulouse, 37 471*
FRANCE   13 T: Contrastin 2, Krawzyk
                     G: Puig Aubert 2
GREAT BRITAIN   13 T: Brown, Helme, Rose
                     G: Ledgard 2

7 Nov *at Marseilles, 20 000*
AUSTRALIA   34 T: Watson 3, Hawick, Bull,
                                Kearney, O'Shea,
                                Diversi
                     G: Pidding 5
NEW ZEALAND   15 T: Ericsen
                     G: McKay 6

11 Nov *at Bordeaux, 14 000*
GREAT BRITAIN   26 T: Kitchen 2, Brown,
                                Ledgard, Rose,
                                Jackson
                     G: Ledgard 4
NEW ZEALAND   6 G: McKay 3

11 Nov *at Nantes, 13 000*
FRANCE   15 T: Contrastin, Merquey,
                                Cantoni
                     G: Puig Aubert 3
AUSTRALIA   5 T: O'Shea
                     G: Pidding

FINAL TABLE

	P	W	D	L	F	A	Pts
Great Britain	3	2	1	0	67	32	5
France	3	2	1	0	50	31	5
Australia	3	1	0	2	52	58	2
New Zealand	3	0	0	3	34	82	0

PLAY-OFF
13 Nov *at Paris, 30 368*
FRANCE   12 T: Cantoni, Contrastin
                     G: Puig Aubert 3
GREAT BRITAIN   16 T: Brown 2, Helme, Rose
                     G: Ledgard 2

1957

In Australia
WINNERS: AUSTRALIA

MATCH RESULTS

15 Jun *at Sydney, 50 077*
FRANCE   5 T: Merquey
                     G: Benausse
GREAT BRITAIN   23 T: Sullivan 2, Boston,
                                Jackson, Stevenson
                     G: Jones 4

15 Jun *at Brisbane, 29 636*
AUSTRALIA   25 T: Moir, Carlson, Provan,
                                O'Shea, Wells
                     G: Barnes 5
NEW ZEALAND   5 T: Johnson
                     G: Sorensen

17 Jun *at Sydney, 57 955*
AUSTRALIA   31 T: McCaffery 2, Moir 2,
                                O'Shea, Wells, Clay
                     G: Carlson 4, Davies
GREAT BRITAIN   6 G: Jones 3

17 Jun *at Brisbane, 28 000*
FRANCE   14 T: Foussat 2
                     G: Benausse 4
NEW ZEALAND   10 T: Sorensen, Hadfield
                     G: Sorensen, Creedy

22 Jun *at Sydney, 35 158*
AUSTRALIA   26 T: Carlson, Marsh, O'Shea,
                                Poole
                     G: Carlson 7
FRANCE   9 T: Benausse
                     G: Benausse 3

25 Jun *at Sydney, 14 263*

GREAT BRITAIN	21	T:	Jackson, Grundy, Sullivan, Little, Jones
		G:	Jones 3
NEW ZEALAND	29	T:	Hadfield, Turner, Menzies, Riddell, McLennan
		G:	Sorensen 7

FINAL TABLE

	P	W	D	L	F	A	Pts
Australia	3	3	0	0	82	20	6
Great Britain	3	1	0	2	50	65	2
New Zealand	3	1	0	2	44	60	2
France	3	1	0	2	28	59	2

1960

In England
WINNERS:
GREAT BRITAIN

MATCH RESULTS

24 Sep *at Odsal, 20 577*

GREAT BRITAIN	23	T:	Myler, Murphy, Ashton, Davies, McTigue
		G:	Fraser 4
NEW ZEALAND	8	T:	Hadfield, Cooke
		G:	Sorensen

24 Sep *at Wigan, 20 278*

AUSTRALIA	13	T:	Raper, Kelly, Gasnier
		G:	Carlson 2
FRANCE	12	T:	Gruppi 2
		G:	A Lacaze 3

1 Oct *at Headingley, 10 736*

AUSTRALIA	21	T:	Carlson 3, Gasnier, Wells
		G:	Carlson 3
NEW ZEALAND	15	T:	Hadfield, Menzies, Turner
		G:	Eastlake 3

1 Oct *at Swinton, 22 923*

GREAT BRITAIN	33	T:	Davies 2, Rhodes 2, Wilkinson, Sullivan, Myler
		G:	Fraser 6
FRANCE	7	T:	Dubon
		G:	A Lacaze 2

8 Oct *at Odsal, 32 773*

GREAT BRITAIN	10	T:	Boston, Sullivan
		G:	Rhodes 2
AUSTRALIA	3	T:	Carlson

8 Oct *at Wigan, 2876*

FRANCE	0		
NEW ZEALAND	9	T:	Reid
		G:	Eastlake 3

FINAL TABLE

	P	W	D	L	F	A	Pts
Great Britain	3	3	0	0	66	18	6
Australia	3	2	0	1	37	37	4
New Zealand	3	1	0	2	32	44	2
France	3	0	0	3	19	55	0

1968

In Australia and
New Zealand
WINNERS: AUSTRALIA

MATCH RESULTS

25 May *at Sydney, 62 256*

AUSTRALIA	25	T:	Coote, Smith, Raper
		G:	Simms 8
GREAT BRITAIN	10	T:	Brooke, Sullivan
		G:	Risman 2

25 May *at Auckland, 18 000*

NEW ZEALAND	10	G:	Wiggs 5
FRANCE	15	T:	Capdouze
		G:	Capdouze 5, Garrigues

1 Jun *at Brisbane, 23 608*

AUSTRALIA	31	T:	King 2, Rhodes, Coote, Jones
		G:	Simms 8
NEW ZEALAND	12	T:	Dunn, Schultz
		G:	Wiggs 3

2 Jun *at Auckland, 15 760*

FRANCE	7	T:	Ledru
		G:	Garrigues, Capdouze
GREAT BRITAIN	2	G:	Risman

8 Jun *at Brisbane, 32 662*

AUSTRALIA	37	T:	Fulton 2, Williamson 2, Coote, Smith, Greaves
		G:	Simms 5, Smith 3
FRANCE	4	G:	Capdouze 2

8 Jun *at Sydney, 14 105*

GREAT BRITAIN	38	T:	Sullivan 3, Burwell 2, Brooke, Shoebottom, Morgan
		G:	Risman 7
NEW ZEALAND	14	T:	Schultz 2
		G:	Wiggs 4

FINAL TABLE

	P	W	D	L	F	A	Pts
Australia	3	3	0	0	93	26	6
France	3	2	0	1	26	49	4
Great Britain	3	1	0	2	50	46	2
New Zealand	3	0	0	3	36	84	0

PLAY-OFF
10 Jun *at Sydney, 54 290*
AUSTRALIA	20	T: Williamson 2, Coote, Greaves
		G: Simms 4
FRANCE	2	G: Capdouze

PLAY-OFF
7 Nov *at Headingley, 18 776*
GREAT BRITAIN	7	T: Atkinson
		G: Dutton, Hynes
AUSTRALIA	12	T: Williamson, Cootes
		G: Simms 3

1970

In England
WINNERS: AUSTRALIA

1972

In France
WINNERS: GREAT BRITAIN

MATCH RESULTS

21 Oct *at Wigan, 9586*
AUSTRALIA	47	T: Cootes 2, McCarthy, Fulton, Simms, Branighan, Turner, Coote, W Smith
		G: Simms 10
NEW ZEALAND	11	T: G Smith
		G: Ladner 4

24 Oct *at Headingley, 15 169*
GREAT BRITAIN	11	T: Hynes
		G: Dutton 3, Hynes
AUSTRALIA	4	G: Fulton, Simms

25 Oct *at The Boulevard, Hull, 3824*
FRANCE	15	T: Marsolan 2, Bonal
		G: Capdouze 3
NEW ZEALAND	16	T: Brereton, Cooksley
		G: Ladner 5

28 Oct *at Castleford, 8958*
GREAT BRITAIN	6	G: Dutton 3
FRANCE	0	

31 Oct *at Swinton, 5513*
GREAT BRITAIN	27	T: Hesketh, Watson, Hynes, Laughton, Atkinson
		G: Dutton 6
NEW ZEALAND	17	T: Kriletich, G Smith, Christian
		G: Ladner 4

1 Nov *at Odsal, 6217*
AUSTRALIA	15	T: Cootes 2, Fulton
		G: Simms 3
FRANCE	17	T: Marsolan 2, Capdouze
		G: Capdouze 3, Garrigues

FINAL TABLE

	P	W	D	L	F	A	Pts
Great Britain	3	3	0	0	44	21	6
Australia	3	1	0	2	66	39	2
France	3	1	0	2	32	37	2
New Zealand	3	1	0	2	44	89	2

MATCH RESULTS

28 Oct *at Marseilles, 20 748*
FRANCE	20	T: Bonal 2, Ruiz
		G: Guilhem 4, Bonal, Frattini (DG)
NEW ZEALAND	9	T: P Orchard 2, Bereton

29 Oct *at Perpignan, 6324*
AUSTRALIA	21	T: Fulton 3, Raudonikis
		G: Langlands 4, McCarthy (DG)
GREAT BRITAIN	27	T: Sullivan, Lowe, Atkinson, O'Neill, Stephenson
		G: Clawson 6

1 Nov *at Grenoble, 5321*
FRANCE	4	G: Bonal, Serrano
GREAT BRITAIN	13	T: Lowe 2, Sullivan
		G: Clawson 2

1 Nov *at Paris, 8000*
AUSTRALIA	9	T: Ward, Fulton
		G: Branighan, Fulton (DG)
NEW ZEALAND	5	T: Whittaker
		G: Wilson

4 Nov *at Pau, 7500*
GREAT BRITAIN	53	T: Holmes 2, Atkinson 2, Nicholls, Sullivan, Nash, Charlton, Hesketh, Stephenson, Jeanes
		G: Holmes 10
NEW ZEALAND	19	T: Whittaker, Coll, Burgoyne, Williams, Eade
		G: Wilson 2

5 Nov *at Toulouse, 10 332*
FRANCE	9	T: Ruiz
		G: Bonal 3
AUSTRALIA	31	T: Harris 2, Sait 2, O'Neill, Fulton, Walters
		G: Branighan 5

Great Britain's 1972 World Cup-winning squad. BACK: Wright, Irving, Dixon, Atkinson, Stephenson, Nicholls, Lockwood, Jeanes, Lowe, Walsh. MIDDLE: Karalius, Clawson, Challinor, Spaven, Simpson, Sullivan, Fallowfield, Hesketh, Charlton, Holmes. FRONT: O'Neill, Redfearn, Topliss, Nash.

1972 FINAL TABLE

	P	W	D	L	F	A	Pts
Great Britain	3	3	0	0	93	44	6
Australia	3	2	0	1	61	41	4
France	3	1	0	2	33	53	2
New Zealand	3	0	0	3	33	82	0

PLAY-OFF
11 Nov at Lyons, 4231

AUSTRALIA	10	T: O'Neill, Beetson
		G: Branighan 2
GREAT BRITAIN	10	T: Sullivan, Stephenson
		G: Clawson 2

(After extra time. Great Britain won the World Cup, having had the best record in the qualifying rounds)

1975

Played in both hemispheres
WINNERS: AUSTRALIA

MATCH RESULTS

2 Mar at Toulouse, 7563

FRANCE	14	T: Terrats, Curt
		G: Serrano 3, Lacoste (DG), Imbert (DG)
WALES	7	T: Wilson
		G: Coslett 2

16 Mar *at Headingley, 10 842*
ENGLAND	20	T: Fielding 2, Millward, Morgan
		G: Gray 4
FRANCE	2	G: Serrano

1 Jun *at Brisbane, 10 000*
AUSTRALIA	36	T: Cronin 2, Langlands 2, Platz, Randall, Fulton, Branighan
		G: Cronin 6
NEW ZEALAND	8	T: Whittaker, Stirling
		G: Collicoat

10 Jun *at Brisbane, 6000*
WALES	12	T: Treasure, Sullivan
		G: Watkins 3
ENGLAND	7	T: Martyn
		G: Fairbairn 2

14 Jun *at Sydney, 25 386*
AUSTRALIA	30	T: Raudonikis, Langlands, Fulton, Harris
		G: Cronin 9
WALES	13	T: Fisher
		G: Watkins 5

15 Jun *at Christchurch, 2500*
NEW ZEALAND	27	T: Jarvis 2, Eade, Stirling, Conroy
		G: D Sorensen 6
FRANCE	0	

21 Jun *at Brisbane, 9000*
AUSTRALIA	26	T: Harris 2, Fulton 2, Cronin, Pickup
		G: Cronin 4
FRANCE	6	G: Calle 3

21 Jun *at Auckland, 12 000*
NEW ZEALAND	17	T: Williams 2, P Orchard
		G: D Sorensen 4
ENGLAND	17	T: Fairbairn 2, Atkinson
		G: Fairbairn 4

28 Jun *at Sydney, 33 858*
AUSTRALIA	10	T: Coote, Anderson
		G: Cronin 2
ENGLAND	10	T: Dunn, Gill
		G: Fairbairn 2

28 Jun *at Auckland, 9368*
NEW ZEALAND	13	T: P Orchard
		G: Collicoat 5
WALES	8	T: Mills, Francis
		G: Watkins

20 Sep *at Warrington, 5034*
ENGLAND	22	T: Holmes, Fielding, Hughes
		G: Fairbairn 6, Bridges (DG)
WALES	16	T: Banner, Coslett
		G: Watkins 5

27 Sep *at Auckland, 20 000*
NEW ZEALAND	8	G: Collicoat 4
AUSTRALIA	24	T: Schubert, Higgs, Quayle, Cronin
		G: Cronin 6

11 Oct *at Bordeaux, 1581*
FRANCE	2	G: Calle
ENGLAND	48	T: Fielding 4, Holmes 2, Dunn 2, Hughes, Hogan, Gill, Forsyth
		G: Fairbairn 4, Milward 2

17 Oct *at Marseilles, 26 879*
FRANCE	12	T: Chauvet 2
		G: Guilhem 3
NEW ZEALAND	12	T: Jarvis, Proctor
		G: Collicoat 3

19 Oct *at Swansea, 11 112*
WALES	6	G: Watkins 3
AUSTRALIA	18	T: Schubert 3, Peard
		G: Cronin 3

25 Oct *at Odsal, 5937*
ENGLAND	27	T: Gill 3, Dunn, Norton, Hughes, Wright
		G: Fairbairn 3
NEW ZEALAND	12	T: Smith, Gordon
		G: Collicoat 3

26 Oct *at Perpignan, 10 440*
FRANCE	2	G: Guilhem
AUSTRALIA	41	T: Rogers 2, Higgs, Platz, Randall, Eadie, Peard, Rhodes, Raudonikis
		G: Eadie 7

1 Nov *at Wigan, 9393*
ENGLAND	16	T: Holmes, Grayshon
		G: Fairbairn 5
AUSTRALIA	13	T: Schubert 3
		G: Cronin 2

2 Nov *at Swansea, 2645*
WALES	25	T: Francis 2, Willicombe, Bevan, Mantle
		G: Watkins 5
NEW ZEALAND	24	T: P Orchard, Gordon, Greengrass, Coll
		G: Gordon 5, Collicoat

6 Nov *at Salford, 2247*

WALES	23	T: Gregory, Willicombe, Bevan, Banner, Francis
		G: Watkins 4
FRANCE	2	G: Guilhem

FINAL TABLE

	P	W	D	L	F	A	Pts
Australia	8	6	1	1	198	69	13
England	8	5	2	1	167	84	12
Wales	8	3	0	5	110	130	6
New Zealand	8	2	2	4	121	149	6
France	8	1	1	6	40	204	2

1977

In Australia and New Zealand
WINNERS: AUSTRALIA

MATCH RESULTS

29 May *at Auckland, 18 500*

NEW ZEALAND	12	T: Smith, Rushton
		G: Collicoat 3
AUSTRALIA	27	T: McMahon 2, Thomas, Harris, Peard
		G: Cronin 6

5 Jun *at Auckland, 10 000*

FRANCE	4	G: Calle 2
GREAT BRITAIN	23	T: Wright, Millward, Dyl
		G: Fairbairn 7

11 Jun *at Sydney, 13 231*

AUSTRALIA	21	T: Eadie 2, Veivers, Fitzgerald, McMahon
		G: Cronin 3
FRANCE	9	T: Laskawiec
		G: Calle 3

12 Jun *at Christchurch, 7000*

NEW ZEALAND	12	T: Fisher, Whittaker
		G: Collicoat 3
GREAT BRITAIN	30	T: Wright 2, Hogan, Nicholls, Bowman, Millward
		G: Fairbairn 6

18 Jun *at Brisbane, 27 000*

AUSTRALIA	19	T: Eadie 2, Randall
		G: Cronin 5
GREAT BRITAIN	5	T: Millward
		G: Fairbairn

19 Jun *at Auckland, 8000*

NEW ZEALAND	28	T: Jordan, Fisher, Smith, Graham
		G: Jordan 8
FRANCE	20	T: Cologni 2, Guigue, Roosebrouck
		G: Moya 4

FINAL TABLE

	P	W	D	L	F	A	Pts
Australia	3	3	0	0	67	26	6
Great Britain	3	2	0	1	58	35	4
New Zealand	3	1	0	2	52	77	2
France	3	0	0	3	33	72	0

PLAY-OFF

25 Jun *at Sydney, 24 457*

AUSTRALIA	13	T: McMahon, Gartner, Kolc
		G: Cronin 2
GREAT BRITAIN	12	T: Pitchford, Gill
		G: Fairbairn 3

1985-88

Played in both hemispheres
WINNERS: AUSTRALIA

MATCH RESULTS

7 Jul 1985 *at Auckland, 19 000*

NEW ZEALAND	18	T: Friend 2, Leuluai
		G: Filipaina 3
AUSTRALIA	0	

9 Nov 1985 *at Elland Road, 22 209*

GREAT BRITAIN	6	G: Crooks 3
NEW ZEALAND	6	T: Graham
		G: D Sorensen

7 Dec 1985 *at Perpignan, 5000*

FRANCE	0	
NEW ZEALAND	22	T: McGahan 2, Kemble, K Sorensen
		G: Filipaina 3

16 Feb 1986 *at Avignon, 4000*

FRANCE	10	T: Dumas
		G: Dumas 3
GREAT BRITAIN	10	T: Hanley
		G: Crooks 3

29 Jul 1986 *at Brisbane, 22 811*

AUSTRALIA	32	T: Kenny 2, Sterling, Lewis, Miles, O'Connor
		G: O'Connor 4
NEW ZEALAND	12	T: Williams 2
		G: Filipaina 2

17 Aug 1986 *at Port Moresby, 15 000*

PAPUA NEW GUINEA	24	T: Haili 2, Ako, Atoi
		G: Kovae 4
NEW ZEALAND	22	T: Brown, Wallace,
		McGahan, Ropati
		G: Brown 3

5 Oct 1986 *at Port Moresby, 17 000*

PAPUA NEW GUINEA	12	T: Numapo 2
		G: Kovae 2
AUSTRALIA	62	T: Kiss 2, O'Connor 2,
		Cleal 2, Mortimer,
		Jack, Lindner, Roach,
		Hasler, Lewis
		G: O'Connor 7

22 Nov 1986 *at Wigan, 20 169*

GREAT BRITAIN	15	T: Schofield 2
		G: Lydon 2, Gill,
		Schofield (DG)
AUSTRALIA	24	T: Lindner, Shearer, Lewis,
		Miles
		G: O'Connor 4

13 Nov 1986 *at Carcassonne, 3000*

FRANCE	0	
AUSTRALIA	52	T: Shearer 4, Jack 3, Folkes,
		Niebling, O'Connor
		G: O'Connor 6

24 Jan 1987 *at Headingley, 6567*

GREAT BRITAIN	52	T: Edwards 2, M Gregory 2,
		Hanley 2, Goodway,
		Lydon, Forster
		G: Lydon 8
FRANCE	0	

24 Oct 1987 *at Wigan, 9121*

GREAT BRITAIN	42	T: Edwards 2, Ford, Hanley,
		Lydon, A Gregory,
		Medley
		G: Stephenson 7
PAPUA NEW GUINEA	0	

15 Nov 1987 *at Carcassonne, 3500*

FRANCE	21	T: Fraisse 2, Pons, Ratier
		G: Bourrel 3 (1 DG)
PAPUA NEW GUINEA	4	T: Kovae

22 May 1988 *at Port Moresby, 12 077*

PAPUA NEW GUINEA	22	T: Kovae 2, Krewanty, Rop
		G: Numapo 3
GREAT BRITAIN	42	T: Schofield 2, Gill 2,
		Medley, Stephenson,
		M Gregory
		G: Loughlin 7

9 Jul 1988 *at Sydney, 15 994*

AUSTRALIA	12	T: Lewis, Backo
		G: O'Connor 2
GREAT BRITAIN	26	T: Gill 2, Offiah, Ford,
		M Gregory
		G: Loughlin 3

10 Jul 1988 *at Auckland, 8392*

NEW ZEALAND	66	T: S Horo 3, K Iro 3,
		Mercer 2, Williams,
		Wallace, A Shelford,
		Graham
		G: Brown 9
PAPUA NEW GUINEA	14	T: Matmillo, Kovae
		G: Numapo 3

17 Jul 1988 *at Christchurch, 8525*

NEW ZEALAND	12	T: Freeman 2
		G: Brown 2
GREAT BRITAIN	10	T: Loughlin, D Hulme
		G: Loughlin

20 Jul 1988 *at Wagga Wagga, 11 685*

AUSTRALIA	70	T: O'Connor 4, Langer 2,
		Meninga 2, Jack,
		Currie, Lewis,
		Fullerton-Smith,
		Miller, Conescu
		G: O'Connor 7
PAPUA NEW GUINEA	8	T: Morea
		G: Numapo 2

FINAL TABLE

	P	W	D	L	F	A	Pts
Australia	7	5	0	2	252	91	12*
New Zealand	7	4	1	2	158	86	11*
Great Britain	8	4	2	2	203	90	10
Papua New Guinea	7	1	0	6	84	325	4*
France	5	1	1	3	35	140	3

* France failed to play her southern hemisphere fixtures with Australia, New Zealand and Papua New Guinea and each was awarded two points.

PLAY-OFF

9 Oct 1988 *at Auckland, 47 363*

NEW ZEALAND	12	T: A Iro, K Iro
		G: Brown 2
AUSTRALIA	25	T: Langer 2, Miller, Shearer
		G: O'Connor 4, Elias (DG)

1989–92

Played in both hemispheres

MATCH RESULTS

23 Jul 1989 *at Auckland, 15 000*
NEW ZEALAND 14 T: Elia, Mercer
G: K Shelford 3
AUSTRALIA 22 T: Meninga, O'Connor,
Shearer, Clyde
G: O'Connor 2, Meninga

11 Nov 1989 *at Wigan, 20 346*
GREAT BRITAIN 10 T: Offiah, Tait
G: Loughlin
NEW ZEALAND 6 T: K Shelford
G: K Shelford

3 Dec 1989 *at Carcassonne, 4200*
FRANCE 0
NEW ZEALAND 34 T: Watson 3, Kemp,
Williams, Kuiti, Bell
G: Sherlock 3

2 Jun 1990 *at Port Moresby, 8000*
PAPUA NEW GUINEA 8 T: Ongogo
G: Numapo 2
GREAT BRITAIN 40 T: Gibson 2, Eastwood,
Goulding, Dixon,
D Powell, Schofield
G: Davies 6

27 Jun 1990 *at Parkes, 12 384*
AUSTRALIA 34 T: Mackay 3, McGaw 2,
Daley, Meninga,
Shearer
G: Belcher
FRANCE 2 G: Dumas

15 Jul 1990 *at Christchurch, 3133*
NEW ZEALAND 21 T: Kemp, Nikau
G: Ridge 6, McGahan (DG)
GREAT BRITAIN 18 T: Schofield, R Powell,
Offiah
G: Davies 3

11 Aug 1990 *at Port Moresby, 10 000*
PAPUA NEW GUINEA 10 T: Waine, Soga
G: Numapo
NEW ZEALAND 18 T: Lonergan, Panapa,
Watson
G: Ridge 3

24 Nov 1990 *at Elland Road, 32 500*
GREAT BRITAIN 0
AUSTRALIA 14 T: Ettingshausen, Meninga,
Elias
G: Meninga

9 Dec 1990 *at Perpignan, 3428*
FRANCE 10 T: Pons, Entat
G: Tisseyre
AUSTRALIA 34 T: Mackay 2, Shearer,
Alexander,
Ettingshausen,
Meninga, Roach
G: Alexander 3

27 Jan 1991 *at Perpignan, 5500*
FRANCE 10 T: Auroy, Fraisse
G: Tisseyre
GREAT BRITAIN 45 T: Offiah 2, Edwards 2,
Schofield 2, Betts,
Platt
G: Eastwood 6,
Schofield (DG)

CURRENT TABLE

	P	W	D	L	F	A	Pts
Australia	4	4	0	0	104	26	8
Great Britain	5	3	0	2	113	59	6
New Zealand	5	3	0	2	93	60	6
Papua New Guinea	2	0	0	2	18	58	0
France	4	0	0	4	22	147	0

(Positions at 28 Jan, 1991)

INDEX

Page numbers in *italics* refer to illustrations

aggregates 189, 201
Ah Kuoi, Fred *66*
All Golds, The 8
Alliance Challenge Cup 96
Alliance Second Division
    Championship 96
American All Star touring team
    1953 *12*
Anderson, Chris *67*
Anderton, Bob *11*
appearances 157, 201
    400 for a club 111–12
    600 in a career 119
Ashby, Ray *65*
Ashcroft, Ernie *206*
Ashton, Eric *174–5*, 176
Ashurst, Bill 181
Atkinson, John *82*, 123, 154
attendances 11, 12, 160, 189 *see
    also* crowds, record
Australia v England, internationals
    187
Australia v Great Britain, Test
    match results 162–71
Australia v Wales, internationals
    188
Australian touring team, 1908–09
    9
Australians to Great Britain, tour
    records 184

ball-back rule 8
BARLA *see* British Amateur Rugby
    League Association (BARLA)
Barnes, Keith *166–7*
Barrow 16
Bath, Harry *44*, 45
Batley 17
Batten, Billy 70, 123
Batten, Eric *70–1*
Batten, Ray 154
BBC2 Floodlit Trophy 13, 98–100
Bentley, Jack 89
Bergin, Tom 89
Bevan, Brian *121*, *122–3*, 157
Bevan, John 46–7, 48
Bishop, Paul *57*, 157
Blan, Billy 154
Board of Directors 15
Boston, Billy 50–1, *121*, 123
bottom 14 competition, 1964–65
    110
Bradford Northern 18–19

Bramley 19
Bridges, Keith *56*
British Amateur Rugby League
    Association (BARLA) 14, 15
British international records 189–
    97
    individual 190–1, 194
    playing summary 189
brothers, who have toured 201
Broughton Rangers *61*
Buck, Harold *10*
Burgess, Bill *197*
Burgess, Bill junior *196*, *197*
Burke, Mick *129*

caps 16–52 *passim*, 191
Captain Morgan Trophy (1973–74)
    110
captains 194
career, longest 157
Carlisle 19–20
Cartwright, John *168–9*
Castleford 20
centuries of goals 157
Challenge Cup Final,
    1901 *59*
    1950 *63*
    1965 65
    1966 *121*
    1982 *139*
    1985 66
    1987 67
    player of the match awards 88–9
    replay 1954 *13*
Challenge Cup semi-final,
    1974 *22*
    1982 26, 27
Challenge Cup winners, 1912 *61*
Charity Shield 15, 87, 88, 89
Cherrington, Norman *36*, 37
Chilcott, Jack 145
Chorley 20–1
Clampitt, JL *61*
Clark, Douglas *83*, 145
Clawson, Terry *52*, *119–20*
Club Championship (1973–74) 110
clubs, Rugby League *see* Rugby
    League clubs
Coetzer, Gert *58*
Colts League 13
competitions,
    current 53–97
    defunct 89–110

Cook, Bert 31
Cooper, Lionel *25*, 123
Coslett, Kel 137
Coulman, Mike 114
County Championship 8
County Cup Finals 89
Crooks, Lee 15
crowds, record 10, 13, 15 *see also*
    attendances
Cunliffe, Jack *102*, *103*

Dalgreen, John 14
Davies, Willie *88*
Davies, Alan *36*, 37
Davies, Jim 145
Dewsbury 21
Dingsdale, Tommy 137
District Development Associations
    15
Dobson, Albert *63*
Doncaster 21
dropout from under the posts 11
Dutton, Ray 154
Dyl, Les *106*
Dyson, Frank *124*, 125

Eastern Division Championships
    13, 109
Eccles, Bob *14*, 114
Edmondson, Harold *157*
Edwards, Allan 70, 123
Edwards, Shaun 157
Egan, Joe 12
Ellaby, Alf 123
Elwell, Keith 157
England v Australia, results 187
England v France, results 186
England v New Zealand, results
    187
England v Other Nationalities,
    results 187
England v Wales, results 185–6
English Rugby Football Union 8
English Schools Rugby League 13
Evans, Bryn *42*, 43

Fairbairn, George *116–17*
Fallowfield, William 11–12
fathers and sons, who have toured
    201
Featherstone Rovers 22–3
Feetham, Jack 114
Fennell, Jackie *52*

Ferguson, Joe *34–5*, 157
Ferguson, John *66*
Fielding, Keith 123
First Division Premiership Trophy
  55–7 *see also* Premiership
  Trophy
first
  £2000 transfer 12
  £5000 transfer 12
  £10 000 transfer 12
  £20 000 transfer 15
  £100 000 transfer 15
  £150 000 transfer 15
  £1 000 000 gate taken 15
  All Four Cups winner 8
  broadcasting 10
  Challenge Cup Final 8
  Champions of the Northern
    Union 8
  Championship Final 8
  club to appear in three
    consecutive Wembley finals 12
  controller of referees 15
  international match 185
  Lions Tour of Australia 10
  man to play and score in every
    club match in a season 10
  national TV broadcast of a
    Wembley Cup Final 12
  Northern Union international
    match 8
  player to kick 100 goals 10
  player to score over 400 points
    in a season 10
  reigning monarch to attend a
    Rugby League match 12
  Rugby League London club 10
  Rugby League varsity match 15
  rule changes 8
  Student Rugby League World
    Cup 15
  Sunday fixtures 13
  team to play in Australia 14–15
  televising of Test match 12
  top 16 play-off and winners 13
  tour of Britain by Australia 10
  tour by Papua New Guinea 15
  touring team to win all games in
    Great Britain 15
  University match 13
  visit to Papua New Guinea 14
  Wales–England international 10
  Wales–France international 10
  winners of both Cup and
    League 8
    in consecutive seasons 15
  winners of four consecutive
    Challenge Cup Finals 15
  winners of the Yorkshire Cup *9*
  World Cup Challenge 15
  World Cup staged in Australia
    12
Fish, Jack 123

five-yard rule 13
four-tackle rule 13
Fox, Neil 126, 132–*3*
France v England, internationals
  186
France v Great Britain, Test match
  results 178–82
France v Wales, internationals
  187–8
free gang-way 15
freedom of contract 15
Freeman, Johnny *24*, 25, 123
Fulham 23

Gabbitas, Brian *65*
Galia, Jean 10, *11*
Ganley, Bernard 12, *74–5*, 137
Gee, Ken *206*
George VI, King *11*, 12
Gilfedder, Laurie *128*
Giltinan, JJ 10
Gleeson, Tommy 145
goal, longest recorded 11
goal-kickers 126, 137, 194
goals,
  200 and 200 tries 135
  300 and 300 tries 135
  500 for a club 116–17
  750 in a career 124–5
  most against Great Britain in a
    match 190
  most centuries of 157
  most for Great Britain in a
    match 190
  most in a match 138–9
  most one-point drop goals 157
  most in a season 143
Goldthorpe, Albert 10
Goulding, Bobby *200*, 201
Gowers, Ken *201*
Gowers, Walter 201
Grayshon, Jeff 194
Great Britain international records
  see British international
  records
Great Britain Lions *see* Lions
Great Britain team, 1926 *172*
Great Britain Test match results *see*
  Test match results
Great Britain tourists 198–211
  individual records 201–11
Great Britain v Australia
  Second Test, 1982 *14*
  Test match results 162–71
Great Britain v France, Test match
  results 178–82
Great Britain v New Zealand, Test
  match results 171–7
Great Britain v Papua New Guinea,
  Test match results 183
Grenoble, 1959 Test *178–9*
Griffiths, Tuss *13*
Gronow, Ben 10, 126, 145, *147*

Gunney, Geoff *58*, 65

Haigh, Bob 13, 114, 154–5
half-centuries of tries 157
Halifax 23–5, *87*
Hallas, D *104*
Hallett, Lyn 157
Halliwell, Steve *158–9*
Harris, Eric 123, 145, 157
Harry Sunderland Trophy 88
Helme, Gerry *63*
Highfield 41
Higson, Willie 145
Hirst, Ken *58*
Hodgson, Martin 11
Hoey, Jim 10
Horne, Willie *16*, 137
Howes, David 14
Huddersfield 25
Hudson, Barney 123
Hughes, Eric *56*
Hull 26–7
Hull Kingston Rovers 28
Hunslet *9*, 29
Hyde, Gary *116–17*

incoming tours 184
individual records,
  British international 190–1, 194
  Rugby League 111–59
  Rugby League clubs 16–52
    passim
  tourists 201–11
International Board 12, 15
international matches 185–8
international records,
  British 189–97
    individual 190–1, 194
    playing summary 189
Invincibles, The *14*, 15
Iro, Kevin *69*
ITV Floodlit Competition 110

Jack Bentley Trophy 89
Jackson, Lee *168–9*
Jackson, Phil *31*
John Player Special Trophy 84
John Player Trophy 13
Jones, Les 154
Jones, Lewis 12, 30–*1*, 132, 137

Kangaroos, The *9, 14*, 89, 145
Keighley 29
Kennedy, Jim *149*
Kielty, Stan *111*
Kindon, Bill 114
Koloto, Emosi 76, 77
Krilich, Max *14*, 15

Lancashire Challenge Cup 8, 72–7
  1914 Final *72*
Lancashire Club Championship 8
Lancashire Combination

Championship 97
Lancashire County Challenge
    Shield 97
Lancashire County Rugby League
    96
Lancashire Cup Final, player of the
    match awards 89
Lancashire League Championship
    8, 13, 107–9
    honours 109
Lancashire Senior Competitions
    53, 107
Lance Todd Trophy 63, 65, 88
League and Cup double 8, 15
Lee, Aaron 145
Leeds 32
Leigh 32–3
Lewis, Wally 15
Leytham, Jim 35, 123
Lindop, Fred 15
Lions 204–11
    1910 199
    1950 206–7
    club representation of 211
    oldest and youngest 201, 211
Lions tours 10, 198
    summaries and records 198, 201
    top performers 204
    see also Tourists
Lister, Peter 19
Liverpool Stanley 41
Lloyd, Sammy (Geoff) 139
Lomas, James 8, 10, 198
Longley, Albany 92
Longstaff, Fred 145
losing run, longest 160
losing season (100%) 160
Loughlin, Paul 195
Lowe, Phil 114
Lydon, Joe 15

MacCorquodale, Iain 125
McLean, Jack 123
McLennan, Bill 212
Man-of-the-Match awards 88–9
Mantle, John 121
Markham, Ray 113
Martyn, Mick 114–15
Millward, Roger 202–3
Moorhouse, Stanley 145
Mortimer, Frank 132
most,
    appearances 201, 157
    centuries of goals 157
    consecutive goal-scoring games
        157
    consecutive tests for Great
        Britain 194
    consecutive try-scoring games
        157
    consecutive wins 160
    games without defeat 160
    goals against Great Britain in a

match 191
    goals for Great Britain in a
        match 190
    goals in a match 138–9
    goals in a season 143
    half-centuries of tries 157
    one-point drop goals 157
    points against Great Britain in a
        match 191
    points for Great Britain in a
        match 190
    points in a match 146
    points in a season 146
    tours 201
    tries against Great Britain in a
        match 190
    tries for Great Britain in a match
        190
    tries in a match 138
    tries in a season 142
Mumby, Keith 18
Murphy, Alex 135, 178–9

Nash, Steve 22
National Amateur Rugby League
    15
national coaching scheme 14
New Zealand v England,
    internationals 187
New Zealand v Great Britain, Test
    match results 171–7
New Zealand v Wales,
    internationals 188
New Zealanders to Great Britain,
    tour records 184
Newlove, Paul 194
Nordgren, Brian 123
Northern Rugby Football League
    10, 53
Northern Rugby Football Union 8
Northern Rugby Football Union
    Challenge Cup 59
Northern Rugby League
    Championship 101–7
    1973 final 106
    honours table 105
    records 105, 107
Northern Union 8–10
Norton, Steve 208
Nottingham City 33
numbering of jerseys 10

Odsal Stadium 13, 104
Offiah, Martin 50, 123
oldest and youngest players 35,
    157, 194, 201, 211
Oldham 36–7
Oliver, Joe 119
Osbourne, Laurie 28
Other Nationalities v England,
    internationals 187
Other Nationalities v Wales,
    internationals 188

Owen, Stan 114
Oxley, David 14

Papua New Guinea v Great Britain,
    Test match results 183
Papua New Guineans to Great
    Britain, tour records 184
Parrish, Mick 134
Paul, Graham 124, 125
Pendlebury, John 67
Perry, Jack 17
Pickerill, Clive 15
Platt, Joseph 8
play-the-ball rule 28
player-of-the-match awards 88
players,
    oldest and youngest 35, 157,
        194, 201, 211
    scored in every game in a season
        134
Player's No 6 Trophy 84
points,
    1000 for a club 118
    1500 in a career 128–9
    most against Great Britain,
        individual records 191
    most by a losing team 160
    most for Great Britain,
        individual records 190
    most in a match 140
    most in a season 146
pre-Northern Union rugby 8
Premiership Trophy 14
    1984 Final 116–17
    1986 Final 57
Prescott, Alan 114, 193
professionalism 8
Prudence, George 72

Quinn, Steve 137

Regal Trophy 13, 84–6, 88, 89
    records 86
registering players 11
Reilly, Mal 26, 27
Reserve Team Rugby League 96–7
Ring, Johnny 123
Risman, Gus 137, 157, 194
Robinson, Bill 114
Robinson, Geoff 57
Rochdale Hornets 37
Rogers, Johnny 145
Rogers, Ned 26
Rorke's Drift Test 10
Rose, David 212
Rosenfeld, Albert 10, 123, 144–5
Roses Match 90–5
    1946 match 92
    records 95
Rugby Football League 10–15
Rugby League Alliance 96
Rugby League Challenge Cup
    59–69

Finals *see* Challenge Cup Final
Rugby League Championship 53–5
   honours table 55
   winners and runners-up 54–5,
      107
Rugby League Charity Shield 15,
   87, 88, 89
Rugby League clubs 16–29, 32–3,
   36–52
   honours, caps and individual
      records 16–52 *passim*
Rugby League Foundation 15
Rugby League Hall of Fame 15, 70
Rugby League records,
   individual 111–59
   other 160–1
Rugby Leaguer Trophy 89
Ryedale-York 37–8

St Helens 38–9
Salford 40
Scarborough Pirates 40
scorers, highest 135, 148–56
scores, highest 135, 161
scoring draw, highest 160
scoring records 141, 147, 201
Scott, Mick *67*
Second Division Championship 58
Second Division Premiership 15,
   59, 88, 89
Sheffield Eagles 40–1
Smith, Stanley 70, 123
Snowden, Billy *174–5*, 176
Sorensen, Kurt 76, *77*, *195*
Southern Amateur Rugby League
   12
Southward, Ike 12, *52*
Steadman, Graham 15
Stephenson, Nigel *106*
Stevenson, Jeff *166–7*
Stone, Charlie *56*
Student Rugby League World Cup
   15
substitutions 13
Sullivan, Clive 123, 154, *181*
Sullivan, Jim 10, 30, 31, *126–7*,
   132, 157
Sullivan, Mick 123, *192–3*, 194
Sunderland, Harry 89
Swinden, Arthur 145
Swinton 42–3

Tabern, Walt 114, *115*
Taylor, Bob 114, 154
Team of All the Talents 144
Test career, longest 194
Test match results,
   Great Britain v Australia 162–71
   Great Britain v France 178–82

Great Britain v New Zealand
   171–7
Great Britain v Papua New
   Guinea 183
Thomas, Dai 145
three-division system 15
time-keepers 13
Todd, Lance 89
Tom Bergin Trophy 89
top 16 play-off 53
top four play-off 53
Topliss, David *208*
Toulouse, 1972 Test *181*
tourists 198–211
   individual records 201–11
   tours, records and summaries 198,
      201
'T'Owd Tin Pot' 8
Trafford Borough 43
Traill, Ken *206*
transfer tribunal 15
triangular international
   tournament 10
tries 193
   200 and 200 goals 135
   200 for a club 113
   250 in a career 121
   300 and 300 goals 135
   most half-centuries of 157
   most in a match 138
   most in a match against Great
      Britain 190
   most in a match for Great
      Britain 190
   most in a season 142
try-scoring records 13, 123
Turley, Norman 157
two-division system 14, 55, 58

Universities Rugby League
   Association 13
USSR, promotional tour of 15

Valentine, Dave *122*, 123, 193
Van Heerden, Attie 123
Vollenhoven, Tom *39*, 50, 123

Wagstaff, Harold 145
Wakefield Trinity 43–4, 132
Wales v Australia, results 188
Wales v England, results 185–6
Wales v France, results 187–8
Wales v New Zealand, results 188
Wales v Other Nationalities, results
   188
War of the Roses 15, 90
Ward, Ernest *11*, *92*
Warrington 44–5, *47*, *48*
   1947–48 *107*

Watkins, David 13, 134, 136–7, 157
Watson, Cliff *121*
Welsh Rugby League 12
Wembley Cup Finals, oldest and
   youngest players 157
West, George 'Tich' 8
Western Division Championships
   13, 109
White Rose Trophy 89
White team 1954 *199*
Whitehaven 45
Whiteley, Johnny 114
Whitfield, Colin *130–1*
Widnes 48
Wigan 48–9
   1989–90 *53*
Williams, Dickie *206*
Wilson, Danny 157
Wilson, John 10
winning season (100%) 160
Wood, Alf *211*
Wood, Peter 157
Workington Town 52
World Cup 189, *212–20*
   1954 213
   1957 213–14
   1960 214
   1968 214–15
   1970 215
   1972 215–*16*
   1975 216–18
   1977 218
   1985–88 218–19
   1989–92 220
Worrall, Albert *33*

Yorkshire Challenge Cup 8, 78–83
   1980 Final *82*
   1982 Final *18*
   1952 semi-final *111*
Yorkshire County Rugby League
   96
Yorkshire Cup Final, player of the
   match award 89
Yorkshire League Championship
   8, 13, *107–9*
   honours table 109
Yorkshire records, Roses matches
   95
Yorkshire Senior Competition 8,
   53, 107
Yorkshire Senior Competition
   Challenge Cup 97
Yorkshire Senior Competition
   Championship Shield 97
youngest and oldest players 35,
   157, 194, 201, 211